Colloquial

Icelandic

The Colloquial Series

Series adviser: Gary King

The following languages are available in the Colloquial series:

Afrikaans
Albanian
Amharic
Arabic (Levantine)
Arabic of Egypt
Arabic of the Gulf and
   Saudi Arabia
Basque
Bulgarian
* Cambodian
* Cantonese
* Chinese
Croatian and Serbian
Czech
Danish
Dutch
Estonian
Finnish
French
German
Greek
Gujarati
Hindi
Hungarian
Indonesian
Italian
Japanese
Korean
Latvian
Lithuanian
Malay
Mongolian
Norwegian
Panjabi
Persian
Polish
Portuguese
Portuguese of Brazil
Romanian
* Russian
Scottish Gaelic
Slovak
Slovene
Somali
* Spanish
Spanish of Latin America
Swedish
* Thai
Turkish
Ukrainian
Urdu
* Vietnamese
Welsh

Accompanying cassette(s) (*and CDs) are available for the above titles. They can be ordered through your bookseller, or send payment with order to Taylor & Francis/Routledge Ltd, ITPS, Cheriton House, North Way, Andover, Hants SP10 5BE, UK, or to Routledge Inc, 29 West 35th Street, New York NY 10001, USA.

COLLOQUIAL CD-ROMs
Multimedia Language Courses
Available in: Chinese, French, Portuguese and Spanish

Colloquial
Icelandic

The Complete Course for Beginners

Daisy L. Neijmann

Routledge
Taylor & Francis Group

LONDON AND NEW YORK

First published 2001 by Routledge
11 New Fetter Lane, London EC4P 4EE

Simultaneously published in the USA and Canada
by Routledge
29 West 35th Street, New York, NY 10001

Reprinted 2002, 2003

Routledge is an imprint of the Taylor & Francis Group

Typeset in Times Ten by Florence Production Ltd, Stoodleigh, Devon.
Printed and bound in Great Britain by
Biddles Ltd, Guildford and King's Lynn

British Library Cataloguing in Publication Data
A catalogue record for this book is available from the British Library

Library of Congress Cataloguing in Publication Data
Neijmann, Daisy L., 1963–
    Colloquial Icelandic: the complete course for beginners/
Daisy L. Neijmann.
        p. cm. – (Colloquials)
    Includes index.
    1. Icelandic language–Textbooks for foreign speakers–English.
    2. Icelandic Language–Spoken Icelandic. I. Title.
    II. Colloquial series.

PD2413 .N45 2001
439´.6983421–dc21   00–047062

ISBN 0–415–20706–1 (book)
ISBN 0–415–20707–X (cassettes)
ISBN 0–415–28690–5 (CDs)
ISBN 0–415–20708–8 (book, CDs and cassettes course)

Contents

Acknowledgements

I am grateful to *Morgunblaðið, Talnakönnun* (formerly *Nesútgáfan*), *DV* and *Tímarit Reykjavík* for permission to use various extracts and articles, to Ferðaskrifstofan Nonni to use their advertisement, to Jón Gíslason and Sigríður Þorvaldsdóttir to use excerpts from their book *Landsteinar*, to Gerður Kristný and Elísabet Þorgeirsdóttir to use excerpts from their articles, to *Hótel Borg* for permission to print their menu. Warmest thanks are extended to my generous and patient Icelandic friends Árni Þór Eymundsson, Katrín Eymundsdóttir and Antonía Sveinsdóttir, who were kind enough to read and correct the manuscript during its various stages, fielded my many questions and contributed valuable insights. Thanks also go to the friendly and helpful staff at Routledge, especially to Gary King whose encouragement and assistance during the early writing stages were important. Final thanks to Wil Neijmann, who passed on to me his love of languages and the joy of language learning, and, as always, to Mark, for his patience and love.

Every effort has been made to obtain permission to reproduce copyright material. If any proper acknowledgement has not been made, or permission not received, we would invite copyright holders to inform us of the oversight.

Abbreviations

acc.	accusative
adj.	adjective
adv.	adverb
comp.	comparative
conj.	conjunction
dat.	dative
dem.	demonstrative
excl.	exclamation
f./fem.	feminine
gen.	genitive
imp.	imperative
impers.	impersonal
indecl.	indeclinable
inf.	infinitive
inter.	interrogative
interj.	interjection
intrans.	intransitive
lit.	literally
m./masc.	masculine
n./neut.	neuter
nom.	nominative
num.	numeral
pl.	plural
pp.	past participle
pref.	prefix
prep.	preposition(al)
pron.	pronoun
refl.	reflexive
sg./sing.	singular
subj.	subjunctive/subject
superl.	superlative
trans.	transitive
v./vb.	verb

Introduction

Icelandic is a fascinating language. Dating back to Viking times, with less than 300,000 speakers and a history that has kept it relatively free from major changes, it has captured the interest of many enthusiasts over the course of time.

People are attracted to Icelandic for many different reasons. For some, it is the romantic lure of learning the language of the Vikings. Others want to be able to appreciate the Icelandic sagas or Eddic poems in the original. You may be intrigued by the linguistic antiquity of Icelandic. Perhaps Icelandic was the language of your ancestors. Or maybe you are simply planning a trip to Iceland, and you wish to communicate with Icelanders in their own language. Whatever it is that motivated you to pick up this book, you are interested in learning Icelandic, or in keeping up and improving your Icelandic. This course may be just what you need.

Iceland

Iceland is an island in the North Atlantic, 103,000 km² in size, hugging the Arctic Circle. Geologically, Iceland is young, and in many ways still 'in the making': volcanic and geothermal activity determine much of Iceland's landscape, as do glaciers, mountains, lava deserts, green valleys, and clear, rich waters. The warm Gulf Stream moderates the climate, with a mean annual temperature in Reykjavík of 5°C.

The island was settled in the ninth century, largely by Norse people from western Norway and the British Isles and their Celtic companions. The settler community established its own national assembly, resembling a parliament and called the Alþingi, and officially adopted Christianity in the year 1000. In 1262–4 Iceland became subject to the Norwegian crown and in 1380 it came under Danish rule. Iceland eventually regained its independence in stages:

it obtained home rule in 1918, and became an independent republic in 1944.

Today, Iceland has approximately 270,000 inhabitants, about half of whom live in the capital Reykjavík and its surroundings. The Icelandic economy largely depends on the fishing industry, which makes up ½ of the GNP. Since only 1 per cent of the land is arable, dairy and sheep farming are more common than arable farming, and woollens and mountain lamb are among Iceland's exports. Iceland is rich in natural energy: geothermal heat is used to heat houses and greenhouses, and electricity is generated from water power.

Icelandic

Icelandic is part of the North Germanic language group, and developed from the Viking Age West Norse speech brought by the settlers. Icelandic first appears as a separate language in the twelfth century, when the anonymous author of *The First Grammatical Treatise* introduced a special alphabet to suit the needs of Icelandic. Writing was introduced by the Church, along with influences from Latin, English and French.

The remarkable body of literature recorded in Iceland during the following centuries, and the translation of the Bible into Icelandic after the Reformation in the sixteenth century, were instrumental for the continuity of Icelandic under foreign domination, when the influence of Danish became pervasive.

During the nineteenth and early twentieth centuries, Icelandic language and literature came to play a crucial role in the nationalist struggle for independence. The nationalists developed language policies to purify Icelandic from foreign influences. Today, many of these policies are still in place: a special language board creates words for new phenomena from the resources of the Icelandic language itself. Nevertheless, Icelandic adopts its share of loan words every year, some of which live a long and happy life alongside their Icelandic neologist equivalents. Where loan words win out, they are usually adapted to Icelandic grammar and spelling, and will often take on a new meaning in the Icelandic context. Icelanders have been remarkably successful in making their ancient language fully compatible with today's global, computerized world: a knowledge of modern Icelandic will allow relatively easy access to a fourteenth-century Icelandic saga as well as a discussion of the latest concepts in marketing or Internet communication.

Colloquial Icelandic

This course is designed to guide the learner, who may not have any previous language-learning experience, from complete beginner to basic communicative competence, enough to converse in a range of common situations. Each of the sixteen lessons contains a systematic presentation of several grammatical issues. The grammar and pronunciation can be learned practically through the accompanying exercises and situational dialogues. The aim is to help the learner achieve a command of contemporary colloquial vocabulary and the basic structures through exposure to dialogues and exercises based on everyday, realistic experiences. By the end of the course, the learner can expect to be able to:

- converse socially, exchange information and relate daily experiences
- obtain information pertaining to travel and tourism
- shop and make business arrangements.

Learning Icelandic

Learning a language is an exciting experience. It is a lot like being a child again: you begin mute, you learn by exposure and repetition, and in the process you are discovering a new world. The main requirements are interest and determination. Enjoying your study will make your progress easier and more fun, and will more than make up for the difficulties you may encounter.

Regular study habits are highly recommended: you'll find that a page a day will pay off more than a chapter once a week. Remember that exposure alone is beneficial, too – you don't always need to be 'studying': listening to your tape in your car or walkman, practising words and phrases while walking or doing dishes will all help.

This is particularly true of Icelandic, which is an inflected language (i.e. words change form to express grammatical information) and has a vocabulary largely new even to speakers of another Germanic language. At first, this may seem rather daunting and your initial progress may appear slow. Don't worry: with time, regular practice and an open mind, even these complex aspects of Icelandic will gradually fall into place. Enjoy!

The sounds and letters of Icelandic

Icelandic pronunciation

Generally speaking, there is a much more direct correspondence between spelling and sound in Icelandic than in English. On the other hand, some Icelandic sounds are either foreign to English speakers, or subtly but importantly different from English or other Icelandic sounds. Students are advised to pay close attention from the start and continue to practise Icelandic pronunciation throughout the course; it is important to develop an ear for the subtleties and intricacies of Icelandic, as well as the ability to integrate them into your own pronunciation. Play with the sounds until they feel good in your mouth. Many Icelanders are proud of their language and will berate Icelander and foreigner alike for treating it with disrespect.

The following is an introduction to Icelandic pronunciation which is meant as a practical guide to which students can refer as they progress through the course. It is by no means exhaustive, but it will allow the learner to grasp the basics and communicate in a comprehensible and acceptable manner. The recordings will help you with the sounds, and the phonetic symbols (based on the International Phonetic Alphabet), enclosed in square brackets, allow you to find out how to produce them exactly.[1] English approximations are also provided where possible, but they are poor substitutes for the actual Icelandic sounds.

---

[1] Guides to the IPA are easily available. Since the phonetic alphabet is based on sound production rather than spelling, it is particularly helpful as a guide to sounds you find difficult to reproduce.

Vowels

We begin with a list of Icelandic vowels and their sounds in Icelandic, divided into monophthongs (one sound) and diphthongs (combinations of two sounds, where one 'slides' towards another):

IPA Symbol	Letter	English approximation	Icelandic examples
Monophthongs			
[a]	a	f*a*ther, t*a*	**taska, kaka**
[ɛ]	e	b*e*d	**drekka**
[jɛ]	é	*y*es	**ég**
[ɪ]	i	w*i*n	**litur**
[i]	í	k*ee*p	**líta**
[ɪ]	y	w*i*n	**þykja**
[i]	ý	k*ee*p	**mýs**
[ɔ]	o	t*o*ffee	**lofa**
[ø]	u	(say 'i' as in 'win', but with rounded lips)	**hundur, upp**
[u]	ú	l*o*se	**þú**
[œ]	ö	g*i*rl	**hönd, ör**
Diphthongs			
[au]	á	n*ow*	**blár**
[ou]	ó	n*o*te[2]	**rós**
[ai]	æ	k*i*nd	**bær**

Note that the accented vowels in Icelandic are individual sounds, completely different in quality from their unaccented counterparts. Compare the following pairs:

ala – ál, te – té, friður – fríður, fyrst – fýst, loga – lóa, utan – út

The following are special vowel combinations which always correspond to the following sounds:

---

[2] Icelandic **ó** is a diphthong, which means that pronunciation starts with the [o] sound, but then moves ('slides') towards an [u] (as in l*o*se). The sound roughly resembles standard southern English pronunciation of 'o' but is more open and rounded.

| [œy] | au | (start with an ö and then gradually lift your tongue) | **auga, haust, þau** |
| [ɛi] | ei/ey | *case* | **skeið** |

Consonants

In English as well as Icelandic, consonants can be voiced or unvoiced. If you pronounce English 'd' and 't', 'v' and 'f', 'z' and 's' while holding your hand against your throat, you will notice the vibration when you pronounce the voiced consonant in each pair. The voiced or unvoiced quality of consonants is subject to change: consonants may become voiced or devoiced when in a voiced or unvoiced environment. This is a significant aspect of Icelandic pronunciation. For instance, an unvoiced consonant surrounded by vowels will usually become voiced in Icelandic, while the fully unvoiced **h** causes any following consonant to become devoiced. Devoicing sometimes causes difficulties for students. It helps if you imagine an **h** before the consonant in question, or try blowing a lot of air when your pronounce the sound. It is important to practise this, as devoicing can mean the difference between two separate words:

vanda – va[h]nta, lambið – la[h]mpi, vergur – ve[h]rkur

You will see in the following list of Icelandic consonants how almost every voiced sound has a devoiced counterpart. Check the examples and notice how the devoiced version occurs before unvoiced consonant(s) or after **h**. There are three consonants that are always voiced in English but never voiced in Icelandic: **b**, **d**, **g**. The only difference in pronunciation between **b**, **d**, **g** and **p**, **t**, **k** is that in initial positions, **b**, **d**, **g** do not become aspirated (burst of air suddenly released, as in English *t*[h]ake), while **p**, **t**, **k** do.

[p]		b	wra*p*	**bera**
[t]		d	we*t*	**dama**
[t]		t	we*t*	**sitja**
[t[h]]	word initial	t	*t*ake	**taka**
[ð]		ð[3]	wea*th*er	**maður**

---

[3] Never occurs initially, and often dropped in final positions: **er þa(ð)? Blaði(ð) er komi(ð).**

[θ]	ð	*th*ought	**maðkur**
[θ]	þ	*th*ought	**íþrótt**
[j]	j	*y*oung	**já**
[ç]	j	[h]*y*es	**hjá, hjarta**
[l]	l	*l*augh	**læra**
[l°]	l	[h]*l*	**stúlka, hlýr**
[m]	m	*m*u*m*	**mamma**
[m°]	m	[h]*m*	**lampi, skammtur**
[r]	r	*r*ed[4]	**ráðherra**
[r°]	r	[h]*r*	**hratt, þurrka**
[s]	s	*s*ong	**sál, vísa[5]**
[xs]	x	wa*x*[6]	**lax, vaxa**

The following consonants can be pronounced in different ways, depending on the combinations in which they occur:

[f]		f	*f*ind	**ferfaldur**
[v]	around vowels	f	*v*oice	**sofa**
[p]	before **l, n**	fl, fn	ta*p*	**Keflavík**
[m]	before **nd**	fnd	ja*m*	**hefnd**
[m°]	before **nt**	fnt	[h]*m*	**nefnt**
[h]		h	*h*ello	**hár**
[kʰ]	before **v**[7]	hv	*qu*ality, without rounding the lips	**hvað**
[k]		k	wi*ck*	**raka** before e, i, í, y, ý, æ, ei/ey, [kʰ]

---

[4] Icelandic has a front rolling **r** much like a Scottish one, where the tip of the tongue trills against the alveolar ridge (behind the upper front teeth). While some people may find this very difficult, it is worth practising since it is a significant feature of Icelandic speech.

[5] In Icelandic, **s** never becomes voiced in pronunciation.

[6] The actual sound [x] does not exist in English and may be hard to produce at first. It is akin to the *ch* in Scottish 'loch' or German 'Dach'. Try pronouncing a **k**, but instead of stopping the airflow altogether, slowly let it through, releasing the air only gradually. The friction this produces creates the distinctive quality of the sound.

[7] **Hv** is also sometimes pronounced with the **h** sounding like the [x] described in footnote 4. This speech variant is found in southern Iceland, and is considered by some to be 'better' Icelandic.

[kʰ]	word initial	k	*k*ing	**kalla**	becomes [cʰ], (i.e. pushed more to the front):
[x]	before **t**	kt, kkt – [8]		**október**	**kisa, keyra**
[n]		n	*n*ame	**nenna**	
[n°]	before **t**	nt	*[h]n*	**svunta, hnerra**	
[ŋ]	before **g**	ng	lo*ng*	**langur**	preceding **a, i, u** become **á, í, ú** and
[ŋ°]	before **k**	nk	*[h]nk*	**blankur**	**e** and **ö** become **ei** and **au**, as in **flinkur, munkur, enginn, söngur**

The pronunciation of **g** in Icelandic often causes problems for students because it varies so much, and some of the variants can be tricky to master, so pay close attention to **g** from the start:

[k]	word initial[9]	g	wic*k*	**glápa**	[c] before **e, i, í, y, ý, æ, ei/ey: geta**[10]
	between vowel and **-l, -n**	g		**logn**	
[ɣ]	after vowels and before **a, u, ð, r**	g	– [11]	**fluga, vegur, dagur**	
	word final	g		**lag**	

---

[8] There is no English equivalent. See footnote 6.

[9] An important exception is the word **Guð** 'God', where a **v** is inserted after **g** in the pronunciation.

[10] This sound is like [cʰ] spelled **k**, but it is not aspirated.

[11] There is no English equivalent. This sound in the voiced counterpart of [x] explained in footnote 6: as you gradually let the air out, try to give the sound more 'voice' (i.e. vocal cords vibrate). You can tell the difference between [x] and [ɣ] if you listen closely: [x] sounds breathy, or 'throaty', while [ɣ] sounds very soft, almost like a [j] (as in *y*oung) but further down in your throat.

[x]	after vowels and before **t, s**	g	–	**dragt**
[j]	between vowel and **-i, -j**	gi, gj	*y*oung	**lygi,** **segja**
–	dropped between **ó, á, ú** and **a, u**	g	–	**fljúga**

Double consonants

Double consonants in Icelandic are twice as long in pronunciation as single consonants, so try to linger on them:

pabbi, Maggi, Snorri, mamma

Some double consonants have a slightly different pronunciation from their single equivalents:

1   **ll** is pronounced **tl**, except in loan words and pet names:

   stóll, bolli, milli, tröll, Páll
   but: **bolla, mylla, troll, Palli**

2   **nn** is pronounced **tn** after an accented vowel or a diphthong:[12]

   fínn, brúnn, einn
   but: **finna, brunnur, enn**

3   **pp, tt, kk** are pronounced as **hp, ht, hk**.[13] This may take some practice:

   stoppa, detta, þakka

Stress and length

In Icelandic the main stress is always on the first syllable of a word. Although that is easy enough to remember, it may demand some extra attention in certain familiar loan words:

---

[12] Such so-called t-insertion also generally occurs between **rl, rn sl, sn**, which become **rtl, rtn, stl, stn** as in **Erla, Örn, rusl, bysna**.
[13] This also usually happens before **pl, pn, tl, tn, kl, kn** when in between vowels: **hnupla, opna, kítla, fitna, Hekla, fíkn**.

'votur, 'töffararnir, 'banani, 'desember[14]

Compound words of which the first element consists of more than one syllable get a secondary stress on the *first* syllable of the *second* element:

'háskóla﹐kennari, 'hjarta﹐knúsari

Unstressed syllables are always short in Icelandic. Stressed syllables are always long, except

1   before double consonants:

    tapa, lama
    but: **labba, djamma**

2   before consonant clusters, excepting **p**, **t**, **k**, **s** followed by **v**, **j** or **r**:

    minstur, haust
    but: **lepja, sítrona**

The Icelandic alphabet

The Icelandic alphabet uses 32 letters. Another four letters are only used for writing foreign words, one of which, **z**, used to be quite common but has since been abolished. Here are the Icelandic letters and their pronunciation:

a	a	**j**	joð
á	á	**k**	ká
b	bé	**l**	ell
d	dé	**m**	emm
ð	eð	**n**	enn
e	e	**o**	o
é	é	**ó**	ó
f	eff	**p**	pé
g	ge	**r**	err
h	há	**s**	ess
i	i	**t**	té
í	í	**u**	u

---

[14] To avoid unclarity in the pronunciation of longer words, secondary stress may also occur on the third syllable of words that are not compounds: **'síga﹐retta, 'appel﹐sína**.

ú	ú	**ý**	ufsilon ý
v	vaff	**þ**	þorn
x	ex	**æ**	æ
y	ufsilon y	**ö**	ö

The following are foreign letters:

c	sé	**w**	tvöfalt vaff
q	kú	**z**	seta

Names can be spelled out as follows: **Sé o ell i enn** = 'Colin', **emm a err ufsilon y** = 'Mary', **ess a ess ká a té sé há e tvöfalt vaff a enn** = 'Saskatchewan'. Can you spell your own name in Icelandic?

You are probably wondering how you can remember all of this. Don't worry; you do not need to absorb this in one go. Remember: a little bit a day works better than a whole chunk at once. Many aspects of Icelandic pronunciation will gradually fall into place as you progress, and in the meantime, you can always come back to this section for practice and reference.

1 Velkomin til Íslands!

Welcome to Iceland!

In this lesson you will learn about:

- singular nominative nouns, pronouns and articles
- gender
- greetings and courtesies
- word order: questions and answers
- **vera/heita** in singular present
- present continuous ('-ing')
- Icelandic names

Dialogue 1

Á flugstöð Leifs Eiríkssonar

Joyce Williams has just arrived at the airport to visit Iceland for the first time. She is looking for information on how to get to her hotel. Can you tell: Where Joyce's hotel is? Where the bus stops?

JOYCE: Góðan daginn.

JÓN: Góðan dag.

JOYCE: Fyrirgefðu, getur þú sagt mér hvar Hótel Ísland er?

JÓN: Hótel Ísland er í Reykjavík.

JOYCE: Er þetta ekki Reykjavík?

JÓN: Nei, flugstöðin er í Keflavík, en það er rúta sem fer til Reykjavíkur. Hún kemur við á Hótel Íslandi. Rútan stoppar hérna rétt fyrir utan.

JOYCE: Þakka þér kærlega fyrir. Ég heiti Joyce Williams.

JÓN: Jón Einarsson heiti ég. Velkomin til Íslands! Hvaðan ert þú?

JOYCE: Ég er Englendingur.
JÓN: En þú talar íslensku!
JOYCE: Svolítið, ég er að læra íslensku. Jæja, takk fyrir hjálpina.
JÓN: Það var ekkert. Vertu blessuð.
JOYCE: Blessaður.

At the Leif Eiriksson airport terminal

JOYCE: *Good afternoon.*
JÓN: *Good afternoon.*
JOYCE: *Excuse me, can you tell me where Hotel Ísland is?*
JÓN: *Hotel Ísland is in Reykjavík.*
JOYCE: *Is this not Reykjavík?*
JÓN: *No, the airport is in Keflavík, but there is a coach that goes to Reykjavík. It stops at Hotel Ísland. The coach stops right outside here.*
JOYCE: *Thank you very much. My name is Joyce Williams.*
JÓN: *Jón Einarsson is my name. Welcome to Iceland! Where are you from?*
JOYCE: *I am English.*
JÓN: *But you speak Icelandic!*
JOYCE: *A little. I am learning Icelandic. Well, thanks for your help.*
JÓN: *Not at all. Goodbye.*
JOYCE: *Goodbye.*

Vocabulary notes

flugstöð Leifs Eiríkssonar	airport terminal Leif Eiriksson (the main terminal at Keflavík International Airport)	**hún**	she (here referring to the coach)
		kemur við	stops at, calls on (from **koma**)
fyrirgefðu	excuse me (*lit.* 'forgive you [me]')	**rétt fyrir utan**	right outside
		þakka þér fyrir	thank you (*lit.* 'thank you for [this]')
getur þú sagt mér ...	can you tell me ...	**heiti**	am called (from **heita**)
það er	it/there is	**hvaðan**	where ... from
rút/a	coach	**Englendingur**	someone from England
fer	goes (from **fara**)		

talar	speak, talk (from **tala**)	**hjálpina**	the help (from **hjálp**)
íslensku	Icelandic (from **íslensk/a**)	**það var ekkert**	don't mention it, not at all, you're welcome (*lit.* 'it was nothing')
að læra	learn (here: learning)		

Language points

Nouns and gender

Nouns in Icelandic are either masculine, feminine or neuter. The gender of Icelandic nouns is grammatical, which means that it relates to the form of a noun rather than its meaning. The endings of nouns often help determine their gender:

> *Masculine nouns* usually end in **-ur**, or **-i**, or **-ll** or **-nn**: **(karl)maður** 'man', **lampi** 'lamp', **stóll** 'chair', **steinn** 'stone'

> *Feminine nouns* often end in **-a**, or have no ending (**-0**) at all, while nouns with final **-ing** or **-un** are usually feminine: **rúta**, **rós** 'rose', **spurning** 'question', **verslun** 'shop'

> *Neuter nouns* generally have no ending (**-0**). Final accented vowels almost always indicate a neuter noun: **borð** 'table', **bakarí** 'bakery'

To help you determine whether a noun has an ending or not, the vocabulary notes and glossary show you by way of a slash where the ending of a noun starts, as in: **mað/ur**, **lamp/i**, **stól/l**, **rút/a**. If there is no slash, the noun has no ending, as is the case in **rós**, **spurning**, **verslun**, **borð** and **bakarí**. Did you notice that in the case of **stóll**, only the second **-l** constitutes the actual ending? This also goes for the second **-n** in nouns ending in **-nn**. The gender of a noun is extremely important in Icelandic, because it determines the form of many other words in the sentence. It is thus essential to learn how to recognize this and quickly get into the habit of determining the gender of nouns.

Exercise 1

Can you determine the gender of the following Icelandic nouns?
flugvöll/ur 'airport', **task/a** 'bag', 'case', **bíl/l** 'car', **dag/ur** 'day', **kon/a**
'woman', **íslensk/a**, **Englending/ur**, **staf/ur** 'letter', **hjálp**, **hótel**,
flugstöð.

Were you able to tell that **hjálp** and **flugstöð** are feminine but **hótel**
is neuter without checking the answers? Most likely not. In the
case of nouns without an ending you will have to rely on memory
(or other clues in the text, if there are any, as you will learn later),
so when you learn a new noun, make it a habit to memorize its
gender along with its meaning. In those cases where it is impos-
sible to determine the gender of a new noun, the vocabulary notes
and the glossary at the back of the book will tell you.

If you go back to Dialogue 1, you will notice that Joyce says: **ég
er Englendingur**, even though **Englendingur** is a masculine noun
and Joyce is a woman. The gender of a noun is predetermined and
always remains the same, irrespective of the sex of the person it
is applied to.

Articles

Icelandic does not have a separate indefinite article like English
'a' or 'an'. This means that a noun like **dagur** can be translated
into English as both 'day' and 'a day'. The Icelandic definite article
(English 'the') is added to the end of a noun like a suffix, and
has different forms depending on the gender of the noun it is
added to:

Masculine nouns get **-inn**, or just **-nn** if the noun ends in a vowel:
dagur*inn*, **lampi*nn***

Feminine nouns get **-in**, or just **-n** if the noun ends in a vowel:
flugstöð*in*, **rúta*n***

Neuter nouns get **-ið**, or just **-ð** if the final letter is an unaccented
vowel: **hótel*ið***, **herbergi*ð*** (from **herbergi**, 'room', a neuter noun of
which the **-i** is not an ending), but: **bakarí*ið***

Exercise 2

Now add the correct form of the definite article to all remaining
nouns in Exercise 1.

Personal pronouns

The definite article is only one example of how the gender of nouns affects other parts of speech in a sentence. Another example is personal pronouns. When referring back to a noun, Icelandic pronouns must reflect the gender of that noun, irrespective of meaning. In Dialogue 1, we heard Jón Einarsson say about the coach: **hún stoppar hérna**, *lit.* 'she stops here'. While it may sound strange in English to refer to an inanimate object as 'he' or 'she', in Icelandic it makes perfect sense to do so. Obviously, however, personal pronouns can also be used to refer directly to a particular individual and will, in that case, reflect the sex of that individual.

The following are the singular personal pronouns in Icelandic:

ég	I
þú	you
hann	he
hún	she
það	it

Dialogue 2

Magnús bumps into his friend Ásdís and her acquaintance Raj. Where is Raj from? Where is he going?

MAGNÚS: Komdu sæl og blessuð Ásdís!

ÁSDÍS: Sæll og blessaður Magnús! Gaman að sjá þig! Hvað segirðu gott?

MAGNÚS: Allt fínt, en þú?

ÁSDÍS: Allt ágætt.

MAGNÚS: Það er gott að heyra. Og hver er þetta?

ÁSDÍS: Þetta er Raj Aluwahlia, kunningi minn.

MAGNÚS: Komdu sæll Raj. Magnús Gíslason heiti ég. Ert þú útlendingur?

RAJ: Já, ég er frá Kanada. Ég er núna í fríi á Íslandi.

MAGNÚS: Þú talar mjög góða íslensku.

RAJ: Takk fyrir, það er gaman að heyra.

MAGNÚS: Jæja, og hvað ætlar þú að gera núna Raj?

RAJ: Ég er að fara í Bláa Lónið. Rútan fer eftir smástund.

MAGNÚS: Má bjóða þér far?

RAJ: Já, þakka þér kærlega fyrir.

Ásdís:	Allt í lagi, vertu blessaður Magnús. Það var gaman að hitta þig.
Magnús:	Sömuleiðis, vertu blessuð.
Ásdís:	Við sjáumst Raj, blessaður.
Raj:	Bless.

Magnús:	*Hello Ásdís!*
Ásdís:	*Hello Magnús! Good to see you! How are you?*
Magnús:	*I'm fine, and you?*
Ásdís:	*I'm fine.*
Magnús:	*That's good to hear. And who is this?*
Ásdís:	*This is Raj Aluwahlia, an acquaintance of mine.*
Magnús:	*Hello Raj. Magnús Gíslason is my name. Are you from abroad?*
Raj:	*Yes, I'm from Canada. I am presently on holiday in Iceland.*
Magnús:	*You speak very good Icelandic.*
Raj:	*Thank you, that's nice to hear.*
Magnús:	*And what are you going to do now, Raj?*
Raj:	*I am going to the Blue Lagoon. The coach is leaving in a little while.*
Magnús:	*Can I offer you a lift?*
Raj:	*Yes, thank you very much.*
Ásdís:	*All right, goodbye Magnús. It was nice to meet you.*
Magnús:	*Likewise. Goodbye.*
Ásdís:	*See you Raj, bye.*
Raj:	*Bye.*

Vocabulary notes

gaman að sjá þig	good to see you (**gaman**, 'fun', 'great', 'nice', and **sjá**, 'see')
það er gott að heyra	that is good to hear (**gott**, from **góður** 'good', and **heyra** 'hear')
útlending/ur, *m.*	foreigner
í fríi	on holidays (from **frí**, *n.* 'holidays', 'vacation', 'off')
Íslandi, from **Ísland**, *n.*	Iceland
Bláa Lónið	the Blue Lagoon, a famous natural pool of warm geothermal sea-water rich in minerals, silica and blue green algae and renowned for its healing powers

allt í lagi	okay, all right
sömuleiðis	likewise, same to you, same here

Greetings and courtesies

As you may have noticed in the preceding dialogue, a number of greetings in Icelandic have slightly different forms depending on whether one is addressing a male or a female. Here are some common Icelandic greetings and courtesies, with their male and female forms where applicable:

How do you do

1 Semi-formal	**Komdu sæll**	to a man
	Komdu sæl	to a woman
2 Informal	**Komdu blessaður**	
	Komdu sæll og blessaður	to a man
	Komdu blessaður og sæll	
	Komdu blessuð	
	Komdu sæl og blessuð	to a woman
	Komdu blessuð og sæl	

Hello how are you

1 Hello	**Sæll**	
	Blessaður	to a man
	Sæll og blessaður	
	Sæl	
	Blessuð	to a woman
	Sæl og blessuð	
2 How are you	Q: **Hvað segirðu (gott)?**	*lit.* 'What do you say?'
	A: **Allt gott,** **Allt fínt,** **en þú?** **Allt ágætt,**	*lit.* 'Everything good/fine/okay, and you?'
	Q: **Hvernig hefurðu það?**	*lit.* 'How do you have it?'
	A: **(Ég hef það) bara** **gott/fínt, en þú?**	*lit.* '(I have it) just fine, and you?'

Q:	**Hvað er að frétta (af þér)?**	*lit.* 'What's the news (from you)'
A:	**Allt gott,** **Allt fínt, en hjá þér?** **Allt ágætt**	*lit.* 'Everything good/fine/okay, and from you?'

Good day

Góðan daginn/ **Góðan dag**	*lit.* 'good day', is the equivalent of English 'good morning' and 'good afternoon', and is a widely used greeting in formal situations (going into shops, classrooms, offices, etc.). It is also used in informal situations first thing in the morning after one gets up.
Gott kvöld/ **Góða kvöldið**	'Good evening', used after 6 p.m. as above.
Góða nótt	Good night

Goodbye

Same as 'how-do-you-do', but replace **komdu** with **vertu**:

vertu sæll/sæl
vertu blessaður/blessuð

In informal situations, it is also common to use:

bless bless, or just: **bless**

the equivalent of '*bye (bye)*' in English, or:

við sjáumst, see you (*lit.* 'we [will] see each other')

Thank you

1 Semi-formal	**Þakka þér (kærlega) fyrir**	*lit.* 'Thank you (kindly/very much)'
2 Informal	**Takk (fyrir)**	'Thanks'
	A: **Það var ekkert**	*lit.* 'It was nothing', not at all

Other common courtesies

1 Excuse me	**Fyrirgefðu** **Afsakið**	
2 Welcome	**Velkominn** **Velkomin**	to a man to a woman
3 Can you tell me (where . . . is?)	**Getur þú sagt mér (hvar . . . er)?**	

4 Q: 'What is your name?' **Hvað heitir þú?**
  A: 'My name is …' **Ég heiti …**

5 Q: 'Where are you from?' **Hvaðan ert þú?**
  A: '(I am) from …' **(Ég er) frá …**

6 'What is this called in **Hvað heitir þetta á íslensku?**
  Icelandic'?

7 'Can I offer you (a ride, **Má bjóða þér (far, sæti, kaffi)?**
  a seat, a coffee)?'

Athugið (NB)

In Iceland, the distinction between semi-formal and informal is not quite the same as in, for instance, the UK. In Iceland, everyone is addressed by their first name, without any titles, irrespective of social standing or age. While it is common to greet a complete stranger with more formality than a friend, it is unlikely you will seriously offend if you use a less formal greeting.

Exercise 3

You are a tourist visiting Reykjavík for the first time. You are looking to find **Dómkirkja**, the cathedral, without much success it seems, so you decide to ask. Fill in the gaps in the following dialogue, using the information provided above.

YOU: (1.*Good day*) ____________.
MAN: Góðan dag.
YOU: (2.*Excuse me, can you tell me where the* Dómkirkja *is?*)
  ____________, ____________ ?
MAN: Dómkirkjan, já, hún er hérna rétt við Hótel Borg.
YOU: (3. *Thank you very much.*) ____________.
MAN: Það var ekkert. Ert þú útlendingur?
YOU: (4.*Yes, I am English*) ____, ____________ .
MAN: Þú talar góða íslensku!
YOU: (5. *Thank you. Goodbye.*) ____________.____________.
MAN: Bless.

Language points

Questions and answers

In Icelandic, the word order of a simple sentence is the same as in English: subject – verb – object. To formulate a question is even easier: you put the (first) verb before the subject: verb – subject – object? To answer the question, the subject goes back to its regular position at the beginning of the sentence:

Talar þú íslensku? Já, **ég tala íslensku**
Do you speak Icelandic? Yes, I speak Icelandic

Ert þú útlendingur? Já, **ég er frá Bretlandi**
Are you from abroad? Yes, I am from Britain

This rule remains in effect when a question is formed, as often happens, with the help of interrogatives such as **hvar**:

Hvar stoppar rútan? Hún stoppar rétt fyrir utan
Where does the coach stop? It stops right outside

Hvað heitir þú? Ég heiti ...
What is your name? My name is ...

In English, interrogatives are usually words beginning with *wh-*. In Icelandic they usually start with **hv-**. Go back to Dialogues 1 and 2, and collect all **hv-** words. Do you remember what they mean? They were:

hvar	where?
hvaðan	where ... from?
hvað	what?
hver	who?

Athugið

It is common for the personal pronoun **þú** to become part of the verb in questions. This often leads to a change or loss of the initial þ:

ert þú útlendingur?	→ **ertu útlendingur?** (þ is dropped*)
hvað segir þú?	→ **hvað segirðu?** (þ changes to voiced ð)

Should a part of speech be moved to the beginning of a regular sentence, for special emphasis for instance, the subject will also 'hide' behind the (first) verb, as in: **Magnús Gíslason heiti ég**, instead of **ég heiti Magnús Gíslason**.

Þetta er/það er

In Dialogue 2, Magnús asked: **hver er þetta**, 'who is this?' **þetta** is a demonstrative pronoun used about something or someone in close visual range, the equivalent of English 'this':

Hvað er þetta? Þetta er kirkja What is this? This is a church

As we saw earlier, the personal pronoun **það** means 'it':

Það er gaman   It is fun/great

It is also often used in combination with singular **er**, 'is' (or plural **eru**, 'are') to mean 'there is' (or 'there are'):

Það er rúta sem fer til Reykjavíkur
There is a coach which goes to Reykjavík

Exercise 4: **Hvað er þetta? Þetta er ...**

Do you remember what the Icelandic words are for the following? Ask and answer for each in Icelandic what it is.

Dæmi ('example') : **blað > Hvað er þetta? Þetta er blað**

1 coach	6 man
2 stone	7 rose
3 table	8 woman
4 chair	9 shop
5 church	10 car

Exercise 5

Now determine the gender of each of these nouns and add the correct form of the definite article.

Vera *and the present continuous*

In Dialogue 1, Joyce said: **ég er að læra íslensku**. This construction translates into the present continuous in English: 'I am learning

Icelandic'. In Icelandic, as in English, this construction is used to indicate a temporary action taking place at the moment of speaking. It is also a relatively easy as well as a very useful way to start using verbs and forming simple sentences in Icelandic. All one needs to do is choose the appropriate form of the verb **vera**, 'to be', followed by **að** and the infinitive form of the verb expressing the action. Here are some examples:

Subject	[vera]		Verb		
Ég	**er**	**að**	**lesa**	–	I am reading
		að	**skrifa**	–	. . . writing
Þú	**ert**	**að**	**fara**	–	You are going
		að	**borða**	–	. . . eating
Hann	**er**	**að**	**drekka**	–	He is drinking
		að	**læra**	–	. . . learning
Hún	**er**	**að**	**tala**	–	She is talking/speaking
		að	**vinna**	–	. . . working

Exercise 6: **Hvað er fólkið að gera?** *'What are the people doing?'*

Look at the pictures below and on p. 24. Can you say in Icelandic what these people are doing, using the verbs listed above to help you?

Exercise 7

Now could you say in Icelandic what you are doing on an ordinary day at the following times?

10 a.m.	Ég er að ________
1 p.m	______________
5 p.m.	______________
9 p.m.	______________

Dialogue 3

Símtal

Richard Johnson is in Reykjavík to meet Gunnar Guðmundsson, a business associate. He has just arrived at his hotel and phones Gunnar to make an appointment. What is the name of the company that Gunnar works for? Where is Richard from?

X:	Eimskip, góðan dag.
RICHARD:	Góðan daginn, Richard Johnson heiti ég. Er Gunnar Guðmundsson við?
X:	Fyrirgefðu, en hvað segirðu að þú heitir?
R:	Richard Johnson, r – i – c – h – a – r – d j – o – h – n – s – o – n.
X:	Richard Johnson.

RICHARD: Já, ég er sölumaður hjá Shell-fyrirtækinu í Aberdeen í Skotlandi, og ég er hér í Reykjavík til að hitta Gunnar.

X: Ég skal athuga það, augnablik.
Allt í lagi, hérna er Gunnar, gjörðu svo vel.

RICHARD: Þakka þér fyrir. Komdu sæll Gunnar.

GUNNAR: Komdu sæll Richard, og velkominn til Íslands!

A telephone conversation

X: *Eimskip, good afternoon.*

RICHARD: *Good afternoon, Richard Johnson is my name. Is Gunnar Guðmundsson there?*

X: *Excuse me, what did you say your name was?*

R: *Richard Johnson, r – i – c – h – a – r – d   j – o – h – n – s – o – n.*

X: *Richard Johnson.*

RICHARD: *Yes, I am a salesperson with the Shell company in Aberdeen in Scotland, and I am here in Reykjavík to meet Gunnar.*

X: *I will check, one moment please.*
All right, here is Gunnar, go ahead.

RICHARD: *Thank you. Hello Gunnar.*

GUNNAR: *Hello Richard, and welcome to Iceland!*

Vocabulary notes

er … við?	is … there?	**augnablik**, *n.*	moment (here: 'one moment please')
fyrirtæki, *n.*	firm, company		
skal	shall (from **skulu**)	**gjörðu svo vel**	here you are, go ahead

Hvað heitir þú?

The Icelandic naming system is different from that in many other countries. Most Icelanders have one or two first names (**skírnarnafn**), and a patronymic (**föðurnafn**), i.e. the father's (or mother's) first name in the possessive case form (see Lesson 4) followed by **-son** or **-dóttir**: Jón Einarsson (i.e. Jón, son of Einar), Vigdís Finnbogadóttir (Vigdís, daughter of Finnbogi). Only a few Icelanders have a family name (**ættarnafn**): Jóhann Briem, Einar H. Kvaran. Women do not change their name after marriage. Thus, in an Icelandic family consisting of a mother, a father, a son and a daughter, each family member will have a different last name.

It is also common for Icelanders to be addressed by relatives and friends with a pet name (**gælunafn**). Most pet names are traditional abbreviations of the first name, ending in **-i** for men, and **-a** for women:

Páll	– Palli	Kolbrún	– Kolla
Sigurður	– Siggi	Sigríður	– Sigga
Guðmundur	– Gummi, Mundi	Ásdís	– Ása, Dísa

Most male names in Icelandic have endings that are identical to those of masculine nouns: **-i**, **-ur**, **-ll**, **-nn**. Female names can be harder to recognize. Some common endings for female names are: **-rún**, **-dís**, **-björg**, **-gerður**, **-hildur**, **-ríður**, **-unn**, and **-ín** (not to be confused with the masculine ending **-inn**).

Earlier we saw that the verb used to indicate someone's name is **heita**, 'to be called'. Its forms in the singular are as follows:

Ég	**heiti**
Þú	**heitir**
Hún/hann	**heitir**

To ask for someone's full name, one uses:

Hvað heitir þú fullu nafni?

To find out a last name (i.e. patronymic), one asks:

Hvers son/dóttir (ert þú)?   Whose son/daughter (are you)?

Exercise 8

The illustration on p. 27 contains a fragment from an Icelandic telephone book. Since Icelanders do not have surnames proper, listings are on a first name basis (as is everything else, even in the most formal of circumstances). Can you distinguish the male from the female names? Do any of these people have a family name?

Helga Björg Árnadóttir Grundargarði 13	472 1234
Helgi Hlynur Pétursson Framnesi	472 7890
Hjalti Eiríksson Bjarkargötu 4	472 5678
Ingigerður Júlíusdóttir Hóli	472 3456
Ingimar Schram Garðarsbraut 8	472 1123
Jakobína Sigurðardóttir Tjörn	472 2345
Kristinn Viðarsson Saltvík	472 4567
Kristín Blöndal Skólagötu 15	472 6789

Reading 1

Fjölskylda frá Íslandi

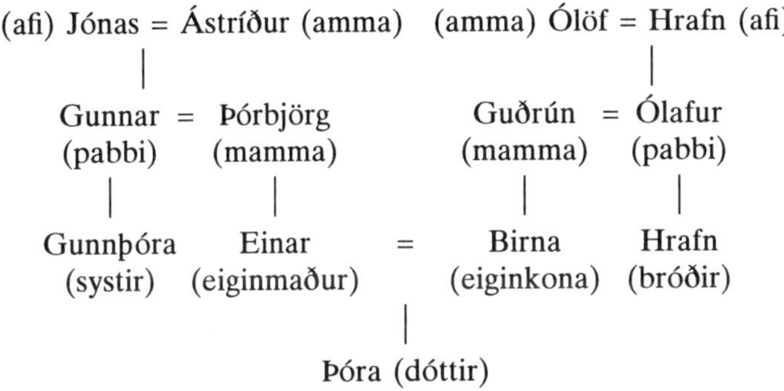

Einar Gunnarsson er Íslendingur. Pabbi hans heitir Gunnar, og þess vegna er Einar Gunnarsson. Afi heitir Jónas, og þess vegna er Gunnar Jónasson. Á Íslandi er það svona.

Einar er eiginmaður. Það þýðir að hann er giftur. Eiginkonan heitir Birna. Hún er kona Einars, en hún heitir samt ekki Birna Gunnarsson, af því að hún er ekki Gunnarsson. Hún er Ólafsdóttir, af því að pabbi hennar heitir Ólafur. Afi heitir Hrafn, og þess vegna er Ólafur Hrafnsson.

Birna og Einar eiga barn. Barnið heitir Þóra. Hvað er barnið að gera? Það er að leika sér. Hvar er Einar? Hann er ekki heima. Hann er að vinna. Hann er sölumaður. Og hvað er Birna að gera? Hún er að vinna heima. Hún er að lesa leikrit. Hún er leikkona og hún er að lesa undir hlutverk.

Vocabulary notes

fjölskyld/a, *f.*	family
þess vegna	therefore
svona	thus, so, like that
eigin-mað/ur, *m.*	husband, wife (**eigin-** is very often left out; the words
eigin-kon/a, *f.*	**maður** and **kona** are commonly used to mean not
	only 'man' and 'woman' but also 'husband' and 'wife')
þýðir	means (from **þýða**)
eins og	like
af því að	because
hennar	her
leika sér	play
heima	at home
lesa undir	prepare, study

Exercise 9: **Spurningar** *('questions')*

Can you answer the following questions in Icelandic?

1 Hvað heitir Gunnþóra fullu nafni?
2 Hvers son er Hrafn, bróðir Birnu?
3 Hvers dóttir er Þóra?
4 Hvað heitir þú fullu nafni?
5 Hvers son/dóttir ertu?

2 Hvaðan ert þú?

Where are you from?

In this lesson you will learn about:

- asking for information and giving information about yourself
- countries, nationalities and colours
- singular nominative adjectives/gender
- professions
- negation, **já/jú**
- verbs in singular present

Dialogue 1

Spjall

Elva Stefansson is looking around for an empty seat to eat her breakfast in the crowded dining room of her Reykjavík hotel. She notices an empty seat at a table with one female occupant. Where does Elva live? And Guðrún? Why does Elva have an Icelandic name?

ELVA: Afsakið, talarðu íslensku?
GUÐRÚN: Já, ég er íslensk.
ELVA: Er þetta laust sæti?
GUÐRÚN: Já, gjörðu svo vel og fáðu þér sæti.
ELVA: Þakka þér fyrir. Elva Stefansson heiti ég.
GUÐRÚN: Elva Stefansson? Er það ekki íslenskt nafn?
ELVA: Jú, ég er vestur-íslensk. Ég er frá Kanada.
GUÐRÚN: Hvaðan í Kanada?
ELVA: Gimli, Manitoba.

GUðRÚN: Nú hvað segirðu, ég á frændfólk í Manitoba. Og það er
          þess vegna sem þú talar íslensku!
ELVA: Já, svolítið. Pabbi minn er íslenskur. Hvaðan ert þú?
GUðRÚN: Ég heiti Guðrún Ásmundsdóttir, og ég er frá Húsavík.

A chat

ELVA: *Pardon me, do you speak Icelandic?*
GUðRÚN: *Yes, I am Icelandic.*
ELVA: *Is this seat taken?*
GUðRÚN: *No, please go ahead and have a seat.*
ELVA: *Thank you. Elva Stefansson is my name.*
GUðRÚN: *Elva Stefansson? Is that not an Icelandic name?*
ELVA: *Yes, I am Western Icelandic. I am from Canada.*
GUðRÚN: *Where from in Canada?*
ELVA: *Gimli, Manitoba.*
GUðRÚN: *Really, I have relatives in Manitoba. And that is why you
          speak Icelandic!*
ELVA: *Yes, a little bit. My dad is Icelandic. Where are you from?*
GUðRÚN: *My name is Guðrún Ásmundsdóttir, and I am from
          Húsavík.*

Vocabulary notes

laus, *adj.*	free (i.e. 'not taken')
fáðu þér sæti	have a seat
vestur-íslensk/ur, *adj.*	Western Icelandic (This term is commonly used by people in Iceland to denote Icelanders who emigrated to North America (mostly around the turn of the century) and their descendants.)
nú hvað segirðu	really (*lit.* 'what do you say?')
frændfólk, *n.*	relatives (Note that although the noun **fólk** implies a plural, it only ever occurs in the singular.)

Language points

Countries and nationalities

Exercise 1

The picture overleaf contains a number of clippings from Icelandic newspapers and brochures with the names of different countries and/or nationalities. Can you pick them out and match them with their English names listed below? Don't worry about forms or endings right now, that will all fall into place later.

1	Thailand	13	France/French
2	South Afrika	14	The United States
3	Faroese/Faroe Islanders	15	Germany
4	Russians	16	England
5	Switzerland	17	Mexico
6	Romania/Romanian	18	Canada
7	Holland	19	Denmark
8	Australia	20	Belgium
9	Norway	21	Israel
10	Malaysia	22	Sweden
11	Scotland	23	Austria
12	Italy	24	Finland

The names of many countries end in the neuter noun **-land** in Icelandic, as for instance in **Indland** (India), **Rússland** (Russia) and **Ungverjaland** (Hungary). The names of inhabitants usually consist of the first part of the country's name, followed by:

1 **-i: Svíþjóð – Svíi, Ítalía – Ítali, Írland – Íri, Japan – Japani**
2 **-lendingur** ('lander'): **Ísland – Íslendingur, Tæland – Tælendingur**
3 **-verji: Pólland – Pólverji, Kína – Kínverji, Spánn – Spánverji**
4 **-maður** (or **-búi): Kanada – Kanadamaður, Bandaríkin – Bandaríkjamaður**

Some national nouns are slightly irregular, for instance **Þýskaland – Þjóðverji, Noregur – Norðmaður**. Can you tell the gender of these nouns? Yes, they are all masculine.

Nationality can also be expressed using an adjective instead of a noun. In Dialogue 1, for instance, Guðrún said that she was **íslensk**, 'Icelandic', rather than **Íslendingur**, an Icelander.

SVISS

á eigin vegum
Bandaríkin

Suður-Afríka í úrslitin á HM

Suður-Afríka er komin í lokakeppni HM í knattspyrnu í fyrsta skipti eftir 1-0 sigur á Kongó á laugardaginn. Phil Masinga skoraði markið dýrmæta.

Taglið er fokið

Roberto Baggio, ítalski knattspyrnusnillingurinn, er búinn að fórna vörumerki sínu, taglinu. Hann mætti stuttklipptur á æfingu á laugardag og ítalskir fjölmiðlar tóku andköf. „Ég var orðinn þreyttur á síða hárinu," var hin einfalda skýring Baggio á tiltækinu.

Holland: PSV meistari meistaranna

PSV Eindhoven varð í gær meistari meistaranna í Hollandi þegar liðið lagði Roda JC að velli, 3-1, en staðan í hálfleik var 1-0 ...

Rússarnir koma!

„Pétur" eftir rúmenska leikskáldið Vlad Zografi

INN kemur kall sem er í jakka eins og ég, hann heimtar ljós og músík, eins og menn eiga til að gera í sýningum Rimasar Tuminasar, og Parísarlífið upphefst. Í París er allt ljósblátt og bleikt og mikið af speglum og gleri, en fyrst og fremst mikið af alls konar hjólum. Tannhjólum, reiðhjólum, vagnhjólum og alls konar gagnslausum hjólum. Annars er þessi sýning leikin í ósköp ómerkilegri skemmu úr múrsteinum og járnbitum; við eigum nóg af svona skemmum heima á Íslandi, tómum; allar ragmagnsleiðshur utanáliggjandi og skólpið líka. Pétur mikli Rússakeisari er kominn til Parísar í heimsókn

ur á eftir sér hauskúpur færi og er með blöðrur Pétur lætur náttúrlega alæer um sig. Honum vont í París og vill frek vasapela sínum. Han kominn til að fá sv heimsins gátum hjá unum í París. En þei eins og hálfgerðar ur, þessir Frakkar. inn sem passar þe piladós.

Upptærða

Það hefur kvis að Pétur sé komir in veisla.
„Má ég k Moskvu?"

Höfundur og leikstjóri

VLAD Zografi fæddist í Búkarest í Rúmeníu árið 1960. Hann lagði stund á eðlisfræði við háskólann í Búkarest og lauk doktorsprófi í kjarnorku- og sameindaeðlisfræði. Hann birtir reglulega ritgerðir um fræði sín á því sviði en hefur frá 1990 jafnframt skrifað smásögur og leikrit og starfað að útgáfumálum. Leikritið Pétur fékk verðlaun gagnrýnenda sem besta rúmenska leikritið árið 1996.

Vlad Zografi

SANDRINE Holt er fjölþjóðleg því hún fæddist í Frakklandi, á kínverska móður og franskan föður en ólst upp í Kanada. Hún lék fyrst í myndinni „Black Robe" árið 1991.

SALMA Hayek kemur frá Mexíkó og sást fyrst í hinni lostafullu mynd „Desperado" með Antonio Banderas árið 1995.

MILI Avital er frá Ísrael og sást fyrst í myndinni „Stargate" árið 1994.

MICHELLE Yeoh er frá Malasíu og vakti fyrst athygli vestra í Bond-myndinni „Tomorrow Never Dies" á móti Pierce Brosnan á síðasta ári.

ASIA Argento er frá Ítalíu og hefur leikið í nokkrum ítölskum myndum sem fáir hafa séð vestra nema gagnrýnendur.

▶**PORTIA** De Rossi er frá Ástralíu og leikur eina af kjánalegu vinkonunum í hrollvekjunni „Scream 2"

TÖFRAR Tælands laða sífellt fleiri íslenska ferðamenn til landsins.

Íslendingar til Tælands

Ferðaskrifstofan Nonni Travel á Akureyri með hringferð um Grænland árið 2000

FÆREYSKUR þjóðbúningur.

vík, Hvítanes, ... Skálavík o.s.frv. Sama máli geg... götuheiti í Þórshöfn, höfuðstað Færeyja. Þau hafa sömu endingar og hér: -ás, -brekka, -gerði, -gata [göta], -hlíð, -hæð, -lág, -teigur, -tröð og - vegur. Það er í raun fátt sem er framandi í augum landans í Færeyjum.

Færeyingar hafa af fjölmörgu að státa.

Exercise 2

In the left-hand column is a list of several countries. Can you pair them with the matching adjectives in the right-hand column? You may recognize some from the previous exercise.

Svíþjóð	japanskur
Spánn	þýskur
Indland	grískur
Skotland	bandarískur
Ítalía	rússneskur
Frakkland	franskur
Ástralía	skoskur
Þýskaland	kínverskur
Grikkland	sænskur
Kína	ástralskur
Kanada	ítalskur
Rússland	kanadískur
Japan	spænskur
Bandaríkin	indverskur

Note that instead of the adjective **bandarískur** Icelanders sometimes use **amerískur**. Did you notice that the nouns denoting countries and nationalities are all capitalized, but the adjectives are not?

Dialogue 2 🔢

Spjall 2

Elva and Guðrún continue their breakfast conversation. What is Elva doing in Reykjavík? Why is Guðrún in Reykjavík?

ELVA:　Hvað ertu að gera hérna?
GUÐRÚN:　Ég er hér á tölvunámskeiði. Ég er kennari.
ELVA:　Hvað kennir þú?
GUÐRÚN:　Ég kenni tölvufræði og ensku. En þú, hvað gerir þú?
ELVA:　Ég er blaðamaður. Ég er að skrifa grein um menningarlíf
　　　í Reykjavík.
GUÐRÚN:　Og hvernig líkar þér hérna?
ELVA:　Mjög vel. Reykjavík er aldeilis skemmtileg og lífleg borg.

GUÐRÚN: Já, hún er það. Hún er náttúrulega ekki stórborg, en það er alltaf mikið um að vera hér.
ELVA: Ferðu oft til Reykjavíkur?
GUÐRÚN: Já, ég fer oft á námskeið og ég á líka frændfólk hér. En heyrðu, ég verð að koma mér af stað. Kannski sjáumst við seinna?
ELVA: Já, ég verð hérna í kvöld. Vertu blessuð Guðrún, og takk fyrir spjallið.
GUÐRÚN: Sömuleiðis takk Elva, vertu blessuð.

A chat 2

ELVA: *What are you doing here?*
GUÐRÚN: *I am here on a computer course. I am a teacher.*
ELVA: *What do you teach?*
GUÐRÚN: *I teach computer science and English. And you?*
ELVA: *I am a journalist. I am writing an article on the cultural life in Reykjavík.*
GUÐRÚN: *And how do you like it here?*
ELVA: *Very much. Reykjavík is really an enjoyable and lively city.*
GUÐRÚN: *Yes, so it is. It is of course not a metropolis, but there is always a lot going on here.*
ELVA: *Do you often go to Reykjavík?*
GUÐRÚN: *Yes, I often go on a course and I also have relatives here. But listen, I must be going. Perhaps we'll see each other later?*
ELVA: *Yes, I'll be here tonight. Goodbye Guðrún, and thanks for the chat.*
GUÐRÚN: *Thanks to you too Elva, goodbye.*

Vocabulary notes

tölvunámskeið, *n.* computer course (from **tölv/a**, *f.* 'computer', and **námskeið**, *n.* 'course')

kennir teach (from **kenna**, *vb.*)

ensk/u English (from **ensk/a**, *f.*)

menningarlíf, *n.* cultural life (from **menning**, *f.* 'culture', and **líf**, *n.* 'life')

hvernig líkar þér? how do you like it?

hún er það	so it is (*lit.* 'she is that')	**verð að**	have to, must (from **verða að**)
mikið,	much from **mikill**, *adj.*	**koma mér af stað**	be going
það er mikið um að vera	there's a lot going on	**í kvöld**	this evening, tonight

Adjectives

Unlike nouns, adjectives do not have a set gender, but reflect instead, through different forms, the gender of the noun or subject they qualify. The form you find in dictionaries or glossaries, and in the above exercise, is the masculine. A slash indicates which part of the adjective is the masculine ending: **íslensk/ur**. The following are the different endings for adjectives:

Masculine	Feminine	Neuter
_____**ur**[1]	_____ $a>ö/u$ 0[2]	_____**t**[3]
_____**ll**		
_____**nn**		
_____**r**		

Athugið (Note)

1 In a few cases, the masculine final **-r** or **-ur** is actually not an ending but part of the stem of the adjective itself. For these adjectives, the masculine and feminine forms are the same, while neuter gets its regular **-t** ending: **stór**, 'big' (**stór**, *f.* and **stórt**, *n.*). The same is the case for a group of adjectives of which the stem ends in **-s** or consonant plus **-n**: **laus** – **laus** – **laust**.

2 In the feminine form of adjectives which have **a** as a stem vowel, the **a** will change into **ö** (or, in unstressed positions, into **u**): **svartur** – **svört** and **gamall** – **gömul**, except in cases where the syllable with the **-a** is followed by a second syllable with a different vowel, as for instance **fallegur** – **falleg**. This phenomenon, known as the U-shift, will be treated in more detail in Lesson 3.

3 The **-t** ending for the neuter form of adjectives sometimes causes preceding letters to change:

- if the **-t** ending is preceded by **ð**, this **ð** will change into **-t**: **góð/ur** – **gott**
- if the ending is preceded by consonant plus **-d** or consonant

plus **-t** respectively, there will be no ending at all, and final **d** will change into **t**: **svart/ur – svart, vond/ur – vont**
- if the ending is preceded by a vowel, the **-t** ending is doubled: **blá/r – blátt**

Here are some examples:

Masculine	*Feminine*	*Neuter*	
íslenskur	íslensk	íslenskt	Icelandic
franskur	frönsk	franskt	French
gamall	gömul	gamalt	old
nýr	ný	nýtt	new

Maðurinn er íslenskur	Guðrún er íslensk	Barnið er íslenskt
Renault er franskur bíll	París er frönsk borg	Franskt brauð
Stóllinn er gamall	Tölvan er gömul	Borðið er gamalt
Þetta er nýr lampi	Þetta er ný kirkja	Þetta er nýtt blað

Note that the neuter forms of the common adjectives **mikill**, 'much', and **lítill**, 'little', are **mikið** and **lítið**.

There are a few adjectives in Icelandic that always stay the same, as adjectives do in English. These are known as indeclinable adjectives. The glossary and vocabulary notes will alert you to them.

Exercise 3

Say what countries the following cities belong to, using adjectives and keeping in mind that the Icelandic word for city, **borg**, is feminine. Note that some cities may be called slightly differently in Icelandic.

Dæmi ('example') **Tókyó er japönsk borg**

1	Róm	5 Delhi
2	Stokkhólmur	6 Amsterdam
3	Berlín	7 Dublin (Dyflinni)
4	Moskva	8 London (Lundúnir)

Exercise 4

Go back to Dialogues 1 and 2 and pick out all the adjectives. Can you tell which gender form they are in and why?

Colours

There are of course many other adjectives than those indicating nationality. Colours are among the frequently used adjectives. Here is a list of colours in Icelandic:

hvítur	white
gulur	yellow
appelsínugulur	orange
bleikur	pink
rauður	red
blár	blue
fjólublár	purple
grænn	green
brúnn	brown
grár	grey
svartur	black

Exercise 5

Below is a list of items. Add the appropriate form of the definite article to each, and then match it with its colour in a sentence, also, of course, using the appropriate gender form. The meaning of each item is given in brackets, and, where this is not obvious from its form, the gender as well. Use the list of colours above, and use each colour only once.

Dæmi: **snjór**, *m. 'snow'* – **hvítur** → **Snjórinn er hvítur**

1 appelsína (orange)
2 banani (banana)
3 gras, *n.* (grass)
4 himinn (sky)
5 rós, *f.* (rose)
6 hundur (dog)

7 kaffi, *n.* (coffee)
8 vínber, *n.* (grape)
9 svanur (swan)
10 fíll (elephant)
11 svín, *n.* (pig)

Now try this for yourself: what objects in your direct environment can you name in Icelandic? Do you know their gender? What colours are they? Solidify your knowledge of Icelandic words and their grammatical features by trying to make a few a day part of your daily routine!

Dialogue 3

Hvernig líkar þér hérna?

The following dialogue takes place at a reception hosted for international students enrolled in an intensive summer course in Icelandic. What does Hiromi do? Does she like Iceland? Where does Luigi work? Why is Aleko working in Iceland?

ALEKO: Komdu sæll, Aleko heiti ég.

LUIGI: Sæll, ég heiti Luigi. Ég er Ítali. Hvaðan ert þú?

ALEKO: Ég er frá Grikklandi. Þetta er Hiromi, hún er frá Japan.

LUIGI: Sæl og blessuð. Hvernig líkar þér hérna?

HIROMI: Ágætlega. Veðrið er búið að vera svolítið kalt og leiðinlegt að vísu, og maturinn og lífsvenjur eru allt öðruvísi en heima í Japan, en landið er mjög fallegt og fólkið alveg indælt.

LUIGI: Maturinn er vissulega óvenjulegur, ég þoli hann ekki. Og það gengur illa að kynnast Íslendingum.

ALEKO: Nú er ég ekki sammála Luigi! Það tekur bara tíma. Ég er búinn að vera hér allt sumarið og mér líkar mjög vel. Af hverju ert þú annars að læra íslensku, Hiromi?

HIROMI: Ég er sölustjóri hjá fyrirtæki sem á mikil viðskipti við Ísland.

LUIGI: Ég er sendiráðsritari hjá ítalska sendiráðinu á Íslandi. Og þú, hvað gerir þú, Aleko?

ALEKO: Ég er háskólanemi. Ég er að læra málvísindi og ég hef áhuga á íslensku. En það er mjög dýrt að búa á Íslandi, þannig að ég vinn í bókabúð hér í Reykjavík.

HIROMI: Er það gott starf?

ALEKO: Já, mjög gott. Ég er afgreiðslumaður og hitti margt fólk, og starfsfólkið er líka skemmtilegt. En heyrðu, þarna kemur maturinn! Fáum okkur að borða!

How are you liking it here?

ALEKO: *Hello, Aleko is my name.*

LUIGI: *Hi, my name is Luigi. I am Italian. Where are you from?*

ALEKO: *I'm from Greece. This is Hiromi, she is from Japan.*

LUIGI: *Hello. How are you liking it here?*

HIROMI: *Fine. The weather has been a little cold and unpleasant to be sure, and the food and customs are completely different from those at home in Japan, but the country is very beautiful and the people quite friendly.*

LUIGI: *The food is certainly unusual, I can't stand it. And it is difficult to get to know Icelanders.*

ALEKO: *I don't agree Luigi! It just takes time. I have been here all summer and I like it very much. Why are you learning Icelandic by the way, Hiromi?*

HIROMI: *I am a marketing director with a company that does business with Iceland.*

LUIGI: *I am an attaché with the Italian Embassy in Iceland. And you, what do you do, Aleko?*

ALEKO: *I am a university student. I am studying linguistics and I am interested in Icelandic. But it is very expensive to live in Iceland, so I work in a bookshop here in Reykjavík.*

HIROMI: *Is it a good job?*

ALEKO: *Yes, very good. I am a shop assistant and meet many people, and the staff are also a lot of fun. But listen, here comes the food! Let's get ourselves something to eat!*

Vocabulary notes

búin/n, *adj.* (**búin**, *f.*, **búið**, *n.*)	finished (The expression **vera búinn að**, *lit.* 'to be finished doing something', is often translated into English as a perfect tense: **það er búið að vera kalt**, 'it has been cold'. See also Lesson 14.)
veðrið,	weather (from **veður**, *n.*)
að vísu	to be sure, actually
lífsvenjur *pl.*	customs (from **líf**, *n.* 'life', and **venj/a**, *f.* 'custom', 'habit')
allt, *n.*	all (here: 'completely', 'totally', from **allur**)
það gengur illa/vel	*lit.* 'it goes badly/well' from **ganga**, *vb.* 'walk', 'go'
sammála, *indecl. adj.*	in agreement (**ég er (ekki) sammála**, 'I (don't) agree')
mér líkar vel hér, *impers.*	I like it here
af hverju	why
annars	by the way (often used when changing the topic of conversation)
viðskipti, *n.pl.*	business

sendiráðsritari	attaché (from **sendiráð**, *n.* 'embassy', and **ritar/i**, *m.* 'secretary')
háskólanem/i	university student (from **háskól/i**, 'university', and **nem/i**, 'student' (also **nemandi**))
áhuga	interest (from **áhug/i**, *m.*)
hafa áhuga á	be interested in
þannig að	so that
bókabúð	bookshop (from **bók**, *f.* 'book' and **búð**, *f.* 'shop')
starfsfólk, *n.*	staff, employees (from **starf**, *n.* 'job', 'employment')
marg/ur, *adj.*	many, a lot
fáum okkur að borða	*lit.* 'let's get us to eat', i.e. 'let's get ourselves something to eat'

Exercise 6

Pick out the adjectives in the above dialogue. Can you tell which gender forms they are in and why? Which are the ones without an ending in the masculine?

Language points

Occupations

In the preceding dialogues, people spoke about what they do for a living. Do you remember the occupations that were mentioned?

They were: **kennari**, **blaðamaður**, **sölustjóri**, **(sendiráðs)ritari**, and **háskólanemi**.

As with the names of nationalities, there are certain patterns to the names of occupations in Icelandic. For instance, the following suffixes are very common in occupational nouns:

-ri	added on to verbs indicating the job activity, for instance: **leika** 'play', 'act' – **leikari** 'player', 'actor' **mála** 'paint' – **málari** 'painter'
-smiður	from the verb **smíða**, 'make' 'build' 'construct', as in: **trésmiður** – 'carpenter'

-fræðingur	from **fræði**, *n.pl.* 'studies', referring to an academic field of study: **lögfræðingur**, 'lawyer' (from **lögfræði**, 'law') **hjúkrunarfræðingur**, 'registered nurse' (from **hjúkrunarfræði**, 'nursing')
-stjóri	referring to a position of management, direction, authority: **leikstjóri**, 'director', **lögreglustjóri**, 'police officer', **(leigu-, vöru-) bílstjóri** ('taxi-', 'lorry'-) 'driver', 'chauffeur'
-virki	'technician' or 'mechanic': **rafvirki**, 'electrician'
-fulltrúi	representative
-sali	sales person

The suffixes **-maður** 'person' and **-fólk** 'people' also commonly indicate an employee or employees respectively in a particular area of work, as for instance in:

afgreiðslumaður	shop assistant (on the floor or behind the counter)
starfsfólk	employees, staff
sjómaður	fisherman
matreiðslumaður	cook (also: **kokkur**)

Did you remember to note the gender of all the above nouns?

Finally, here are a few common occupations not included in the above:

læknir (tann-, dýra-), *m.*	doctor (dentist, vet)
skáld (tón-, leik-), *n.*	poet (composer, playwright)
rithöfundur, *m.*	writer, novelist
forseti, *m.*	president
(forsætis-)ráðherra, *m.*	(Prime) Minister
þjónn, *m.* **þjónustustúlka**, *f.*	waiter, waitress (from **þjónusta**, *f.* 'service')

Exercise 7

Can you guess what the following occupations might be?

flugstjóri, skipstjóri, fiskifræðingur, bókari, bílasali, læknaritari, píanóleikari, rútubílstjóri

Negation

In Icelandic, the word **ekki**, 'not', is used to make a sentence negative. It is usually combined with initial **nei**, 'no', in negative answers:

Ertu kennari?   **Nei, ég er ekki kennari**

In most cases, **ekki** comes directly after the first verb in affirmative sentences. In questions where subject and verb change places, **ekki** follows the subject:

Talar hún ekki íslensku? **Nei, hún talar ekki íslensku**

We have already seen in previous dialogues that the antonym to **nei** is **já**, 'yes'. However, when replying positively to a negative question, Icelandic uses **jú** instead of **já**. Compare the following examples:

Talar hún ensku?   **Já, hún talar ensku**
Talar hún ekki íslensku? **Jú, hún talar íslensku**

Exercise 8 

Look at the pairing of the following people and occupations, and construct positive or negative sentences as appropriate, taking into account gender. In the cases where the answer is negative, can you give the correct answer instead, using the correct option from the column?

Dæmi: **Hrafn** **– leikstjóri** > **Hrafn Gunnlaugsson**
  Gunnlaugsson   **er leikstjóri**
Vilhjalmur Stefansson **– bílstjóri** > **Vilhjalmur Stefansson er**
           ekki bílstjóri. Hann er
           landkönnuður ('explorer')

Björk	söngkona
Ólafur Ragnar Grímsson	hjúkrunarkona
Halldór Laxness	forseti
Sigmund Freud	sálfræðingur
Leifur Eiríksson	alþingismaður
Florence Nightingale	málari
Nelson Mandela	rithöfundur
Edvard Munch	tölvufræðingur
Gérard Dépardieu	leikari
Bill Gates	landkönnuður

Exercise 9

Go back to the previous exercise and write down the nationality of each of the individuals listed, using adjectives and taking into account gender. Some might be a little difficult, but just review the patterns outlined above and give it a try – after all, creativity is an important part of language learning!

Verbs

In Dialogue 3, you encountered the following verbs in their singular present forms:

líkar, þoli, gengur, tekur, gerir, hef, vinn, kemur

These singular forms are in many cases different from the infinitive forms of the verbs which you learned to use in forming the present continuous. The infinitive form of virtually all Icelandic verbs ends in **-a**. To put verbs in their singular forms, this **-a** is taken off, and endings reflecting the subject, i.e. the 'I' or 'you' or 's/he/it' forms, are added to the remaining stem to create the so-called simple present: **ég tala**, 'I speak'.

In Icelandic, verbs can be roughly divided into three groups, depending on which endings they receive in the singular present. The first group, which could be called the **-a** group, consists of verbs of which the first-person 'I' ending is **-a** (just like the infinitive form), and the second and third person 'you' and 's/he/it' endings are **-ar**:

	tal-a	*borð-a*	*skrif-a*
ég	tal-a	borð-a	skrif-a
þú	tal-ar	borð-ar	skrif-ar
hún	tal-ar	borð-ar	skrif-ar

The second group, or **-i** group, closely resembles the first one, except where the first group has **-a** in its endings, this group has **-i**:

	þol-a	*lær-a*	*hitt-a*
ég	þol-i	lær-i	hitt-i
þú	þol-ir	lær-ir	hitt-ir
hann	þol-ir	lær-ir	hitt-ir

Finally, the **-ur** group is slightly more diverse. For now, it is enough to remember that the first person has no ending at all, while the other two get **-ur**:

	vinn-a	*verð-a*	*tak-a*
ég	vinn-	verð-	tek-
þú	vinn-ur	verð-ur	tek-ur
það	vinn-ur	verð-ur	tek-ur

Quite a few verbs belonging to the **-ur** group, like **taka** above, are subject to a vowel change, as are, for instance, other verbs found in Dialogue 3: **kemur** from **koma**, **gengur** from **ganga**, and **hef** from **hafa.** We will come back to this in Lesson 7.

Some verbs in Icelandic have infinitive forms ending in **-ja** rather than just **-a**. This **-j** does not occur in the singular present forms demonstrated above. Thus, a verb like **syngja**, 'sing', becomes **syng** in the first person, and **syngur** for the other two.

Since verbs contain no indication of which group they belong to, you have to learn as you go. Therefore, whenever you encounter a new verb, find out what group it belongs to and memorize this. To help you along, the vocabulary notes will list all new verbs with their 'I' forms. This will also alert you to any vowel changes that may occur. For instance, **gera – geri** tells you that **gera** is an **-i** verb and that the second and third persons therefore are **gerir**, while **láta – læt** informs you that a vowel change occurs here, and that the other two singular forms of this verb are **lætur**.

Any new irregular verbs will be listed in all forms necessary to work with them:

fara – (ég) fer – (þú) ferð – (hún) fer
lesa –   les –   lest –   les

Exercise 10

Go back to Exercises 6 and 7 in Lesson 1, and rewrite your answers using the simple present form of the verbs represented there.

Exercise 11

How would you say the following in Icelandic? Use previous dialogues to help you, trying not to translate too literally but rather use the vocabulary and constructions you have learned so far:

My name is Mark. I am Canadian. I am a novelist from Calgary. I work at home. I speak English and I am learning Icelandic. Calgary is a pleasant city. There is always much going on and the people are friendly.

Exercise 12

Pair the professions listed below with a verb from the column on
the right. Use each verb only once. Can you construct sentences,
adding the correct form of the definite article to the nouns?

Dæmi: **söngkona – syngja**: **söngkonan syngur**

skáld	kenna	
kokkur	fiska	**(-ar)**
kennari	skrifa	
nemandi	spila á píanó	**(-ar)**
ritari	elda, borða	
sölumaður	læra	
sjómaður	vélrita	**(-ar)**
píanóleikari	selja	**(-ur)**

Exercise 13

Ásdís is giving a description of herself, but some of the verbs have
been left out. Fill in the gaps, using the verbs listed and putting
them in their appropriate forms. You can use each verb as often
as you need.

vinna, elda, kenna, heita, spila, vera, lesa

Ég ___________ Ásdís. Ég ___________ íslensk. Ég ___________
dökkhærð og hávaxin. Ég ___________ kennari. Ég _________ í
grunnskóla á Akureyri. Ég ___________ ensku og frönsku.
Maðurinn minn _________ Jónas. Hann _________ í bókabúð.
Þegar ég ___________ í fríi _________ ég á píanó eða ég
___________, meðan Jónas ___________. Hann ___________ svo
góður kokkur!

Vocabulary notes

hávaxin/n, *adj.* tall (*vs.* **lágvaxin/n**, 'short' (in build),	**grunnskól/i**, *m.* **meðan**, *conj.*	elementary school while
dökkhærð/ur dark-haired (*vs.* **ljóshærð/ur**, 'fair-haired')	**svo**	such

Exercise 14

Imagine you are at a reception. Introduce the following people in Icelandic:

1 An Australian man called Tom, tall and fair-haired, married and working as a baker in Brisbane.
2 A Scottish woman from Glasgow called Helen, university student studying (= learning) law, married, husband is Irish.
3 And now it's your turn! Describe yourself as well as you can, using the vocabulary and constructions introduced in this chapter. Of course there is no set answer to this exercise, it depends on you.

3 Hvert förum við?

Where are we going?

In this lesson you will learn about:

- directions: adverbs of place
- plural personal pronouns
- verbs in the plural present
- U-shift
- cardinal numbers/gender
- plural nouns, articles and adjectives
- money, measurements, asking for amounts
- time: hours, days, months, seasons, years
- suggested action: 'let's . . .'

Dialogue 1

Á Akureyri

Þór and Harpa are walking around Akureyri, the capital of northern Iceland and the largest urban centre outside the larger Reykjavík area. Harpa is reading from a guidebook while Þór is looking around. Do Þór and Harpa go inside Akureyrarkirkja? Where did Matthías Jochumsson live? What time of day is it?

Þór:	Hvert förum við?
Harpa:	Þangað niður eftir.
Þór:	Hvað er þetta?
Harpa:	Þetta er Akureyrarkirkja.
Þór:	Mjög áberandi bygging. Hvað er hún gömul?
Harpa:	Ég veit það ekki, en hún er opin. Eigum við að fara inn og athuga það?

ÞÓR: Nei, kannski seinna. Höldum áfram. Veðrið er svo fallegt
         og það er svo mikið eftir að sjá.
HARPA: Hérna eru Sigurhæðir. Matthías Jochumsson skáld og
         prestur bjó hér. Húsið er frá 1902.
ÞÓR: Er opið?
HARPA: Nei, ekki ennþá. Það er opið milli klukkan tvö og fjögur.
ÞÓR: Förum þangað eftir hádegi.

In Akureyri

ÞÓR: *Where are we going?*
HARPA: *Down this way.*
ÞÓR: *What is that?*
HARPA: *That's the church of Akureyri.*
ÞÓR: *A very striking building. How old is it?*
HARPA: *I don't know, but it is open. Should we go in and check?*
ÞÓR: *No, later perhaps. Let's continue. The weather is so beau-
         tiful and there is so much left to see.*
HARPA: *Here is Sigurhæðir. Matthías Jochumsson, the poet and
         minister, lived here. The house is from 1902.*
ÞÓR: *Is it open?*
HARPA: *No, not yet. It is open between two and four o'clock.*
ÞÓR: *Let's go there in the afternoon.*

Vocabulary notes

vita (veit – veist – veit)	know
opin/n (opið, *n.*), *adj.*	(from **opna (opna)**) 'open'
eiga (á – átt – á) að	have to, should
halda (held) áfram	continue, go on
vera eftir	be left
Matthías Jochumsson	famous Icelandic minister and poet (1835–1920) who composed the lyrics for the Icelandic national anthem
bjó	lived (past tense of **búa**)
eftir hádegi	in the afternoon

Language points

Directions: adverbs of place

In Dialogue 1, you may have noticed the use of different words for 'where?', 'here' and 'there' from the ones you learned: **hvert** and **þangað**, instead of **hvar?**, **hér(na)** and **þarna**. Adverbs indicating location in Icelandic take different forms depending on whether a motion is implied, and if so, whether the motion is towards or away from the speaker. English has this distinction as well ('hence', 'hither', 'whence', 'whither', 'thence', 'thither'), although it is no longer common usage. The following are the Icelandic forms:

Hvar?	Where?	**Hvaðan?**	Where from?	**Hvert?**	Where to?
Hér(na)	Here	**Héðan**	From here	**Hingað**	(To) here
Þarna	There	**Þaðan**	From there	**Þangað**	(To) there

In English, the 'from' or 'to' parts are usually left out, as in 'where is she going?' In Icelandic, however, it would be ungrammatical to use **hvar** in this instance, since the verb 'going' implies a motion away from the speaker. Can you think of the proper way to phrase this question in Icelandic?

It should be: **hvert er hún að fara?** You may have noticed the brackets around -na in **hérna**. This is because **hér** and **hérna** are interchangeable, while **þar** and **þarna** are not:

- **þarna** is exclusively used as a demonstrative pronoun, indicating something in visual range: **kirkjan er þarna**, 'the church is there (i.e. within view).
- **þar** is used to refer to a location mentioned earlier, as in, for instance: **Akureyri. Þar er gott að vera. Þar** is also found in the combination **þar sem**, which means 'where', but can only be used to connect two clauses: **húsið *þar sem* Matthías Jochumsson bjó**, 'the house *where* Matthías Jochumsson lived' (not: *****húsið *hvar* Matthías Jochumsson bjó**).

The adverbs **upp** and **niður** are similar in usage to English 'up' and 'down' in their reference to areas which are perceived to be 'up' or 'down' in relation to the location from which one is speaking. If the implication is *not* one of motion, they have a slightly different form in Icelandic: **uppi** and **niðri**:

Ég er að fara niður í bæ	**Ég er niðr'í (niðri í) bæ**
I am going to the city centre	I am in the city centre

Ég fer upp á sjúkrahús   **Ég er upp'á (uppi á) sjúkrahúsi**
I am going up to the hospital I am (up) at the hospital

Where the reference is sufficiently clear, **upp** and **niður** are often used only in combination with the prepositions **frá** (static, i.e. no motion) or **eftir** (implied motion):

Kaffihúsið er (þarna) upp frá (not ***uppi frá!**)
The cafe is up there

Hann er að fara upp eftir
He's going up there

Plural personal pronouns

In Lesson 1 you learned the singular personal pronouns in Icelandic. Here are their plural counterparts:

ég	>	**við**	we
þú	>	**þið**	you
hann/hún/það	>	**þeir/þær/þau**	they *m./f./n.*

Note how the third person plural in Icelandic, unlike English 'they', continues to have separate gender forms. In cases where reference is made to a combination of different genders, Icelandic uses the neuter plural form **þau**:

Þarna eru Jón (*m.sg.*) **og Stefán** (*m.sg.*) – **Þeir** (*m.pl.*) **eru frá Reykjavík**

but:

Þarna eru Þór (*m.sg.*) **og Harpa** (*f.sg.*) – **Þau** (*n.pl.*) **eru á Akureyri**

Verbs in the plural present

In the previous chapter you learned how to make present verb forms agree with the singular subject of a sentence (I, you, or someone or something else). These verb forms change when the subject is plural rather than singular (we, you, they). These are the plural forms for Icelandic verbs in the present tense:

	borð-a	*lær-a*	*verð-a*	*syng-j-a*
við	borð-um	lær-um	verð-um	syngj-um
þið	borð-ið	lær-ið	verð-ið	syngj-ið
þeir	borð-a	lær-a	verð-a	syngj-a

The process of making verb forms agree with their subject is called conjugation.

Whereas the three different verb groups have different endings in the singular, the plural endings are the same for all groups. Note in the conjugation of **syngja** that the **-j-**, which disappears in the singular, returns in the plural.

U-shift: a > ö/u

We already briefly encountered the U-shift in Lesson 2 when dealing with the feminine form of adjectives. The U-shift is a vowel change where a stem vowel **a** changes into an **ö**, or an **u** in unstressed syllables, under the influence of a visible or invisible (i.e. lost) **u** in the next syllable. You might say that **a**'s in Icelandic are allergic to **u**'s, and break out into **ö**'s or **u**'s as soon as any **u**, whether visible or invisible, gets too close.

The U-shift occurs throughout the Icelandic language and affects all words, so it is helpful to start training yourself to look out for when it might occur. As soon as there is an intermediate syllable that separates the two, however, the effect is neutralized and nothing happens. Note that a U-shift only affects the individual vowel **a**, not **á** or **au**, which are separate vowels in Icelandic.

Back to plural verb forms: whenever there is an **a** in the stem of the verb, it will change into **ö** under the influence of the **-u-** in the first person plural ending **-um**. Here are some examples:

	tal-a	*far-a*	*tak-a*
við	töl-um	för-um	tök-um
þið	tal-ið	far-ið	tak-ið
þær	tal-a	far-a	tak-a

With the exception of the U-shift, there are no vowel changes in the plural forms as there sometimes are in the singular (**taka – tek**).

Note the plural forms of **vera** and **eiga**:

	vera	*eiga*
við	erum	eigum
þið	eruð	eigið
þau	eru	eiga

Exercise 1

Answer the following questions positively, using **já** or **jú** as appropriate and answering 'you' questions in the first person ('we'). Be sure to adjust the verb form to the subject where necessary, and mind the possibility of a U-shift!

> *Dæmi*: **Bakið þið ekki brauð? – Jú, við bökum brauð**
> Don't you bake bread? Yes, we bake bread

1 Talið þið ekki íslensku?
2 Farið þið ekki þangað?
3 Eiga þau húsið?
4 Kennið þið ekki tölvufræði?
5 Vinna þær ekki?
6 Ganga þeir niður í bæ?
7 Lærið þið ekki íslensku?
8 Eruð þið í fríi á Íslandi?

Language points

Cardinal numbers

In Icelandic, the numbers 1 to 4, like adjectives and articles, have different gender forms, depending on whether they refer to a masculine, a feminine or a neuter noun. However, after 4 it becomes easier. Here are the numbers:

1	**einn**	**ein**	**eitt**
2	**tveir**	**tvær**	**tvö**
3	**þrír**	**þrjár**	**þrjú**
4	**fjórir**	**fjórar**	**fjögur**

5	**fimm**	8	**átta**
6	**sex**	9	**níu**
7	**sjö**	10	**tíu**

11	**ellefu**	21	**tuttugu og einn**
12	**tólf**	22	**tuttugu og tveir ...**
13	**þrettán**		
14	**fjórtán**	30	**þrjátíu**
15	**fimmtán**	40	**fjörutíu**
16	**sextán**	50	**fimmtíu**
17	**sautján**	60	**sextíu**
18	**átján**	70	**sjötíu**
19	**nítján**	80	**áttatíu**
20	**tuttugu**	90	**níutíu**

100	**(eitt) hundrað**	1,000	**(eitt) þúsund**
101	**hundrað og einn**	5,121	**fimm þúsund eitt hundrað tuttugu og einn**
121	**hundrað tuttugu og einn**		
0	**núll**	1,000,000	**(ein) miljón**

Note that in number combinations, **og** is used only to connect the last two digits. For general counting, the masculine forms of 1–4 are used, including the reading out of phone numbers and doing arithmetic.

Exercise 2

Practise the Icelandic numbers by reading and writing out the following phone numbers:

464 1409	451 3268
568 1543	566 7123
487 1172	854 3789

And your own phone number?

Now listen to the speakers and see if you can write down the phone numbers they read out.

Exercise 3

Listen to the additions (+ **plús**) and subtractions (– **mínus**) read out by the speakers. Can you give the correct answer in Icelandic?

Plural nouns and articles

In Icelandic, the plural form of a noun depends on its gender. In some cases, the singular ending is replaced by a plural one; in others, there will be a vowel change but no ending; and sometimes there is no change at all. Definite articles in Icelandic also have different forms if they are added to a plural rather than a singular noun. Here are the nouns and articles for the three genders in their singular and plural forms:

	Masculine				*Feminine*		

Masculine
sing.   plural

____ur	-inn	
____i	-nn	____ ar -nir
____ll	-inn	
____nn	-inn	

Feminine
sing.   plural

____0 -in > ______ ir-nar

____a -n > __U-shift__ ur-nar

Neuter
 sing.   plural

 ____0 -ið > __U-shift__0 -in

Some examples:

dagurinn > dagarnir	borgin > borgirnar	húsið > húsin
skólinn > skólarnir	rósin > rósirnar	borðið > borðin
stóllinn > stólarnir	rútan > rúturnar	barnið > börnin
steinninn > steinarnir	taskan > töskurnar	hundraðið >
		hundruðin

The U-shift is at work here as well: it occurs in feminine nouns which have a plural **-ur** ending, as well as in neuter plural nouns with a stem **-a-**. A U-shift is also at work in feminine nouns which have no ending in the singular and **-ö-** or **-u-** in the stem, such as **gjöf** 'present' and **verslun** 'shop', 'business'. Note that in the plural the U-shift is neutralized by the **-ir** ending and these nouns get their original **-a-** back: **gjöf > gjafir, verslun > verslanir**.

The plural of **maður** is irregular > **menn**. With the definite article it becomes **mennir-nir**. Whenever the plural of a noun does not conform to the patterns outlined above, the correct plural ending will be added in brackets in the vocabulary notes and glossary.

Exercise 4

Can you put the following nouns into the plural? You will need to determine the gender of each noun, so this is a good test for you to see if you are beginning to get the hang of doing this. If you still find it a little difficult, read through the relevant sections of Lesson 1 again. Mind the possibility of a U-shift!

bíll – blað – kirkja – penni – amma – rós – brauð – tölva – kennari – nafn – fyrirtæki – þökk (f.) – kona – spjall – búð – starf

Now add the correct form of the definite article, first in the singular and then in the plural.

Dialogue 2 ▢▢

Enn á Akureyri

Harpa and Þór continue their stroll through the town. What's to be found in the Lystigarður? What's the oldest house in Akureyri called? Where do Þór and Harpa go instead?

ÞÓR: Hvar er Lystigarðurinn? Hann á að vera mjög fallegur.

HARPA: Við skulum sjá. Lystigarðurinn. Hann var stofnaður árið 1912, og það er plöntusafn þar sem í má finna flestar íslenskar plöntur.

ÞÓR: Já, en hvar er hann?

HARPA: Hann er ekki langt héðan, við erum bara fimm mínútur að ganga niður Eyrarlandsveg, þar sem við vorum rétt áðan. En við skulum frekar fara að skoða Laxdalshús fyrst.

ÞÓR: Laxdalshús, hvaða hús er það?

HARPA: Elsta hús á Akureyri. Það er frá 1795 og stendur þar sem fyrsta byggðin var.

ÞÓR: Nú, en klukkan er ekki nema tíu. Er opið svona snemma?

HARPA: Já, það er nú það. Það er ekki opnað fyrr en klukkan eitt. Hvað eigum við að gera?

ÞÓR: Fáum okkur kaffi og förum svo í Lystigarðinn!

HARPA: Góð hugmynd, gerum það! Er kaffihús nálægt?

ÞÓR: Já, það eru tvö kaffihús hérna upp frá.

HARPA: Förum þangað!

Still in Akureyri

ÞÓR: *Where is the Lystigarður? It is supposed to be very beautiful.*

HARPA: *Let's see. The Lystigarður. It was founded in the year 1912, and there is a plant collection where most Icelandic plants may be found.*

ÞÓR: *Yes, but where is it?*

HARPA: *It's not far from here, we only have to walk five minutes down Eyrarlandsveg where we were just now. But rather let's go and have a look at Laxdal house first.*
ÞÓR: *Laxdal house, what house is that?*
HARPA: *The oldest house in Akureyri. It is from 1795 and stands where the first settlement was.*
ÞÓR: *I see, but it is only ten o'clock. Is it open that early?*
HARPA: *Yes, well, there we are. It doesn't open until one o'clock. What shall we do?*
ÞÓR: *Let's have a coffee and go to the Lystigarður!*
HARPA: *Good idea, let's do that! Is there a cafe nearby?*
ÞÓR: *Yes, there are two cafes up the road here.*
HARPA: *Let's go there!*

Vocabulary notes

Lystigarð/ur, *m.*	public park and botanical garden in Akureyri
skulum sjá	let's see (from **skulu (skal – skalt – skal)** 'shall')
plöntusafn, *n.*	plant collection (from **planta**, *f.* 'plant' and **safn**, *n.* 'collection', 'museum')
finna (finn)	find
má finna	may be found
var – vorum	were (past tense of **vera**)
rétt áðan	just now
skoða (skoða)	(have/take a) look at
hvaða	what kind of
elsta	from **elst/ur** (*superl.*) 'oldest'
nema, *adv.*	except
ekki nema	only
það er nú það	(infinitely flexible phrase usually meaning something like 'that's how it is', 'there we are')
fyrr en	before, until

Language points

Numbers again

When counting something specific, the grammatical gender of what it is you are counting determines which forms of the numbers you should use. For instance, in Icelandic, houses are counted in the neuter (**eitt, tvö, þrjú, fjögur hús**), because **hús** is a neuter noun, while roses are counted in the feminine (**ein, tvær, þrjár, fjórar rósir**), because **rós** is a feminine noun.

When counting larger numbers, it is important to realize that the words **hundrað**, **þúsund** and **miljón** are nouns which have their own gender. As a result, when you speak of more than one hundred, thousand or million, these nouns have to be in their plural forms, and you need to use the appropriate gender form of 1–4 when using them in combination with these nouns:

hundrað (*n.*) > **hundruð:**	**eitt hundrað**	– **tvö, þrjú, fjögur hundruð**	
þúsund (*n.*) > **þúsund:**	**eitt þúsund**	– **tvö, þrjú, fjögur þúsund**	
miljón (*f.*) > **miljónir:**	**ein miljón**	– **tvær, þrjár, fjórar miljónir**	

This is not as complicated as it may look at first. Rather, it is a matter of keeping close track of the gender of each noun you are dealing with and, just as with adjectives, remaining aware every step of the way which number qualifies which noun. For instance, think carefully how you would say in Icelandic: two thousand and fifty-two computers.

The answer is **tvö þúsund fimmtíu og tvær tölvur**. Did you remember to use two different forms of 'two', the neuter form with **þúsund** (*n.*) and the feminine form with **tölvur** (*f.*)?

Exercise 5

Put the following nouns in their plural forms, adding the appropriate forms of the numbers 1–4.

Dæmi: **eitt, tvö, þrjú, fjögur hús**

borg – Íslendingur – fíll – appelsína – sæti – banani – sjómaður – skáld

Money

The Icelandic currency is the **króna**, plural **krónur** (*f.*) If there is one thing we all tend to count a lot, it is money. So, you need to determine what form of the numbers 1–4 to use when counting your **krónur**. Exactly: Icelanders count their money in the feminine!

Icelandic notes and coins:

5000 krónur	100 krónur
2000 krónur	50 krónur
1000 krónur	10 krónur
500 krónur	1 króna

Krónur are also often popularly referred to as **kall** (equivalent to 'quid' or 'bucks'), as in, for instance, **tíkall** (= **tíu 'kall'**, a 10-**krónur** piece).

Iceland uses the metric system, which means that larger amounts of money are separated by dots rather than by commas. For example: **44.352** is **fjörutíu og fjögur þúsund þrjú hundruð fimmtíu og tvær krónur**.

Exercise 6

Read and write out the following amounts in Icelandic:

260 kr. – 4.373 kr. – 640 kr. – 17.750 kr. – 372.465 kr. – 4.000.000 kr.

Now listen to the amounts read out by the speakers and see if you can write them down.

Years

The Icelandic word for 'year' is **ár**, *n*. This means that years are counted in the neuter forms of 1–4. As in English, centuries are counted in the hundreds rather than the thousands: **1993 – nítján hundruð níutíu og þrjú**.

Exercise 7

Read and write out the following years in Icelandic. Can you match them with the appropriate Icelandic historical events listed on the right? Try to do this exercise first without help from the vocabulary notes and see how much you can guess and piece together from the context.

874	Jón Arason biskup hálshöggvinn, Ísland tekur lútherska trú
1000	Biblían prentuð á íslensku

1402–(til) 1404	Tveir íslenskir stúdentar ganga fyrstir upp á Heklutind
1550	Ingólfur Arnarson byggir bæ sem heitir Reykjavík
1584	Halldór Laxness fær Nóbelsverðlaun
1700	Um 2000 Íslendingar flytja til Kanada
1750	Kristnitaka á Íslandi – Leifur Eiríksson finnur Norður Ameríku
1787	Ísland gengur í NATO
1874	Svartidauði á Íslandi – 1/3 Íslendinga deyr
1886	Verslun á Íslandi gefin frjáls
1940	Bretar hernema Ísland
1944	Reagan og Gorbatsjof funda í Reykjavík
1949	Vigdís Finnbogadóttir verður forseti Íslands
1955	Heklugos
1980	1000 ára byggð á Íslandi – Ísland fær stjórnarskrá
1986	Ísland verður sjálfstætt lýðveldi
2000	Íslendingar taka upp gregoríanskt tímatal

Vocabulary notes

hálshöggvin/n, *adj.*	beheaded	**frjáls**, *adj.*	free
		hernema, *vb.*	occupy (military)
trú, *f.*	faith, belief	**funda (funda)**, *vb.*	hold a meeting
Heklutind/ur, *m.*	top of Mt Hekla	**gos**, *n.*	eruption
fá (fæ – færð – fær), *vb.*	get, obtain	**stjórnarskrá (-r)**, *f.*	constitution
flytja (flyt), *vb.*	move (house)	**sjálfstæð/ur**. *adj.*	independent
deyja (dey – deyrð – deyr), *vb.*	die	**lýðveldi**, *n.*	republic
		tímatal, *n.*	calendar

Measurements – How far? How much? How heavy?

In Dialogue 1, Þór asks Harpa how old the church is: **Hvað er hún gömul?** English uses 'how' to ask for amounts, followed by the appropriate adjective: how old, how much, how far, how heavy, how deep? Icelandic, on the other hand, uses **hvað**, followed by the remainder of the question, keeping the adjective until the very last:

hvað er hann stór?	how big/tall is he? (*lit.* 'what is he big?')
hvað er hún sterk?	how strong is she?
hvað er bíllinn gamall?	how old is the car?
hvað er þetta þungt?	how heavy is that?

Did you notice how the form of the adjective reflects the gender of the subject in each sentence?

Now look at the following measurements in Icelandic:

(desí)lítri	(deci)litre
kíló(gramm), *n.*	kilogram
gramm, *n.*	gram
(kíló)metri	(kilo)metre

Exercise 8

Answer the following questions, using the numbers given and making sure to use the correct gender forms of the numbers and the correct plural forms of the nouns involved:

1 Hvað er þetta þungt? (2 kg)
2 Hvað er þetta mikið? (4 l)
3 Hvað er barnið þungt? (1543 gr)
4 Hvað er langt frá Kaupmannahöfn til Lissabon? (3115 km)
5 Hvað er langt frá París til Róm? (1531 km)
6 Hvað er langt frá Amsterdam til Búdapest? (1464 km)

Dialogue 3 ▢

Hvað eigum við að gera?

While having lunch, Þór and Harpa are discussing their plans for the afternoon in Akureyri. Is Laxdalshús open on weekdays? Does Harpa want to go and see Listagil? Are Þór and Harpa going to see a play?

Þór: Eigum við að fara í Laxdalshúsið strax á eftir?
Harpa: Æ já, gerum það, ég ætla endilega að skoða Laxdalshús.
Þór: En það er sunnudagur í dag. Er opið sunnudaga?
Harpa: Já, meira að segja bara sunnudaga.
Þór: En sú heppni!
Harpa: Já, er það ekki! Og hvað gerum við svo?

ÞÓR:	Við skoðum Listagilið! Ég er búinn að heyra mikið um Listagilið.
HARPA:	Hvað er Listagilið?
ÞÓR:	Þú ert leiðsögumaðurinn!
HARPA:	Skulum sjá, já, hérna er Listagil: 'heil gata í miðbæ þar sem eru listasafn, gallerí, vinnustofur listamanna, menningarkaffihús . . .' En gaman! Förum endilega þangað!
ÞÓR:	Hvað um Leikhúsið, er ekki leikfélag hér á Akureyri? Hvernig væri að fara í leikhús í kvöld?
HARPA:	Nei, það er ekki hægt, Leikhúsið er bara opið á veturna, frá september til júní, stendur hér.
ÞÓR:	Nú hvað! Ekkert á sumrin?
HARPA:	Nei, en hins vegar eru sumartónleikar í Akureyrarkirkju.
ÞÓR:	Hvenær?
HARPA:	Bíddu, já, það stendur hérna: frá júlí til ágúst, sunnudaga kl. 5.
ÞÓR:	Það passar ágætlega! Jæja, þá er örugglega best að fara af stað. Bærinn bíður!

What shall we do?

ÞÓR:	*Shall we go the Laxdal house directly after?*
HARPA:	*Oh yes, let's do that, I really want to see the Laxdal house.*
ÞÓR:	*But it's Sunday today. Is it open on Sundays?*
HARPA:	*Yes, what's more, only on Sundays.*
ÞÓR:	*What luck!*
HARPA:	*Yes, isn't it. And what do we do then?*
ÞÓR:	*We'll have a look at the Listagil! I have heard a lot about the Listagil.*
HARPA:	*What is the Listagil?*
ÞÓR:	*You're the guide!*
HARPA:	*Let's see, yes, here's Listagil: 'a whole street in the city centre area where there is an art museum, galleries, artists' studios, cultural cafes . . .' Great! By all means let's go there!*
ÞÓR:	*What about the theatre, is there not a theatre company here in Akureyri? How would it be to go to the theatre tonight?*
HARPA:	*No, that's not possible, the theatre is only open in the winter, from September to June, it says here.*
ÞÓR:	*Really! Nothing in the summer?*

HARPA: *No, but on the other hand there is a summer concert in the Akureyri church.*

ÞÓR: *When?*

HARPA: *Wait, yes, it says here: from July until August, Sundays at 5.*

ÞÓR: *That suits just fine! Well, then it's surely best to be on our way. The town awaits!*

Vocabulary notes

strax, *adv.*	immediately
endilega, *adv.*	by all means
ég ætla endilega	I would really like, I really want to
í dag	today
meira að segja	what's more
miðbæ/r (-ir), *m.*	town centre (from **bæ/r** 'town')
en gaman!	how lovely, how wonderful
hvernig væri	how would it be
(Það) stendur hérna	it says here (from **standa (stend)** 'stand')
ekkert	nothing
hins vegar	on the other hand, however
sumartónleikar, from **sumar**, *n.* and **tónleikar**, *m.pl.*	summer concert
bíddu!	wait! (*imp.* of **bíða (bíð)** 'wait')
örugglega, *adv.*	surely, certainly

Language points

Telling time 1: hours, days, months, seasons

To find out what time it is, you ask in Icelandic: **Hvað er klukkan?** lit. 'What's the clock?' The answer will be: **klukkan er . . .** 'the clock is . . .'. Surprisingly, although **klukka** is a feminine noun, Icelanders tell the time in the neuter: **klukkan er eitt, klukkan er tvö, klukkan er . . ., . . ., klukkan er fimm . . .**

Can you fill in the gaps?

When asking or saying that something happens *at* such and such a time, the verb **vera** must be left out, as in:

Klukkan hvað borðar þú?   At what time do you eat?

Ég borða *klukkan eitt*   I eat at one (o'clock)

In written language, **klukkan** is often abbreviated to **kl.**

Exercise 9

Answer the following questions in Icelandic:

1 Hvað er klukkan?
2 Klukkan hvað ferð þú að vinna?
3 Klukkan hvað kemur þú heim?
4 Klukkan hvað ferð þú að sofa?
5 Klukkan hvað opna búðirnar?
6 Klukkan hvað fer rútan af stað? (2 o'clock)

Now go back to Lesson 1, Exercise 7, and add the appropriate hours to the sentences you constructed there, as in:

'10 a.m.' Ég ... klukkan ...

Weekdays, months and seasons

Vika = sjö vikudagar		*Mánuðir*	*Árstíðir*
mánudagur		**janúar**	
þriðjudagur		**febrúar**	**vetur**, *m.*
miðvikudagur	**virkir dagar**	**mars**	
fimmtudagur		**apríl**	**vor**, *n.*
föstudagur		**maí**	
laugardagur	**helgi**, *f.*	**júní**	
sunnudagur		**júlí**	**sumar**, *n.*
		ágúst	
		september	
		október	**haust**, *n.*
		nóvember	
		desember	**vetur**, *m*

daglega	**vikulega**	**mánaðarlega**	**árlega**
daily	weekly	monthly	yearly

Note that in sentences, references to parts of the week or the seasons often occur in different forms if they are not the subject of the sentence:

	weekday /	*a particular* *weekend* /	*season*
Singular	**á sunnudaginn**	**um helgina**	**í vor/um vorið**
	on Sunday	on the weekend	in the spring

		always on/in those particular	
Plural	*weekdays* /	*weekends* /	*seasons*
1 with	**á sunnudögum**	**um helgar**	**á vorin**
preposition	on Sundays	on weekends	in spring
	á virkum dögum		**á sumrin**
	on working days		**á haustin**
			á veturna
2 without	**sunnudaga**	–	–
preposition	Sundays		
	virka daga		
	weekdays		

The names of the months in Icelandic never change their form.
The masculine noun **mánuður** has **-ir** as a plural ending instead of
-ar: **mánuðir**.

Exercise 10

Answer the following questions in Icelandic:

1 Vinnur þú um helgar?
2 Ert þú í fríi á sumrin?
3 Ert þú heima á virkum dögum?
4 Í hvaða mánuði átt þú afmæli ('birthday')?

Exercise 11

On p. 65 is a listing of museums and exhibitions in and around
Hafnarfjörður (near Reykjavík). Study it, and see if you can answer
the following questions:

1 Er Siggubær opinn á sunnudögum?
2 Er Gallerí Klettur opið á sunnudögum?
3 Hvenær er ekki opið í Hafnarborg?
4 Er hægt að skoða Sjóminjasafnið á veturna?
5 Er Sívertsen-hús opið á sumrin?

ÞJÓNUSTA

Söfn/sýningar: *Byggðasafn Hafnarfjarðar*,
☎ 565 5420 / 897 0102; *Sívertsens-hús*, Vesturgötu 6. Fyrrum
heimili Bjarna Sívertsen. Opið daglega 1.6.-31.8. frá kl. 13.00-
17.00. Á veturna er opið 13.00-17.00 um helgar. *Siggubær*,
Kirkjuvegi 10. Gamalt heimili alþýðufólks. Opið um helgar 1.6. -
31. 8. frá kl. 13.00-17.00. *Smiðjan*, Strandgötu 50, sýningar-
salur. Opið alla daga 1.5.-30.9. frá kl. 13.00-17.00. *Gallerí Jörð*,
Reykjavíkurvegi 66, ☎ 555 2436, myndlist, íslensk listiðn og
glerlist. *Gallerí Klettur* Helluhraun 16 e.h., ☎ 565 0785.
Vinnustofur og gallerí 5 listamanna. Opið laugardaga kl. 10.00-
14.00, og eftir samkomulagi. *Hafnarborg*, Strandgötu 34,
☎ 555 0080 / 565 5580. Opið frá kl. 12.00-18.00 alla daga nema
þriðjudaga. *Kvikmyndasafn Íslands*, Vesturgötu 11-13,
☎ 565 5993. Opið virka daga kl. 9.00-12.30. *Halli rakari-hár
og list*, Strandgötu 39, ☎ 5551066, gallerí á hársnyrtistofu.
Póst- og símaminjasafnið, Austurgötu 11, ☎ 555 4321. Opið
þri. og sun. kl. 15.00-18.00 og eftir samkomulagi.
Sjóminjasafn Íslands Vesturgötu 8, ☎ 565 4242. Opið:
daglega 1.6.-30.9. frá kl. 13.00-17.00. Á veturna er opið lau. og
sun. kl. 13.00-17.00 og eftir samkomulagi. *Vinnustofa Gests
og Rúnu*, Austurgötu 17, ☎ 555 3960. Opið eftir samkomulagi.
Listamiðstöðin í Straumi v/ Reykjanesbraut, ☎ 565 0128.
Gisti- og vinnuaðstaða fyrir íslenska og erlenda listamenn.
Hafnarfjarðarleikhúsið Hermóður og Háðvör, Vesturgötu
11, ☎ 555 0553.

Language points

Plural adjectives

Adjectives in Icelandic reflect not only the gender of the noun they
describe, but also, like articles, its number, i.e. whether it is singular
or plural. These are the plural endings for adjectives:

Masculine	*Feminine*	*Neuter*
____ir	____ar	a>ö/u ____0

Here are some examples:

heil/l	heilir	heilar	heil
sjálfstæð/ur	sjálfstæðir	sjálfstæðar	sjálfstæð
svart/ur	svartir	svartar	svört
	heilir bananar	heilar appelsínur	heil vínber
	sjálfstæðir menn	sjálfstæðar konur	sjálfstæð börn
	svartir hundar	svartar töskur	svört hús

Adjectives which have two syllables in the stem, like **lítil/l**, lose the
second vowel in the masculine and feminine plural:

lítil/l	litlir	litlar	lítil
mikil/l	miklir	miklar	mikil
opin/n	opnir	opnar	opin

Exercise 12

Connect the following adjective–noun combinations by putting the adjectives in the appropriate gender forms, and then change both noun and adjective into their correct plural forms.

Dæmi: **grænn, rúta** → **græn rúta – grænar rútur**

1 grár, fiskur
2 skemmtilegur, blað
3 fallegur, mynd
4 hár, borð
5 gamall, maður

6 langur, vika
7 indæll, fjölskylda
8 rauður, rós
9 þungur, steinn
10 sterkur, kona

Suggested action

In Dialogue 1, Harpa asks Þór: **Eigum við að fara inn ...?** 'Should we go in?' Þór says no, and suggests: **Höldum áfram**, 'Let's go on'. The first person plural form of verbs is commonly used in Icelandic to suggest a course of action 'let's ...', 'shall/should we ...'/ 'shouldn't we ...', sometimes by itself, and sometimes with the help of other verbs. Here are some common constructions to suggest a particular action:

1 The first person plural form of the verb without a subject, as in:

Höldum áfram	Let's move on/continue
Förum þangað	Let's go there
Fáum okkur kaffi	Let's get (ourselves) a coffee
Gerum það	Let's do that

2 The first person plural form of **eiga** followed by **að** plus the infinitive form of the main verb, usually in the form of a question:

Eigum við að fara inn?	Should we go in?
Hvað eigum við að gera?	What should we do?

3 The first-person plural form of **skulu** followed by the infinitive
form of the main verb:

(Við) skulum sjá	Let's see
Við skulum frekar fara þangað	Let's rather go there

Exercise 13

You and your friend are in Reykjavík, planning your first day
of sightseeing. You cannot quite agree on what to do first, so each
of you keeps suggesting an alternative. Write the dialogue in
Icelandic:

1 You suggest going to have a look at the Parliament House
  (**Alþingishús**), but your friend suggests rather walking up
  Laugaveg and looking at the shops.
2 You observe that it is Saturday today and the shops are not
  open until 10 o'clock on Saturdays. You suggest going there in
  the afternoon.
3 Your friend then suggests going to the National Ethnographic
  Museum (**Þjóðminjasafn**). You remark that it is far away from
  where you are, 'from here', and should you not rather take a
  look at the Town Hall (**Ráðhús**) and get yourselves a coffee
  there?
4 Your friend asks where the Town Hall is. You reply that it's
  down the road, 'down there'.
5 Your friend thinks it's a good idea and suggests you walk down
  there.

4 Ég ætla að fá . . . Hvað verður þetta mikið?

I would like to get . . . How much will that be?

In this lesson you will learn about:

- shop talk: buying something, ordering a snack/drink
- asking for availability: **vera með**, **fást**, **eiga til**, **vera til**
- amounts and prices: how much? how many?
- the declension of nouns and articles
- the use of cases after verbs and prepositions
- intentional future: **ætla**
- asking for permission: **mega**
- impersonal **maður**
- addresses, **búa** and **eiga heima**

Dialogue 1 🎧

Í bókabúð

*Joyce wants to see something of the country and goes to a book-shop to buy a guidebook with a road map in it. She finds some postcards she likes, but no maps or guidebooks, so she decides to enlist the help of the person at the counter (**afgreiðslumaður**). Which part of the country does Joyce plan to visit? Why is the map provided by a rental car agency insufficient for Joyce's needs? Why does Joyce need to find Austurstræti?*

JOYCE: Góðan daginn, ég ætla að fá þessi póstkort.
AFGR.: Hvað eru þau mörg?

JOYCE: Fjögur.

AFGR.: Fleira?

JOYCE: Já, ég ætla að ferðast út á land, og mig vantar leiðsöguhandbók með vegakorti.

AFGR.: Einmitt. Við skulum sjá. Hvaða landshluta ætlarðu að heimsækja? Það eru til mjög góðar bækur um alla landshluta.

JOYCE: Ég ætla að leigja bíl og keyra hringveginn.

AFGR.: Nú já. Ef þú leigir bíl færðu yfirleitt Íslandskort með, en það sýnir manni bara lauslega aðalvegina og merkisstaði. Þessi bók hérna er mjög vinsæl. Hún er ítarleg og skýrir frá öllum einkennum í landslaginu, og kortin í bókinni eru mjög nákvæm. Þau sýna til dæmis líka fjallvegina. Ætlarðu líka að keyra yfir hálendið, Sprengisandsleiðina kannski?

JOYCE: Já, ég hugsa það.

AFGR.: Þá þarftu mjög góða leiðsögn. Ég mæli með bókinni hér.

JOYCE: Má ég skoða bókina aðeins?

AFGR.: Að sjálfsögðu, gjörðu svo vel.

JOYCE: Takk. Já, hún er fín, ég ætla þá að fá þessa bók. Hvað kostar hún?

AFGR.: Hún er nú ekki ódýr, hún kostar 2.850 kr.

JOYCE: Jæja, það verður bara að hafa það.

AFGR.: Eitthvað fleira?

JOYCE: Nei, þá er það komið. Heyrðu jú, ertu með frímerki?

AFGR.: Nei, því miður, en þau fást á pósthúsinu.

JOYCE: Hvar er það, með leyfi?

AFGR.: Hérna niður frá, í Austurstrætinu.

JOYCE: Nú já, takk. Hvað verður þetta þá mikið?

AFGR.: Þetta eru 3.250 kr.

JOYCE: Má ég borga með greiðslukorti?

AFGR.: Gjörðu svo vel.

In a bookshop

JOYCE: *Good morning, I would like to get these postcards.*

AFGR.: *How many are they?*

JOYCE: *Four.*

AFGR.: *Anything else?*

JOYCE: *Yes, I'm planning to travel out into the country and I need a guidebook with a road map.*

AFGR.: *Right. Let's see. Which part of the country will you be visiting? There are many good books available about all areas of the country.*

JOYCE: *I intend to rent a car and drive around the ring-road.*

AFGR.: *I see. If you rent a car you will generally get a map along with it, but it shows you only roughly the main roads and sights. This book here is very popular. It is detailed and explains all the landmarks, and the maps in the book are very accurate. They also show the mountain roads, for instance. Do you intend to drive across the interior, the Sprengisandur route perhaps?*

JOYCE: *Yes, I think so.*

AFGR.: *Then you need a very good guide. I recommend this book here.*

JOYCE: *May I just have a look at the book?*

AFGR.: *Of course, here you are.*

JOYCE: *Thanks. Yes, it's fine, I'd like to get this book. What does it cost?*

AFGR.: *It is not cheap, it costs 2.850 kr.*

JOYCE: *Well, there's nothing to be done about that.*

AFGR.: *Anything else?*

JOYCE: *No, that's it. Listen, yes, do you have stamps?*

AFGR.: *No, unfortunately, but they are available from the post office.*

JOYCE: *Where is that, please?*

AFGR.: *Down the road here, in Austurstræti.*

JOYCE: *I see, thanks. How much does that come to?*

AFGR.: *That's 3.250 kr.*

JOYCE: *May I pay by credit card?*

AFGR.: *By all means.*

Vocabulary notes

(eitthvað) fleira — (anything) more (in shops often meaning 'anything else?')

þessi — this

leiðsöguhand-bók (-ar, -bækur) — guidebook (derived from **leiðsögn (-ar, -ir)** 'guidance')

veg/ur (-ar/-s, -ir) *m.* — road (The **hringvegur** is the ring-road around Iceland, which connects most towns and villages and is a popular route for tourists to see the country.

	Fjallvegir are unpaved roads, sometimes no more than unmarked routes, across the uninhabited interior (**hálendi**), of which the **Sprengisandsleið**, the route across the Sprengisandur desert, is the most famous.)
einkenni (-s, -), *n.*	characteristics
einkenni í landslaginu	landmarks
þurfa (þarf, þarft, þarf)	need
mæla (mæli) með, *dat.*	recommend
dýr – ódýr, *adj.*	dear – cheap
það verður bara að hafa það	an expression of resignation, meaning something like 'we'll just have to put up with it/that'
(þá er það) komið	that's it, that's all

Language points

We are now at the point where the inevitable can no longer be postponed: declensions. In Icelandic, nominals (that is to say, nouns, articles, adjectives, numbers and pronouns) change their form to reflect their function in a sentence. These different forms are known as cases. So far, we have dealt with the subject form of nominals, known as the nominative case. This is also the form in which nominals are found in dictionaries.

When a nominal is used as an object, it can take on one of three object cases: the accusative, the dative, or the genitive. This is determined by the main verb or preposition governing the object in question. An example: the verb **keyra** 'drive' takes the accusative case, which means that whatever is being driven will be in its accusative form. Consequently, while the Icelandic word for car will be listed in the dictionary as **bíll** (**Þetta er bíll**), when you are driving it, it becomes **bíl** (**Ég keyri bíl**). A verb like **skipta** ('change'), on the other hand, requires its object to be in the dative, so that in Icelandic you can never change **peningar** 'money' but must always change **peningum**, the dative form. If there is a preposition in the sentence, it, rather than the verb, will determine the case of the object: **frímerki fást á pósthúsinu** (dative of **pósthús-ið**).

You have just grown accustomed to memorizing new nouns along with their gender. Similarly, whenever you come across a new verb (or preposition), make it a habit to check which case it governs and memorize both at the same time. The glossary will tell you, but you can also find out yourself once you have mastered the various declensions, or case forms, of nouns and their articles. In the table opposite they are listed, in the singular and the plural, for each gender.

The process of putting nominals in their various case forms is known as declension.

Of course there are deviations from the pattern outlined here. Most nouns, however, conform to it. As of now, information will be included in brackets following each new noun which tells you what you need to know about that noun grammatically in order to work with it: the first dash is followed by the genitive singular ending of the noun, and the second by the plural nominative ending. These endings alert you to any possible deviations, and show you how a noun may deviate from the pattern you have just learned:

stað/ur (-ar, -ir) place

The **-ur** tells you that this is a masculine noun. The singular genitive ending **-ar** informs you of a deviation. Since the plural ending is listed as **-ir**, you know that this noun belongs to the masculine **-ir** subgroup. You can now fill in the rest of the picture by concluding that its accusative plural ending must therefore be **-i** instead of **-a**: **staði -na**.

Exercise 1

Can you, with the help of the information in brackets, derive the complete singular and plural declensions of **hlut/i (-a, -ar)**, **skeið (-ar, -ar)** and **kort (-s, -)**?

Exercise 2

Go back to Dialogue 1 and write down all verbs and prepositions followed by an object (of course you only need to do each verb or preposition once). Study the objects you find and see if you can determine in which case they are and, by extension, which case the verb or preposition in question governs (note that sometimes it could be more than one case).

		Masculine		Feminine		Neuter
sg.	nom.	___ur/l/n -inn	___i -nn	___0 -in	___a-n	___0 -ið
	acc.	___0 -inn	___a -nn	___0 -ina	___u³-na	___0 -ið
	dat.	___(i)¹ -num	___a -num	___0 -inni	___u³-nni	___i -nu
	gen.	___s -ins	___a -ns	___ar -innar	___u³-nnar	___s -ins
pl.	nom.	___ar² -nir		___ir -nar		^{U-shift}___0 -in
	acc.	___a -na		___ir -nar	___ur³ -nar	^{U-shift}___0 -in
					___ur³ -nar	
	dat.	___u(m)³,⁴ -num		___u(m)³,⁴ -num		___u(m)³,⁴ -num
	gen.	___a -nna		___(n)a -nna		___a -nna

Athugið

[1] A substantial number of masculine nouns do not have **-i** nor any other ending in the dative singular, for instance **bíll** (*dat.sg.* **bíl -num**) and **skápur** (*dat.sg.* **skáp -num**). Unfortunately, there are no rules to help us distinguish these nouns from other masculine nouns; as with so many things in Icelandic, you can only learn through usage.

[2] There is a subgroup of masculine nouns which has **-ir** instead of **-ar** in the nominative plural and **-i** in the accusative plural.

[3] Whenever an ending starts with a **-u** and the preceding syllable has an **-a-** in it, the U-shift will occur: for instance the feminine weak noun **taska** becomes **tösku** in all singular object cases and all plural cases except the genitive.

[4] The definite article in the plural dative case, **-num** always causes the preceding 'm' in the noun ending to be dropped to facilitate pronunciation, so we get, for instance, **bílunum** instead of ***bílumnum**. Note that the dative plural **-unum** ending is often pronounced '**onom**'.

Did you notice that one verb, **sýna**, had two objects, an indirect (**manni**) and a direct one (**aðalvegina og merkisstaði**)? In cases where a verb can take two objects, the first one will be in the dative and the second one in the accusative. Such verbs are indicated in the glossary list by *dat. + acc.*

If you possibly can, make it a habit of doing this with every new text or dialogue.

Exercise 3

In the following sentences, the objects are given in brackets in the nominative, in the singular or plural and with or without the article as appropriate in each instance. Can you put them in the proper cases? You will need to know, of course, which case the verbs or prepositions govern, so this information is provided for each sentence. However, to help you train yourself, those verbs and prepositions occurring in Dialogue 1 have been left blank. Do you remember what they govern without checking?

1 Þóra vinnur á ____________ (hótel). Hún er frá (dat.)
____________ (Ísland) en hún vinnur á ____________ (Ítalía).
Hún talar (acc.) ____________ (ítalska-n) mjög vel. Hótelið er
á ____________ (aðalgata-n).
2 Jón skoðar ____________ (myndir-nar) og ____________
(merkisstaðir-nir). Hann ætlar líka að heimsækja ____________
(Hallgrímskirkja).
3 Má ég loka (dat.) ____________ (gluggi-nn)?
4 Hvað ætlarðu að fá? Ég ætla að fá ____________ (fiskur).
5 Afgreiðslumaðurinn hjálpar (dat.) ____________ (kona-n) að
finna leiðsöguhandbók.

Intentional future: ætla

In Icelandic, it is very common to state an intention of doing something, expressed by the verb **ætla**. There is no exact equivalent for this in English, but it comes close to the idea of 'going to' or 'plan to', although it is also used in cases where we might say 'I'm thinking of' or 'I'm wanting to'. For example: **ég ætla að leigja bíl** means: 'I intend/plan/am going to rent a car'. **Ætla** is an -a verb, so its forms are familiar, and it is always followed by **að** plus the infinitive form of whatever it is that you intend to do:

Joyce ætlar að ferðast	Joyce is going to travel
Þú ætlar að keyra yfir hálendið?	Do you plan to drive across the interior?

In those cases where the intention is to 'go' somewhere, the Icelandic verb in question, **fara**, is often left out altogether:

Ég ætla í pósthús	I intend to go to the post office
Joyce ætlar í bókabúð	Joyce intends to go to a book shop

Exercise 4

You are a tourist in Iceland, and today is your first day. You are in your Reykjavík guest house, making a list of all the things you plan to do today. Here are some suggestions, with the verbs in their infinitive forms. Can you make them into full sentences using **ætla**? Which of the suggestions has the least chance of succeeding? See if you can add some of your own plans to the list.

 1 ganga niður í bæ
 2 fara (!) á Austurvöllinn
 3 skoða Alþingishúsið og Dómkirkjuna
 4 fara í bókabúð
 5 kaupa póstkort
 6 fara á kaffihús
 7 skrifa póstkortin
 8 ganga upp Laugaveginn
 9 skoða búðirnar
10 heimsækja forsetann á Bessastöðum
11 ...

Exercise 5

How would you say what your plans are for tomorrow? This exercise has of course no set answer. It depends on you.

Saying what you'd like to get

Ætla is also commonly used to say what you would like to get in a shop or restaurant, as Joyce does in the dialogue: **Ég ætla að fá póstkortin**, and **Ég ætla að fá þessa bók**. **Ætla að fá** is thus a very useful construction to use to get what you want. Remember, however, that the verb **fá** governs the accusative, so be prepared to know your shopping list and favourite menu items in their accusative forms.

Fá is a very common and useful verb to know. It is conjugated as follows:

ég	fæ	við	fáum
þú	færð	þið	fáið
hann ⎫ hún ⎬ fær það ⎭		þeir ⎫ þær ⎬ fá þau ⎭	

Another expression often heard instead of **ég ætla að fá** is **mig vantar**, an impersonal construction meaning 'I need', 'I'm in need of', also followed by an accusative. Don't hesitate to use it if you would like to add some variety to your 'shopping' vocabulary, but be aware that this construction is grammatically more complex (we shall come back to it in Lesson 8), less widely applicable (it is not used to place an order in a restaurant for instance) and easily confused with English 'want' (of course it does mean 'want', but strictly in the sense of 'lack' alone).

Do you have . . .?

To ask if something is available you can use the following expressions:

1 **Vera með** is a very common and very useful construction. It means 'carry', 'have on you', or 'have available'. It will be easy for you to start using it, since you are already familiar with the forms of **vera**, and all you need to do is add **með** and have it followed by an accusative:

Ertu með penna? Nei, við erum ekki með ritföng
Do you have pens? No, we don't carry any writing materials

2 The verb **fá** also exists in a slightly different form: **fást** (we shall come back to this **-st** form in Lesson 12), which can be translated as 'be available', 'to be had/got'. The final **-st** does not change the forms of **fá** listed above, so it's easy to use. It generally occurs in questions and statements regarding where or whether something is available:

Ritföng fást ekki hér	Stationery is not available here
Hvar fæst þetta?	Where is that available? Where can I get that?

3 As an alternative to the above, you can also ask if it is possible to get something by using **vera hægt að fá**:

Er hægt að fá vegakort hér?	Is it possible to get a road map here?
Er hægt að fá mjólk?	Is it possible to get milk?

Note that in these questions, an equivalent for 'it' is usually left out.

4 Finally, the expressions **eiga til** 'have in one's possession' (*acc.*) and **vera til** 'exist', 'be available' are also heard:

Það eru til margar góðar bækur um alla landshluta
There are many good books available on all areas of the country

Áttu til gosdrykki?
Do you have any soft drinks?

How much? How many?

Now that you are able to ask for the things you want, the shop assistant will want to know how much you want, and you'll want to know what it's going to cost you. Like English, Icelandic distinguishes between countable and uncountable quantities which, when large, are referred to as **margir**, 'many' or **mikill** (irregular neuter **mikið**) 'much' respectively. Although individual coins and notes are very countable, when speaking about the cost of something, or a final amount, **mikið** is the word to use. So, when asking for the price of something or for the final bill, you say:

Hvað kostar þetta (mikið)?	How much is it/does it cost?
Hvað verður þetta mikið?	How much will it be/does it come to?

Verða means 'become', but it is frequently used in Icelandic as a future form of **vera**. Unlike **vera**, its forms are regular: it is an **-ur** verb. **Kosta** is … (did you remember to note?) an **-a** verb.

Dialogue 2

Michael and his friends have been strolling and sightseeing in Reykjavík all day and are in need of a break and some refreshments. It's one of those rare, gloriously sunny and warm days, however, and all the pavement cafes are full. They don't want to go inside on a wonderful day like this, so they decide to shop at a **sölu-turn** *(a kiosk) and buy some drinks and snacks to enjoy in the sunshine on the grass. Michael offers to order since he speaks Icelandic. Donald and Michael both want a Coke (***kók***, f.). Joan prefers a fruit juice (***ávaxtasaf/i***, m.). Margaret would like to know if it is possible to have a coffee (***kaffi***, n.), if not she will have a Coke as well. Donald and Margaret want a hot dog (***pylśa***, f.). Michael would prefer a hamburger (***hamborgar/i***, m.), and Joan wants an ice-cream (***ís***, m.).*

Exercise 6

Listen to the following dialogue. Can you say Michael's words, given in English in brackets, in Icelandic? See if you can bring some variety to your vocabulary.

M.: (1 *Good day*) _____________
AFGR.: Góðan dag
M.: (2 *Do you have any coffee?*)__________
AFGR.: Nei, við erum bara með gosdrykki
M.: (3 *Is it possible to get hamburgers?*)__________
AFGR.: Nei, bara pylsur
M.: (4 *Then we'll have three Cokes and . . . is there any fruit juice?*)__________
AFGR.: Já, það er til Trópíkana
M.: (5 *. . . and one Tropicana, and then three hot dogs and one ice-cream*)__________
AFGR.: Pylsur með öllu?
M.: (6 *Yes. How much will that come to?*)__________
AFGR.: 1.135 kr.
M.: (7 *Here are 2000*)__________
AFGR. 865 gjörðu svo vel
M.: (8 *Thanks*)__________

May I . . .? Can I . . .?

Asking permission to do something is done in Icelandic with the help of the verb **mega** 'may' which, like its English counterpart, is very irregular. Its forms are as follows:

Ég	má	við	megum
þú	mátt	þið	megið
hann		þeir	
hún	má	þær	mega
það		þau	

It is followed by a verb in the infinitive but without **að**:

Má ég skoða bókina?	May/Can I have a look at the book?
Má ég borga með greiðslukorti?	May/Can I pay by credit card?
Má ég fá penna?	May/Can I have a pen?

You may have noticed in previous dialogues that Icelandic seldom uses words equivalent to English 'please'. Icelanders are much more direct in their dealings with other people, and tend to express politeness in very different ways. Here are some polite phrases. Be careful not to overuse them – in Icelandic it is not necessary to be overly polite.

Með leyfi – 'with permission' often added to a straightforward question, as in the dialogue above: **hvar er það, með leyfi?** *Do not use it together with* **mega**; *choose one or the other*

Gjörðu svo vel – difficult to translate literally; it serves many purposes. It is often used as a polite 'go ahead', 'please be my guest', or 'here/there you are' (when handing somebody something). Also used as an invitation to begin eating or drinking.

Viltu gjöra svo vel að	Would you please . . .
Með ánægju	With pleasure

Impersonal *maður*

The noun **maður** can mean different things. You have already encountered it as a short form of **karlmaður** 'man'. Most often, however, it is used to mean 'person' or 'one':

Hvernig gerir maður það? How does one do this?
Hvernig segir maður það á How does one say this in
íslensku? Icelandic?

In Dialogue 1 you saw it used in the sentence: **það sýnir** *manni* **bara lauslega aðalvegina og merkisstaði**. The form of **maður** in this sentence already indicates its irregularity as a masculine noun. Its complete declension follows here, along with the definite article:

maður	**-inn**	**menn**	**-irnir**	!
mann	**-inn**	**menn**	**-ina**	!
manni	**-num**	**mönnu(m)**	**-num**	
manns	**-ins**	**manna**	**-nna**	

Dialogue 3

Á pósthúsinu

Joyce goes to the main post office in Reykjavík to post a package to Britain. How long will Joyce still be in Reykjavík? Will she stay in a guest house in Borgarnes?

JOYCE: Góðan daginn, ég ætla að senda smápakka til útlanda.
AFGR.: Hvert til útlanda?
JOYCE: Til Bretlands.
AFGR.: Ætlarðu að senda hann í flugpósti eða með skipi?
JOYCE: Hvað kostar að senda með flugi?
AFGR.: Það fer eftir því hvað pakkinn er þungur. Sjáum til, 715 grömm. Það verða þá 1.115 kr. flugleiðis.
JOYCE: Allt í lagi.
AFGR.: Viltu gjöra svo vel að fylla út þetta fylgibréf. Þú verður að skrifa heimilisfang viðtakanda og líka þitt heimilisfang.
JOYCE: En ég bý ekki á Íslandi, ég er ferðamaður frá Bretlandi. Ég gisti í Þverholti 4.
AFGR.: Er það gistihús?

JOYCE: Já, það heitir Egilsborg.
AFGR.: Verðurðu lengi í bænum?
JOYCE: Nei, ég verð hjá vinum í Borgarnesi eftir helgina.
AFGR.: Þá er örugglega best að nota það heimilisfang. Hvar eiga þeir heima í Borgarnesi?
JOYCE: Þórunnargötu 16.

At the post office

JOYCE: *Good afternoon, I would like to send a small package abroad.*
AFGR.: *To what country?*
JOYCE: *To Britain.*
AFGR.: *Would you like to send it by airmail or surface mail?*
JOYCE: *What does it cost to send it by air?*
AFGR.: *It depends on how heavy the package is. Let's see, 715 grams. That will be 1.115 kr. by air.*
JOYCE: *All right.*
AFGR.: *Would you please fill in this form. You must write the address of the addressee and also your address.*
JOYCE: *But I don't live in Iceland, I'm a tourist from Britain. I am staying at Þverholt 4.*
AFGR.: *Is that a guest house?*
JOYCE: *Yes, it's called Egilsborg.*
AFGR.: *Will you be long in town?*
JOYCE: *No, I will be with friends in Borgarnes after the weekend.*
AFGR.: *Then it's undoubtedly best to use that address. Where do they live in Borgarnes?*
JOYCE: *Þórunnargata 16.*

Vocabulary notes

smápakk/i (-a, -ar)	small package	**flugpóst/ur (-s)**	air mail
það fer eftir því	it depends on	**heimilisfang (-s, -)**	address
flugleiðis	by air	**gista (gisti)**	stay (overnight)

Hvar áttu heima?

Addresses in Icelandic are usually in the dative, because they are often preceded by the prepositions **í** 'in' or **á** 'on', which, in this instance, govern the dative case. The implication is so strong that even when the prepositions themselves do not occur, for example on an envelope or in the telephone directory, the address, that is to say the street or farm and place-name, will retain the dative form:

Þóra Árnadóttir, Laugavegi 15 . . . . 561 6320
Jón Friðfinnsson, Hvammi 461 2345

Note that house numbers in Icelandic are always in the neuter.

Like English, Icelandic distinguishes roads, streets, lanes, avenues, etc., and, as in English, one needs to know whether one lives 'in' or 'on' them. What follows are some of the most common Icelandic terms, listed under the appropriate preposition:

(á +)		*(í +)*	
gat/a (-u, -ur), *f.*	street	**stræti (-s, -)**	street
veg/ur (-ar, -ir), *m.*	road	**tún (-s, -)**	field
stígur (-s, -ar), *m.*	path	**mel/ur (-s, -ar)**	hillock
torg (-s, -), *n.*	square		

There are two ways of saying one lives somewhere, using either **búa** 'live' or **eiga heima** (*lit.* 'have one's home'). **Búa** is conjugated as follows:

ég	bý	við	búum
þú	býrð	þið	búið
hún		þeir	
hann	býr	þær	búa
það		þau	

You already know the forms of **eiga**. When followed by **heima** it is equivalent to, and just as common as, **búa**:

Jón og Ásdís búa á Þórunnargötu 16 = Jón og Ásdís eiga heima á Þórunnargötu 16
Þau eiga heima í Sigtúni
Forsetinn býr á Bessastöðum

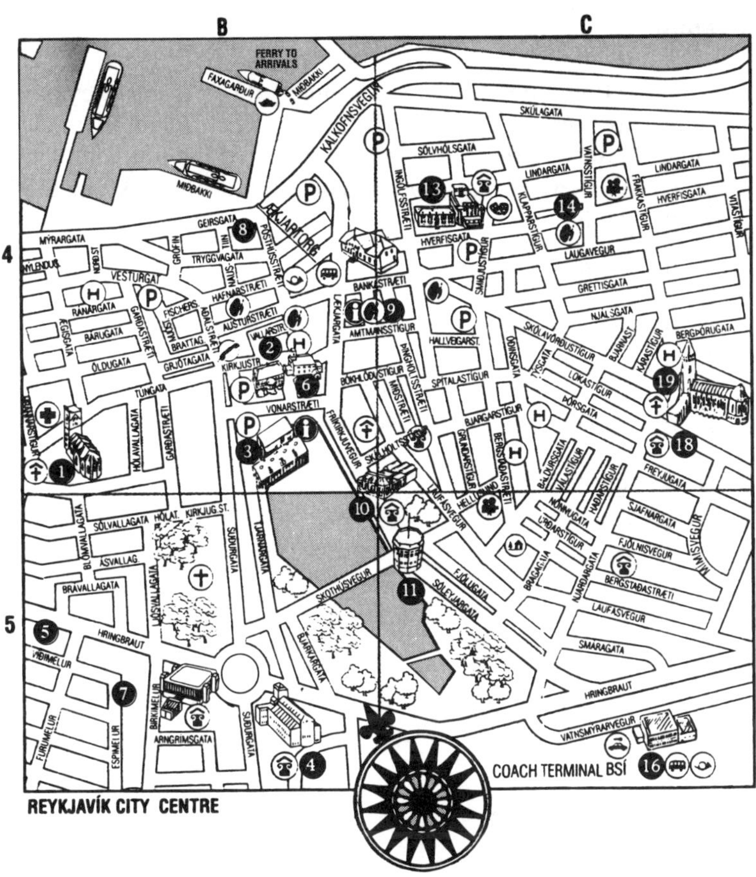

1 Landakotskirkja
2 Alþingishúsið
3 Ráðhús
4 Þjóðminjasafnið
5 Kristín
6 Dómkirkjan
7 Einar
8 Kolaportið
9 Upplýsingamiðstöð
  Ferðamála

10 Listasafn Íslands
11 Hljómskálinn
13 Safnahúsið – Þjóðleikhúsið
14 Nýlistasafnið
16 Umferðarmiðstöðin BSÍ
18 Listasafn Einars Jónssonar
19 Hallgrímskirkja

Exercise 7

The illustration above shows an inner-city map of Reykjavík
marked with sights and the addresses of Kristín and Einar. Use
the map to answer the following questions (if it's not completely
clear which of several streets is the correct one, just pick one that's
close and likely):

1 Hvar er Listasafn Íslands?
2 Hvar er Ráðhúsið?
3 Hvar er Hallgrímskirkja?
4 Hvar er Hljómskálinn?
5 Hvar tekur maður rútu? (coach terminal BSÍ)
6 Hvar stoppa margir strætisvagnar?
7 Hvar býr Kristín?
8 Hvar á Einar heima?
9 Og hvar býrð þú?

5 Föt

Clothing

In this lesson you will learn about:

- descriptions of clothing and appearances
- the declensions of adjectives and numbers 1 to 4
- the use of cases continued
- the seasons in Iceland
- fraction: nouns and adjectives
- interrogative pronoun declensions
- antonyms and compounds

Dialogue 1

Göngufatnaður

Joyce is preparing for a hiking trip in the interior of Iceland. She phones up her friend Brynja to consult with her on what clothing to take. Where in Iceland will Joyce be hiking? When is she leaving? What does she need to buy?

JOYCE: Brynja, sæl vertu. Ég ætla í gönguferð á Vatnajökul. Það er viku-hópferð, og við leggjum af stað á morgun, en ég hef enga hugmynd um hverju maður klæðist í svona ferð og hvers konar föt á að taka með.

BRYNJA: Maður verður alltaf að búast við breytilegu veðri á Íslandi. Það er auðvitað alveg nauðsynlegt að vera með regngalla. Áttu ullarnærföt og lopapeysu?

JOYCE: Nei, ég kom bara með sumarföt.

BRYNJA: Sko, veðrið breytist oft á svipstundu, og það er aldrei eins hlýtt á fjöllum eða á jöklum. Það má jafnvel búast við snjó þar, líka á sumrin! Margir eru í léttum fötum, til dæmis bol, og svo peysu. Ef sólin sýnir sig er maður enga stund að fara úr peysunni og í sólbað! Svo er ullarfatnaður alltaf mjög góður þegar maður verður blautur í rigningu eða fer yfir á vaði. Það er verst að vera í gallabuxum í svona ferð, því þær eru svo lengi að þorna.

JOYCE: Nú er það! Ég er bara með gallabuxur, boli, og bómullarpeysur. Það er greinilegt að ég verð að skreppa í búð.

BRYNJA: Já, það þýðir ekkert annað. En áttu gönguskó?

JOYCE: Já, reyndar. En hvað um yfirhöfn? Ég er með flísjakka og regngalla.

BRYNJA: Fínt að vera með flísfatnað. Ef þú kaupir svo síð ullarnærföt og lopapeysu þá ertu tilbúin.

JOYCE: Þakka þér kærlega fyrir heilræðið.

BRYNJA: Það var nú lítið Joyce. Góða ferð, og góða skemmtun!

Hiking clothes

JOYCE: *Brynja, hello. I am going on a hiking trip on Vatnajökull. It's a week's group journey and we leave tomorrow, but I have no idea about what one wears on such a trip and what kind of clothing one should take along.*

BRYNJA: *One must always expect changeable weather in Iceland. It's of course absolutely necessary to have rainwear. Do you have woollen underwear and a woollen sweater?*

JOYCE: *No, I only have summer clothes with me.*

BRYNJA: *You see, the weather often changes in an instant, and it's never as warm in the mountains or on the glaciers. One can even expect snow there, also in the summer. Many wear light clothes, for instance, a shirt, and then a jumper. If the sun shows itself it doesn't take a moment to take off the jumper and sunbathe! Woollen clothing is also very good when you get wet in the rain or ford a river. It's worst to wear jeans on such a trip because they take so long to dry.*

JOYCE: *Really. I only have jeans, shirts and cotton jumpers with me. It's obvious I must pop out to a shop.*

BRYNJA: *Yes, quite right. Do you have hiking boots?*

JOYCE: *I do, as a matter of fact. But what about outer garments? I have a fleece jacket and a rain suit.*

BRYNJA: *It's good to have fleece clothing. If you then buy long, woollen underwear and a woollen sweater you'll be all set.*

JOYCE: *Thanks very much for the good advice.*

BRYNJA: *Not at all, Joyce. Have a good trip and have fun!*

Vocabulary notes

göngu-	walking, hiking (from **ganga (geng)** 'walk')
gönguferð (-ar, -ir), *f.*	hiking trip
Vatnajökul/l (-s, -ar), *m.*	the largest glacier in Iceland, located in the south-east
sko	common interjection meaning something like 'you see', 'look here'
búast (býst) við, *dat.*	expect
lopapeys/a (-u, -ur), *f.*	Icelandic sweater (The wool used in the traditional Icelandic sweater, called **lop/i**, is normally an unspun and undyed wool.)
á svipstundu	in an instant
maður er enga stund (að, *inf./dat.*)	it takes no time at all (to)
fara í sólbað (-s, -), *n.*	sunbathe
blotna (blotna) *intrans.*	become wet
vað (-s, -), *n.*	ford
fara yfir á vaði	ford a river
þorna (þorna) *intrans.*	(become) dry
skreppa (skrepp)	take a quick trip, pop out
það þýðir ekkert annað	that's all there is to it, quite right (*lit.* 'it means nothing else')
reyndar *adv.*	as a matter of fact
síð/ur *adj.*	long (vertical: hair, dress, etc.)

Language points

Klæðnaður (clothing)

The following verbs and verb combinations are often used in connection with clothing:

klæðast (klæðist), *dat.*	be dressed in, wear
vera í, *dat.*	wear, have on
fara í, *acc.*	put on
fara úr, *dat.*	take off

Did you notice the cases these expressions govern? You always wear your clothes in the dative in Icelandic, but you put them on in the accusative. Here is some vocabulary to practise these expressions as well as the noun declensions involved:

Föt (klæðnaður, fatnaður)

bol/ur	shirt	**bux/ur**, *f.pl.*	trousers
blúss/a	blouse	**stuttbux/ur**	shorts
skyrt/a	button shirt	**sokkabux/ur**	tights
peys/a	sweater, jumper	**pils**, *n.*	skirt
vesti, *n.*	waistcoat	**sokk/ur**	sock
kjól/l	dress		
dragt, *f.*	female suit		
jakkaföt, *n.pl.*	male suit		
gall/ar, *m.pl.*	outfit, suit		

e.g. **regngallar**, rain suit; **íþróttagallar**, jogging suit

Yfirhafnir

(regn)káp/a	(rain)coat
frakk/i	man's overcoat
úlp/a	parka
jakk/i	jacket

Skór (skófatnaður)

skó/r	shoe
íþrótta-*	trainers
spari-*	dress-
striga-	sneakers
inni-	slippers
kulda-*	winter boots
göngu-*	hiking boots
stígvel, *n.*	boot
kloss/i	clog

* These prefixes are also commonly used with other clothing items, e.g. **spariföt**, dress clothes, **göngubuxur**, hiking trousers, etc.

Ýmislegt:

sundföt, *n.pl.*	swimwear	**nærföt**, *n.pl.*	underwear
sundbol/ur	bathing suit	**náttföt**, *n.pl.*	night wear
sundskýl/a	swimming trunks		

The declension of the masculine noun **skó/r** is rather irregular in Icelandic. Here it is:

skór	-inn	skór	-nir
skó	-inn	skó	-na
skó	-num	skó(m)	-num
skós	-ins	skóa	-nna

Icelandic vocabulary makes a distinction between actual clothing items that are worn, like the above, and what might be termed accessories, such as glasses, hats, jewellery, etc. For these items, the following verbal expressions are used:

vera með *acc.*
setja á sig *acc.*
taka af sér *acc.*

The first expression you already know of course; it is used in many other situations as well. So, in Icelandic, you 'are inside' your clothes but you 'carry' any accessories:

Ég *er í* **bol og gallabuxum**, **og ég** *er með* **sólglerauga og tösku**
I *am wearing* a shirt and jeans, and I *am carrying* sunglasses and a case

Here are some accessories in Icelandic that are 'carried' rather than 'worn':

bindi, *n.*	tie	**hatt/ur**	hat
spenn/a	buckle, clasp	**húf/a**	woollen hat
gleraug/u, *n.pl.*	glasses, specs	**hett/a**	hood
veski, *n.*	purse, wallet	**hansk/i**	glove
pok/i	bag	**vettling/ur**	mitten
		Skartgripir:	
(vasa)klút/ur	(hand)kerchief	**úr,** *n.*	watch
sjal, *n.*	shawl	**armband,** *n.*	bracelet
trefil/l	woollen scarf	**hálsfesti,** *f.*	necklace
hnapp/ur (tal/a)	button	**hring/ur**	ring
rennilás, *m.*	zip	**eyrnalokk/ur**	earring
		næl/a	brooch

Exercise 1

Study the grammatical properties of the vocabulary above. Use this information to help you describe what each person in the pictures overleaf is wearing. What are you wearing today?

Exercise 2

Now change the sentences you have just constructed, using the expression for putting on clothes instead, and adding the definite article in its appropriate form:

1 Hún fer í úlpuna og . . .
2 . . .

More adjectives

Here are some more adjectives to help you describe people's clothing and appearances:

létt/ur, léttklædd/ur	light, lightly dressed
þykk/ur, hlý/r, velklædd/ur	thick, warm, well/warmly dressed
þægileg/ur	comfortable
klæðileg/ur	dressy
skrautleg/ur	decorative, colourful

jákvæður (positive)
smekklegur 'tasteful', **myndarlegur** 'handsome', **glæsilegur**

'elegant', **snyrtilegur** 'neat', 'smart', **sætur** 'sweet', 'pretty',
flottur 'smart', 'cool', **fínn** 'elegant', 'dressy'
neikvæður (negative)
ósmekklegur 'tasteless', **druslulegur** 'untidy', 'sloppy', **ljótur**
'ugly', **fáránlegur** 'ridiculous', **gamaldags** *indecl.* 'old-fashioned'

As in English, you can often extend the vocabulary you already know by adding certain prefixes to adjectives. For instance, the following prefixes are often used to further qualify colours:

ljós-	light-	**dökk-**	dark-
skær-	bright-	**föl-**	soft-, pastel

The prefix **ó-** is used with many adjectives to create the opposite, like English 'un-':

smekklegur – ósmekklegur, þægilegur – óþægilegur

Exercise 3

Go back to the pictures in Exercise 1. Write sentences for each, describing the clothing depicted there according to your own opinion. Remember to pay attention to the correct gender forms of the adjectives you used:

Dæmi: 1. Úlpan er flott. Hún er hlý. Hún er hvít, etc.

Adjectives take on not only the gender and number but also the case of the noun(s) they describe, so in order to start using adjectives more elaborately, you need to learn their case forms. Before proceeding to the adjectival declensions, however, you should first make sure that you have a fairly firm grasp of the noun and article declensions so that you will not mix them up.

		masculine	feminine	neuter
sg.	*nom.*	______ur/l/n/r	______*U-shift* 0	______t
	acc.	______an	______a	______t
	dat.	______um	______ri*	______u
	gen.	______s	______rar*	______s
pl.	*nom.*	______ir	______ar	______*U-shift* 0
	acc.	______a	______ar	______*U-shift* 0
	dat.	______um	______um	______um
	gen.	______ra*	______ra*	______ra*

Athugið
*Adjectives whose stem ends in a vowel, like **hlý/r**, get a doubling of **-r** before an **-r** ending: **hlýrri**, **hlýrrar**, **hlýrra**. Adjectives with **-l/l** or **-n/n** get assimilation of **-r** in **-r** endings: **lítilli**, **lítillar**, **lítilla**, **fínni**, **fínnar**, **fínna**.

Can you indicate where else in the above a U-shift may occur?

J-insertion

According to Icelandic spelling, a **-j-** is inserted whenever an **-a-** or **-u-** ending follows **-ý-**, **-æ-** or **-ey-**. This is particularly relevant for adjectives of which the stem ends in one of these vowels, like **nýr**: **nýjan**, **nýjum**, but: **nýs**, **nýrri**, **nýrrar** (see *Athugið* above).

Exercise 4

Decline the following pairs in the singular and the plural:

> **svartur jakki, skrautlegt pils, fínn kjóll, þykk peysa, ljótt bindi, ný dragt**

Exercise 5

Put the adjectives in brackets into the sentences in their appropriate gender and case forms:

1 Konan á ________ (blár) bíl.
2 Ég ætla að kaupa ________ (nýr) peysu og ________ (grár) skó.
3 Maðurinn er í ________ (hvítur) skyrtu, ________ (svartur) buxum og ________ (nýr) spariskóm.
4 Konan klæðist ________ (gulur) blússu, ________ (brúnn) pilsi, ________ (gulur) sokkabuxum og ________ (grænn) klossum.
5 Stelpan fer í ________ (rauður) úlpu og setur á sig ________ (hlýr) húfu, ________ (langur) trefil og ________ (stór) vettlinga.

Reading 1

Árstíðir á Íslandi

Veturinn er frá janúar til mars. Hann er langur og frekar kaldur. Oftast er éljagangur, snjór og frost, og oft er mjög hvasst. Dagarnir eru stuttir í skammdeginu.

Vorið er frá apríl til júní. Þá fer að hlýna, dagarnir lengjast og lóan kemur til landsins. Náttúran vaknar úr vetrarsvefni og allt byrjar að blómstra.

Sumarið er frá júlí til september. Þá er bjart allan sólarhringinn, og þegar sólin skín er oft mjög hlýtt og þægilegt, allt upp í 20–25 stig. Það eru margar útihátíðir, og margir fara í útilegu. En það getur líka verið svalt, jafnvel kalt, sérstaklega á hálendinu, og það má alltaf búast við úrkomu. Í ágúst og september fara menn í berjamó.

Haustið er frá október til desember. Haustlitirnir eru mjög fallegir, en um haustið fer líka að kólna og það er oft rigning og hvasst.

Vocabulary notes

éljagang/ur (-s)	intermittent snow or hailstorms
hvass, *adj.*	windy, blowing hard
skammdegi (-s)	short days of winter
hlýna (hlýna), *intrans.*	become warm(er)
lengjast (lengist), *intrans.*	become longer
ló/a (-u, -ur)	golden plover (The return of the plover traditionally heralds the coming of spring in Iceland.)
sólarhring/ur (-s)	24 hours, around the clock
útihátíð (-ar, -ir)	outdoor festival
fara í berjamó	go berry-picking
kólna (kólna), *intrans.*	cool down, become cold(er)

Exercise 6

Read the text above carefully. Imagine you are in Iceland for a full year. What kind of clothing will you wear during each season?

1 Vetur: ég ætla að vera í ______.
2 Vor: ég ____________.
3 Sumar:
4 Haust:

Language points

Fraction

In Dialogue 1 we encountered such forms as **jöklum**, from **jökull**, and **veðri**, from **veður**. Icelandic nouns and adjectives that have two syllables in the stem, such as **jökul/l** and **veður**, lose the second stem vowel whenever a vowel ending is added:

> **jökul-i → jökli, veðuri → veðri, gamal-an → gamlan, opin-ir → opnir**

This phenomenon is known as fracture (**brottfall**). Note that there are some important exceptions to this rule:

1 Fraction only occurs before noun or adjective endings, not before the suffixed article: **sumr-i** (*dat. sg.*), but: **sumar-ið.**
2 Fraction does not occur in adjectives ending in **-legur**: **falleg/ur → falleg-an, falleg-ir.**

Exercise 7

Put the nouns and adjectives in brackets into the following sentences in their correct forms. You will have to determine the appropriate number, case and gender as well as consider the possibility of fraction.

1 Það eru margir ____________ (jökull) á Íslandi.
2 Börn setja ____________ (trefill) á sig.
3 Peysurnar eru ____________ (gamall).
4 Mamma á ____________ (fallegur) bíl.
5 Söfnin eru ____________ (opinn).
6 Ert þú með ____________ (lykill-inn)? Já, ég er með alla ____________ (lyklar-nir).
7 Hundarnir eru ____________ (lítill) og ____________ (sætur).
8 Winston Churchill reykti (*acc.*) ____________ ____________ (stór, vindill, *pl.*).

Reading 2

Draumur um brúðkaup í hvítum kjól

Where is Muriel from? What is her greatest wish?

Ástralska gamanmyndin, Brúðkaup Muriel, sem nú er sýnd í Háskólabíói fjallar um unga stúlku sem býr í litlum strandbæ. Stúlkan heitir Muriel og á sér þá ósk heitasta að finna ástina sína og gifta sig í hvítum brúðarkjól. Því miður reynist Muriel erfitt að fá ósk sína uppfyllta því hún er óframfærin og óörugg með sig.

Tónlist sænsku hljómsveitarinnar ABBA er mikilvæg í lífi Muriel. Þar er tilveran svo björt og áhyggjulaus og gjörólík þeirri sem Muriel þarf að takast á við. Hogan* er mikill aðdáandi ABBA og lagði hann á sig ómælt erfiði til að fá leyfi hljómsveitarmeðlima til að fá að leika tónlistina í myndinni.

Brúðkaup Muriel hefur hlotið góðar viðtökur bæði hér á landi og erlendis.

Adapted from Gerður Kristný, 'Brúðkaup Muriel',
Nýtt líf 18.5 (júlí/ágúst 1995: 30)

Vocabulary notes

gamanmynd (-ar, -ir)	comedy film	**takast á við**	struggle with
á sér þá ósk heitasta	has as her greatest wish	**leggja á sig (legg)**	take on
gifta sig (gifti)	get married	**lagði hann á sig ómælt erfiði**	he spared himself no trouble
reynast erfitt	prove difficult	**hefur hlotið góðar viðtökur**	has been well received (from **hljóta (hlýt)**, 'receive')
ólík/ur, *adj.*	unlike, different from		
gjörólík þeirri sem	completely different from the one that	**bæði**, *n.* of **báðir**	both

Language points

Declension of numbers 1–4

The numbers 1–4 in Icelandic not only have different gender forms, but, like adjectives, they have different case forms as well. These are the declensions:

---

* P.J. Hogan, leikstjóri myndarinnar

1	*masc.*	*fem.*	*neut.*	2	*masc.*	*fem.*	*neut.*
nom.	einn	ein	eitt		tveir	tvær	tvö
acc.	einn	eina	eitt		tvo	tvær	tvö
dat.	einum	einni	einu			tveimur	
gen.	eins	einnar	eins			tveggja	

3	*masc.*	*fem.*	*neut.*	4	*masc.*	*fem.*	*neut.*
nom.	þrír	þrjár	þrjú		fjórir	fjórar	fjögur
acc.	þrjá	þrjár	þrjú		fjóra	fjórar	fjögur
dat.		þremur				fjórum	
gen.		þriggja				fjögurra	

As you see, there are twelve ways of saying, 1, 2, 3 and 4 in Icelandic, depending on the gender of the noun and its position in the sentence.

Exercise 8

Put the correct case and gender forms of the numbers 1–4 into the following sentences. Remember to change the nouns into the correct plural and case forms after 1.

1 Strákurinn á _________________________ (1,2,3,4, **hjól**, *n.*, 'bike').
2 Brynja er í _________________________ (1,2,3,4, **peysa**).
3 Jón fer í _________________________ (1,2,3,4, **jakki**).
4 Afi á _________________________ (1,2,3,4, **mynd**).
5 Hérna eru _________________________ (1,2,3,4, **króna**).
6 Við förum til (*gen.*) _________________________ (1,2,3,4, **land**).

Exercise 9

Football (**knattspyrn/a, fótbolt/i**) is one of the most popular sports in Iceland. Listen closely to the radio broadcast. Can you fill in the scores? Note that **mark**, 'score', 'goal' is neuter and that, depending on the sentence, the numbers may occur in different case forms. Also note that 'zero' can be **núll**, but also **ekkert**, *dat.* **engu** 'nothing'.

<table>
<tr><td>Skagamenn – Valsmenn</td><td>____ – ____</td></tr>
<tr><td>KR – Breiðablik</td><td>____ – ____</td></tr>
<tr><td>Grindavík – Vestmannaeyingar</td><td>____ – ____</td></tr>
<tr><td>Blik – ÍBA</td><td>____ – ____</td></tr>
</table>

More interrogatives

By now you are familiar with most interrogatives in Icelandic: **hver**, **hvað**, **hvaða**, **hvar**, **hvenær**, **hvernig**, **hvert** and **hvaðan**. They are not all grammatically similar, however. The first two are interrogative pronouns, whereas the others are interrogative adverbs. Adverbs of any kind are easy in Icelandic because they are not declined, but pronouns are declined, including interrogative pronouns: if you are asking for an object rather than a subject, the verb or preposition in the sentence will determine the case of **hver** or **hvað**.This can be tricky, because interrogatives usually start off the question, so that you need to think in advance of the verb you are going to use and which case it governs:

Hvað (*subj.*) **er þetta?**
but:
Hverju (*neut. dat.*) **svarar** (*dat.*) **þú?**   What do you answer?

With prepositions it is a little easier, because they can be put before the interrogative pronoun and can help clue you in on the case form that is to follow:

Í (*dat.*) **hverju er hún?** What is she wearing? (*lit.* 'In what is she?')

Með (*dat.*) **hverjum förum við?** With whom do we go?

These are the forms:

		masculine	feminine	neuter
sg.	*nom.*	hver	hver	hvað
	acc.	hvern	hverja	hvað
	dat.	hverjum	hverri	hverju
	gen.	hvers	hverrar	hvers
pl.	*nom.*	hverjir	hverjar	hver
	acc.	hverja	hverjar	hver
	dat.		hverjum	
	gen.		hverra	

In general, the masculine form is used when asking about people, unless you know you are specifically asking about a woman or women. The neuter is used to ask about some thing or things.

Exercise 10

Construct questions for the following answers, using the (correct form of the) appropriate interrogative:

1 _________________? Pósthúsið er *í Austurstræti*.
2 _________________? Það kostar *11.000 krónur*.
3 _________________? Ég segi *allt gott*.
4 _________________? Ég fer *í kvöld*.
5 _________________? Þetta er *kunningi minn*.
6 _________________? Ég er að fara *niður í bæ*.
7 _________________? Hún klæðist *blússu og buxum*.
8 _________________? Hann saknar ('misses', *gen.*) *barnsins*.

Adjectives 2: opposites

Exercise 11

Match the adjectives in the left-hand column with their opposites on the right:

góður/ágætur	kaldur
hlýr	leiðinlegur
svartur	stór/mikill
síður/langur	vondur/slæmur
heitur	stuttur
nýr	svalur
lítill	hvítur
fölur	auðveldur
ljós	þungur
léttur	snyrtilegur
skemmtilegur	ljótur
fallegur	gamall
druslulegur	dökkur
erfiður	skær

Most of the other adjectives introduced in this chapter make their opposites by adding (or taking off) **-ó-**. Fill in the gaps: **breytilegur – óbreytilegur**; **þægilegur – ...** ; **smekklegur – ...** ; **myndarlegur ...** ; **óöruggur – ...** ; **ólíkur – ...**

Exercise 12

Fill in the gaps with adjectives: what words can you think of to describe the following? (Think of the appropriate gender forms!)

Hár	*Munnur*	*Veður (n.)*	*Bíómynd*
(hair, *n.*)	(mouth, *m.*)		(film, *f.*)
sítt	stór	. . .	. . .
. . .	. . .	. . .	. . .
. . .	. . .	. . .	. . .
. . .	. . .	. . .	. . .

Language points

Compounds

Compounds are nouns made up of two or more individual words which are put together in certain ways to form a new word, like 'schoolbag' or 'toothpaste'. In Icelandic, compounds are constructed as follows (in order of frequency):

1 The first word is added to the next word in the genitive form singular or plural, whichever makes more sense: *ullar*fatnaður (ull + fatnað/ur), *lopa*peysa (lop/i + peys/a), *bíla*sali (bíl/l + sal/i).
2 The stem of one word is added to another word: *hóp*ferð (hóp/ur + ferð), *bíl*stjóri (bíl/l + stjór/i).
3 Individual words are combined with the help of connective letters, usually -i- or -u-, or -an- or -in-: *spar-i*-skór, *mán-u*-dagur, *fár-an*-legur, *leið-in*-legur.

In all compounds, the final part determines the gender and thus its declension.

Exercise 13

On the left is a list of materials. How many compounds can you construct, matching the various materials up with clothing items listed on the right?

bómull (-ar, *f.* cotton)	**sokkar**
leður (-s, *n.* leather)	**skór**
galli (-a, *m.* denim)	**jakki**
gull (-s, *n.* gold)	**bolur**
tré (-s, *n.* wood)	**stígvél**
plast (-s, *n.* plastic)	**buxur**
gúmmí (-s, *n.* rubber)	**poki**
lop/i (-a, *m.* unspun wool)	**hringur**
ull (-ar, *f.* wool)	**húfa**

Now do the same for the following columns:

sól (*f.*)	**úr**
spara (spara)	**spenna**
brúður (-ar, -ir, *f.* bride)	**frakki**
vas/i (pocket)	**band**
hár	**efni** (-s, *n.* material)
hett/a	**gleraugu**
teygj/a (stretch)	**kjóll**
vetur (-rar, -ur, *m.*)	**peysa**

Exercise 14

Look at the advertisement below. Which items are on sale?
(**afslátt/ur**, *m.* 'discount'). Which items are expected before the
weekend? Are all advertised items clothing items?

Reading 3 ⏺⏺

Skuggi skammdegisins

Skammdegi *refers to the midwinter period in Iceland when the days
are at their shortest, with only 4–6 hours of daylight. The influence
of the winter darkness on the mind and body has been a favourite
topic of speculation and research. This is what some Icelanders have
to say on the topic. Which period does Hermann find the most difficult? Is Sóley active during the winter? What time of the year does
Nína Björk prefer?*

Hermann Ragnar, danskennari:
'Mér finnst haustið yndislegur tími. Þá hefja skólarnir og leikhúsin
starfsemi sína. Haustlitirnir eru svo fallegir og lerkitrén í garðinum
mínum verða fagur-gulbrún. Ég hlakka alltaf til jólanna en þegar
slökkt hefur verið á jólaljósunum á þrettándanum fer í hönd erfiðari
tími.'

Sóley, leikkona:
'Ég er fremur lífsglöð að eðlisfari en á haustin verð ég löt og
niðurdregin. Þá langar mig helst til að kúra undir sæng allan daginn.
Ég verð líka vör við að börnin mín eiga erfiðara með að vakna á
morgnana. Jólin létta mér lundina en í byrjun febrúar verð ég
aftur löt.'

Nína Björk, skáld:
'Ég verð vör við þunglyndi fyrst á vorin þegar það fer að birta
á nýjan leik. Mér líður aftur á móti vel í rökkrinu við kertaljós.
Þess vegna er haustið skemmtilegasti árstíminn og september
uppáhaldsmánuðurinn minn.'

Adapted from Gerður Kristný, 'Skuggi skammdegisins',
Nýtt líf 17.8 (1994: 126–8)

Vocabulary notes

mér finnst, *impers.*	I find
lerkitré (-s, -), *n.*	larch
þegar slökkt hefur verið á jólaljósunum	when the Christmas lights have been turned off
þrettánd/i (-a)	6 January (lit. 'the thirteenth', or 'twelfth night', Epiphany, traditionally the end of the Christmas season.)

fara í hönd	approach
lífsglað/ur, *adj.*	cheerful
lat/ur, *adj.*	lazy
kúra (kúri) undir sæng	snuggle down into bed
verða var (vör, *f.***) við**, *acc.*	notice, experience
eiga erfiðara með	have a harder time
létta mér lundina	raise my spirits
þunglyndi (-s), *n.*	depression
á nýjan leik	once more, again
mér líður vel, *impers.*	I feel good
aftur á móti	on the other hand

6 Á ferð og flugi

On the move

In this lesson you will learn about:

- travelling by bus and air
- booking and buying tickets
- telling the time 2
- schedules
- personal pronoun declensions
- expressions of necessity and future intention
- radio and television programmes

Dialogue 1

Að panta flug

Richard has a few extra days to spare in Iceland and would very much like to visit the Vestmannaeyjar ('Westmen Islands'), off the south coast of Iceland, before he goes home. He decides to phone Flugfélag Íslands ('Air Iceland') for flight information, and dials the central information number. When can Richard leave? On which day does the conversation take place? How long is Richard going to stay in the Vestmannaeyjar? At what time does he have to be at the airport?

SÍMSVARINN: Þetta er Flugfélag Íslands. Veldu einn fyrir upplýsingar, veldu tvo fyrir bókanir. (*Richard chooses 1, but the automated information is of no use to him, so he tries again, this time choosing 2.*)

SÍMSVARINN: Því miður eru allar línur uppteknar sem stendur. Símtölum er svarað í röð. (*Richard waits his turn until someone answers the phone.*)

Afgr.: Flugfélag Íslands, góðan dag.

Richard: Góðan daginn, ég ætla að fá upplýsingar um flug til Vestmannaeyja.

Afgr.: Það er flogið þrisvar á dag, kl. 07:05, 14:00 og 16:50, mánudaga til laugardaga, og kl. 8, 13:30 og 16:50 á sunnudögum.

Richard: Nú já, og eru öll flugin bein?

Afgr.: Já, það eru engar millilendingar.

Richard: Hvað er lengi verið að fljúga þangað?

Afgr.: Flugið tekur 25 mínútur.

Richard: Og hvað kostar miðinn?

Afgr.: Skulum sjá ... Hann kostar 4.965 báðar leiðir.

Richard: Er laust sæti í vélinni sem fer seinni partinn í dag?

Afgr.: Nei, hún er fullbókuð, en það eru nokkur laus sæti í fyrramálið.

Richard: Jæja, þá ætla ég að panta miða með fluginu í fyrramálið.

Afgr.: Og hvenær viltu koma aftur?

Richard: Ekki á morgun heldur hinn daginn.

Afgr.: Á föstudaginn.

Richard: Já, með síðdegisflugi ef hægt er.

Afgr.: Já, það er hægt. Hvað er nafnið?

Richard: Richard Johnson.

Afgr.: Heimilisfang og símanúmer?

Richard: Ég gisti á Hótel Íslandi, herbergisnúmerið er 364.

Afgr.: Ertu með síma í Vestmannaeyjum þar sem hægt er að ná í þig?

Richard: Nei, ég veit ekki ennþá hvar ég ætla að gista.

Afgr.: Allt í lagi, en hafðu þá samband við umboðsmann á flugvellinum áður en þú ferð.

Richard: Já, ég geri það.

Afgr.: Brottfarartími í fyrramálið er kl. 07:05, mæting á flugvelli er klukkan hálf sjö.

Richard: Fínt er, þakka þér fyrir.

Afgr.: Gjörðu svo vel.

Vocabulary notes

símsvar/i (-a, -ar)	answering machine
veldu, *imp.sg.* of **velja (vel)**, *acc.*	choose
upptekin/n, *adj.*	busy
sem stendur	as it is, right now
símtölum er svaraðí röð	telephone calls are answered in sequence
fljúga (flýg)	fly
það er flogið	there are flights, flights are running (*lit.* 'it is flown')
seinni partinn	in the afternoon
í fyrramálið	tomorrow morning
hinn daginn	the day after tomorrow
síðdegis	in the afternoon
ná (næ, nærð, nær) í, *acc.*	reach
hafðu samband við, *imp.sg.*	get in touch with
umboðsmaður	agent (i.e. of the airline)
brottfarartím/i (-a, -ar)	time of departure
mæting (-ar, -ar)	attendance, 'be there at. . .' (In this case the expression refers of course to the check-in time.)

Language points

Travelling in Iceland

Travel in Iceland is conducted mostly by car, bus or aeroplane. There are no trains or railways, but most of the larger towns can be reached by plane, and nearly all towns and villages are on or connected to a conch route.

Vocabulary

General travel

ferð, *f.*	trip, journey	**seinkun**, *f.*	delay
ferðalag, *n.*	journey, voyage	**fara/leggja af stað**	depart
far, *n.*	ride, passage	**ferðast (ferðast)**	travel
fargjald, *n.*	fare	**koma til**, *gen.*	arrive
(far)mið/i (farseðil/l)	(travel) ticket	**komast (kemst)**	get (to)
(far)kort	(travel) pass	**panta (panta)/ bóka (bóka)** *acc.*	book
farmiðasal/i/ afgreiðslustaður	booking office, reservations	**aðra leið**	one-way

fram og aftur/	return		**verðskrá (-ar, -r)** *f.*	list of fares
fram og til baka/				
báðar leiðir			*Aeroplane*	
lágmarksdvöl	minimum		**(flug)vél** *f.*	aeroplane
	required stay		**flugvöll/ur**	airport
farþeg/i	passenger		**fljúga (flýg)**	fly
(ferða)áætlun, *f.*	schedule		**innanlands**	domestic
tímatafl/a	timetable		**utanlands**	international
mæting	check-in time		**millilending**	stop-over
brottför, *f.*	departure		*Coach*	
kom/a, *f.*	arrival		**rút/a**	coach
gildistím/i	time of validity		**(áætlunarbíl/l)**	
biðlist/i	waiting list		**umferðarmiðstöð**	main coach
fullbókað/ur, *adj.*	fully booked		**BSÍ (-var,**	terminal
leið, *f.*	route		**-var),** *f.*	
á leiðinni	en route, on		**viðkomustað/ur**	stop
	the way		**(stoppistöð)**	
um borð	on board			

Telling time 2

ein klukkustund (-ar, -ir)/	
einn klukkutím/i (-a, -ar)	one hour
hálftím/i (-a, -ar)	half an hour
korter (-s, -)	a quarter (of an hour)
mínút/a (-u, -ur)	a minute
sekúnd/a (-u, -ur)	a second
hádegi (-s), *n.*	noon
miðnætti (-s), *n.*	midnight

01:00/13:00	**klukkan er eitt**
01:05/13:05	**klukkan er fimm mínútur yfir eitt***
01:15/13:15	**klukkan er korter yfir eitt**
01:30/13:30	**klukkan er hálf tvö**
01:40/13:40	**klukkan er tuttugu mínútur í tvö***
01:45/13:45	**klukkan er korter í tvö**
02:00/14:00	**klukkan er tvö**

* more formally also: **klukkan er fimm mínútur gengin í tvö**
* more formally also: **klukkuna vantar tuttugu mínútur í tvö**

Note that Icelanders do not use a.m. and p.m. Usually the context makes clear whether it is before or after noon (**árdegis** or **síðdegis**,

fyrir hádegi/miðnætti, eftir hádegi/miðnætti). In programming and schedules, the 24-hour clock is used: **klukkan fjórtán fimmtíu** is 2:50 p.m.

Exercise 1

Read and write out the following times:

6:25, 18:30, 15:10, 4:45, 12:55, 23:35, 5:20, 20:40, 10:50, 21:00, 11:15

Exercise 2

Listen to and write out the times read out in the recording.

To say in Icelandic how many times something happens you use the dative form of **sinn** (**-s, -**), *n.* in the singular or plural as appropriate. When used in combination with a number 1 or 4, the numbers must also be in the dative, while the numbers 2 and 3 have special forms: **tvisvar** and **þrisvar**, which can be followed by **sinnum** or used on their own:

einu sinni	once
tvisvar (sinnum)	twice
þrisvar (sinnum)	three times
fjórum sinnum	four times
fimm sinnum	five times, etc.

Exercise 3

Look at the flight and coach schedules on pp. 108 9 and answer the following questions in Icelandic:

1 Klukkan hvað er flogið til Ísafjarðar á fimmtudögum?
2 Er hægt að fljúga til Hornafjarðar á laugardagsmorgnum?
3 Hvað er flogið oft á viku til Færeyja?
4 Klukkan hvað fer kvöldrútan frá Bifröst til Reykjavíkur?
5 Klukkan hvað kemur þú til Borgarness ef þú tekur rútu frá Reykjavík kl. átta um morguninn?

NORÐURLEIÐ
LANDLEIÐIR

Skógarhlíð 10 · Reykjavík · Sími 551 1145
Bréfasími 552 6550

FERÐAÁÆTLUN

	S	M	Þ	M	F	F	L
Allt árið (all year)..							
Frá Reykjavík........	08.00	08.00	08.00	08.00	08.00	08.00	08.00
(From):.................	17.00					17.00	
– Akureyri............	09.30	09.30	09.30	09.30	09.30	09.30	09.30
	17.00					17.00	
15/6-15/8							
Frá Reykjavík........	17.00	17.00	17.00	17.00	17.00	17.00	17.00
– Akureyri............	17.00	17.00	17.00	17.00	17.00	17.00	17.00

AFGREIÐSLUSTAÐIR:

Reykjavík: Bifr.st. Íslands (B.S.Í.), Umferðarmiðst., sími 552 2300
Staðarskáli: sími 451 1150
Hvammstangi: Söluskálinn, sími 451 2465
Skagaströnd: Hótel Dagsbrún, sími 452 2730
Blönduós: Blönduskálinn, sími 452 4350
Varmahlíð: Hótel Varmahlíð, sími 453 8170
Sauðárkrókur: Verslun Haraldar Júlíussonar, sími 453 5124
Akureyri: Umferðarmiðstöðin Hafnarstræti 82,
símar 462 4442 & 462 4729

Viðkomustaðir og brottfarartímar
Árdegisferðir

Kl.	FRÁ	TIL	KL.
08.00	Reykjavík..........................		16.00
09.00	Þyrill, Hvalfirði		14.55
09.15	Akranesvegamót		14.40
09.45	Borgarnes		14.20
10.10	Bifröst............................		13.55
10.45	Brú		13.20
11.20	Staðarskáli		13.15
11.40	Norðurbraut......................		12.25
12.30	Blönduós		11.35
13.20	Varmahlíð........................		10.45
14.30	Akureyri..........................		09.30
	TIL	FRÁ	

Síðdegisferðir

Kl.	FRÁ	TIL	KL.
17.00	Reykjavík..........................		23.25
18.00	Þyrill, Hvalfirði		22.25
18.15	Akranesvegamót		22.10
18.45	Borgarnes		21.50
19.10	Bifröst............................		21.25
19.45	Brú		20.55
20.15	Staðarskáli		20.50
20.35	Norðurbraut......................		20.00
21.25	Blönduós		19.10
22.15	Varmahlíð........................		18.20
23.20	Akureyri..........................		17.00
	TIL	FRÁ	

SUMARÁÆTLUN FLUGFÉLAGS ÍSLANDS

Gildistími: 26. mai – 31. ágúst 1998

Frá/til REYKJAVÍKUR Reykjavíkurflugv., sími: 570 3030, fax: 570 3132

Til/frá AKUREYRI (AEY) Flugvöllur, sími: 460 7000, fax: 460 7010

Gildistími	Dagar	Brottf.	Koma	Brottf.	Koma	Flugnr.	Teg.	Um
25. mai - 31. ágú	MÁN-FÖS	08:50	09:35	07:45	08:30	FI8546/8545	SWM	
25. mai - 31. ágú	DAGLEGA	07:30	08:15	08:30	09:15	FI8112/8113	F-50	
25. mai - 31. ágú	DAGLEGA	11:00	11:45	12:10	12:55	FI8122/8123	F-50	
25. mai - 31. ágú	DAGLEGA	14:00	14:45	15:10	15:55	FI8132/8133	F-50	
25. mai - 31. ágú	DAGLEGA	17:00	17:45	18:10	18:55	FI8142/8143	F-50	
25. mai - 31. ágú	MÁN-FÖS/SUN	19:30	20:15	20:40	21:25	FI8162/8163	F-50	
25. mai - 31. ágú	MÁN-FÖS/SUN	21:15	22:00	22:25	23:10	FI8172/8173	F-50	
25. mai - 31. ágú	LAU	21:45	22:30	22:55	23:40	FI8174/8175	F-50	

Til/frá EGILSSTÖÐUM (EGS) Flugvöllur, sími: 471 1210, fax: 471 2208

Gildistími	Dagar	Brottf.	Koma	Brottf.	Koma	Flugnr.	Teg.	Um
25. mai - 31. ágú	DAGLEGA	07:45	09:30	09:55	10:55	FI8216	F-50	HFN
25. mai - 31. ágú	MÁN/MIÐ/FIM/FÖS	14:10	15:10	15:35	16:35	FI8332/8333	F-50	
25. mai - 31. ágú	ÞRI/LAU/SUN	14:10	15:10	15:35	16:35	FI8334/8335	SWM	
25. mai - 31. ágú	DAGLEGA	19:30	20:30	20:55	21:55	FI8354/9355	F-50	

Til/frá HORNAFIRÐI (HFN) Flugvöllur, sími: 478 1250, fax: 471 1297

Gildistími	Dagar	Brottf.	Koma	Brottf.	Koma	Flugnr.	Teg.	Um
25. mai - 31. ágú	DAGLEGA	07:45	08:40	09:05	10:55	FI8216	F-50	EGS
25. mai - 31. ágú	MÁN-MIÐ/FÖS/SUN	16:50	17:45	18:05	19:00	FI8362/8363	F-50	
25. mai - 31. ágú	FIM	16:50	17:45	18:05	19:00	FI8364/8365	SWM	
25. mai - 31. ágú	LAU	18:40	19:35	19:55	20:50	FI8366/8367	SWM	

Til/frá HÚSAVÍK (HZK) Flugvöllur, sími: 464 1080, fax: 464 1084

Gildistími	Dagar	Brottf.	Koma	Brottf.	Koma	Flugnr.	Teg.	Um
25. mai - 31. ágú	MÁN-FÖS	08:15	09:05	09:25	10:15	FI8302/8303	SWM	
25. mai - 31. ágú	LAU - SUN	11:00	11:50	12:15	13:05	FI8306/8307	SWM	
25. mai - 31. ágú	MÁN-FÖS/SUN	18:30	19:20	19:40	20:30	FI8314/8315	SWM	
1. jún - 15. júl	MÁN/MIÐ (mds)	18:45	19:35	23:00	00:20	FI8614/8316	SWM	

Til/frá ÍSAFIRÐI (IFJ) Flugvöllur, sími: 456 3000, fax: 456 4074

Gildistími	Dagar	Brottf.	Koma	Brottf.	Koma	Flugnr.	Teg.	Um
25. mai - 31. ágú	MÁN-LAU	08:30	09:10	09:35	10:15	FI8014/8015	F-50	
25. mai - 31. ágú	SUN	10:45	11:25	11:50	12:30	FI8026/8027	F-50	
25. mai - 31. ágú	MÁN/MIÐ-FÖS	12:00	12:40	13:05	13:45	FI8044/8045	F-50	
25. mai - 31. ágú	ÞRI	12:00	12:40	13:00	13:40	FI8046/8047	SWM	
25. mai - 31. ágú	MÁN-FÖS/SUN	18:30	19:10	19:35	20:15	FI8052/8053	F-50	
25. mai - 31. ágú	LAU	19:30	20:10	20:35	21:15	FI8056/8057	F-50	

Til/frá VESTMANNAEYJUM (VEY) Flugv., sími: 481 3300, fax: 481 3299

Gildistími	Dagar	Brottf.	Koma	Brottf.	Koma	Flugnr.	Teg.	Um
25. mai - 31. ágú	MÁN-LAU	07:05	07:30	07:40	08:05	FI8400/8401	F-50	
25. mai - 31. ágú	SUN	08:00	08:25	08:40	09:05	FI8404/8405	F-50	
25. mai - 31. ágú	SUN	13:30	13:55	14:10	14:35	FI8414/8415	F-50	
25. mai - 31. ágú	MÁN-LAU	14:00	14:25	14:40	15:05	FI8420/8421	SWM	
25. mai - 31. ágú	MÁN-MIÐ/FÖS/LAU	16:50	17:15	17:30	17:55	FI8434/8435	SWM	
25. mai - 31. ágú	MÁN-MIÐ/FÖS/LAU	17:00	17:25	17:40	18:05	FI8440/8441	SWM	
25. mai - 31. ágú	FIM/SUN	16:50	17:15	17:30	17:55	FI8436/8437	F-50	

MILLILANDAFLUG UM REYKJAVÍKURFLUGVÖLL

Frá/til REYKJAVIK Reykjavíkurflugvöllur, sími: 570 3030, fax: 570 3132

Til/frá FÆREYJAR (FAE) Vágar

Gildistími	Dagar	Brottf.	Koma	Brottf.	Koma	Flugnr.	Teg.	Um
25. mai - 31. ágú	ÞRI/LAU	11:45	14:35	15:10	16:00	FI8264/8265	F-50	
25. mai - 31. ágú	MIÐ			17:30	17:45	FI267	BAE	RC255
25. mai - 31. ágú	FIM	08:30	10:45			FI266	BAE	RC250

Til/frá KULUSUK (KUS) Grænland

Gildistími	Dagar	Brottf.	Koma	Brottf.	Koma	Flugnr.	Teg.	Um
15. jún - 28. ágú	MÁN-MIÐ/FÖS	10:00	09:50	14:00	18:00	NY243/244	F-50	
18. jún - 29. ágú	FIM/LAU	09:40	09:30	14:40	18:40	NY241/242	F-50	
25. mai - 14. jún	FIM/LAU	14:00	14:00	15:00	19:00	NY253/254	F-50	
25. mai - 28. okt	ÞRI "KEF"	13:45	13:45	08:45	12:45	GL721/720	DH7	
18. jún - 29. ágú	FIM/LAU "KEF"	14:20	14:10	10:00	13:50	NY246/245	F-50	

Til/frá NARSARSUAQ (UAK) Grænland

Gildistími	Dagar	Brottf.	Koma	Brottf.	Koma	Flugnr.	Teg.	Um
10. jún - 2. sept	MIÐ	18:30	18:30	19:30	23:30	FI237/236	BAE	
6. jún - 5. sept	LAU	16:30	17:55	18:30	23:55	NY235/234	F-50	

Til/frá CONSTABLE POINT (CNP) Grænland

Gildistími	Dagar	Brottf.	Koma	Brottf.	Koma	Flugnr.	Teg.	Um
27. mai - 28. ágú	MIÐ/FÖS	11:30	13:20	14:30	16:20	GL753/752	SWM	

Frá/til FÆREYJA

Til/frá GLASGOW (GLA) Skotland

Gildistími	Dagar	Brottf.	Koma	Brottf.	Koma	Flugnr.	Teg.	Um
22. jún - 6. ág.	MÁN/FIM	12:00	13:15	13:50	16:10	FI8184	BAE	

Dialogue 2

Exercise 4: Til Hafnar í Hornafirði

*You would like to travel from Reykjavík to Höfn in Hornafjörður, in the far south-eastern corner of Iceland, by coach, so that you will see something of the spectacular landscape in southern Iceland, in particular **Jökulsárlón** (-s, n.; the famous lagoon where the Vatnajökull runs into the sea). You go to the main coach terminal BSÍ in Reykjavík in order to get some travel information. Can you fill in the gaps in Icelandic according to the English prompts given in brackets in the following dialogue?*

AFGR.: Hver er næstur?
YOU: (1 *I am next. Good afternoon.*) _______________
AFGR.: Góðan dag
YOU: (2 *I would like to travel to Höfn í Hornafjörður by coach if that's possible.*)

____

AFGR.: Já, það er hægt. Austurleið fer tvisvar á dag
YOU: (3 *At what time?*)_______________.
AFGR.: Hálf níu á morgnana og klukkan fimm á kvöldin
YOU: (4 *At what time does the bus arrive in Höfn?*)

_______________.

AFGR.: Ef þú ferð frá Reykjavík hálf níu þá ertu komin til Hafnar klukkan fimm.
YOU: (5 *What does the ticket cost?*)_______________.
AFGR.: Hann kostar 3.965 kr.
YOU: (6 *Does the bus make a stop at Jökulsárlón?*)

_______________.

AFGR.: Já, en hún stoppar bara í smátíma, ekki nógu lengi til að fara í skoðunarferð. En Austurleið býður upp á sérstakar dagsferðir frá Höfn á Vatnajökul og að Jökulsárlóni.
YOU: (7 *I see. Is it possible to buy a ticket to Höfn now?*)

_______________.

AFGR.: Báðar leiðir?
YOU: (8 *No, one-way, I intend to fly back*)_______________.
AFGR.: Hvenær ætlar þú að fara?
YOU: (9 *Tomorrow morning*)_______________.
AFGR.: 3.965 krónur
YOU: (10 *There you are, thank you very much*)

_______________.

Language points

Time of day/week/year

fyrr   ⟵   núna   ⟶   seinna

í morgun ⟵ í dag ⟶ í kvöld ⟶ í nótt
(in the morning,   (today)   (this evening)   (tonight)
this morning)

fyrir hádegi   eftir hádegi

árdegis   síðdegis

um morguninn seinni partinn

í gærmorgun	í fyrramálið
í gær	á morgun
í gærkvöld	annað kvöld
í fyrradag	hinn daginn
í fyrriviku	næstu viku
í fyrra	næsta ár

Prepositions commonly used with adverbial phrases of time

fyrir + *dat.*	*í* + *acc.*	*eftir* + *acc.*
______ ago	for ______	after ______
fyrir ári	**í ár**	**eftir ár**
a year ago	for a year	after a year
fyrir tveimur dögum	**í tvo daga**	**eftir tvo daga**
two days ago	for two days	after two days

When an adverbial phrase of time is not preceded by a preposition and is not in a subject position, it is in the accusative case. For example:

Hvað er lengi verið að fljúga til Vestmannaeyja? Rúmlega 25 *mínútur*

Hvað ertu búin að vera lengi á Íslandi? (Ég *(subj.)* **ætla að vera hér í)** *fjóra daga*

Exercise 5

Imagine you have travelled to Höfn and found accommodation there. At breakfast you are planning the day ahead and the following morning as well. Here are some suggestions in English, including the time of day. Can you make them into full Icelandic sentences? See if you can add some of your own ideas to the list.

1 In the morning: walk around (**um**, *acc.*) town
2 After that: have a coffee
3 Before noon: get information about sightseeing trips to Vatna-jökull and Jökulsárlón
4 At (**í**, *dat.*) noon: lunch (**hádegismat/ur**, *m.*)
5 Afternoon: take a look at the museum
6 Tomorrow morning: go on (**í**) sightseeing trip
7 Tomorrow evening: take a coach to Egilsstaðir (*m.pl.*!)
8 . . .

Dialogue 3 ▢▢

Í strætó

Joyce has been sightseeing all day in Reykjavík and gone for a refreshing swim afterwards in the magnificent swimming pool in Laugardalur. She feels too tired to do any more walking and decides to hop on a bus back to her guest house. She finds a bus stop nearby and asks a waiting bystander for information.

JOYCE: Afsakið, getur þú sagt mér hvernig ég kemst héðan í miðbæinn?

MAÐUR: Með því að taka fimmuna. Hún fer niður í bæ og stoppar við Hlemm og Lækjartorg.

JOYCE: Hvenær er hún væntanleg?

MAÐUR: Rétt fyrir sex. Hún hlýtur að koma bráðum. Ég er að bíða eftir henni.

JOYCE: Hvað kostar í vagninn?

MAÐUR: 120 krónur farið ef þú ert ekki með farmiða eða græna kortið.

JOYCE: Ég er ekki með kort eða miða, ég hef aldrei farið með strætisvagni hér áður.

MAÐUR: Nújá. Áttu smámynt? Þú verður að staðgreiða, og vagnstjórinn gefur ekki til baka.

JOYCE: Já, ég held það. En er hægt að skipta yfir í annan vagn án þess að borga aftur? Ég gisti á Rauðarárstig og ég er svo þreytt að ég nenni ekki að ganga þangað frá Hlemmi.

MAÐUR: Þá biður þú vagnstjórann um skiptimiða þegar þú kemur upp í vagninn, og við Hlemm skiptir þú svo yfir í vagn númer sex sem fer að Breiðholtskjöri. Hann stoppar við Rauðarárstig.

JOYCE: Þakka þér kærlega fyrir! Jæja, þarna kemur vagninn!

Vocabulary notes

strætisvagn (-s, -ar)/strætó city bus (Although the form of the popular abbreviation **strætó** would suggest the neuter gender, the underlying reference to the masculine noun **vagn** prevents it from being treated as a neuter noun. As a result, **strætó** is only used in this form. When its position in the sentence demands a change, for instance a definite article or a plural form, the word **strætisvagn**, or just **vagn**, is used instead.)

fimm/a (-u), *f.* 'the five' (i.e. bus number five. Buses 2–5 are generally referred to with the following nouns based on their numbers: **tvist/ur, þrist/ur, fjark/i, fimm/a.** Other buses/routes are referred to as **vagn númer** . . . or **leið** . . ..)

bíða (bíð) eftir, *dat.* wait for

hvað kostar í vagninn how much does it cost to get on the bus

græna kortið 'the green card' (monthly bus pass)

smámynt (-ar, -ir) change

staðgreiða (greiði), *acc.* to pay cash

gefa til baka give change

ég held það I think so

skipta yfir í annan vagn change buses

án þess að without

biðja (bið) um, *acc.* ask for

vagnstjór/i (-a, -ar) bus driver

skiptimið/i (-a, -ar) transfer ticket

koma upp í vagninn get onto the bus

Exercise 6

Look at the pages from the *Leiðabók Strætisvagna Reykjavíkur (SVR)* on p. 115 and see if you can answer the following questions:

1 If it takes Joyce about 10 minutes to get from Laugardalur to Hlemmur, at what time could she catch the next number 6, given that it's a weekday?
2 What if it were a Saturday?
3 When would be the earliest Joyce could get to Lækjartorg by bus from her guest house on Rauðarárstígur on a Sunday morning?
4 How much would it cost Joyce to get a green card?
5 How much money would she save per ride if she got a **spjald** rather than pay cash for her fares?
6 How much would it cost to take a bus back after a night out on the town?

Vocabulary notes

frest/ur (-s), *m.*   interval, every . . .
akstur (-s), *m.*   drive (from **aka (ek, ók, óku, ekið)** *dat.* drive)

Exercise 7

Answer the following questions in complete Icelandic sentences:

1 Hvert fer vagn númer sex?
2 Stoppar hann á Laugavegi?
3 Hvað kostar farið?
4 Hvað gerir þú ef þú verður að skipta á leiðinni?
5 Hvað segir þú við vagnstjórann ef þú þarft skiptimiða?
6 Ferð þú oft með strætisvagni? Hvaða vagn tekur þú?
7 Hvað kostar í vagninn þar sem þú átt heima?
8 Er hægt að kaupa kort þar? Ef svo er, hvað kostar það?

Language points

Personal pronoun declensions

As the function of a pronoun is to replace a noun, so it, too, changes form according to its position in the sentence. These are the case forms for the personal pronouns in Icelandic:

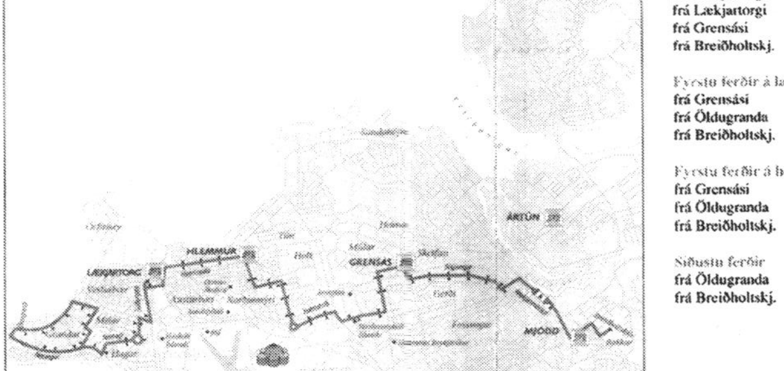

Fyrstu ferðir á mánud. - föstud.

frá Lækjartorgi	06:46	- ekið að Öldugranda
frá Lækjartorgi	06:48	- ekið að Mjódd.
frá Grensási	06:47	- ekið að Öldugranda.
frá Breiðholtskj.	06:57 og síðan á 20 mín fr.	

Fyrstu ferðir á laugardögum

frá Grensási	06:47	- ekið að Öldugranda.
frá Öldugranda	06:44 og síðan á 30 mín fr.	
frá Breiðholtskj.	07:08 og síðan á 30 mín fr.	

Fyrstu ferðir á helgidögum

frá Grensási	09:47	- ekið að Öldugranda.
frá Öldugranda	09:44 og síðan á 30 mín fr.	
frá Breiðholtskj.	10:08 og síðan á 30 mín fr.	

Síðustu ferðir

frá Öldugranda	00:14	- ekið að Hlemmtorgi
frá Breiðholtskj.	00:08	- ekið að Hlemmtorgi

Leið 6

Endastöðvar: Breiðholtskjör og Eiðisgrandi við Öldugranda.
Aksturleið: Breiðholtskjör - Arnarbakki - Álfabakki - Mjódd - Álfabakki - Reykjanesbraut - Bústaðavegur - Sogavegur - Grensásvegur(Grensás) - Fellsmúli - Háaleitisbraut - Listabraut - Kringlumýrarbraut - Hamrahlíð - Langahlíð - Flókagata - Rauðarárstígur - Hlemmur - Laugavegur - Snorrabraut - Hverfisgata - Lækjartorg - Lækjargata - Vonarstræti - Suðurgata - Hringbraut - Birkimelur - Neshagi - Hofsvallagata - Ægisíða - Nesvegur - Suðurströnd - Eiðsgrandi - Grandavegur - Meistaravellir - Flyðrugrandi - Kaplaskjólsvegur - Ægisíða - Hofsvallagata - Neshagi - Birkimelur - Hringbraut - Suðurgata - Aðalstræti - Vesturgata - Grófin - Tryggvagata - Lækjartorg - Hverfisgata - Hlemmur - Rauðarárstígur - Flókagata - Langahlíð - Hamrahlíð - Kringlumýrarbraut - Listabraut - Háaleitisbraut - Fellsmúli - Grensásvegur(Grensás) - Sogavegur - Bústaðavegur - Reykjanesbraut - Álfabakki - Mjódd - Álfabakki - Arnarbakki - Breiðholtskjör

Mjódd-Grandar	Á 20 mín. fresti: mán. - fös. kl. 07-19			Á 30 mín. fresti: mán. - fös. kl. 19-24 laug. kl. 07-24 helgid. kl. 10-24	
Taflan sýnir mín. yfir heila klst.					
Frá Breiðholtskjöri	17	37	57	8	38
Mjódd	19	39	59	10	40
Grensás	27	47	7	17	47
Verslunarskóli	32	52	12	22	52
Hlemmur	41	1	21	29	59
Lækjartorg	46	6	26	34	4
Frá Öldugranda	56	16	36	44	14
Lækjartorg	8	28	48	55	25
Hlemmur	13	33	53	59	29
Verslunarskóli	22	42	2	6	36
Grensás	27	47	7	11	41
Mjódd	35	55	15	18	48
Að Breiðholtskjöri	37	57	17	20	50

fyrirmyndar ferðamáti

FARGJÖLD SVR

Fullorðnir:
Einstök fargjöld.....................................120 kr.
Farmiðaspjald
   - almennt með 10 miðum ....1.000 kr.
   - fyrir aldraða með 20 miðum .....1.000 kr.
   - fyrir öryrkja með 20 miðum ....500 kr.

Græna kortið..3. 400 kr.

Unglingar 12 - 15 ára:
Einstök fargjöld.......................................60 kr.
Farmiðaspjald
   - með 20 miðum..........................1.000 kr.

*Unglingar greiða fullt gjald eftir
1. júní það ár sem þeir verða 16 ára.*

Börn innan 12 ára:
Einstök fargjöld.......................................25 kr.
Farmiðaspjald
   - með 22 miðum...........................300 kr.

**Börn innan 6 ára eru gjaldfrí séu þau
í fylgd með fullorðnum.**

Næturvagnar 200 kr. staðgreitt

1. október 1995

		1st person	2nd person	3rd person		
				Masculine	*Feminine*	*Neuter*
sg.	*nom.*	ég	þú	hann	hún	það
	acc.	mig	þig	hann	hana	það
	dat.	mér	þér	honum	henni	því
	gen.	mín	þín	hans	hennar	þess
pl.	*nom.*	við	þið	þeir	þær	þau
	acc.	okkur	ykkur	þá	þær	þau
	dat.	okkur	ykkur		þeim	
	gen.	okkar	ykkar		þeirra	

Examples:

Hvenær kemur fimman? *Hún* **kemur bráðum. Ég er að bíða
eftir** (*dat.*) ***henni***
Við* ætlum í bíó. Nennið þið að koma með** (*dat.*) ***okkur?

Exercise 8

Replace the italicized nouns in the following sentences with the
appropriate personal pronouns. Remember to check which number
and gender (what/whom does it refer to?) and which case form
(what is its position in the sentence?) to use.

1 Ég trúi *sögunni*. Ég trúi______.
2 *Flugin* eru sein. ______.
3 *Konurnar* skoða *bílana*. ________.
4 *Barnið* fer til *mömmu*. ________.
5 *Strákarnir* taka *rútuna*. ________.

Exercise 9

Read the following text and fill in the gaps with the correct forms
of the appropriate personal pronouns. Take care to note what
noun(s) each pronoun refers to in order to determine its number
and gender (remember: a combination of different genders makes
a neuter plural). Looking at the forms of adjectives in the same
sentence can also be helpful.

Pétur er að skoða myndir í fjölskyldu-albúmi. ______ eru
gamlar, gular og skemmtilegar. Hérna er mynd af mömmu frá
1970. ______ er hippaleg, með sítt hár. ______ er líka með

ofsa stór gleraugu. _______ eru fáranleg! Hérna kemur mynd af pabba. _______ er líka með sítt hár, og _______ er í útvíðum buxum. _______ eru líka svakalega hlægilegar! Hér er mynd af hjónunum þegar _______ eru gift. Og hérna er mynd af fyrsta barninu, systur Péturs. _______ er lítil og rauð og krumpuð. Og þarna er Pétur sjálfur. _______ er ofsalega sætur! Það er líka mynd af Pétri og litla bróður hans þegar _______ eru 5 og 3 ára gamlir. Svo er stór mynd af Pétri og systkinum. _______ eru öll í sparifötunum. Loksins kemur mynd af allri fjölskyldunni þegar _______ er í fríi í Frakklandi.

Vocabulary notes

hippaleg/ur, *adj.* hippi-ish, like a hippy

hlægileg/ur, *adj.* ridiculous, funny

útvíðar buxur bell-bottoms

krumpað/ur, *adj.* wrinkled

Expressions of necessity and future intention

The following verbal constructions express different degrees of necessity in Icelandic:

eiga að + infinitive 'have to' (because someone else says so, implied authority)

hljóta að + infinitive 'must' (because it is inevitable)

verða að + infinitive 'have to', 'must' (because it is unavoidable)

þurfa að + infinitive 'need to' (like **verða að** but weaker, not completely unavoidable but preferable nevertheless)

Examples:

> **Michael *verður að* flýta sér** (hurry) **af því að hann *á að* mæta á flugvöllinn klukkan hálf sjö**
>
> **Ég *verð að* flýta mér, annars missi ég af strætó**
>
> **Ég *þarf að* flýta mér af því að það er svo mikið að gera**
>
> **Þetta *hlýtur að* vera bróðir þinn, þið eruð svo lík**

Icelandic has no special verbs to indicate future tense, like English 'will'. Instead, the simple present is used to express both present and future. The context usually makes clear whether a future tense is implied:

Hann fer á morgun	He will leave tomorrow
Ég gleymi þér aldrei	I will never forget you

A notable exception is **vera**, which becomes **verða** in the future tense:

Verður þú heima á morgun? Will you be home tomorrow?

The verb phrases **ætla að** and **fara að**, however, are often used to express a future intention. **Ætla** emphasizes the intention, as we saw earlier, while **fara** emphasizes an action that is about to take place:

Ég *fer að* **kaupa miða**	I am going to buy a ticket
Hann *fer að* **horfa á**	He is going to/about to watch
sjónvarpið	television

Reading 1 ◧

Útvarp og sjónvarp á Íslandi

What is the most popular radio programme? What kind of television programmes are in the majority? Do state radio and television have a monopoly?

Útvarpsstöð Íslands, kölluð Ríkisútvarpið (RÚV) síðan 1934, var stofnuð árið 1928. Síðan 1983 rekur RÚV tvær rásir, Rás 1 og Rás 2. Rás 1 fer með fjölbreytta dagskrá sem leggur áherslu á fréttir, menntun og tónlist, og íslenskt efni. Rás 2 er í loftinu allan sólarhringinn og fer aðallega með dægurtónlist og samtalsþætti fyrir almenning. Aðalfréttirnar á báðum rásum eru hádegisfréttir kl. 12 og kvöldfréttir kl. 7, og njóta þær mestu vinsælda í útvarpinu. Upphaflega átti RÚV einkaleyfi, en síðan útvarps- og sjónvarps-bylgjur voru gefnar frjálsar árið 1985 hafa ýmsar einkastöðvar verið stofnaðar. Margar þeirra útvarpa aðeins á höfuðborgarsvæðinu.

Fyrstu sjónvarpsútsendingar á Íslandi komu frá bandarísku herstöðinni í Keflavík. Árið 1966 var sjónvarpað á íslensku í fyrsta skipti þegar Ríkissjónvarpsstöð, eða Sjónvarpið, hóf starfsemi. Dagskráin var stutt í mjög langan tíma, 4–5 klukkutímar á kvöldin, og ekki sjónvarpað á fimmtudögum. Nú á dögum er, auk Sjón-varpsins, Stöð 2, einkastöð sem maður verður að borga fyrir.Vegna peningaskorts er meirihluti dagskrár erlent efni, mest frá Bretlandi og Bandaríkjunum og sýnt með íslenskum texta; barnaefni er með íslensku tali. Helstu nýju stöðvarnar sem sjónvarpað hafa síðan 1995 eru Sýn, Bíórásin og Skjár 1. Aðalefnið á dagskrá aðalsjónvarpsstöðvanna eru fréttir kl. 7 ('Fréttir' í Sjónvarpinu og '19>20' á Stöð 2).

Vocabulary notes

útvarp (-s, -)	radio (broadcast)	**njóta (nýt)**, *gen.*	enjoy
útvarpa (útvarpa)	(radio) broadcast	**einkaleyfi (-s, -)**	monopoly
sjónvarp (-s, -)	television	**bylgj/a (-u, -ur)**	wave
sjónvarpa (sjónvarpa)	televise	**einkastöð (-var, -var)**	private (commercial) station
fjölbreytt/ur, *adj.*	varied		
dagskrá (-r, -r), *f.*	daily programme	**útsending (-ar, -ar)**	broadcast
leggja áherslu á, *acc.*	emphasize	**nú á dögum**	nowadays
		peningaskort/ur (-s), *m.*	lack of money
fréttir, *f.pl.*	news		
menntun (-ar, -ir)	culture, education	**meirihlut/i (-a, -ar)**	majority
dægurtónlist (-ar), *f.*	popular music	**text/i (-a, -ar)**	text (here 'subtitles')
samtalsþáttur (-ar, þættir), *m.*	chat show	**með íslensku tali**	dubbed in Icelandic
almenning/ur (-s) fyrir almenning	general public, popular	**helst**, *adv.superl.*	most prominent

The Icelandic word for a film is **mynd (-ar, -ir)**, *f.* from **kvikmynd** 'moving picture'. Films can be **bíómyndir** or **sjónvarpsmyndir**. A television programme is generally referred to as a **þáttur**, and a TV series as a **myndaflokkur**.

Exercise 10

There are many genres of films and television shows. Can you guess what genre the following refer to? The Icelandic television programme on p. 121 and the examples in brackets provide clues to help you:

1 Gamanmynd   (Monty Python)
2 Teiknimynd   (The Simpsons)
3 Heimildarmynd   (National Geographic)
4 Vestri   (John Wayne)
5 Spennumynd   (Hitchcock, Bruce Willis)

6 Sakamálamynd   (Sherlock Holmes)
7 Stórmynd   (*Ben Hur, Titanic*)
8 Hryllingsmynd   (*Friday the 13th*)

Exercise 11

Carefully study the TV programme opposite. Can you find Icelandic words/terms that correspond to the following?

1 Main roles (in the lead roles)
2 Translator and narrator (translated and narrated by)
3 A musical
4 Nominated for an Oscar
5 Direct (live) broadcast
6 Programme for children and young people

Exercise 12

Now answer the following questions in Icelandic:

1 Klukkan hvað byrjar dagskrá í Sjónvarpinu?
2 Er sakamálamynd eða spennumynd á dagskrá?
3 Klukkan hvað byrja fyrstu fréttir kvöldins?
4 Klukkan hvað er dagskráin búin á Stöð 2?
5 Frá hvaða landi kemur heimildarmyndin 'Pílagrímsferð til Mekka'?
6 Hvað eru margir erlendir þættir sýndir í Sjónvarpinu?
7 Hvað er uppáhaldssjónvarpsþátturinn þinn?

Sjónvarpið 20.10 Frönsk heimildarmynd um ferð norður-
afríska pílagríma til Mekka, könnunarleiðangur til eins helg-
asta staðar á jörðu og þess sem er hjúpaður hvað mestri
leynd.

SJÓNVARPIÐ

11.30 ▶ **Skjáleikurinn**
16.50 ▶ **Leiðarljós** [6540900]
17.35 ▶ **Táknmálsfréttir**
[5141639]
17.45 ▶ **Beverly Hills 90210**
(Beverly Hills 90210 VIII)
Bandarískur myndaflokkur.
(17:34) [1242368]
18.30 ▶ **Tabalugi** *(Tabaluga)*
Þýskur teiknimyndaflokkur um
drekann Tabaluga og vini hans í
Grænumörk . Ísl. tal. (5:26)
[6813]
19.00 ▶ **Fréttir, íþróttir**
og veður [77900]
19.45 ▶ **Becker** *(Becker)*
Bandarískur gamanmynda-
flokkur. Aðalhlutverk: *Ted
Danson og Terry Farrell.* (9:22)
[5876707]
20.10 ▶ **Pílagrímsferð til**
Mekka *(La Mecque secrète: Au
coeur de l'islam)* Frönsk heimildarmynd um ferð norður-
afrískra pílagríma til Mekka.
Þýðandi og þulur: *Jón B. Guð-
laugsson.* [494455]
21.10 ▶ **Veggurinn hái** *(The
Ruth Rendell Mysteries: The
Orchard Walls)* Bresk sjón-
varpsmynd byggð á sögu eftir
Ruth Rendell. Sextán ára
stúlka í enskri sveit á stríðsár-
unum ljósta að upp leyndarmáli
með hörmulegum afleiðingum.
Aðalhlutverk: *Honeysuckle
Weeks og Sylvia Syms.* [3250962]
22.10 ▶ **Dansað í gegnum sög-**
una Seinni þáttur um sögu dans
á Íslandi og hlutverk hans í
menningu okkar. Umsjón:
Ragna Sara Jónsdóttir. (2:2) (e)
[350287]
22.40 ▶ **Pétur Ísland Östlund**
Stutt heimildarmynd eftir
Helga Felixson. (e) [9934504]
23.00 ▶ **Ellefufréttir og íþróttir**
[20252]
23.15 ▶ **Sjónvarpskringlan**
23.30 ▶ **Skjáleikurinn**

STÖÐ 2

13.00 ▶ **Samherjar** (12:23) (e)
[43523]
13.45 ▶ **Orðspor** *(Reputations)*
Billie Jean gerði tennis kvenna
að þeirri virtu keppnisgrein
sem hún er í dag. (4:10) (e)
[8595271]
14.45 ▶ **Verndarenglar** (1:30) (e)
[6037349]
15.30 ▶ **Ástir og átök** (22:25)
(e) [4233]
16.00 ▶ **Köngulóarmaðurinn**
[26691]
16.25 ▶ **Sögur úr Andabæ**
[277504]
16.50 ▶ **Í Barnalandi** [4191233]
17.10 ▶ **Simpson-fjölskyldan**
[3994320]
17.35 ▶ **Glæstar vonir** [39368]
18.00 ▶ **Fréttir** [33788]
18.05 ▶ **Sjónvarpskringlan**
[2759558]
18.30 ▶ **Nágrannar** [4455]
19.00 ▶ **19>20** [675962]
20.05 ▶ **Barnfóstran** (17:22)
[920455]
20.35 ▶ **Dharma og Greg**
(Dharma and Greg) Gaman-
myndaflokkur. (2:23) [558252]
21.05 ▶ **Bílslys** *(Crash)* Myndaflokkur í þremur hlutum sem
fjallar um bílslys og hvernig
reynt er að sporna við þeim.
(2.3) [3764349]
22.00 ▶ **Daewoo-Mótorsport**
(10:23) [368]
22.30 ▶ **Kvöldfréttir** [79504]
22.50 ▶ **Geimveran** *(Alien)* Víð-
fræg bíómynd um áhöfn geim-
fars sem er ofsótt af geimveru.
Þau urðu ekki vör við að þessi
óvætt færi um borð en þau fá
svo sannarlega að vita af henni
þegar hún lætur til skarar
skríða. Aðalhlutverk: *Ian Holm,
John Hurt, Sigourney Weaver,
Tom Skerritt og Harry Dean
Stanton.* 1979. Stranglega
bönnuð börnum. (e) [6313707]
00.45 ▶ **Dagskrárlok**

SÝN

18.00 ▶ **Dýrlingurinn**(The Saint)
[84813]
18.55 ▶ **Strandgæslan** *(Water
Rats)* Myndaflokkur um lög-
reglumenn í Sydney í Ástralíu.
(2:26) [180639]
19.50 ▶ **Coca-Cola bikarinn**
Bein útsending frá leik Keflavíkur og ÍBV í 16 liða úrslitum.
[63005523]
22.00 ▶ **Sjóræninginn** *(The
Pirate)* ★★★ Söngleikur þar
sem ástin svífur yfir vötnum.
Manuela er heitbundin efnuðum
manni. Hún leyfir sér samt að
dreyma um aðra karlmenn.
Myndin var tilnefnd til Óskarsverðlauna. Aðalhlutverk: *Judy
Garland, Gene Kelly, Walter
Slezak, Gladys Cooper og Reg-
inald Zucco.* 1948. [226610]
23.40 ▶ **Glæpasaga** *(Crime
Story)* (e) [883349]
00.30 ▶ **Dagskrárlok og skjá-**
leikur

OMEGA

17.30 ▶ **Ævintýri í Þurragljúfri**
Barna- og unglingaþáttur.
[152252]
18.00 ▶ **Hasar inni** Barnaefni. [153981]
18.30 ▶ **Líf í Orðinu** [161900]
19.00 ▶ **Þetta er þinn dagur**
með Benny Hinn. [576748]
19.30 ▶ **Frelsiskallið** [176287]
20.00 ▶ **Kærleikurinn mikils-**
verði [376900]
20.30 ▶ **Kvöldljós** Bein útsending. Stjórnendur þáttarins:
*Guðlaugur Laufdal og Kolbrún
Jónsdóttir.* [405981]
22.00 ▶ **Líf í Orðinu** [271356]
22.30 ▶ **Þetta er þinn dagur**
með Benny Hinn. [621897]
23.00 ▶ **Líf í Orðinu** [140417]
23.30 ▶ **Lofið Drottin**

BÍÓRÁSIN

06.00 ▶ **Whity** Aðalhlutverk:
Gunther Kaufmann o.fl. [6749900]
08.00 ▶ **Kaffivagninnn** *(Diner)*
★★★ Aðalhlutverk: *Steve
Guttenberg* o.fl. 1982. [6736436]
10.00 ▶ **Bananar** *(Bananas)*
★★★★ Aðalhlutverk: *Woody
Allen* o.fl. 1971. [3551271]
12.00 ▶ **Whity**.(e) [478417]
14.00 ▶ **Kaffivagninnn** (e)
[849981]
16.00 ▶ **Bananar** ★★★★ (e)
[836417]
18.00 ▶ **Hasar í Minnesota**
(Feeling Minnesota) 1996.
Stranglega bönnuð börnum.
[290691]
20.00 ▶ **Dominion** Aðalhlutverk: *Tim Thomerson* o.fl. 1995.
Stranglega bönnuð börnum.
[71146]
22.00 ▶ **Ítölsk örlög** *(Looking
Italian)* 1994. Stranglega bönnuð börnum. [84610]
24.00 ▶ **Hasar í Minnesota** (e)
Stranglega bönnuð börnum.
[865585]
02.00 ▶ **Dominion** (e) Stranglega bönnuð börnum. [5229653]
04.00 ▶ **Ítölsk örlög** (e) Stranglega bönnuð börnum. [5216189]

SKJÁR 1

16.00 ▶ **Fóstbræður** [50078]
17.00 ▶ **Dallas** (51) (e) [69726]
18.00 ▶ **Svíðsljósið** með
Prodigy. [3962]
18.30 ▶ **Barnaskjárinn** [1981]
19.00 ▶ **Dagskrárhlé**
20.30 ▶ **Pensacola** (7) (e)
[22271]
21.30 ▶ **Dallas** (51) [28455]
22.30 ▶ **Hausbrot** [19707]
23.30 ▶ **The Young Ones** (8) (e)
[41184]
00.05 ▶ **Bak við tjöldin** [85943]
00.35 ▶ **Dagskrárlok**

7 Daglegt líf

Daily life

In this lesson you will learn about:

- aspects of daily life in Iceland
- the simple present conjugation of strong verbs
- vowel change: the I-shift
- more about prepositions and their cases
- customs and holidays

Reading 1

Dagur í lífi íslenskrar fjölskyldu

How many children do Jón and Sigríður have together? How many individuals make up their family? Where do Jón and Sigríður work? Who dresses the children in the morning? Who does the cooking?

Jón Grétarsson og Sigríður Ólafsdóttir eiga heima í Kópavogi, sem er rétt hjá Reykjavík. Þau búa í stórri íbúð í blokk og eiga saman dótturina Höllu. Sigríður er fráskilin og á líka Ásgeir af fyrra hjónabandi, og Jón á Einar frá fyrra sambandi. Strákarnir búa hjá þeim. Sigríður er deildarstjóri hjá Íslandsbanka, og Jón er trésmiður en er nú heimavinnandi húsfaðir.

Dagurinn hefst á því að Jón og Sigríður vakna og fara á fætur kl. 7, og meðan Sigríður fer í sturtu og klæðir sig vekur Jón krakkana og gefur þeim morgunmatinn í eldhúsinu og lætur þá taka lýsið. Hann lagar líka kaffi handa þeim hjónunum. Áður en Sigríður fer í vinnu hjálpar hún Jóni að klæða börnin. Eftir að Sigríður er farin fara Jón og krakkarnir í gönguferð. Í hádeginu borðar fjölskyldan samlokur við eldhúsborðið og hlustar á hádegisfréttir. Svo er tími til að fara með krakkana í leikskólann. Jón fer aftur heim, tekur til, ryksugar og kaupir í matinn.

Sigríður er mjög upptekin í vinnunni. Dagurinn er stífbókaður og hún er stöðugt á fundum, en hún er samt mjög ánægð í vinnunni. Vinnufélagarnir eru hressir og skemmtilegir, og þau hittast í kaffinu eða borða saman hádegismat þegar tækifæri gefst.

Þegar Sigríður kemur heim kl. 7 eftir langan vinnudag er Jón búinn að elda matinn og hún fer beint að kvöldmatarborði. Fjölskyldan spjallar saman – krakkarnir segja frá því sem þeir gerðu í skólanum í dag. Svo þakka þeir fyrir matinn (þakka fyrir sig) og fara út að leika sér eða gera heimaverkefni fyrir morgundaginn. Sigríður ber fram af borðinu, vaskar upp og brýtur saman þvottinn á meðan Jón horfir á fréttirnar í sjónvarpinu. Síðan bjóða allir góða nótt og hátta.

Vocabulary notes

fráskilin/n, *adj.*	divorced	**samlok/a (-u, -ur)**	sandwich
blokk (-ar, -ir)	block of flats, apartment building	**leikskól/i (-a, -ar)**	kindergarten
		taka til	clean up
		ryksuga (ryksuga)	vacuum, hoover
deildarstjór/i (-a, -ar)	branch manager, department head	**kaupa (kaupi) í mat**	buy groceries
		fund/ur (-ar, -ir)	meeting
fara á fætur	get up (out of bed)	**fara á fund**	go to a meeting
		vera á fundi	be in a meeting
fara í sturtu	have a shower	**heimaverkefni (-s, -)**	homework (from **verkefni** 'task', 'project', 'assignment')
láta (læt) *acc.*	let		
lýsi (-s), *n.*	fish liver oil (traditionally taken at breakfast, esp. by young children, in liquid form or capsules (lýsisperlur))	**bera (ber) fram af borðinu**	clear the table
		vaska (vaska) upp	do the dishes
		brjóta (brýt) saman, *acc.*	fold
		þvott/ur (-s, -ar)	laundry
		hátta (hátta)	go to bed

Language points

Simple present conjugation of strong verbs

Most so-called **-ur** verbs discussed in Lesson 2, as well as a number of other verbs, are strong verbs. Strong verbs, like weak ones (that is, those belonging to the **-a** and **-i** groups and most of those with a **-j** before the infinitive final **-a**), can be divided into three subgroups based on their conjugation patterns. Here, too, the patterns are distinguished by the singular conjugations only; the plural conjugation is always the same. The following are the three conjugation patterns for strong verbs in the simple present tense:

1 The first group generally corresponds to the **-ur** pattern outlined in Lesson 2, and is by far the largest:

	bíð-a	*vinn-a*	*tak-a*
ég	bíð-	vinn-	tek-
þú	bíð-ur	vinn-ur	tek-ur
hann	bíð-ur	vinn-ur	tek-ur

2 The second group consists of verbs whose stem ends in a vowel— many of them do not have the infinitive final **-a**:

	fá	*sjá*	*bú-a*
ég	fæ-	sé-	bý-
þú	fæ-rð	sé-rð	bý-rð
það	fæ-r	sé-r	bý-r

3 The last group includes verbs of which the stem ends in **-r** or **-s**. Note how the ending of the second-person singular is a **-t** rather than a **-ð** when the stem ends in **-s**:

	far-a	*les-a*	*ber-a*
ég	fer-	les-	ber-
þú	fer-ð	les-t	ber-ð
hann	fer-	les-	ber-

Now, of course, you would like to know how you can tell a weak verb from a strong one. If you happen to encounter it in a singular conjugated form you should be able to recognize its conjugation pattern, or you may remember having encountered it before. Generally, however, as with so many other aspects of Icelandic, you have to learn through practice. As always, the vocabulary notes and glossary list will help you along by including the first person singular form so that you can derive the conjugation pattern on your own.

What most distinguishes a strong verb from a weak one is the likely occurrence of a change in the stem vowel of the verb. Many strong verbs are subject to the influence of the so-called I-shift in the singular present, the result of an **-i** or **-j** that once occurred in the ending but has since been lost.

The I-shift

The I-shift involves the following vowel changes:

a	changes to	**e**	as in	**taka – tek, fara – fer**
o	changes to	**e**	as in	**koma – kem**
á	changes to	**æ**	as in	**fá – fæ**
ú				**búa – bý**
jú →	change to	**ý**	as in	**fljúga – flýg**
jó				**brjóta – brýt**
au	changes to	**ey**	as in	**auka – eyk** (increase)

Whenever the infinitive of a strong verb has one of the vowels listed on the left, it will change into the vowel on the right in the singular present conjugation. Note that the I-shift never occurs in the plural. The influence of the I-shift extends far beyond the realm of present tense verb conjugation, so it is important to begin familiarizing yourself with it now. It will make what lies ahead much easier.

Exercise 1

Put the strong verbs in brackets into the sentences in their correct present tense form. Remember that a vowel change may occur.

1 Þú _______ (verða) blaut ef þú _______ (standa) í rigningunni.
2 Pabbi _______ (skera) brauðið í eldhúsinu.
3 Hvert _______ (fara) þú? Ég _______ (fljúga) til Vestmannaeyja
   á morgun.
4 Fjölskyldan _______ (búa) í Kópavogi.
5 Ég _______ (fá) mér kaffisopa í vinnunni.
6 Börnin _______ (sofa) uppi í rúminu en mamma _______ (sofa)
   í stólnum við sjónvarpið.

7 Hún _______ (bjóða) góða nótt.

8 _______ (ganga) þið upp á jökulinn? Já, við _______ (ganga) upp jökulinn, en þú? Nei, ég _______ (ganga) ekki, ég _______ (aka) í staðinn.

Exercise 2

The following are some of the things Einar does on an ordinary work day. The verbs are all in the infinitive. Can you turn them into sentences using Einar (or 'he') as a subject? Note that in this exercise, not all verbs are strong.

Dæmi: 1 Vakna kl. 6. → Einar vaknar klukkan sex

2 Fara á fætur kl. 7:15. 3 Borða morgunmat og drekka kaffi, klæða sig. 4 Taka strætó í vinnu. 5 Vinna á skrifstofu. 6 Fara út í búð og fá sér samloku kl. 12. 7 Fara á fund eftir hádegi, sjá um matarinnkaup. 8 Koma heim kl. 7. 9 Elda matinn og horfa á fréttir. 10 Taka til og lesa yfir skjöl ('documents', 'files'). 11 Hátta kl. 11:30. 12 Sofa eins og steinn alla nóttina ...

Now rewrite the sentences as if you were doing all these things:

Dæmi: 1 Ég vakna klukkan sex ...

Can you adapt the sentences to reflect some of the things that you do on an ordinary working day? There are of course no set answers to this, as the answers depend on you.

Exercise 3

Hulda has been telling you about herself. Can you tell someone else what she said, i.e. rewrite her words so that you are talking about her in the third person? You will need to change the endings of the verbs from the 'I' to the 'she' form:

Dæmi: Ég heiti (1) Hulda → Hún heitir Hulda

Ég er (2) bókhaldari og rek (3) stórt hrossasölufyrirtæki.* Ég sé (4) um sölu og útflutning á hrossum. Ég bý (5) á Laugarvatni og á (6) 30 hross. Ég nýt (7, *inf.* njóta) þess að ríða út í náttúrunni. Ég fæ (8) marga útlendinga hingað til að skoða og kaupa íslenska hesta. Ég vakna (9) snemma á morgnana og vinn (11) við bókhaldið, og svo fer (11) ég út til að sjá um hestana. Oftast kem (12) ég ekki heim fyrr en seint á kvöldin.

* **hross (-, -)**, *n.* also **hest/ur (-s, -ar)**, *m.* horse

Simple present versus **vera að**

Now that you have met all the main conjugation patterns for the simple present tense, you no longer need to rely on the construction **vera að** (+ *inf.*) to use verbs in sentences. In fact, there is a difference between the use of the simple present and that of the **vera að** construction, one that resembles the difference between the simple present and the present continuous in English in many ways:

- The *simple present* is used in Icelandic to indicate a general situation or to indicate that the activity expressed by the verb takes place on a regular basis:

  ég drekk alltaf kaffi á morgnana
  I always drink coffee in the mornings

  hún vaknar sjaldan fyrir kl. 8
  she seldom wakes up before 8 o'clock

  þau borða aldrei í hádeginu
  they never eat lunch (*lit.* 'at noon')

- **vera að** plus infinitive is used to indicate an activity that is happening right now and is of temporary duration:

  ég er að drekka morgunkaffið núna
  I'm drinking my morning coffee now

  ég er að vinna í bili
  I'm working at the moment

It is also commonly used in combination with verbs indicating an activity that only lasts a brief moment, such as **sofna** 'fall asleep', **detta** 'fall', **fara** and **koma**, often in combination with the adverb **alveg**. In those instances, the combination with *vera að* indicates that the acitivity is just about to happen:

hann er að koma	he is on his way
ég er alveg að sofna	I'm about to fall asleep

Because the construction with **vera að** emphasizes temporary action, it is not possible to use it in Icelandic in combination with verbs denoting a situation rather than an activity, such as **vera, sitja, liggja**, etc. This means, for instance, that English 'he is sitting' cannot be translated into Icelandic as **hann er að sitja**; it should be **hann situr.**

Dialogue 1

Samtal við nýbúa

On his way home to Iceland from a conference, Einar Gunnarsson initiates a conversation with Hilton Peters from the Turk Islands, who is sitting next to him on the plane. Where in Iceland does Hilton live? What does he like about Iceland? What doesn't he like? How does he get along with Icelanders?

EINAR: Ertu að fara til Íslands í fyrsta sinn?

HILTON: Nei, ég er reyndar á leiðinni heim.

EINAR: Þú býrð á Íslandi?

HILTON: Já, síðan 1996. Ég vinn í fiski á Ísafirði.

EINAR: Nú er það. Og hvernig líkar þér?

HILTON: Ég kann mjög vel við mig á Íslandi. Sérstaklega þegar það er hlýtt. Ég reyni að ferðast og sjá eins mikið af landinu og ég get. Náttúran er alveg einstök, og það er hægt að gera skemmtilega hluti á sama stað.

EINAR: Eins og?

HILTON: Til dæmis að fara á skíði á Snæfellsjökli og svo í sólbað á ströndinni á eftir, eða að fara í sund þegar það er snjór og frost! Loftið hér er líka alveg frábært.

EINAR: Og hvað um fólkið, hvernig kanntu við Íslendinga?

HILTON: Ágætlega. Íslendingar eru mjög hjálpsamir og hafa tekið mér vel. Það kemur manni reyndar svolítið á óvart því Ísland er lítið land, lítið samfélag. En Íslendingar koma vel fram við mig, vinnufélagar, og aðrir líka.

EINAR: Var ekki erfitt að kynnast fólki svona til að byrja með?

HILTON: Jú, svolítið, þegar maður skilur ekki tungumálið er stundum erfitt að komast í samband við fólk, og svo gleymir fólk stundum að maður skilur ekki, en þetta er eðlilegt svona fyrst í stað, býst ég við.

EINAR: En eru Íslendingar ekki frekar lokaðir, að þínu mati?

HILTON: Til að byrja með kannski, en það lagast fljótlega, sérstaklega þegar maður fer út að skemmta sér með Íslendingum! Þá losnar fólkið við feimni, verður sama um allt og hugsar bara um að skemmta sér. Það líkar mér vel við, lifa fyrir augnablikið og njóta þess sem mest!

EINAR: En það hlýtur að vera eitthvað sem þér mislíkar!

HILTON: Það er alltof kalt og dimmt á veturna. En þó, ég er alltaf hissa hvað það er mikið fjör og félagslíf einmitt þá. Það er alltaf eitthvað að gerast!

EINAR: Ekkert annað?

HILTON: Ef til vill það hvað er dýrt að búa á Íslandi. En þar sem
          ég bý út á landi er maður ósjálfrátt sparsamur því að það
          er ekki hægt að kaupa mikið. En það eru líka margir
          kostir við að búa á Íslandi. Ég er bara mjög ánægður að
          búa hér.

Vocabulary notes

nýbú/i (-a, -ar)	immigrant to Iceland
vinna í fiski	work in the fishing industry
kunna (kann, kannt, kann) vel/illa við, *acc.*	like/dislike
hlut/ur (-ar, -ir)	thing
hafa tekið mér vel	have made me welcome
koma á óvart	surprise (**það kemur manni á óvart** 'it is surprising')
samfélag (-s, -)	society
koma fram	behave, come across
fyrst í stað	at first
að þínu mati	in your estimation/opinion
lagast (lagast)	get better
skemmta sér	have fun, have a good time, party
feimni, *f.indecl.*	shyness, timidity
losna (losna) við, *acc.*	lose, get rid of
vera sama, *impers.*	not care
mér er sama	I don't care
fjör (-s), *n.*	vitality, fun
ósjálfráð/ur, *adj.*	involutary, unintentional
sparsam/ur, *adj.*	economical, thrifty
félagslíf (-s), *n.*	social life, social activity
kost/ur (-ar, -ir)	advantage

Language points

Prepositions and their cases

In the previous chapters you have learned that in Icelandic prepositions, like verbs, determine the case of their object(s). Prepositions are among the trickiest aspects of a language to learn, their
usage being often a matter of idiom. The translation of a preposition

is therefore usually only tentative. For instance, the preposition **um** generally translates into 'about', as in:

Hann talar *um* ferðina He speaks *about* the trip

However, in combination with the verb **sjá** the translation changes:

Ég sé *um* fyrirtækið I look *after* the company

Similarly, one may live 'in' (**í**) or 'on' (**á**) a place in Icelandic:

Þú býrð á Íslandi but **Ég bý í Englandi**
Hann á heima á Húsavík but **Hún á heima í Reykjavík**

Using the correct preposition is something that is learned through extensive practice. Using the correct case form after a preposition, on the other hand, is something that can be more easily charted, at least to begin with. What follows are the most common prepositions in Icelandic, listed by the case they govern:

acc.		*dat.*		*gen.*	
um	about	**að**	towards	**til**	to
gegnum	through	**frá**	from	**án**	without
kringum	around	**af**	off	**auk**	in addition,
við	at, against	**hjá**	beside, by, with		apart from
		úr	out of	**milli**	between
		handa	for	**vegna**	because of,
		á móti	opposite		due to
		undan	from under		
		nálægt	near		

These are all prepositions that govern one particular case. There is also a group of prepositions that govern two cases, accusative or dative, usually depending on:

1 whether the preposition refers to location (place) or time
2 whether, in the case of location, the preposition refers to a static (unchanging) situation or whether a motion with direction (change) is implied.

Prepositions of place

The prepositions **á** 'on', **í** 'in', **undir** 'under' and **yfir** 'over' all govern a dative when they are used in a context which implies a static or unchanging situation, something that is often indicated by the verb. Examples:

Ég bý á Laugavegi	I live on Laugavegur
Hann er í fríi/í nýrri peysu	He is on holidays/wears a new sweater
Hundurinn liggur undir borðinu	The dog lies under the table
Myndin hangir yfir stólnum	The picture hangs over the chair

In all of these sentences, the situation depicted is static, as the verbs, 'live', 'be', 'lie', 'hang', indicate. Compare these examples with the following:

Hann fer í frí/í nýja peysu
He is going on holiday/putting on a new sweater

Hún setur pokann undir borðið
She puts the bag under the table

Hann hengir myndina yfir stólinn
He hangs the picture over the chair

These sentences all imply a motion which causes a change in situation, from working to being on holiday, from not wearing a sweater to wearing one, etc. This difference is reflected by the difference in case. Now study the following sentences:

Barnið skríður undir rúminu and **Barnið skríður undir rúmið**

The difference in case implies that the sentences have a different meaning. In the first instance, the child is crawling around under the bed, not going anywhere in particular, an unchanging situation captured by the dative case: **rúminu**. In the second sentence, the child is crawling from one location to another, ending up under the bed. This change in situation is reflected by the accusative: **rúmið**.

Finally, note that in Icelandic, the following prepositions form pairs of opposite movement but do not follow the same case rules:

í	in/to, *dat/acc.*	↔	**úr**	out of, *dat.*
á	on/to, *dat/acc.*	↔	**af**	off, *dat.*
undir	under, *dat/acc.*	↔	**undan**	from under, *dat.*

Prepositions of time

These were briefly introduced in Lesson 6. However, it is important to pay specific attention to how these prepositions behave differently when used in a non-temporal or other context:

	Time	Place	Other
fyrir	ago: *dat.*	in front of: *dat.*	for: *acc.*
	fyrir þremur dögum	**tjöldin eru fyrir glugganum**	**hann gerir það fyrir mig**
í	for: *acc.*	in/into: *dat/acc.*	____
	í þrjá daga	**hún er í skólanum/ hún fer í skólann**	____
eftir	after *acc.*	behind, along: *dat.*	by: *acc.*
	eftir þrjá daga	**þú ert eftir mér ég geng eftir götunni**	**bókin er eftir hana**

Finally, the preposition **á** is a story in itself: it can be followed by an accusative and a dative in temporal sentences as well as in sentences of place. If something happens on a certain day or time, **á** governs the accusative, but if it concerns something that always happens on that day/those days, it is followed by a dative. Compare the following:

á *a certain day/time → acc.*   *repeated event(s) → dat.*
    ég fer heim á sunnudaginn   **ég fer alltaf heim á sunnudögum**
    hann fer í frí á föstudaginn   **hann fer í sund á föstudögum/ á hverjum föstudegi**

Other prepositions ruling more than one case

The preposition **með** 'with' is arguably one of the trickiest prepositions for students of Icelandic, but because it is so common, you will want to start using it, so here are some pointers: **Með** governs the dative when:

- it implies that the accompanying element is there of their own agency and free will:

  ég kem með þér   I'm coming with you

- it is used in an instrumental sense (as the tool to perform an action):

  Jón smíðar með hamri   Jón builds with a hammer

Með is followed by an accusative:

- when control or agency lies with the subject, not with the accompanying element:

  hún kemur með hundana
  she's coming with the dogs (i.e. bringing the dogs along)

- in many verb combinations, such as **vera með** (when it means 'have', 'carry')

Exercise 4

Put the (pro)nouns in brackets into the following sentences in the correct case forms. Remember to assess the gender and number of the (pro)nouns in question.

 1 Stelpan gengur kringum _________ (húsið).
 2 Þið farið til _________ (útlönd).
 3 Þau fá bréf frá _________ (skólinn).
 4 Hann er reiður við _________ (ég).
 5 Garðurinn er milli _________ (húsin).
 6 Borðið stendur á _________ (gólfið).
 7 Hundurinn kemur undan _________ (borðið).
 8 Hjónin ganga eftir _________ (vegurinn).
 9 Börnin gista hjá _________ (afi og amma).
10 Ég þakka fyrir _________ (hjálpin).
11 Ferð þú með _________ (hann) í bíó?
12 Það er ekki flogið vegna _________ (veður!).

Exercise 5

Now see if you can insert the right prepositions. Be careful to check that the case each of the objects is in matches the preposition. Sometimes you have more than one choice.

1 Við förum í frí ____ mánuð. 2 Hún stendur ____ þér.
3 Kennarinn situr ____ borðið ____ stólnum. 4 Hann býr ____
Bandaríkjunum. 5 Ætla börnin að koma ____ þér ____
Englands? 6 Jón fer ____ gallabuxunum og fer ____ jakkafötin.
7 Ég ætla að vera á Íslandi ____ fjóra daga. 8 Á morgnana
skríður Páll ____ rúminu, fer ____ eldhúsið, tekur glas ____
hillunni (shelf) og mjólk ____ ísskápnum (fridge) og drekkur
mjólkina. Svo setur hann glasið ____ borðið og fer ____ það.
Hann syngur lag ____ baðinu, kemur svo ____ baðinu og fer
____ fötin. Svo fer hann ____ skóla ____ strætisvagni.

Reading 2

Hátíðir og merkisdagar á Íslandi

Bolludagur var áður mánudagurinn fyrir löngöföstu. Á bolludag fær fólk sér bollukaffi og borðar rjómabollur.

Sprengidagur var síðasti dagur fyrir byrjun föstu. Það er gömul venja að borða eins mikið og hægt er af kjöti og öðru sem bannað var að borða á föstu. Margir borða saltkjöt og baunir á sprengidag.

Öskudagur var fyrsti dagur löngöföstu og er nú frídagur á Íslandi.

Páskar. Það eru ekki margar íslenskar venjur sem tengjast páskum fyrir utan kirkjuhátíðina. Nú á dögum borðar fólk súkkulaðiegg (páskaegg) en það er ekki mjög gamall siður.

Margar ævagamlar venjur virðast hins vegar tengjast *Sumardeginum fyrsta*, sem hefur lengi verið stór hátíð á Íslandi. Það var gamall siður að fólk færði hvort sumargjafir. Sumardagurinn fyrsti er fyrsti fimmtudagur eftir 18. apríl og er enn frídagur í dag. Á sumardaginn fyrsta býður fólk gleðilegt sumar.

Sjómannadagur er fyrsti sunnudagur í júní, fyrst haldinn hátíðlegur 1938. Þá eru margar útihátíðir, og sjómenn, útgerðarmenn og sjávarútvegsráðherra halda ræður.

Sautjándi júní er þjóðhátíðardagur Íslendinga. Ísland varð lýðveldi 17. júní 1944, og á sautjánda júní er mikil hátíð um allt land. Það er stór samkoma við Alþingishúsið á Austurvelli í Reykjavík þar sem forseti Íslands og forsætisráðherra halda ræður og fjallkonan flytur ávarp. Síðdegis eru margs konar hátíðahöld.

Verslunarmannahelgi er fyrsta helgi í ágúst. Mánudagurinn er frídagur, og margir fara í skemmtiferðir, í útilegu og á útihátíðir.

Jólin: 23. desember er Þorláksmessa. Á mörgum stöðum landsins borðar fólk skötu á þessum degi. Fólk sker líka laufabrauð, sérstaklega á Norðurlandi. Á aðfangadagskvöld 24. desember kl. 6 hringja klukkur inn jólin. Þá borða menn góðan mat jólagrautinn, rjúpur eða annan hátíðamat, og opna svo jólagjafirnar. Á aðfangadag kemur líka síðasti jólasveinninn. Jólasveinarnir eru 13 og koma til bæja til að færa börnunum gjafir, sá fyrsti 13 dögum fyrir jól. Svo fara þeir aftur, sá fyrsti á jóladag. Á jóladag borða margir hangikjöt og drekka jólaöl, og allir klæðast sparifötunum. Ef þú færð ekki nýja flík fyrir jól kemur jólakötturinn og borðar jólamatinn, og þig líka ef hann getur!

Áramótin eru gamlárskvöld og nýársdagur. Um nóttina flytja álfarnir (huldufólkið) búferlum. Nú á dögum eru áramótabrennur á gamlárskvöld, og um miðnætti er líka mikið af flugeldum.

Þrettándinn (þrettándakvöld) er síðasti dagur jóla. Þá eru álfabrennur og fólk dansar í gervi álfa og trölla í kringum eldinn.

Vocabulary notes

merkisdag/ur (-s, ar)	important day, holiday
langafast/a (-u)	lent
boll/a (-u, -ur)	bun
rjómabolla	bun filled with whipped cream traditionally eaten on 'bun day'
saltkjöt (-s), *n.*	salted meat
pásk/ar, *m.pl.*	Easter
annar í páskum/jólum	second day of Easter/Christmas
sið/ur (-ar, -ir)	custom
ævagamal/l, *adj.*	ancient
færði *past sg.* **færa (færi)**	move, bring
færa hvort öðru gjafir	bring each other gifts
útgerðarmað/ur (manns, menn)	(fishing) shipowner
sjávarútveg/ur (-s), *m.*	fishing industry
þjóðhátíð (-ar, -ir)	national day, national celebration
fjallkon/a (-u, -ur)	*lit.* 'lady of the mountain', national figurehead of Iceland
flytja (flyt), *acc.*	deliver, recite **flytja búferlum**, move house
ávarp (-s, -)	address
laufabrauð (-s)	paper-thin wheatbread carved with decorative patterns and fried for Christmas
skat/a (-u, -ur)	skate
rjúp/a (-u, -ur)	ptarmigan
jólasvein/n (-s, -ar)	one of the thirteen Icelandic Christmas lads/ elves
hangikjöt (-s)	smoked lamb
jólaöl (-s), *n.*	traditional Christmas ale
flík (-ar, -ur)	piece of clothing
jólakött/ur (kattar, kettir)	Christmas cat
flugeld/ar, *m.pl.*	fireworks
álf/ur (-s, -ar), also **huldufólk (-s)**, *n.*	elf, elfin people, 'hidden people'
brenn/a (-u, -ur)	(bon)fire, burning
gervi (-s, -)	costume

Exercise 6: Rétt eða rangt?

Are the following statements true or false?

1 Það er gömul venja að borða ekki kjöt á sprengidag.
2 Íslendingar eru í fríi á Öskudag.
3 Íslendingar borða súkkulaðiegg um páska.
4 Það eru margar ævagamlar íslenskar venjur sem tengjast páskum.
5 Sumardagurinn fyrsti er ekki lengur frídagur.
6 Sjómannadagur er aðeins 60 ára gamall.
7 Það er aðeins haldið upp á 17. júní á höfuðborgarsvæðinu.
8 Margir Íslendingar eru á ferðinni um verslunarmannahelgi.
9 Á Norðurlandi sker fólkið laufabrauð.
10 Jólasveinarnir koma til bæja með jólagjafir á jóladag.

Some customary phrases

Thanking

Þakka þér (takk) fyrir matinn	Thank you for the meal
fyrir mig/okkur	Thank you for having/inviting me/us
fyrir síðast	Thank you for last (i.e. last time spent together)
fyrir skemmtunina	Thank you for the entertainment
samveruna/samvinnuna	Thank you for the time spent/ working together
fyrir liðna árið	Thank you for the past year (traditionally added to a New Year's wish)

Response

Verði þér/ykkur að góðu	*approx.* 'May it be of good to you' (Host's/cook's response to thank you's; also said to invite people ('help yourself/ves') and to wish people bon appetit.)

Invitation

Gakktu/gangið í bæinn   Please come in

Good wishes

Gleðilega hátíð/páska *acc.*   Happy celebration/Easter
Gleðileg jól *acc.*   Merry Christmas
Gleðilegt sumar/(nýtt) ár *acc.* Happy Summer/New Year

Exercise 7: Dagbók

Record in Icelandic your daily activities during one week in your life, using the simple present tense. There are of course no set answers to this exercise – it depends on you!

Dæmi: **mánudagur: ég fer á fætur klukkan sex. Ég ...**

8 Verði þér að góðu!

Enjoy your meal!

In this lesson you will learn about:

- buying groceries 1
- food and taste
- meals and cooking
- impersonal constructions
- expressing likes and dislikes
- indefinite pronouns: **einhver/enginn**

Dialogue 1

Í matarbúð

On their way home from work, Þór and Harpa stop off at the grocery shop to buy some food. Why are Þór and Harpa not buying any fish? What do they decide to have for supper instead? What else do they need to pick up?

HARPA: Jæja, hvað eigum við að hafa í matinn í kvöld?

ÞÓR: Ég veit það ekki. Komum okkur að kjötborðinu. Hvað langar þig í? Kótilettur kannski? Eða kjötbollur?

HARPA: Nei, mig langar eiginlega ekki í kjöt. En þarna eru ný ýsuflök.

ÞÓR: Höfum fisk annað kvöld. Það er svo mikið vesen að elda fisk, og það er orðið framorðið. Ég er líka hryllilega svangur! Búum til pastarétt í staðinn. Það er þægilegt, ódýrt og fljótlegt.

HARPA: Eigum við allt til í pastarétt?

ÞÓR: Allt nema tómatsósu, held ég.

HARPA: Ég skal ná í dós. Okkur vantar líka skyr og brauð.
Nennirðu að taka eina dollu af rjómaskyri, og líka eina
fernu af nýmjólk, þá næ ég í brauðið.

ÞÓR: Ekki gleyma kaffinu, það er allt búið!

HARPA: Við eigum nóg af kaffi heima, það er til heill pakki í
eldhússkápnum!

ÞÓR: Nú er það. Jæja, er þá ekki allt komið?

HARPA: Jú, ég held það.

ÞÓR: Drífum okkur heim að borða!

Vocabulary notes

hafa/kaupa í mat(inn)	have/buy for supper (or lunch, or breakfast) (*from* **mat/ur** (**-ar**) 'food', 'meal')
kjötborð (-s, -)	meat counter
kótilett/a (-u, -ur)	(lamb) chop (Unless specifically indicated otherwise, references to meat in Icelandic tend to be to lamb.)
kjötboll/a (-u, -ur)	meatball
ýsuflök	from **ýs/a (-u, -ur)** 'haddock', and **flak (-s, -)**, (fish) 'fillet'
búa til, *acc.*	prepare
vesen (-s), *n.*	bother, fuss
svang/ur, *adj.*	hungry
(pasta)rétt/ur (-ar, -ir)	(pasta) dish
dós (-ar, -ir)	tin
skyr (-s), *n.*	a very popular and healthy traditional Icelandic dairy product consisting of milk curds and often eaten stirred with milk or cream and sugar.
doll/a (-u, -ur)	pot
fern/a (-u, -ur)	carton
eldhússkáp/ur (-s, -ar)	kitchen cupboard
allt búið/allt komið	all finished/have everything
drifum okkur heim	let's hurry home (from **drífa (dríf) sig** 'hurry (up)', 'get going')

Vocabulary connected with food

Matur

Kjöt (-s), n.		*Fiskur (-s,-ar), m.*	
lambakjöt	lamb	**ýs/a**	haddock
nautakjöt	beef	**þorsk/ur**	cod
svínakjöt	pork	**lax (-, -ar)**, *m.*	salmon
kjúkling/ur	chicken	**síld**, *f.*	herring
fuglakjöt	poultry	**rækj/a**	prawn
hvalkjöt	whale	**hum-ar (-ars, -rar)** *m.*	lobster

Brauð, kökur og sætindi (n.pl.)		*Korn (-s, -), n.*	
franskbrauð (-s, -)	white bread	**korn**	grain, corn
hveiti, *n.*	flour	**haframjöl**, *n.*	oatmeal
heilhveitibrauð	wholemeal bread	**hrísgrjón**, *n.pl.*	rice
þriggjakornabrauð	granary bread	**kornmat/ur**	cereal
snittubrauð	baguette	**(hafra)graut/ur**	porridge
rúnstykki, *n.*	roll	*Annað*	
rúgbrauð	ryebread	**sykur**, *m.*	sugar
bak/a	pie, quiche	**egg**, *n.*	egg
tert/a	tart		
kak/a	cake		
smákak/a	cookie		
kex, *n.*	cracker, biscuit		

Grænmeti (-s), n.		*Ávextir*	
baun, *f.*	pea, bean	*(sg. ávöxt/ur, m.)*	
kál, *n.*	cabbage	**appelsín/a**	orange
gulrót (-ar, -rætur), *f.*	carrot	**epli**, *n.*	apple
kartafl/a	potato	**banan/i**	banana
lauk/ur	onion	**per/a**	pear
hvítlauk/ur	garlic	**sítrón/a**	lemon
svepp/ur (-s, -ir)	mushroom	**ferskj/a**	peach
tómat/ur	tomato	**vínber**, *n.*	grape
gúrk/a	cucumber	**bláber**	blueberry
paprík/a	pepper	**jarðarber**	strawberry
(gul)róf/a	swede	**rúsín/a**	raisin
salat, *n.*	lettuce	**hnet/a**	nut

Mjólkurmatur		*Drykkir (sg. drykk/ur, m.)*	
súrmjólk (-ur), *f.*	soured milk (buttermilk)	**kaffi**, *n.*	coffee
		te, *n.*	tea
nýmjólk	fresh milk	**gos**, *n.*	soft drink

léttmjólk	semi-skimmed milk	**vatn**, *n.*	water
undanrenn/a	skimmed milk	**saf/i (djús**, *n.*)	juice
jógúrt, *n.*	yoghurt	**bjór**, *m.*	beer
ost/ur	cheese	**léttvín**, *n.*	wine
rjóm/i	cream	**rauðvín**	
smjör, *n.*	butter	**hvítvín**	
smjörlíki, *n.*	margarine	**(sterkt) vín**	alcohol, liquor
		léttöl, *n.*	light beer

Skyndimatur (convenience food)

pyls/a	wiener, hot dog
bjúga, *n.*	sausage
hamborgar/i	hamburger
fransk/ar (kartöfl/ur), *f.pl.*	chips
hakk, *n.*	minced meat
kjötfars, *n.*	sausage meat
steik, *n.*	steak
skink/a	ham

Note: the spelling of the names of many imported foods often fluctuates between foreign and Icelandic forms. Thus it is common to find, for instance, both **pizz/a** and **píts/a**, or **bacon** and **beikon**, *n.*

Matartímar: *the meals of the day*

Morgunmatur	**t.d. ristað brauð með osti eða marmelaði, kornmatur, hafragrautur, kaffi, te eða mjólk, og lýsi**
Hádegismatur	**t.d. skyr, smurt brauð: brauð með áleggi** 'open sandwich with luncheon meat or cheese etc.', **eða samloka**
(Síðdegis)kaffi/ kaffitími:	**kaffisop/i** 'cup of coffee' **og kökubit/i** 'piece of cake', **kaffibrauð, kex**
Kvöldmatur	**forréttur (t.d. súp/a), aðalréttur (kjöt eða fiskur með kartöflum og grænmeti), og eftirréttur (t.d. ís, grautur eða sætsúpa).**
Snarl *n.*	'snack', 'light meal'
Nesti *n.*	'meal box', 'provisions taken to school/work/on a trip'

What case does the preposition **með** rule here?

Matargerð/matreiðsla: *preparing food*

Elda/búa til mat cooking (a meal)

Verb	*Adjective*	
(ofn) baka	**bakaður**	(oven) baked
djúpsteikja	**djúpsteiktur**	deep fried
pönnusteikja	**pönnusteiktur**	pan fried
sjóða	**soðinn**	cooked, boiled
grilla	**grillaður**	grilled, barbecued
reykja	**reyktur**	smoked
blanda	**blandaður**	mix(ed)
hita		heat
setja (út í)		add
hræra		stir
þeyta		whip
krydda		spice
saxa		chop
bræða		melt
bera fram		serve
– og borða		
matinn! Verði þér		
að góðu!		

Exercise 1

Answer the following questions in Icelandic:

1 Hvað borðar þú í morgunmat?
2 Hvað borðarðu í hádegismat?
3 Tekurðu nesti með þér í vinnu, eða borðarðu heima, á kaffistofu ...?
4 Tekur þú kaffitíma?
5 Hvað borðarðu helst ('preferably') á kvöldin?

Language points

Impersonal constructions

Before certain verbs or verb constructions in Icelandic, the noun or pronoun that fills the subject position and would normally be in the nominative case will actually be in the dative or accusative. One example you have already encountered is **hvernig líkar þér**, where the 'subject' is in the dative form (**þér**) rather than the nominative

þú. As there are no subjects in these impersonal sentences, it follows that the verb cannot take its form from them. Instead, it will always be in the third person singular: **þér lík**_ar_, **mig lang**_ar_, **okkur vant**_ar_. Most impersonal sentences indicate a state of mind or body. Here are some of the most common impersonal expressions:

acc. + **langa í**	long, feel like, would like	**hana langar í fisk** she feels like having fish, she would like some fish
acc. + **vanta**	need	**vantar þig sítrónu?** do you need a lemon?
acc. + **hrylla við**	shudder at	**mig hryllir við tómötum** I shudder at tomatoes
acc. + **þyrsta**	be thirsty	**Guðmund þyrstir** Guðmundur is thirsty
acc. + **dreyma**	dream	**mig dreymir oft illa** I often have bad dreams
dat. + **finnast**	think, find	**mér finnst gaman að synda** I like swimming
dat. + **líða**	feel	**honum líður illa út af þessu** he feels bad about this
dat. + **lítast á**	like	**hvernig líst þér á það?** how do you like it?
dat. + **leiðast**	be bored	**barninu leiðist í skólanum** the child is bored at school
dat. + **sýnast**	seem	**henni sýnist það vera rangt** it seems to her that this is wrong
dat. + **þykja**	think, find	**okkur þykir gott að fara út að ganga** we like going out for a walk

As you can see from the examples above, many of the verbs used impersonally take an object. There is no relation between the case of these objects and the case of the 'subject'. For instance, the noun or pronoun preceding **hrylla við** is in the accusative, but the object (**tómatar**) is in the dative.

There are also impersonal constructions which consist of a combination of the verb **vera** (in the third person singular), **finnast**, or **þykja**, and an adjective:

mér er *kalt*	I am *cold*
mér finnst *gott* **að fara út að ganga**	I like going out for a walk

Since there is no subject for the adjective to base its form on, it will always be in the nominative neuter singular in these sentences, as in the examples above: **kalt**, and **gott**.

Finally, whenever a verbal phrase follows the object or adjective, its verb will be in the infinitive, with **að** after an adjective, and without **að** after an object.

Exercise 2

Put the words in brackets into the sentences in their correct form:

1 Langar __________ (þú) í kaffi?
2 (Við) __________ vantar nýja skó.
3 (Barnið) __________ er heitt.
4 (Jónína) __________ finnst gaman í bíó.
5 (Hann) __________ líður vel hér.
6 (Hún) __________ dreymdi skrýtinn draum.
7 Þyrstir __________ (þið)?
8 (Maðurinn) __________ leiðist heima.
9 (Konan) __________ þykir gaman að vinna.
10 (Þeir) __________ hryllir við sveppum.

Athugið. Some verbs can be used in personal as well as impersonal constructions. Often the meaning changes when the verb is used in a personal sentence:

tíminn líður, trúðu mér ...	time flies, believe me ...
vs. **henni líður illa**	she feels unwell
vatnið er kalt	the water is cold
vs. **barninu er kalt**	the child is cold

Likes and dislikes

In Icelandic, likes and dislikes are often expressed through impersonal constructions, using verbs such as **finnast**, **þykja** and **líka**. Whereas **líka** is used in combination with an adverb (**líka** *vel* or *illa*), **finnast** and **þykja** are usually followed by a noun or pronoun and an adjective in the nominative case, with the adjective taking on the number and gender of the (pro)noun:

mér finnst *lambakjöt gott*	I like lamb
honum þykir *mjólk vond*	he does not like milk

Huldu finnst *fiskur góður*	Hulda likes fish
okkur þykir *grænmeti* ekki *gott*	we do not like vegetables

Finnast and **þykja** should be in the third person plural (rather than singular) if the following noun is in the plural: **henni** *þykja hnetur vondar*; **þér** *finnast kótilettur góðar*.

All this may seem confusing at first, but with some practice you will soon get the hang of it. The adjectives **góður** and **vondur** can be qualified by many intensifying adjectives, from the straightforward **mjög** to such popular colloquials as **ofsalega**, **rosalega**, **æðislega**, **svakalega**, **óskaplega** (roughly equivalent to English 'awfully', 'tremendously', etc.), so you can easily be a little more expressive than just 'good' or 'bad'. Or you can replace **góður** or **vondur** with one of the following:

ljúffengur	delicious	**óætur**	inedible
gómsætur	succulent		

Exercise 3

Look at the food items and adjectives paired below and make sentences out of them, using **finnast** or **þykja** and making sure the adjectives are in the appropriate forms:

Dæmi: **sítrónur – vondur:** *mér þykja sítrónur vondar*

1 mjólk – ofsalega góður
2 epli – mjög góður
3 franskar kartöflur – óætur
4 appelsínusafi – ofsalega vondur
5 reyktur lax – æðislega góður
6 pylsur – hryllilega vondur
7 ofnbakaður kjúklingur – ljúffengur
8 svart kaffi – mjög vondur

Now have another look at the vocabulary describing food. Pick out ten items which you like or dislike to various degrees, and construct an Icelandic sentence for each describing how much you like or dislike that particular food. Try to be a little adventurous and combine, for instance, some of the food items with an adjective describing their preparation. Remember to make sure all the adjectives are in the appropriate forms.

Exercise 4A

Below are the ingredients for five different recipes. Can you match them with the right recipe from the following list?

1 Laukbaka
2 Rjómapönnukökur
3 Síldarsalat
4 Pasta með valhnetum og sveppum
5 Lambagúllas

i
3 soðnar kartöflur
2 laukar
2 epli, súr
2 rauðrófur
3 síldarflök
1 dl. sýrður rjómi
1 tsk. sinnep
3 harðsoðin egg

ii
250 gr. hveiti
125 gr. smjörlíki
1 dl. vatn
½ tsk. salt
8 laukar
2 tómatar
6–8 svartar ólífur
Provence krydd
svartur pipar
4 msk. ólífolía

iii
1½ kíló lambakjöt
1 laukur
1 msk. tómatsósa
½ l. kjötkraftur
1 tsk. papríkuduft
1 tsk. karrí
rósmarín
kúmen
salt, pipar
2 dl. rjómi

iv
4 bollar hveiti
½ bolli sykur
1 tsk. salt
2 tsk. lyftiduft
2 egg
vanilludropar
1 bolli smjörlíki
1 bolli þeyttur
   rjómi
jarðarberjasulta

v
2–3 skalotlaukar
2 msk. ólífólía
safi úr ½ sítrónu
600gr. nýir sveppir
600gr. ferskt tag-
   liatelli
1 dl. valhnetur
1 stykki af
   parmesan osti

Exercise 4B

You are hosting a dinner party. Compare the dislikes and/or dietary restrictions of your guests outlined below. Which of the recipes from Exercise 4A would you be unable to use for each? What menu would you be left with that would satisfy all? What adjustments would you need to make?

1 Raj: *grænmetisæta* (vegetarian).
2 Joyce: er *með ofnæmi fyrir* hnetum (allergic to).
3 Jón: þykir fiskur ofsalega vondur.
4 Margrét: er *í megrun* (on a diet).

Dialogue 2

Á veitingastað

Áslaug is taking her friend Joyce out for dinner at Hotel Borg, in the centre of Reykjavík. They have been studying the menu (**matseðill**, *m.*) *as the waiter* (**þjónn**) *joins them to take their order. Why does Áslaug persuade Joyce to have a starter? Are they having anything to drink? What's wrong with Áslaug's dish? Are they having anything after the main course?*

ÞJÓNN: Góða kvöldið. Eruð þið búnar að ákveða ykkur?
JOYCE: Ég ætla að fá lambahrygginn. Mig langar að smakka íslenskt lambakjöt.
ÞJÓNN: Lambahrygginn, já. Og í forrétt?
JOYCE: Enginn forréttur fyrir mig, takk.
ÁSLAUG: Jú, víst verður þú að smakka forrétt! Maturinn er alveg einstakur hér. Er ekkert sem þér finnst girnilegt á matseðlinum?
ÞJÓNN: Kannski má bjóða þér eitthvað létt, blandað salat til dæmis.
JOYCE: Já takk, mér líst vel á það.
ÁSLAUG: Og ég ætla að fá fiskisúpuna, og svo lunda.
ÞJÓNN: Þakka ykkur fyrir. Eitthvað að drekka á meðan þið bíðið?
ÁSLAUG: Þykir þér gott rauðvín Joyce? Eigum við að fá okkur rauðvínsflösku með matnum?
JOYCE: Það væri indælt!

During the main course:

ÞJÓNN: Jæja, hvernig bragðast þetta?
JOYCE: Lambakjötið er ljúffengt, en það vantar svolítinn pipar.
ÞJÓNN: Augnablik, ég skal ná í piparkvörnina. Hvernig er lundinn á bragðið?
ÁSLAUG: Mér finnst hann vera aðeins of mikið soðinn, en annars er hann meyr og bragðgóður.

Later, as the waiter clears the table:

ÞJÓNN: Hvað má bjóða ykkur í eftirrétt?
JOYCE: Ekkert, þakka þér fyrir, ég er orðin södd.
ÁSLAUG: Ekki heldur fyrir mig, takk.
ÞJÓNN: Kaffi og koníak í kaffistofunni kannski? Gott fyrir
         meltinguna!
ÁSLAUG: Já, er það ekki Joyce? Tvo kaffi og koníak, og reik-
         ninginn, takk.

Vocabulary notes

veitingastað/ur (-ar, -ir)	restaurant
smakka (smakka), *acc.*	taste
lambahrygg/ur (-jar, -ir), *m.*	rack of lamb
girnileg/ur, *adj.*	appetizing
lund/i (-a, -ar)	puffin
það væri indælt	that would be lovely
hvernig bragðast . . ./hvernig er . . . á bragðið	how does . . . taste?
piparkvörn (-kvarnar, -kvarnir), *f.*	pepper mill
orðin/n sadd/ur, *adj.*	full, eaten one's fill (It is not at all impolite in Icelandic to say that one is **saddur**. One should, on the other hand, be careful not to say **ég er fullur** instead, which means 'I am drunk'.)
melting (-ar), *f.*	digestion
reikning/ur (-s, ar)	bill

Language points

Food and taste

Exercise 5

The following adjectives describe the taste and other qualities of
foods. They are paired with their opposites where applicable. Can
you guess their meaning?

súr/beiskur	sour/bitter	sætur	. . . . .
seigur	tough	meyr	. . . . . .
þurr	dry	safaríkur	. . . . . .
harður	hard	mjúkur	. . . . . .
saltur	salty	bragðlaus	. . . . . .
stökkur	crispy, crunchy	linur	. . . . . .
ferskur/nýr	fresh	skemmdur	. . . . . .
(of mikið) soðinn	over cooked	ósoðinn, hrár	. . . . . .
bragðgóður	tasty	bragðvondur	. . . . . .
feitur	fatty	magur	. . . . . .

Exercise 6

Use as many adjectives as you can think of to describe each of the
following food items. Think of qualities such as size, colour, taste,
etc. Make sure that the adjectives are in the right forms.

Dæmi: **appelsína: stór, appelsínugul, (súr)sæt, safarík, bragðgóð**
. . .

1 tómatur 2 sítróna 3 rjómaterta 4 rúsína 5 kaffi 6 ís
7 rúgbrauð 8 rækja

Now construct a sentence for each of the items describing your
dis/like of them and why, along the lines of the following example
(remember to use the correct personal pronoun!):

Mér þykja appelsínur góðar af því að þær eru sætar og safaríkar.

1 Mér finnst tómatar . . .
There are of course no set answers to this part of the exercise.

Exercise 7

You are going to listen to the descriptions of four food items. Can
you tell from the descriptions what they are? Try to do this exercise purely as a listening exercise first. If you find it very difficult
to understand, use the descriptions below to help you.

1 Þetta er ávöxtur sem er lítill, rauður, safaríkur, sætur, mjúkur og
  bragðgóður.
2 Kjöt sem kemur frá mjög stórum fiski.
3 Grænmeti sem er appelsínugult, hart, stökkt, og sætt.
4 Stór fiskur sem er vinsæll og ljúffengur á bragðið. Hann er
  bleikur á litinn þegar hann er soðinn.

Ordering food

Dishes and food items are often ordered by the portions or containers in which they tend to be served, and, in many cases, these are formed into one compound. In Dialogue 2, for instance, Áslaug ordered a **rauðvínsflaska** rather than just **rauðvín** or a **flaska af rauðvíni**. Other common examples are a **kaffibolli** 'cup of coffee', a **vatnsglas** 'glass of water', or a **kökustykki** 'piece of cake'. As with all compounds, it is the final element that determines gender and thus form, so that a cup of coffee is ordered in the masculine, but a glass of water in the neuter, even if you leave out the word **bolli**: 'two coffees' will be **tvo kaffibolla**, or **tvo kaffi** for short. Similarly, one orders **eina kók** because the implication is **eina kókflösku**, and **eitt Lion's** because a chocolate bar is ordered by the piece (**stykki**). Dishes which are not served in such specific amounts are generally ordered by the **skammt/ur (-s, -ar)**, *m*. If you want chips for two, you order **tvo (skammta) af frönskum**. Dishes which already form separate portions in themselves, such as a sandwich or a hamburger, are, however, just ordered as they are: **eina samloku**, and **tvo hamborgara**. It will not always be equally obvious how to order things, sometimes you have to take your cue from a menu, and sometimes you just have to guess (but always listen closely to the server repeating your order to find out if you guessed right).

Exercise 8

Look at the menu on p. 151 and the order the waiter has marked on. As she goes and repeats the order to the kitchen, can you fill in the right forms of the amounts?

Dialogue 3

Exercise 9

You and three of your friends have been sightseeing all day and are ready for a break and a bite to eat. You decide to go into Hotel Borg for afternoon coffee. Since you speak Icelandic, you ask for a menu and tell the waiter what everyone will have after they have made their choice. You may not recognize all the items on the menu, but, as you explain to your friends, sometimes one has to

Víkurgrill

1 Ristuð samloka m/sk. og osti		9 Smurt br. m/hangikj. og salati	
2 Ristað brauð með osti		10 Smurt brauð m/roastbeef	
3 Samloka m/rækjusalati	*1*	11 Smurt brauð m/eggi og síld	
4 Samloka m/skinku og salati		12 Franskar kartöflur 1/1	
5 Samloka m/hangikj. og salati		13 Franskar kartöflur 1/2	*2*
6 Samloka m/roastbeef		14 Hrásalat	
7 Smurt brauð m/rækjum		15 Cokteilsósa	
8 Smurt brauð m/skinku og salati			

	Fj.	Fra	Sósa	Salat	Egg	An.	Annað
19 Hamborgari							
20 Ostborgari	3						
21 Eggborgari							
22 Píta m/buffi							
23 Píta m/grænmeti	1						
24 Pizza							
25 Skinka og egg m/ristuðu br.							
26 Bacon og egg m/ristuðu br.							
27 Lambakótilettur							

		Drykkir				
28 Marineraðar lambasneiðar						
29 Hangikjöt		36 Kók	4	16 Kaffi		2
30 Kjúklingur		37 Diet kók		17 Kakó		
31 Djúpsteiktur fiskur		38 Appelsín		18 Mjólk		3
32 Laxadiskur m/ristuðu br.		39 Malt				
Pönnusteikt bleikja		40 Pilsner				
33 Súpa dagsins		41 Annað				
34 Skyr með rjóma		42 Réttur dagsins				
35 Ís og ávextir						
36 Djúpsteiktur Camembert						

Nr. 47

HÓTEL BORG
Stofnað 1930

SÍÐDEGISSEÐILL

KÖKUR OG SÆTINDI

Vöfflur með sultu og rjóma   kr. 395
(Aðeins fáanlegar frá kl. 14:00 - 18:00)

Kransakökustykki   kr. 250

Heimabökuð súkkulaðikaka með rjóma   kr. 490

Marmaraostakaka með mokkasósu   kr. 540

Gulrótarkaka með þeyttum rjóma   kr. 490

Napóleonshattur   kr. 250

Úrvals konfekt (6 stk.)   kr. 250

BRAUÐMETI OG SNARL

Maísbaka með gráðosti, blönduðu grænmeti, hunangs-chilisósu   kr. 990

Súpa dagsins með brauði   kkr. 490

Kartöfluflögur með aiole   kr. 390

Grillaður lúxusborgari með osti. steiktum laukhringum
og frönskum kartöflum   kr. 990

Heit samloka með skinku, osti og tómötum   kr. 590

Grænmetissamloka með grænu salati   kr. 590

KAFFI OG TE

· Kaffi   kr. 195

· Úrval af jurta- og ávaxtateum   kr. 195

Espresso   kr. 195

Tvöfaldur Espresso   kr. 295

Cappuccino   kr. 225

Swiss Mocca   kr. 225

Heitt kakó með þeyttum rjóma   kr. 225

Matreiðslumeistari: Sæmundur Kristjánsson

kal 9.6.95

take chances! Fill in the gaps of the following dialogue. Don't forget to place the orders in the correct case.

You: (*to a passing waiter:* 1 *May I have a menu?*)
______________.

Þjónn: Viljið þið fá kvöldmatarseðil eða síðdegisseðil?
You: (*2 The afternoon menu, thank you.*) ______________.
Þjónn: Gjörið svo vel.

After you have explained the menu to the best of your abilities and everyone has made a choice:

Þjónn: Eruð þið búin að ákveða ykkur?
You: (*To friend 1*): what would you like?
Friend 1: 3 *A coffee and a piece of carrot cake.*
You: (*To the waiter*)______________.
             (*To friend 2*): And you?
Friend 2: 4 *Cocoa and waffles.*
You: (*To the waiter*): ______________.
             (*To friend 3*): And what will you have?
Friend 3: 5 *A vegetarian sandwich and a Coke.*
You: (*To the waiter*):______________.
Þjónn: Og hvað má bjóða þér?
You: (*6 A double espresso and a big piece of chocolate cake!*)
______________.

Some indefinite pronouns

In Icelandic, if you use a noun in a general sense without the article, it is indefinite. If you want to emphasize this indefiniteness, you use a form of the indefinite pronoun **einhver** 'some':

Einhver maður er í símanum til þín
Some guy is on the phone for you

Einhverjir strákar eru að leika sér í götunni
Some boys are playing out in the street

Einhver takes on the gender, case and number of the noun it stands with. It is declined exactly like the interrogative pronoun **hver** (Lesson 5), except that the neuter singular form is **eitthvert** in the nominative and accusative. **Einhver** can also be used on its own; then its case is determined by its position in the sentence, and its gender and number by what it is referring to. When used independently, the neuter singular form is **eitthvað** instead of **eitthvert**:

> **Er einhver heima?**   Is someone home?
> **Heyrir þú eitthvað?**   Do you hear something?

The negative form of **einhver** is **enginn** 'no', 'no one'. It, too, can be used either with a noun or independently. The neuter singular form is **ekkert** 'nothing'. Also note the irregular masculine and neuter genitive singular form **einskis**. Here are some examples:

> **Enginn forréttur fyrir mig**   No starter for me
> **Enginn er eins**   No one is alike
> **Ég heyri ekkert**   I hear nothing
> **Það var allt til einskis**   It all came to nothing

The declension of **enginn** is as follows:

	masc.	*fem.*	*neut.*		*masc.*	*fem.*	*neut.*
sg.	enginn	engin	ekkert	*pl.*	engir	engar	engin
	engan	enga	ekkert		enga	engar	engin
	engum	engri	engu		engum	engum	engum
	einskis	engrar	einskis		engra	engra	engra

Exercise 10

Insert the appropriate form of **einhver** or **enginn** into the following sentences:

1 Kemur _______ til þín í kvöld? Nei, _______ (einhver, enginn).
2 Ég heyri _______ (einhver).
3 Kennslan var til _______ (enginn).
4 Hún heimsækir _______ (enginn).
5 Hann er að tala við _______ konu í síma (einhver).
6 Það er bréf til þín frá _______ manni (einhver).
7 Er _______ glas í skápnum? Nei, það eru _______ glös hér (einhver, enginn).
8 Ég hef _______ tíma til að fara út (enginn).

Dialogue 4

Gestaboð

Hrafn og Jónína fá gesti í mat í kvöld. Þrír viðskiptafélagar Jónínu frá Bandaríkjunum koma í heimsókn og borða hjá þeim. Þau hjónin ætla að bjóða upp á þorramat. Þau eru búin að elda fullt af séríslenskum réttum og ætla að vera með hlaðborð í stofunni. Það hringir: gestirnir eru komnir! Hrafn fer til dyra:

HRAFN: Komið þið sæl, og velkomin! Gjörið svo vel og gangið í bæinn!

Gestirnir taka af sér og fara inn í stofu. Jónína er búin að leggja á borðið og maturinn er til, en fyrst býður Hrafn gestunum í glas og allir skála.

JÓNINA: Jæja, maturinn er til. Viljið þið ekki gjöra svo vel og fá ykkur að borða.

1. GESTUR: Með ánægju, þakka þér fyrir. Þetta lítur allt ljómandi út!

HRAFN: Þetta er hefðbundinn íslenskur vetrarmatur.

2. GESTUR: Hvers konar réttir eru hér?

JÓNINA: Fyrst er hérna harðfiskur, þurrkaður fiskur sem við borðum með íslensku smjöri. Og þarna er hangikjöt, reykt lambakjöt, með kartöflum í hvítri sósu.

1. GESTUR: Og hvað er þetta?

HRAFN: Við köllum þetta svið, það eru kindahausar sem eru sviðnir og klofnir í tvennt, og svo soðnir.

2. GESTUR: En augun og nefið sjást ennþá! Það er að horfa á mann! En hryllilegt!

HRAFN: Það lítur kannski ekki svo fallega út, en kjötið er mjúkt og bragðgott. Sumum þykir gott að borða augun, en ykkur er velkomið að sleppa því ...

JÓNINA: Þetta hérna er súrhvalur. Í gamla daga var matur látinn í sýru til að geyma hann yfir veturinn. Mörgum útlendingum finnst súrmatur ekki góður, og reyndar sumum Íslendingum ekki heldur, en það er alltaf gaman að prófa, ekki satt?

HRAFN: Svo eru hérna hrútspungar. Þá verðið þið bara að smakka, svo segi ég ykkur frá þeim á eftir.

3. GESTUR: Nú fer ég að hafa áhyggjur!

HRAFN: Það er engin þörf á því. Þeir eru eins og kjúklingabringur á bragðið.

2. GESTUR: En það er ekki fuglakjöt? Er það kannski ekki kjöt?
HRAFN: Jújú, það er lambakjöt. Það voru engar grænmetisætur hér á Íslandi í gamla daga! Svo er slátur, lifrapylsa og blóðmör. Mjög gott með rófustöppunni hér!
JÓNINA: En fyrir þá sem borða helst ekki kjöt er hérna pönnusteikt ýsa. Svo er líka rækjusalat, og rauðkál og baunir, og flatbrauð með.
HRAFN: En við byrjum á því að bjóða ykkur brennivínsglas og hákarlsbita, íslenskt góðgæti! Vilt þú rétta okkur glösin, Jónína?
1. GESTUR: Það er virkilegur veislumatur sem þið bjóðið okkur hér! Við þökkum kærlega fyrir okkur. Ég segi skál fyrir gestgjöfunum!
JÓNINA: Þakka ykkur kærlega fyrir, og verði ykkur að góðu! Skál!

Vocabulary notes

gestaboð (-s, -)	party of guests. *From* **gest/ur (-s, -ir)**, 'guest'
þorramat/ur (-ar)	traditional Icelandic midwinter food, often eaten at **þorrablót**, feasts held all over the country during the old Icelandic month of Þorri (January and February)
hlaðborð (-s, -)	smorgasbord, buffet
bjóða í glas	offer an (alcoholic) drink
skál (-ar, -ar), *f.*	toast
skál!	cheers!
skála (skála)	touch glasses
skál(a) fyrir ...	drink to ...
kindahaus (-s, -ar), *m.*	sheep's head
sviðnir og klofnir í tvennt	singed and split (cloven) in two
sjást (sést)	be seen
augun sjást ennþá	you can still see the eyes
ykkur er velkomið að, *impers.*	you are welcome to
láta í sýru	pickle
súrmat/ur	pickled food
ekki satt?	'isn't that so?' (*lit.* 'not true?')
hrútspung/ur (-s, -ar)	ram's testicle
kjúklingabring/a (-u, -ur)	chicken breast

slátur (-s, -)	sheep innards, made into **lifrapyls/a (-u, -ur)**, liver sausage, and **blóðmör (-s)**, *m.* blood sausage
stappa (-u, -ur)	mash
flatbrauð (-s, -)	Icelandic flatbread, made of ryemeal and baked on a hot plate
veislumat/ur	feast meal
brennivín (-s, -)	Icelandic aquavit
hákarl (-s, -ar), *m.*	shark, matured (buried) in sand
góðgæti (-s, -)	delicacy

9 Fjölskyldan

The family

In this lesson you will learn about:

- the family tree: family and relatives
- some common irregular nouns and their declensions
- ownership
- possessive constructions and pronouns

Reading 1

Fjölskyldan mín

Kristín is preparing to go to Italy for a year as an exchange student. She writes the following description of her family in Iceland for her prospective host family in Italy. Is Kristín the oldest child? How many of Kristín's siblings are still at school? Who are Hulda's parents? With whom does Kristín go riding? What are the names of Kristín's grandfathers?

Ég heiti Kristín Ragnarsdóttir. Ég er sautján ára gömul. Pabbi minn heitir Ragnar Hjálmarsson. Hann er prentari, alveg eins og Sveinn langafi minn. Mamma mín heitir Eyrún Jónsdóttir. Hún er skólaritari. Ég á þrjú systkini, tvo bræður og eina systur. Jón bróðir er elstur. Hann er tuttugu ára gamall og er á sjó. Hann er giftur Lilju. Ég er næst elst, og svo kemur Soffía systir. Hún er nýorðin sextán og er komin í menntaskólann. Palli litli er yngstur. Hann er ennþá í grunnskóla. Hulda bróðurdóttir er fyrsta barnabarn mömmu og pabba. Jón og Lilja eru nýbúin að eiga hana. Lilja mágkona er jafn gömul mér og við erum góðar vinkonur.

Við fjölskyldan eigum heima á Selfossi, sem er kaupstaður á Suðurlandi. Við búum í gömlu húsi niðri í bæ. Verkstæðið hans pabba er við hliðina á húsinu. Mamma er mikil hestakona. Hún á nokkra hesta, og oft þegar við erum komnar úr skólanum förum við mæðgurnar á hestbak.

Afi Hjálmar og amma Soffía eiga bóndabæ upp í sveit. Sigurbjörg langamma mín býr hjá þeim. Við förum oft í heimsókn til þeirra þegar við erum í fríi. Þau eiga margar kindur og kýr, og það er alltaf gaman að koma þangað. Ég var skírð eftir ömmu Kristínu sem býr í Reykjavík með Gústaf, stjúpa mömmu. Afi dó þegar mamma var ennþá lítil. Við heimsækjum þau alltaf þegar við förum til Reykjavíkur.

Mamma er einkabarn, en ég á margar frænkur og frændur úr ættinni hans pabba. Við ætlum á ættarmót næsta sumar, og ég hlakka til að hitta alla ættingjana mína þar.

Vocabulary notes

elst/ur, *adj.superl.* oldest

vera á sjó   be at sea (i.e. a fisherman)

nýorðin/n, *adj.* newly turned, just become

yngst/ur, *adj.superl.* youngest

eru nýbúin að eiga hana   have just had her (i.e. the baby)

jafn gamal/l, *adj dat.* the same age as

við hliðina á, *dat.* to the side of

bóndabæ/r (-jar, -ir), *m.* farm

upp í sveit (-ar, -ir)   (up) in the countryside

kýr (-, -), *f.* cow

skírð/n eftir, *dat.* be called after

dó, past tense of **deyja (dey – deyrð – deyr)** die

einkabarn (-s, -) only child

ætting/i (-ja, -jar) relative (from **ætt (-ar, -ir)**, 'family lineage', 'kin')

ættarmót (-s, -) family reunion

Language points

Ættartréð (the family tree)

Family relations in Iceland are extensive and complex for anyone unfamiliar with them. Genealogy has been a national obsession ever since Iceland was settled and is still very popular. Most Icelanders today can trace their family or **ætt** back for several generations, hence the existence in Icelandic of such terms as **fimm-menningar** (*m.pl.*) for people who share the same great-great-grandfather or grandmother.

Vocabulary

mamma/móðir	mother	**mæðgur**, *f.pl.*	mother and daughter
pabbi/faðir	father		
foreldrar, *m.pl*	parents	**mæðgin**, *n.pl.*	mother and son
systir	sister	**feðgar**, *m.pl.*	father and son
bróðir	brother	**feðgin**, *n.pl.*	father and daughter
frændi	male relative (uncle, cousin)	**bróðursonur/ dóttir**	nephew/niece on brother's side
frænka	female relative (aunt, cousin)	**systursonur/ dóttir**	same on sister's side
móðurbróðir/ systir	uncle/aunt on mother's side	**mágur**	brother-in-law
föðurbróðir/ systir	same on father's side	**mágkona**	sister-in-law
systkini, *n.pl.*	siblings	**tengdafaðir/ móðir**	father/mother-in-law
amma	grandmother	**tengdasonur/ dóttir**	son/daughter-in-law
afi	grandfather		
barnabarn	grandchild	**tengdafólk**	in-laws
lang-	great-	**stjúpfaðir/móðir**	stepfather/mother

Note that in Icelandic, the words **faðir** and **móðir** are rarely used except in very formal situations or by older people. The words **frænka** and **frændi** indicate a general family relationship, while a word like **móðursystir** would only be used in a situation where it was felt that specific detail was desirable. Finally, the word **stjúpi** used in the text (**stjúpa**, *f.*) is only used informally.

Exercise 1

Answer the following questions about Kristín's family in full Icelandic sentences:

1 Hvað heitir tengdafólk Lilju?
2 Hvað heitir afi Kristínar í föðurætt fullu nafni?
3 Hvað heita amma og afi Huldu?
4 Hvað heitir Hulda fullu nafni?
5 Kristín er _________ Huldu.

Exercise 2

Look at the following family tree, and complete the sentences below with the right word:

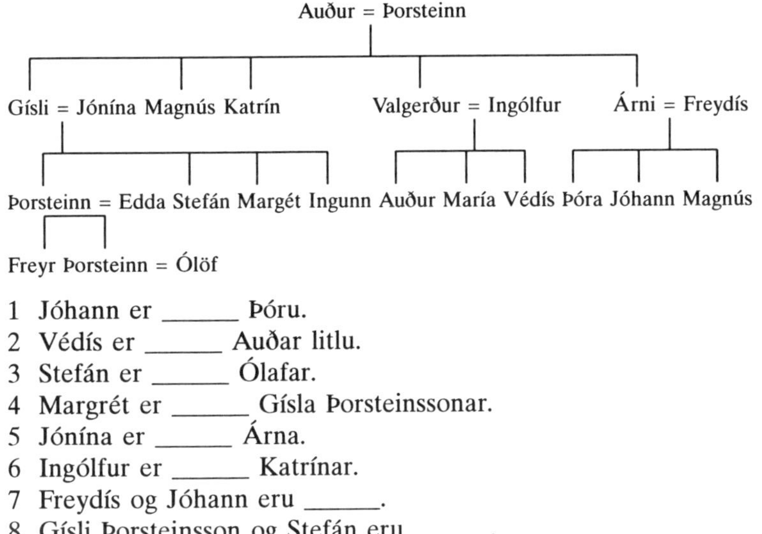

1 Jóhann er _______ Þóru.
2 Védís er _______ Auðar litlu.
3 Stefán er _______ Ólafar.
4 Margrét er _______ Gísla Þorsteinssonar.
5 Jónína er _______ Árna.
6 Ingólfur er _______ Katrínar.
7 Freydís og Jóhann eru _______.
8 Gísli Þorsteinsson og Stefán eru _______.

Exercise 3

Kristín has drawn her family tree (**ættartré**) (see p. 162).

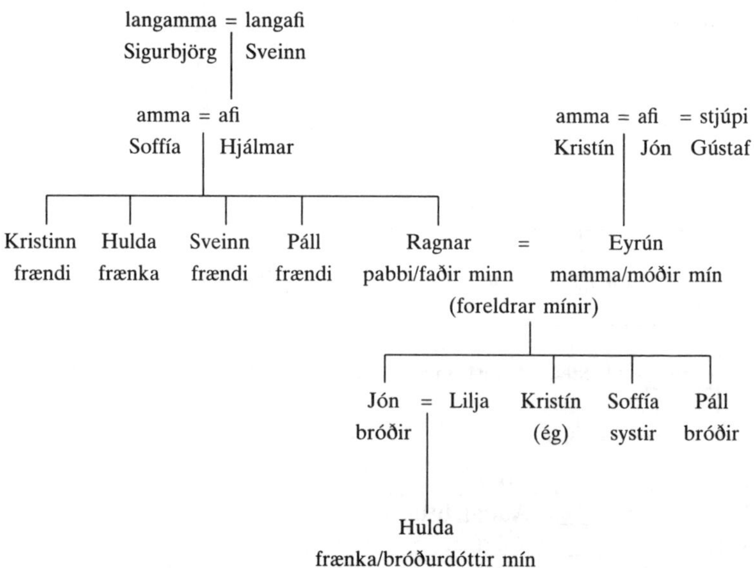

Draw your **ættartré** for an Icelandic friend.

Some irregular nouns

Many nouns indicating family relations have irregular endings and declension patterns. Since they are so common, it is good to pay particular attention to them right from the start. Here are the declension patterns for the most common irregular nouns:

		Masculine				
sg.	*nom.*	faðir	bróðir	sonur	frændi	bóndi
	acc.	föður	bróður	son	frænda	bónda
	dat.	föður	bróður	syni	frænda	bónda
	gen.	föður	bróður	sonar	frænda	bónda
pl.	*nom.*	feður	bræður	synir	frændur	bændur
	acc.	feður	bræður	syni	frændur	bændur
	dat.	feðrum	bræðrum	sonum	frændum	bændum
	gen.	feðra	bræðra	sona	frænda	bænda

		Feminine			('bridge')	Neuter
sg.	nom.	móðir systir dóttir	kýr	brú -in		tré -ið
	acc.	móður systur dóttur	kú	brú -na		tré -ið
	dat.	móður systur dóttur	kú	brú -nni		tré -nu
	gen.	móður systur dóttur	kýr	brúar -innar		trés -ins
pl.	nom.	mæður systur dætur	kýr	brýr -nar		tré -n
	acc.	mæður systur dætur	kýr	brýr -nar		tré -n
	dat.	mæðrum systrum dætrum	kúm	brú(m)-num		trjá(m) -num
	gen.	mæðra systra dætra	kúa	brúa -nna		trjá(a) -nna

Exercise 4

Put the correct form of the nouns in brackets into the following sentences. Remember to look closely at the sentence to determine whether the noun should be in the singular or the plural form and in which case it should be:

1 Jón á fjóra __________ (bróðir) en enga __________ (systir).
2 Hvað áttu margar __________ (systir)?
3 __________ eru komnar til að ná í börnin (móðir-in).
4 Óðal __________ heitir íslensk kvikmynd (faðir-inn, *gen.pl.*).
5 Njáll átti þrjá __________ (sonur).
6 Systir mín á þrjár __________ (dóttir).

Language points

Possession

A Verbs

There are two Icelandic verbs that indicate possession: **eiga** and **hafa**. **Eiga** is used to indicate ownership and close relations (family, friends, etc.), whereas **hafa** is used in combination with more abstract concepts that cannot really be 'owned' as such, for instance 'time' or 'idea'. Both verbs govern the accusative case. The expression **vera með**, encountered earlier, indicates rather that someone is carrying or wearing something instead of ownership *per se*. In other words, **Jón er með penna** means that Jón has a pen on him which he does not necessarily own, although he might.

B Possessive pronouns

Icelandic only has two possessive pronouns proper: **minn** 'my' or 'mine' and **þinn** 'your' or 'yours'. As you may already have noticed in the text and examples above, these pronouns follow the noun they qualify (i.e. what is owned), and, like all pronouns, take on its gender, number and case. They are declined as follows:

		masculine	*feminine*	*neuter*	*masculine*	*feminine*	*neuter*
sg.	*nom.*	minn	mín	mitt	þinn	þín	þitt
	acc.	minn	mína	mitt	þinn	þína	þitt
	dat.	mínum	minni	mínu	þínum	þinni	þínu
	gen.	míns	minnar	míns	þíns	þinnar	þíns
pl.	*nom.*	mínir	mínar	mín	þínir	þínar	þín
	acc.	mína	mínar	mín	þína	þínar	þín
	dat.	mínum	mínum	mínum	þínum	þínum	þínum
	gen.	minna	minna	minna	þinna	þinna	þinna

(NB: whenever double **-nn** follows the stem vowel of the pronoun, the vowel is unaccented.)

Note that when a noun is followed by a possessive pronoun, it must have the definite article:

hesturinn minn	my horse
bókin þín	your book
verkstæðið mitt	my workshop

There are, however, two important exceptions to this rule:
1 Personal names and nouns which exclusively indicate a family or friendly relation:

Ásta mín	**vinkonur þínar**	but	**maðurinn minn**
Pabbi minn	**foreldrar þínir**		**barnið þitt**

2 Nouns indicating abstractions that cannot be 'owned' as such (in verbal phrases used in combination with **hafa** rather than **eiga**):

Þú hefur ákveðna skoðun	**Þetta er skoðun þín**
	This is your view
Ég hef margar góðar hugmyndir	**Þetta eru hugmyndir mínar**
	These are my ideas

C The genitive case

Possessive constructions where the owner is someone else than the speaker or the addressee are made with the noun or pronoun indicating the owner in the genitive case:

Hann á bókina	He owns the book
Þetta er bókin *hans*	This is his book
Hún á hestinn	She owns the horse
Þetta er hesturinn *hennar*	This is her horse
Barnið á boltann	This child owns the ball
Þetta er boltinn *þess*	This is its ball
Við eigum bílinn	We own the car
Þetta er bíllinn *okkar*	This is our car
Þið eigið húsið	You own the house
Þetta er húsið *ykkar*	This is your house
Þeir/þær/þau eiga hjólið	They own the bike
Þetta er hjólið *þeirra*	This is their bike

Here, too, the preceding noun must have the definite article, with the same exceptions as listed under B:

Þetta er pabbi hans	This is his dad
but **Þetta er kona*n* hans**	This is his wife

Instead of pronouns, nouns can also be used in the genitive case to indicate ownership. They will then also be placed after the noun indicating what is owned, but whenever a genitive noun (rather than a pronoun) follows, the preceding noun does not get the definite article:

Þetta er bók*in* *hennar*	This is her book
but **Þetta er bók *konunnar***	This is the book of the woman

Þetta er barn*ið* *þeirra*	This is their child
but **Þetta er barn *foreldranna***	This is the parents' child

Personal names follow the same rule:

Þetta er hús*ið* *hans*	This is his house
but **Þetta er hús *Stefáns***	This is Stefán's house

Athugið

Nouns or pronouns that are in the genitive case as part of a possessive construction cannot change case along with the noun they qualify but will remain in the genitive. Compare the following examples:

Ég fer með dætrum mínum   but   **Ég fer með dætrum hans**

Why does **dætrum** not have the definite article?

D Icelandic vs. English

There are certain instances where English uses a possessive construction where in Icelandic you cannot, notably in combination with body parts and ailments, which cannot be 'owned' and therefore get the definite article instead (usually the context makes it quite clear whose body parts or ailments they are anyway):

Hann réttir mér höndina	He gives me his hand
Hún er að blása hárið	She is blow-drying her hair
Kvefið er að versna	My cold is getting worse

Exercise 5

Fill in the correct form of **eiga**, **hafa** or **vera með** as appropriate:

1 Magnús ____________ tölvu.
2 Amma og afi ____________ fjögur barnabörn.
3 Þú ____________ nógan tíma til að ná í strætó.
4 Ég ____________ fullt af pennum en mamma ____________ þá alla.
5 Barnið ____________ slæmt kvef.
6 Hún ____________ lítið að segja.

Exercise 6

Reword the following sentences, using the possessive pronoun or pronoun in the genitive case as appropriate

Dæmi: **Ég á myndina** – *þetta er myndin mín*

1 Hún á útvarpið.
2 Við eigum skápinn.
3 Þau eiga börnin.

4 Þið eigið fötin.
5 Ég á peningana.

Exercise 7

Answer the following questions with the help of the genitive case.

> *Dæmi:* **Á hjúkrunarkonan bílinn? Já, þetta er bíll hjúkrunarkonunnar.**

1 Á strákurinn peysuna?
2 Á kennarinn pennann?
3 Eiga börnin boltann?
4 Á fólkið húsið?
5 Á amma myndirnar?

Dialogue 1

Brúðkaup

Dagný runs into her friend Guðrún on the street. They have not seen each other for a while, so they stop and have a brief chat. Who is getting married? Is it going to be a big wedding? What people are they expecting from Canada? Where is Guðrún going?

DAGNÝ: Sæl og blessuð Guðrún!
GUÐRÚN: Sæl Dagný! Hvað segirðu gott?
DAGNÝ: Allt fínt, en þú?
GUÐRÚN: Mest lítið. Það er langt síðan maður hefur séð þig! Hvað er að frétta af þér?
DAGNÝ: Allt ágætt. Bróðir minn er að gifta sig á laugardaginn kemur.
GUÐRÚN: Nú hvað ertu að segja, hann Palli ætlar að gifta sig!
DAGNÝ: Já, það er komið að því. Þau Hólmfríður kærasta hans eiga von á barni í vor.
GUÐRÚN: En gaman að heyra! Á hún annars ekki líka börn með fyrrverandi manni?
DAGNÝ: Jú, stelpu og strák.
GUÐRÚN: Jæja, eru foreldrar þínir ekki spenntir?
DAGNÝ: Jú, mjög spenntir. Það verður fyrsta brúðkaupið í fjölskyldunni. Svo verður stór veisla eftir giftinguna á Hótel Íslandi, þannig að við mamma erum alveg á fullu. Fullt

af ættingjum ætlar að koma í brúðkaupið, jafnvel frænd-
fólkið hans pabba frá Kanada.

GUÐRÚN: Nú, eigið þið frændfólk þar?

DAGNÝ: Já, langamma mín og maðurinn hennar fluttu til Kanada
með fimm af börnunum. Hvað er að frétta af þér annars?

GUÐRÚN: Það er alltaf nóg að gera hjá mér. Enda verð ég víst að
halda áfram, ég er að fara á fund. Svo segi ég bara góða
skemmtun á laugardaginn, og ég bið kærlega að heilsa
heim til þín.

DAGNÝ: Þakka þér fyrir Guðrún, ég skila því.

Vocabulary notes

það er langt síðan maður hefur séð þig	it's been a long time since I (*lit.* 'one') have seen you
það er komið að því	the time has come, it has come to that
kærast/a (-u, -ur)	girlfriend (*'boyfriend'* is **kærast/i (-a, -ar)**)
eiga von á, *dat.*	expect
gifting (-ar, -ar)	wedding (particularly the wedding ceremony)
vera á fullu (í), *dat.*	be very busy (with)
fluttu, past tense of **flytja**	move
enda, *conj.*	and what's more, in fact
biðja að heilsa, *dat.*	give one's regards **Ég bið að heilsa heim til þín**, give my regards to everyone at home
skila (skila), *dat.*	pass on

Language points

Personal pronouns once more

In Icelandic, there are some usages of the personal pronoun that
do not occur in English. First, it is commonly used just before a
personal name or noun to indicate familiarity. This happens, for
instance, often in combination with references to relatives:

hann pabbi	**hann Palli**
hún systir mín	**hún Halldóra**

One could compare this with English 'our', as in 'our dad', although
it isn't always easily translated. Compare for instance the following
title of a famous Icelandic folk tale (and pop band): **Sálin hans
Jóns míns** 'the soul of my John'. As you can see, the pronoun is

declined along with the noun or name it stands with, and when used in a genitive (possessive) construction, the preceding noun must have the definite article in accordance with the rules explained above. Compare the following:

sál Jóns but **sál*in* *hans* Jóns**

Some other examples:

Þetta er hús*ið* *hans* Stefáns
This is the house of our Steven

Þetta eru frænkar og frændur úr ætt*inni* *hans* pabba
These are aunts and uncles from my dad's side of the family

Next, the plural personal pronoun is often used in Icelandic in combination with a name or noun that is to be included in the reference. Thus, the phrase **við mamma** is translated into English as 'mum and I': **við** already includes the speaker, so all that needs to be added is the reference to who else is included:

við fjölskyldan	my family and I
þið afi	you and granddad
við systkinin	my brothers and sisters and I
þau Halldóra	he and Halldóra

Note the use of the definite article in the examples.

Exercise 8

Answer the following questions as prompted, using the possessive construction:

Dæmi: **Er þetta greiðslukortið þitt?** (Yes)
Já, þetta er greiðslukortið mitt
Er þetta hjólið þitt? (No → granddad)
Nei, þetta er hjól afa míns. Þetta er hjólið hans afa.

1 Er þetta taskan þín? (Yes)
2 Er þetta bíllinn þinn? (No → mother)
3 Er þetta bókin þín? (No → brother)
4 Er þetta úlpan þín? (No → aunt)
5 Eru þetta gleraugun þín? (Yes)
6 Eru þetta dæturnar þínar? (No → sister)

Dialogue 2

Exercise 9

As you are walking down the street in Húsavík with your mother (3), who has only been here since yesterday (5) and is visiting you in Iceland (4), you bump into Magnús, a local acquaintance. You stop for a brief chat (1–2), but then you have to be on your way (6): you are going to meet your friend, Brynja, in the town centre (7) and after that you intend to go on a sightseeing trip into Ásbyrgi (n., 8), a magnificent rock formation which, according to legend, is a hoofprint of Odin´s eight-legged horse Sleipnir. Can you fill in the gaps in the following dialogue accordingly?

MAGNÚS:	Komdu sæl(l)!
YOU:	(1) ________________________________.
MAGNÚS:	Hvað er að frétta af þér?
YOU:	(2) ________________________________?
MAGNÚS:	Allt ágætt. Og hver er þetta?
YOU:	(3) ________________________________.
	(4) ________________________________.
MAGNÚS:	Jæja, það er gaman að heyra. Hvað er hún búin að vera lengi?
YOU:	(5) ________________________________.
MAGNÚS:	Er það já.
YOU:	(6) ________________________________.
	(7–8) ________________________________.
MAGNÚS:	Nújá, ég ætla ekki að halda ykkur. Ég segi bara góða ferð.
YOU:	(9) ________________________________.
MAGNÚS:	Verið þið blessaðar.
YOU:	(10) ________________________________.

Exercise 10

Write a brief description of your family in Icelandic.

10 Stefnumót

Appointments

In this lesson you will learn about:

- using the phone and writing letters
- arranging meetings and appointments, making plans
- ordinal numbers and dates
- the weak declension of adjectives
- the imperative
- the verbs **munu** and **skulu**

Dialogue 1

Er Hrafn Jökulsson við?

Mary Scanlon is phoning from Dublin to arrange a meeting next week to discuss a business project. When would Mary like to meet Hrafn? What does Hrafn suggest they do?

MARY: Góðan daginn, er Hrafn Jökulsson við?

RITARI: Hver er þetta, með leyfi?

MARY: Mary Scanlon heiti ég, frá D&M-fyrirtæki í Dyflinni.

RITARI: Andartak, ég skal gefa þér samband.

MARY: Þakka þér fyrir.

HRAFN: Halló, Hrafn hér.

MARY: Blessaður Hrafn, þetta er Mary Scanlon hérna, frá Dyflinni.

HRAFN: Já, sæl og blessuð Mary, hvernig hefurðu það?

MARY: Gott, takk. Ég ætla til Íslands i næstu viku, og mig langar að hitta þig til að ræða nýja verkefnið okkar.

HRAFN: Góð hugmynd. Hvenær kemurðu og hvað verðurðu lengi?

MARY: Ég kem á þriðjudaginn og mun líklega fara aftur á föstudag.
HRAFN: Einmitt. Verðurðu laus fimmtudaginn 17. nóvember?
MARY: Bíddu, ég skal athuga það. 17. nóvember er fimmtudagur, segirðu. Nei, því miður, ég er upptekin allan fimmtudaginn.
HRAFN: Er það já. Væri hægt að hittast á miðvikudaginn?
MARY: Já, en þá helst seinni partinn.
HRAFN: Þá sting ég upp á að við hittumst um sexleytið og ég býð þér í kvöldmat. Hvernig væri það?
MARY: Alveg ljómandi, þakka þér kærlega fyrir. Hvar hitti ég þig?
HRAFN: Hittumst á Hótel Óðinsvéum klukkan sex í veitingasalnum.
MARY: Allt í fína. Ég hlakka til að sjá þig.
HRAFN: Sömuleiðis. Sjáumst á miðvikudaginn!

Vocabulary notes

andartak (-s, -)	moment	**... leytið**	around ... o'clock
ræða (ræði), *acc.*	discuss		
líklega, *adv.*	probably, likely	**væri**, *past subj.* *of* **vera**	would be
bíddu, *imp. of* **bíða (bíð)**	wait	**veitingasal/ur (-ar, -ir)**	restaurant
stinga (sting) upp á, *dat.*	suggest		

Language points

Dagsetningar (dates)

Dates in Icelandic involve the use of ordinal numbers. (Note: cardinal numbers were given in Lesson 3). Here are the ordinals:

1 **fyrsti**	11 **ellefti**	30 **þrítugasti**
2 **annar**	12 **tólfti**	40 **fertugasti**
3 **þriðji**	13 **þrettándi**	50 **fimmtugasti**
4 **fjórði**	14 **fjórtándi**	60 **sextugasti**
5 **fimmti**	15 **fimmtándi**	70 **sjötugasti**
6 **sjötti**	16 **sextándi**	80 **áttugasti**
7 **sjöundi**	17 **sautjándi**	90 **nítugasti**
8 **áttundi**	18 **átjándi**	100 **hundraðasti**
9 **níundi**	19 **nítjándi**	
10 **tíundi**	20 **tuttugasti**	205 **tvö hundraðasti og fimmti**
	21 **tuttugasti og fyrsti**	...
		1000 **þúsundasti**

Note that ordinal numbers in Icelandic are always followed by a full stop, and also in dates.

Exercise 1

Say the following dates in Icelandic:

17. júní, 1. maí, 25. desember, 29. febrúar, 2. ágúst

Weak declension of adjectives

As you probably noticed, all the ordinals except one end in **-i**. This is the masculine nominative singular ending in the weak declension of adjectives. Whenever an adjective qualifies a definite noun, that is to say a noun with a definite article, demonstrative or possessive pronoun, or a personal name, its declension will be weak rather than strong (as learned in Lesson 5). The good news is that the weak declension pattern is much easier to memorize than the strong one. Here it is:

		masculine	*feminine*	*neuter*
sg.	*nom.*	______**i**	______**a**	______**a**
	acc.	______**a**	U-shift ______**u**	______**a**
	dat.	______**a**	U-shift ______**u**	______**a**
	gen.	______**a**	U-shift ______**u**	______**a**
pl.			U-shift ______**u**	

(for all genders and cases)

Ordinal numbers always follow the weak declension pattern. In dates, they will be in the masculine, because the months are masculine. The only ordinal that has a completely different declension pattern is **annar**:

		masculine	*feminine*	*neuter*
sg.	*nom.*	annar	önnur	annað
	acc.	annan	aðra	annað
	dat.	öðrum	annarri	öðru
	gen.	annars	annarrar	annars
pl.	*nom.*	aðrir	aðrar	önnur
	acc.	aðra	aðrar	önnur
	dat.	öðrum	öðrum	öðrum
	gen.	annarra	annarra	annarra

Annar is used in a variety of other ways as well. It can also mean, for instance, 'one out of two', 'another' and 'else'.

In certain cases, adjectives are always declined weakly. Examples are **næsti** and **síðasti**. More about this in Lesson 12.

Exercise 2

Put the adjectives in brackets into the following sentences in their appropriate form.

1 Hann var hér í _________ (síðasti) viku.
2 Stelpan fer í _________ (nýr) kjólinn.
3 Við ætlum að heimsækja ömmu og afa _________ (næsti) vor.
4 Þóra _________ (stór) systir mín kemur ekki með okkur.
5 Mamma og pabbi ætla að halda (*acc.*) _________ (stór) veislu (!).
6 _________ (bandarískur) forsetafrúin kemur til Íslands.

Exercise 3

Answer the following questions in Icelandic according to the English prompts given in brackets. Write out all numbers.

1 Hvenær kemurðu? (Monday 3 September)
2 Hvenær ferðu heim? (next week)
3 Við sjáumst _________. (on Friday)
4 Hvenær ætlarðu að heimsækja foreldra þína? (on Sunday)
5 Hvenær á Ólafur afmæli? (2. apríl)
6 Hvenær ætlarðu að hitta vini þína? (tomorrow around 8 o'clock)

Síminn (the telephone): vocabulary

hringja í, *acc.*	ring/telephone	**er ... við?**	is ... there?
símaskrá	telephone	**þetta er hann/hún**	speaking
(-r, -r), *f.*	directory	**augnablik/**	one moment
halló?/ já?	used to answer	**andartak**	
	the telephone	**á ég að/viltu taka**	can I/would you
hver er þetta	who is calling	**skilaboð**	take a
(með leyfi)?	(please)?		message
þetta er ... /...	this is ... /...	**síma-vörð/ur**	operator
hérna	speaking	**(-varðar, -verðir)**	

(það er) sími til þín	there's a telephone call for you	**leggja (símtólið) á**	hang up (the phone)
gefa samband	connect	**ég heyri illa í þér/það er slæmt samband**	I can't hear you/ we have a bad connection
farsím/i (GSM sím/i, also called gems/i)	mobile phone	**velja (vel) númer**	dial a number
símsvar/i	answering machine	**hann/hún er í símanum**	s/he is on the phone
þetta er símsvarinn hjá …	this is the answering machine of …	**bréfsím/i**	fax
gjörið svo vel að skila eftir skilaboð	please leave a message	**hringja utanbæjar/ til útlanda**	phone long distance/abroad
símalín/a	extension	**hringja innanbæjar**	make a local call
símaklef/i	telephone box		
símkort	telephone card	**landsnúmer/ svæðisnúmer/ símanúmer**	country code, area code, phone number
halda línunni	hold the phone		
það er á tali/ línan er upptekin	the line is busy	**svargreitt símtal**	collect call

Dialogue 2

Að panta tíma

Árni telephones to make a dental appointment. Who does Árni want to make an appointment with? Why can't Árni make it on Tuesday?

MÓTTAKA: Tannlæknastofan góðan dag.

ÁRNI: Já blessuð, mig langar að panta tíma hjá Sigurjóni tannlækni.

MÓTTAKA: Já, það er hægt. Er eitthvað alvarlegt að eða ætlarðu í skoðun?

ÁRNI: Ég ætla bara í skoðun.

MÓTTAKA: Allt í lagi. Sigurjón á lausan tíma á þriðjudaginn kemur.

ÁRNI: Klukkan hvað?

MÓTTAKA: Rétt eftir hádegi.

ÁRNI: Nei, það hentar mér ekki, þá er ég í vinnu.

MÓTTAKA: Mánudaginn hálf fimm?

ÁRNI: Hvaða mánaðardagur er það?

MÓTTAKA: 6. júní.

ÁRNI: Já, það er fínt.

Vocabulary notes

móttak/a (-u, -ur)	reception	**alvarleg/ur**, *adj.*	serious
panta (panta), *acc.*	book	**skoðun (-ar, -ir)**	examination, check-up
panta tíma	make an appointment (at the doctor's, etc.)	**það hentar mér ekki**	that doesn't suit me
tannlæknastof/a	dental clinic	**mánaðardag/ur (-s, -ar)**	day of the month (i.e. date)
er eitthvað að	is something wrong		

Reading 1

Bréf

Where did John get the idea to write Þórhallur? What information is he looking for?

23 Main Street
Minnesota, Minnesota
56264 USA
4. október 1999

Þórhallur Höskuldsson
Bókabúð Máls og menningar
Laugavegi 18
101 Reykjavík
Iceland

Kæri Þórhallur,

Sigrún Jónsdóttir frá íslenska sendiráðinu í Washington ráðlagði mér að hafa samband við þig. Ég er að læra íslensku upp á eigin spýtur af því að það er engin íslenskukennsla í boði hér í nágrenninu. Málið er að mig vantar bækur til að æfa mig í málinu. Viltu gjöra svo vel að senda mér bókaskrá og upplýsingar um pantanir og greiðslu.

Með fyrirfram þökk,
virðingarfyllst,

John Anderson

Vocabulary notes

kær, *adj.*	dear (in salutations always in the weak declension)
ráðlagði	past tense of **ráðleggja (ráðlegg)**, *dat. + acc.* advise
upp á eigin spýtur	on one's own
boð (-s, -)	offer
í boði	offered, on offer
mál (-s, -)	matter, case (also short for **tungumál** 'language')
æfa (æfa) sig í, *dat.*	practise (oneself) in
greiðsl/a (-u, -ur)	payment
fyrirfram	in advance
virðingarfyllst, *adj.superl.*	sincerely, respectfully

	REYKJAVÍK	KÓPAVOGUR	SELTJ.NES	HAFNARFJ. GARDABÆR BESSAST.HR.	MOSFELLSBÆR
LÖGREGLA	0112	41200	0112	5 11 66	0112
SJÚKRABIFREIÐ / SLÖKKVISTÖÐ	1 11 00 til vara 0112	1 11 00 til vara 0112	1 11 00 til vara 0112	5 11 00	1 11 00 til vara 0112
ALMANNAVARNIR	2 20 40	41200	61 11 66	5 11 66 5 11 00	5 11 66 5 11 00
Læknavakt VIRKA DAGA KL. 17-08, LAUGARDAGA OG HELGIDAGA ALLAN SÓLARHRINGINN	2 12 30	2 12 30	2 12 30	5 13 28	66 62 01
Neyðarvakt lækna EF EKKI NÆST Í HEIMILISLÆKNI EÐA STADGENGIL Á VIRKUM DÖGUM KL. 08-17	69 66 00	69 66 00	69 66 00		
Neyðarvakt tannlækna LAUGARDAGA OG HELGIDAGA KL. 10-12	69 66 00	69 66 00	69 66 00	69 66 00	69 66 00
Upplýsingar um vaktir lækna og lyfjabúða	1 88 88	1 88 88	1 88 88	5 11 00	66 62 01

Almannavarnir ríkisins	Neyðarsími	(91) 1 11 50
Kvennaathvarf OPIÐ ALLAN SÓLARHRINGINN	Neyðarsími	(91) 61 12 05
Rauðakrosshúsið OPIÐ ALLAN SÓLARHRINGINN	Neyðarsími	(91) 62 22 66
Rauðakrosshúsið -grænt númer	Neyðarsími	99 66 22
Vímulaus æska NEYÐARSÍMI FORELDRA OPINN ALLAN SÓLARHRINGINN	Neyðarsími	985- 2 96 00
Stígamót SAMTÖK KVENNA GEGN KYNFERÐISLEGU OFBELDI	Neyðarsími	(91) 62 68 68
Landhelgisgæslan	Neyðarsími	(91) 1 30 99
Leit og björgun LANDSBJÖRG • SLYSAVARNARFÉLAG ÍSLANDS	Neyðarsími	(91) 62 71 11
Vinnueftirlit ríkisins	Neyðarsími	(91) 67 25 05
Borgarstofnanir NÁTTÚR- OG HELGARVARSLA		(91) 2 73 11
Upplýsingar um veður (sjá auglýsingu á bls.5)		99 06 00

PÓSTUR OG SÍMI
sími: 63 60 00

Exercise 4: Neyðarsímanúmer

Look at the information on p. 177 from an Icelandic telephone directory and say which number you would call if you were in Reykjavík and:

1 You saw a building on fire.
2 You saw someone knocked down by a car.
3 You noticed your wallet had been stolen.
4 You urgently needed a doctor in the middle of the night.
5 You needed to know the exact time.
6 You wanted to know the phone number of someone in Iceland not yet listed in the directory.

Dialogue 3 ▣

Komdu með mér í bíó!

Þórey rings Kristinn to ask him to go to the cinema with her. Why does Þórey want to go to the cinema tonight? What are Kristinn's plans for the evening? Why do they have to be there early?

KRISTINN: Já.
ÞÓREY: Hver er þetta?
KRISTINN: Kristinn.
ÞÓREY: Sæll, Þórey hérna. Heyrðu, það er alveg mögnuð spænsk mynd sýnd í Háskólabíói í kvöld, og mig langar svo óskaplega að sjá hana. Nennirðu að koma með mér?
KRISTINN: Ekki í kvöld. Ég er nefnilega að klára verkefni sem ég á að skila á morgun, og ég mun líklega ekki vera búinn fyrr en seinna í kvöld.
ÞÓREY: Hvað áttu mikið eftir að skrifa?
KRISTINN: Fimm blaðsíður eða svo.
ÞÓREY: Þú verður enga stund að því! Haltu áfram að skrifa þangað til í kvöld og kláraðu það sem eftir er í fyrramálið!
KRISTINN: Æ, Þórey, ég veit ekki ...
ÞÓREY: Myndin er bara sýnd í kvöld! Láttu námið vera í þetta sinn og komdu með mér í bíó, gerðu það!
KRISTINN: Jæja þá, hvenær byrjar sýningin?
ÞÓREY: Klukkan 9, en það væri best að mæta snemma svo að

> við fáum örugglega miða. Ég kem og sæki þig korter
> yfir átta. Vertu tilbúinn!
KRISTINN: Allt í lagi. Ég sé þig hér korter yfir átta.

Vocabulary notes

magnað/ur, *adj.*	brilliant, super	**í þetta sinn**	this once, for once
nefnilega, *adv.*	namely, you see		
klára (klára), *acc.*	finish	**nám (-s, -)**	studies
seinna, *adj.comp.*	later	**gerðu það!**	please!
þú verður enga stund að því	it will take you no time at all	**sýning**, *f./* **sýnd/ur**, *adj.*	show(n)

Language points

Imperative

You have already encountered examples of the imperative, for
instance:

heyrðu listen   **bíddu** wait   **sjáðu** look   **vertu tilbúinn** be ready

The imperative is a verb form used to tell people what or what
not to do. The singular imperative is formed in Icelandic by taking
the stem of the verb, and by adding, with certain modifications, the
suffix **-ðu** (from **þú**), as in **farðu** (**far-** and **-ðu**, 'go!' from infinitive
fara). The rules for the modifications are as follows:

1 Verbs belonging to the **-a-** group keep the infinitive **-a** in the
imperative singular:

borðaðu (from **borða**, 'eat')   **kláraðu** (from **klára**, 'finish')

2 **-ðu** will change to **-du** when the stem of the verb ends in **-l**,
-m or **-n**:

veldu (from **velja**, 'choose')   **komdu** (from **koma**)
kenndu (from **kenna**, 'teach')

The **-ð** will assimilate to **-d** when the stem ends in **-ð**:

leiddu (from **leiða**, 'lead', 'conduct')

3 **-ðu** will change to **-tu** whenever the stem ends in **-p**, **-t**, **-k** or **-s**:

hlauptu (from **hlaupa**, 'run') **brostu** (from **brosa**, 'smile')
láttu (from **láta**, 'let')

Note: if the stem already ends in **-dd** or -tt, no extra **-d** or **-t** will
be added:

hættu (from **hætta**, 'stop', 'quit')

In the plural, the second person plural form of the verb is used,
sometimes followed by its (separate) subject **þið**, and sometimes
with **-i** (from **þið**) added as a suffix, as in: **farið** (**þið**), or **fariði**,
although in the plural it is fairly common to use only the verb.

The following are among the more common verbs which have
an irregular singular imperative:

ganga	**gakktu**	**gangið(i)**
vera	**vertu**	**verið(i)**
þegja (be quiet)	**þegiðu**	**þegið(i)**
hringja	**hringdu**	**hringið(i)**
senda	**sendu**	**sendið(i)**
halda	**haltu**	**haldið(i)**
binda	**bittu**	**bindið(i)**
standa	**stattu**	**standið(i)**

The imperative is commonly used in Icelandic for straightforward
requests. This is not at all considered impolite. Less direct constructions using **Viltu** (**gjöra svo vel að**) ... or the subjunctive (see
Lesson 16) always remain an option if desired, but when it concerns
a simple request made of someone familiar, it would be considered unnecessarily wordy in Icelandic. Compare for instance the
following:

Náðu í mjólk fyrir mig, elskan	Get me some milk (would you), love
Réttu mér saltið	Pass me the salt (please)
Láttu ekki svona!	(Would you) stop acting up!

Exercise 5

The following cooking instructions are from a recipe for pasta with
smoked salmon. Add the verbs in brackets, first in the singular and
then in the plural imperative form.

1 __________ smjörið (bræða)
2 __________ laukinn mýkjast (láta)

3 __________ helminginn af laxinum (saxa)
4 __________ hann út í smjörið (setja)
5 __________ þetta varlega (hita)
6 __________ til slétta sósu (búa)
7 __________ það sem eftir er af laxinum (skera)
8 __________ pastað (sjóða)
9 __________ saman við laxasósuna (hræra)
10 __________ með salti og pipar (krydda)
11 __________ laxarestinni saman við (blanda)
12 __________ réttinn fram (bera)

The verbs munu *and* skulu

The verb **munu** usually indicates futurity moderated by uncertainty
or doubt:

Ég mun (líklega) fara aftur á föstudaginn
I will probably leave again on Friday

Hann mun ekki klára ritgerðina fyrr en seinna
He (probably) won't finish the essay until later

Skulu indicates (a) strong intention or obligation or (b) advice or
promise:

a **Ég skal ná prófinu, hvað sem það kostar**
   I will pass the exam, no matter what

b **Þú skalt ekki gera þetta strax**
   Don't (= you shouldn't) do this right away

Ég skal ná í kaffi fyrir þig
I will get you some coffee

Note: when used in the second person, the meaning of **skulu** resembles that of an imperative. In the first person plural, the meaning
of **skulu** is closely related to that of the first person plural without
við, indicating a suggestion or encouragement (English 'let's'):

Við skulum fara í bíó!   = Förum í bíó!

Munu and **skulu** are the only Icelandic verbs with an infinitive
ending in **-u**, and their conjugation is rather irregular:

	munu	*skulu*
ég	mun	skal
þú	munt	skalt
hún	mun	skal
við	munum	skulum
þið	munið	skulið
þær	munu	skulu

Another important characteristic of these two verbs is that they are followed by a main verb in the infinitive without **að**.

Exercise 6

Add the correct form of **munu** or **skulu**, as appropriate, to the following sentences:

1 Þið __________ fara heim strax!
2 Ég __________ fara út með hundinn fyrir þig.
3 Þú __________ sjá eftir þessu.
4 Þú __________ gera heimaverkefnin þín!
5 Hann __________ sækja þig klukkan níu.

11 Gisting

Accommodation

In this lesson you will learn about:

- booking accommodation
- indefinite dual and plural pronouns: **báðir, allir, sumir, nokkrir, ýmsir**
- the genitive case with adjectives
- the dative of difference
- numerals with plural nouns
- more noun groups

Dialogue 1

Að panta herbergi

After having spent several days in Reykjavík, Michael and his friends are preparing to tour the Icelandic countryside. Michael phones up a guest house to book accommodation for the first two nights. What kind of rooms does Michael want? Are they available? How will the little boy be accommodated?

MICHAEL: Eigið þið nokkur herbergi laus annað kvöld?
GESTGJAFI: Eins eða tveggja manna herbergi?
MICHAEL: Tveggja manna herbergi.
GESTGJAFI: Hvað mörg?
MICHAEL: Tvö, með baði, ef hægt er.
GESTGJAFI: Hvað margar nætur?
MICHAEL: Tvær.
GESTGJAFI: Bíddu við . . . Við eigum eitt herbergi laust með baði, hitt hefur sameiginlegt bað og snyrtingu, en það er handlaug á herberginu.

MICHAEL: Hvað kostar gistingin?
GESTGJAFI: Herbergi með baði kostar 9.500 kr á nótt, og hitt 7.800 kr.
MICHAEL: Er morgunverður innifalinn?
GESTGJAFI: Já, hann er innifalinn, og auk þess eru öll herbergin búin síma, sjónvarpi, litlum kæliskáp og örbylgjuofni.
MICHAEL: Við erum líka með lítinn strák með okkur. Væri hægt að setja aukarúm inn í herbergið?
GESTGJAFI: Það er enginn vandi. Hvað er strákurinn gamall?
MICHAEL: Hann er þriggja ára.
GESTGJAFI: Þá fáið þið 5000 kr. í afslátt. Börn að fjögurra ára aldri greiða 4.500 kr.
MICHAEL: Er það já. Frábært. En segðu mér, er langt að fara í sundlaug?
GESTGJAFI: Nei, það er örstutt, aðeins nokkra mínútna ganga.
MICHAEL: Allt í fína, þá ætla ég að panta herbergin tvö og aukarúm.

Vocabulary notes

hitt, *n.sg. of* **hinn**, the other one
  dem. pron.
sameiginleg/ur, common, shared
  adj.
snyrting (-ar, -ar) toilet, washroom
handlaug wash basin
  (-ar, -ar)
innifalin/n, *adj.* included
auk þess apart from (that), in addition

búin/n, *dat.* *here* 'fitted out with'
aukarúm (-s, -) extra bed (from **auka-** 'extra', 'additional')
vand/i (-a, -ar) problem
greiða (greiði), pay
  dat. + acc.
ör-, *pref.* very
sundlaug (-ar, -ar) swimming pool

Language points

The genitive with adjectives

In Icelandic, the genitive case is used with an adjective, actual or implied, indicating a measure in space or time, i.e. how old, big, deep, wide, far, etc., someone or something is. For instance, in the dialogue above, Michael wanted a *tveggja manna* (**stórt**) **herbergi**, as well as an extra bed for a *þriggja ára* (**gamall**) **strákur**, while the distance to the swimming pool was said to be only *nokkurra* *mínútna* (**löng**) **ganga**. In these instances, there are no specific verbs or prepositions to remind you which case to use, and, as you can see, more often than not the adjective itself is absent from the sentence, so that it can be tricky to remember to use the genitive case in the appropriate instances. As always, practice will help you get into the habit. It may also help to memorize a particular common example, such as telling (some)one's age.

Exercise 1

Fill in the blanks with the correct form of the words in brackets:

1 Hvað er þetta hús hátt? Þetta er __________ (3 hæðir) hús.
2 Hvað er sundlaugin djúp? Hún er __________ (2 metrar) laug.
3 Hvað er íbúðin stór? Hún er __________ (4 herbergi) íbúð.
4 Hvað verður mikil seinkun á fluginu? Það verður __________ (20 mínútur) seinkun.
5 Hvað er ferðin löng? Það er __________ (1 dagur) ferð.

Now can you answer the following questions?

6 Hvað er lýðveldið Ísland gamalt?
7 Hvað er *Njáls saga* gömul?
8 Og hvað ert þú gamall/gömul?

Indefinite dual and plural pronouns: báðir, allir, sumir, nokkrir, ýmsir

All of these pronouns are declined as strong adjectives, with only a few exceptions, outlined below.

Báðir, 'both', is always in the plural and must be followed by a noun with the definite article, unless the noun refers to something which only comes in a pair. Compare the following examples:

Hann á báða bíla*na*	He owns both (the) cars
but **bæði augu**	both (the) eyes

Note that **báðir** has irregular forms in the neuter nominative and accusative, **bæði**, and in the genitive for all genders, **beggja**.

Allir, 'all'/'everyone', can occur in both the singular and the plural. When modifying a noun it means 'all' or 'whole'. The noun must have the definite article:

Hann á alla bílana	He owns all (of the) cars

| **Hún drekkur allt kaffið** | She drinks all of the coffee |

When used as a pronoun, on its own, **allur** means 'everybody' or, in the neuter, 'everything':

| **Allt í fína** | *lit.* 'Everything fine', i.e. all right |
| **Allir eru heima** | Everyone is (at) home |

Sumir, 'some', is almost always used in the plural, with or without a noun:

| **Sumir útlendingar borða ekki svið** | Some foreigners don't eat svið |
| **Sumir trúa á drauma** | Some (people) believe in dreams |

Nokkrir usually means 'several' when used in the plural:

Ég á nokkrar bækur eftir Laxness
I own several books by Laxness

However, it can also mean 'any(one)/(thing)', in which case it can occur in the singular or the plural, and can be on its own or followed by a noun. As the implication is negative, a positive answer will have **jú** rather than **já**:

Er nokkur hér? Nei, enginn
Is anyone here? No, no one

Heyrir þú nokkuð? Jú, ég heyri eitthvað
Do you hear anything (at all)? Yes, I do hear something

Eiga þau nokkurt barn? Jú, þau eiga stelpu
Do they have a child? Yes, they have a girl

Note that the neuter singular form is different depending on whether it is followed by a neuter noun (**nokkurt barn**) or is used independently (**nokkuð**).

Ýmsir, 'various', can be used in the singular or the plural, both as a subject and as an adjective:

Ýmsir halda því fram að ...	Various people claim that ...
Hann þekkir ýmsa stjórnmálamenn	He knows various politicians
af ýmsu tagi	of various kinds
á ýmsan hátt	in various ways

Dialogue 2

Á *ferðaskrifstofu*

While in Iceland, Joyce would like to take the opportunity to visit Greenland for a few days. She goes to a travel agent to enquire after organized trips and fares. How long does Joyce want to go for? On what day would she depart? Can she stay longer if she chooses?

JOYCE: Góðan daginn. Mig langar að fá upplýsingar um pakkaferðir til Grænlands.

STARFSMAÐUR: Hvað ætlar þú að vera lengi? Við erum með þriggja daga eða vikuferðir í boði.

JOYCE: Ég var að hugsa um helgarferð. Hvað er innifalið í þriggja daga ferð?

STARFSMAÐUR: Það eru flogið til Narsarsuaq, og svo gisting með hálfu fæði, grænlenskt kynningarkvöld á hótelinu, og hálfs dags eða heils dags skoðunarferðir, til dæmis til Brattahlíðar, þar sem eru rústirnar af bæ Eiríks rauða, og sigling út með Eiríksfirði.

JOYCE: Hvað kostar ferðin?

STARFSMAÐUR: Hún kostar 43.500 á mann í tvíbýli, eða 47.000 í einbýli. Brottför er á föstudögum ef þú ætlar að vera yfir helgina.

JOYCE: Er hægt að bæta aukadegi við?

STARFSMAÐUR: Nei, það er tveggja nátta hámarksdvöl á þessu verði.

JOYCE: Og hvenær þarf að borga fargjaldið?

STARFSMAÐUR: Þú borgar 7000 kr. í staðfestingargjald innan viku frá pöntun. Fullnaðargreiðsla þarf að fara fram þremur vikum fyrir brottför.

JOYCE: Þakka þér kærlega fyrir upplýsingarnar.

Vocabulary notes

pakkaferð (-ar, -ir)	package trip
með hálfu fæði	half board
rúst (-ar, -ir)	ruin
Eiríkur rauði	father of Leifur Eiríksson, settled in Greenland and founded a community there which survived until the fourteenth century
ein-, tvíbýli (-s, -)	single, double (room)

bæta (bætir) við, *dat.*   add
hámarksdvöl (-ar, -ir)   maximum length of stay
staðfestingargjald (-s, -)   deposit
innan, *prep. gen.*   within
fullnaðargreiðsl/a (-u, -ur)   final payment

Exercise 2

Study the advertisements on p.189 from the brochure of the
Ferðaþjónusta bænda (Icelandic farm holidays) and the explan-
ations of the various symbols.

1 Which farm(s) would you choose to stay at if you were particularly interested in:

a   riding
b   hunting and fishing
c   cycling
d   going for a swim in the morning
e   cooking your own meals

2 Imagine you are planning to stay at one of these farms during a
trip to Iceland and have decided to ring the farm of your choice
to book your accommodation there. How would you ask for the
following information in Icelandic:

1 Do they have a room available in June?
2 Is it possible to book a four-day stay for one?
3 You would like a made-up (**uppbúið**) bed if possible.
4 Is there a possibility for you to cook your own meals
    (**eldunaraðstað/a**, *f.*)?
5 What would the accommodation cost?
6 You would like to make your reservation now.

Language points

Dative of difference and comparison

In Dialogue 2, the travel agent told Joyce that her full payment
was due **þremur vikum fyrir brottför**. The dative case (**þremur
vikum**) is used here and elsewhere in Icelandic to denote a difference or comparison:

BÆIR/GESTGJAFI	AÐSTAÐA FJÖLDI				FJÖLDI HERB. EFTIR STÆRÐ			AÐSTAÐA FLOKKUN			ELDUNARAÐSTAÐA FÆÐI			
	Gisting alls	Sumarbúst./sumarhús	Heimagisting	Gisting í sérhúsi/sérhúsum	Eins og tveggja manna	þriggja manna og stærri	Gisting í sal	Sumarbúst./sumarhús	Uppbúin rúm	Svefnpokapláss	Eldunaraðstaða í heimagistingu	Eldunaraðstaða í sérhúsi	Morgunverður	Máltíð samkvæmt beiðni
B180 Breiðavik vid Látrabjarg, 451 Patreksfj.	32			32	12	3			I	S		x	x	x
B185 Alviðra í Dýrafirði, 471 þingeyri	20	6		14	3	3		C	I	S		x	x	x
AB232 Bær í Strandas., 520 Drangsnes	16	8	8		4			G	I	S		x	x	x
AB234 Snartartunga í Bitrufirði, 500 Brú	5		1	4	2				I	S		x	x	x
BD240 Staðarskáli í Hrútafir i, 500 Brú	48	6		42	21			C	II/III	S			x	x
B250 Melstaður í Miðfirði, 531 Hvammstangi	12			12	5	1			II	S		x	x	
BC260 Brekkulækur í Miðfirði, 531 Hvammstangi	22			22	9	2			I/III				x	x
B265 Barkarstaðir í Miðfirði, 531 Hvammstangi	6			6	2	1			I	S		x	x	x

B180 Breiðavik — Gistiaðstaðan er í skólahúsnæði. Aðallega svefnpokapláss, en uppbúin rúm í 3 herbergjum. Látrabjarg er í 12 km fjarlægð. Mikið fuglalíf og falleg fjara. Silungsveiði í nágrenninu og fjallavötnum. Breiðavík stendur við veg nr. 612, sem liggur til Látrabjargs. **Opið:** 1.maí-30.sept. **Næsta þéttbýli/sundlaug/verslun:** Patreksfjörður 50 km.

B185 Alviðra — 1 x 6 manna sumarhús (2 svefnh.). Einnig er í boði gisting í sérhúsi á 2 hæðum. Máltíðir þarf að panta. Vel staðsett til skoðunarferða um Vestfirði, er miðsvæðis, 8 km frá vegi nr 60 við veg nr. 624. Gestgj. búa á Alviðru III, 150 m fjær, gestir snúi sér þangað. **Opið:** 1.maí - 30.sept. **Búskapur:** Kindur, hundur. **Næsta þéttbýli/golf/sundlaug:** Þingeyri 25 km, Flateyri 21 km, Ísafjörður 33 km.

AB232 Bær — 1 x 2ja eininga smáhýsi (1 svefnh. í hvorri ein). Vel staðsett til skoðunarf. um Strandirnar. Skammt frá landi er Grímsey í Steingrímsfirði. Hægt að fá skoðunarf. í eyjuna og siglingu í kringum hana, ef pantað er fyrirfram. Gæsa- og rjúpnav. Berjaland. Silungsv. í Kjalarvatni og Bæjarvötnum. Bær við veg nr. 645. **Opið:** allt árið. **Næsta þéttbýli:** Drangsnes 3 km. **Sundlaug:** Laugarhóll 17 km.

AB234 Snartartunga — 1 x 4 manna séríbúð (1 svefnherbergi) og 1 herbergi í heimagistingu. Vel staðsett til skoðunarferða um Strandirnar, Vestfirði, Dali og Hólmavík. Góðar gönguleiðir. Hestaleiga. Snartartunga stendur við veg nr. 61. **Opið:** 1.júní - 31.des. **Búskapur/gæludýr:** Kindur, hestar, hundur, köttur. **Næsta þéttbýli:** Hólmavík 54 km. **Verslun:** Óspakseyri 5 km. **Sundlaug:** Laugarhóll 75 km.

BD240 Staðarskáli — Nýtt vel búið gistihús, gisting á sérhæð í Staðarskála og 1 x 6 manna sumarbúst. (1 svefnh. og loft). Veitingastaður þar sem í boði eru heitar og kaldar máltíðir samkv. matseðli. Gæsav. á haustin. Hjólaleiga. Byggðasafn 12 km. Við veg nr.1, miðja leið milli Akureyrar og Reykjavíkur. **Opið:** Allt árið. **Næsta þéttbýli:** Hvammstangi 34 km. **Sundlaug:** Reykjaskóli 12 km.

B250 Melstaður — Uppbúin rúm á efri hæð. Svefnp.pláss í 4ra m. séríbúð í kjallara. Vatnsneshringurinn tilvalin dagsferð. Miðfjörður söguslóð Grettissögu. Mikið fuglalíf. Silungs- og gæsaveiði. Melstaður við veg nr. 704, vestan Miðfjarðarár, 1,5 km frá vegi nr. 1. **Opið:** Allt árið. Panta þarf fyrirfram 1.9.-1.6. **Búskapur/gæludýr:** Kindur, gæsir. **Næsta þéttbýli/sundlaug:** Laugarbakki 4 km, Hvammstangi 12 km. **Nettang:**Melstaður@mmedia.is.

BC260 Brekkulækur — Mikil áhersla lögð á lengri hestaferðir, 7-13 daga. T.d. eru ferðir yfir Arnarvatnsheiði í Húsafell, í Dalina og á Snæfellsnes. Einnig eru í boði skipulagðar göngu- og hjólaferðir. Brekkulækur er við veg nr. 704, 8 km frá vegi nr. 1. **Opið:** Allt árið. Panta þarf fyrirfram sept. - maí. **Búskapur:** Hestar. **Næsta þéttbýli:** Laugarbakki 10 km. **Sundlaug:** Hvammstangi 18 km.

B265 Barkarstaðir — Gistiaðstaða á sérhæð á bænum. Ókeypis veiði fyrir dvalargesti í Barkarstaðarvatni. Aðrir áhugaverðir veiðimöguleikar: Vötnin á Arnarvatnsheiði. Gæsa og rjúpnaveiði á haustin. Góðar gönguleiðir. Barkarstaðir eru við veg 704, 17 km frá vegi nr. 1.**Opið:** Allt árið. **Búskapur:** Kindur, hestar. **Næsta þéttbýli/sundlaug:** Laugarbakki 17 km, Hvammstangi 25 km.

Aðfangadagur er einum degi fyrir jól
Christmas Eve is one day before Christmas

Hann var fimm mínútum á eftir mér
He was five minutes behind me

Sumir koma alltaf nokkrum mínútum of seint
Some people are always several minutes too late

More about comparison in the next lesson.

Dialogue 3

Í skóbúð

*Þór needs a pair of winter boots. His friend Ragnar is coming along
with him to the shoe shop to advise him.*

AFGREIÐSLUMAÐUR: Góðan daginn, get ég aðstoðað ykkur?
ÞÓR: Já, ég er að leita að kuldaskóm.
AFGREIÐSLUMAÐUR: Við eigum nóga kuldaskó, hérna til hægri.
Þessir til dæmis eru mjög vinsælir.
ÞÓR: Já, mér líst vel á þá.
AFGREIÐSLUMAÐUR: Viltu máta þá?
ÞÓR: Já, takk.
AFGREIÐSLUMAÐUR: Hvaða númer notarðu?
ÞÓR: Númer 42. Þakka þér fyrir. Þeir passa
ágætlega. Hvað segirðu Ragnar, eru þetta
ekki flottir skór?
RAGNAR: Jú, mér sýnist það. Þeir líta út fyrir að vera
traustir og þægilegir.
AFGREIÐSLUMAÐUR: Góð gæði líka, og þú færð þá á mjög
hagstæðu verði, þeir kosta aðeins 5000 kr.
ÞÓR: Nú! Úr því að ég geri svona góð kaup ætla
ég að fá mér tvenna skó! Ég er nefnilega
mjög hrifinn af þessum fjólubláu hér. Ég ætla
að máta þá líka. Hvað kosta þeir?
AFGREIÐSLUMAÐUR: Þeir kosta 12.000 kr.
ÞÓR: Það er fjandi dýrt! Jæja, hvað um það, mig
vantar einmitt svona fína skó fyrir árs-
hátíðina. En þessir eru fullstórir. Áttu
númeri minna?
AFGREIÐSLUMAÐUR: Gjörðu svo vel.

ÞÓR:	Já, þeir virðast passa sæmilega. Hvað finnst þér Ragnar?
RAGNAR:	Já, ég er sammála þér, þeir eru alveg einstakir og fara þér mjög vel.
AFGREIÐSLUMAÐUR:	Nokkuð fleira fyrir ykkur?
ÞÓR:	Ég ætla að fá þrenna sokka, þessa íþróttasokka hér. Þá er það komið.

Vocabulary notes

get ég aðstoðað, *acc.*	can I help		**fjandi dýr**	darned expensive
leita (leita) að, *dat.*	look for		**hvað um það**	who cares
máta (máta), *acc.*	try on		**árshátíð (-ar, -ir)**	annual celebration/ staff party
númer (-s, -)	size			
gæði, *n.pl.*	quality		**full-**, *pref.*	very
hagstæð/ur, *adj.*	economical		**minni**, *comp.*	less, smaller
nú!	really!		**sæmilega**, *adv.*	fairly well
gera góð kaup	get a bargain		**þeir fara þér vel**	they look good on you
vera hrifin/n af, *dat.*	be very taken/ infatuated with			

Language points

Numerals with plural nouns

In the dialogue above, Þór thinks of buying **tvenna skó**, 'two pairs of shoes', and also purchases **þrenna sokka**, 'three pairs of socks'. These forms of the numbers 2 and 3 are different from the ones you already know. They are used specifically when counting items which come in pairs, such as **hanskar** 'gloves', and plural nouns such as **buxur**, **skæri**, 'scissors', **tónleikar** and **dyr**. These plural forms of the numbers 1–4 are: **einir, tvennir, þrennir, fernir**, and they are declined like strong adjectives – only in the plural of course. Plural nouns can only ever be counted with these forms of the numerals. In the case of items such as socks or gloves, however, the plural forms of the numerals are only used when the reference is to a pair, while an individual sock or glove is counted with the ordinary form of the numeral.

Exercise 3

Count the following items from 1 to 4, using the correct forms of the numerals depending on the gender of the individual nouns and whether they are plural nouns/pairs.

> *Dæmi:* **1, 2, 3, 4 skór: einir, tvennir, þrennir, fernir skór**

1, 2, 3, 4 gleraugu
1, 2, 3, 4 vettlingar
1, 2, 3, 4 skæri
1, 2, 3, 4 armbandsúr
1, 2, 3, 4 buxur
1, 2, 3, 4 dyr (*f.pl.*)

Language points

More noun groups

In Lesson 4, you learned about noun declensions in Icelandic. As you may have noticed since then, not all nouns conform to those patterns. There are various masculine and feminine nouns in particular which correspond to declension patterns that deviate in certain ways from the main pattern. These will be outlined here in so far as they are relevant for daily usage. Before moving on, however, it might be a good idea to brush up on the main declension patterns as well as on the vowel changes involved in the I-shift (Lesson 7).

Masculine nouns

There are two main subgroups for masculine noun declension. The first is not so very different from the main pattern: it has **-ir** and **-i** in the nominative and accusative plural where the main group has **-ar** and **-a**. In addition, many nouns belonging to this group (but not all) have **-ar** as a singular genitive ending, rather than the regular masculine genitive **-s**. So far so good, but where things can get a bit tricky is that the **-i** endings cause an I-shift where the stem vowel of the noun is susceptible. These are examples of the main patterns involved:

				á > æ	*ö > i/e and a*	*o > y*
sg.	*nom.*	fundur	bær	þáttur	fjörður/köttur	sonur
	acc.	fund	bæ	þátt	fjörð/kött	son
	dat.	fundi	bæ	þætti	firði/ketti	syni
	gen.	fundar	bæjar	þáttar	fjarðar/kattar	sonar
pl.	*nom.*	fundir	bæir	þættir	firðir/kettir	synir
	acc.	fundi	bæi	þætti	firði/ketti	syni
	dat.	fundum	bæjum	þáttum	fjörðum/köttum	sonum
	gen.	funda	bæja	þátta	fjarða/katta	sona

There is really no way to tell whether a masculine noun belongs to the main group or this one except by looking in the dictionary. You have to learn as you go. The second group, however, can be recognized very easily. It consists of nouns ending in **-andi**. In the singular, these nouns conform to the weak masculine declension pattern, but in the plural, **-i** changes to **-ur** in the nominative and accusative, with a vowel change occurring in the preceding syllable: **-andi** > **-endur**, as in **nemandi** > **nem*e*nd*u*r**.

Feminine nouns

For feminine nouns, too, there are two main subgroups. The first and largest makes its plural nominative and accusative with an **-ar** rather than an **-ir** ending. To these belong a significant number of feminine nouns without an ending, as well as all feminine nouns (a) of which the stem ends in **-ing** or (b) which have an **-i** ending. Note that these last two also have some special features in the singular: **-ing** nouns have a **-u** ending in the accusative and dative singular, while nouns ending in **-i** change the **-i** for **-ar** in the singular genitive as well as plural nominative and accusative. The second group has **-ur** in the plural nominative and accusative, with the **-u-** causing a vowel shift where the stem vowel is susceptible. Note that some (although not all) of the nouns with plural **-ur** also take **-ur** in the genitive singular. Here are some common examples:

						ó > æ	*ö > e and a*
sg.	*nom.*	laug	gisting	helgi	vík	bók	önd
	acc.	laug	gisting*u*	helgi	vík	bók	önd
	dat.	laug	gisting*u*	helgi	vík	bók	önd
	gen.	laugar	gistingar	helg*ar*	vík*ur*	bókar	*a*ndar

pl.	*nom.*	laug**ar**	gisting**ar**	helg**ar**	vík**ur**	bæk**ur**	end**ur**
	acc.	laug**ar**	gisting**ar**	helg**ar**	vík**ur**	bæk**ur**	end**ur**
	dat.	laugum	gistingum	helgum	víkum	bókum	öndum
	gen.	lauga	gistinga	helga	víka	bóka	**a**nda

Finally, note that there are also some feminine nouns with a stem ending **-i** that are indeclinable. Unfortunately you cannot tell them apart from nouns like **helgi**, so you will have to learn to recognize them yourself. Among the more common ones is **fræði**. Female personal names that do not end in **-a** take either an **-i** or **-u** ending in the accusative and dative: **Hildur** > **Hildi**, **Áslaug** > **Áslaugu**.

Neuter nouns

Fortunately for the student of Icelandic, there are very few deviating neuter nouns. There are some common weak neuter nouns ending in **-a** which keep **-a** throughout the singular and have **-u** (plus U-shift where applicable) in the plural, like **auga** – **augu** and **hjarta** – **hjörtu**. Then there are a few nouns with stem ending **-é** which changes to **-já** in the dative and genitive plural, like **tré** and **hné** (**trjám** – **trjáa** and **hnjám** – **hnjáa**), with the exception of **hlé** (no vowel change) and **fé** (no plural, **-já** in the genitive singular: **fjár**).

Exercise 4

Answer the questions below using the plural, as outlined in the example:

Dæmi: **Áttu vin?** →   **Já, ég á**
marga vini

1 Kaupirðu ávöxt?
2 Borðarðu rétt?
3 Sérðu ísbjörn?
4 Þekkirðu nemanda?
5 Kemurðu við á flugvelli?
6 Skoðarðu sýningu?
7 Heyrirðu í flugvél?
8 Lestu bók?
9 Ertu með skemmda tönn?
10 Ferðu í sundlaug?

Exercise 5: Nokkrar vegalengdir í kílómetrum

Can you tell the distances between the following Icelandic places in grammatically correct Icelandic sentences (writing out or saying the numbers in full)? Remember that the prepositions **frá** and **til** govern the dative and genitive case respectively.

Dæmi: **Akranes – Höfn, 493 km:** *frá Akranesi til Hafnar eru fjögur hundruð níutíu og þrír kílómetrar.*

1 Akureyri – Vík, 561 km
2 Borgarnes – Ísafjörður, 384 km
3 Grindavík – Reykjavík, 52 km
4 Selfoss – Þingvellir, 44 km
5 Kirkjubæjarklaustur – Egilsstaðir, 440 km
6 Ólafsfjörður – Akureyri, 61 km
7 Þingvellir – Borgarnes, 95 km

Reading 1

Hringferð um Grænland árið 2000

How long will the trip around Greenland be? What is the occasion for the organization of the trip? How much does the trip cost? Whose attention has it attracted?

Ferðaskrifstofa á Akureyri hyggst á aldamótaárinu 2000 bjóða upp á tveggja vikna flugferð í kringum Grænland með viðkomu á yfir tuttugu stöðum.

Þar mun þátttakendum getast kostur á að sjá ísbjarnabyggðir, sögufræga firði og njóta útsýnis yfir jakabreiður. Hringferðin um Grænland kostar eina milljón króna og er skipulögð í tilefni af þúsund ára landnámi Inúíta á Grænlandi.

Hringferðin hefur náð athygli manna erlendis ef marka má úttekt tímaritsins *For Him Magazine* á spennandi ævintýraferðum. Á lista yfir eitt hundrað spennandi ferðamöguleika fyrir þá sem vilja reyna eitthvað alveg nýtt er hún í öðru sæti.

Af öðrum spennandi ferðum á listanum má nefna flúðasiglingu niður Ganges-fljót, ferð niður að *Titanic*, átta mánaða rútuferð um Bali og hjólreiðaferð um Kúbu.

Announced in Morgunblaðið, 9 August 1998: 56

Vocabulary notes

hyggjast (hyggst) intend, plan
+ *inf.*

þátttakand/i participant
(-a, -ur)

gefast kostur be offered the
á, *dat.* possibility of

sögufræg/ur, *adj.* historically
famous

jakabreið/a glacial run-off
(-u, -ur) area

í tilefni af on the occasion of

marka (marka), take seriously, **ef
acc. marka má**, if
we may take
seriously

úttekt (-ar, -ir) appraisal, study

spennandi, exciting
adj.indecl.

í öðru sæti in second place

flúðir, *f.pl.* rapids

12 Tómstundir

Spare time

In this lesson you will learn about:

- sports and leisure activities
- reflexive verbs and pronouns
- the middle voice
- adverbs and intensifiers, making a point
- word order
- comparison
- negative pronouns **ekki neinn/nokkur** and **hvorugur**, emphatic negation

Dialogue 1

Íþróttaiðkun

Joyce has been invited to a party hosted by her friend Áslaug. There she meets and engages in an animated conversation with Höskuldur and his partner Birna. Why does Joyce not practise many sports? Why does Höskuldur exercise every day? What does Birna like doing after work?

HÖSKULDUR: Og hvað gerirðu þegar þú ert ekki að vinna Joyce?
JOYCE: Þá fer ég til Íslands til að slappa af og hvíla mig! Ég verð að viðurkenna að ég er ekki mikið fyrir hándavinnu og er lítil íþróttamanneskja, nema hvað ég syndi á morgnana, en þar með eru upptalin afskipti mín af íþróttum. Minn veikleiki er að ég tek alltaf vinnuna með mér heim.

HÖSKULDUR: Ég er ekki mjög spenntur fyrir íþróttum heldur, en mér finnst voða gott að fá útrás með líkamlegri áreynslu fyrst ég vinn kyrrsetustarf. Mér líður illa þegar ég fæ ekki tækifæri til að hreyfa mig, þess vegna skokka ég á hverjum degi. Ég vil komast í gott form ...

BIRNA: Og léttast!

HÖSKULDUR: Og leggja af, já! En hún Birna hérna, hún er mjög flink í lyftingum og vaxtarrækt, og fæst við handbolta líka ... keppir í liði. Hún leggur mikinn metnað í íþróttamennsku!

BIRNA: Já, ég hef óskaplega gaman af að keppa og stunda líkamsrækt. Íþróttaæfingar eru ómissandi hluti af daglegu lífi mínu! Mér finnst gott að koma heim eftir vinnudag og snúa mér að líkamsæfingum, þannig losna ég við streitu. Heilbrigð sál í hraustum líkama!

JOYCE: Satt segirðu! Ég er bara ekki nógu dugleg. Ég er afar upptekin í vinnunni og má bara ekki vera að því að fara á æfingu. En ég er farin að fá áhuga á að fara meira á gönguskíði þegar ég er í fríi. Ég hyggst meira að segja koma aftur til Íslands næsta vetur og taka þátt í gönguskíðaferð.

HÖSKULDUR: Þá höfum við sama áhugamálið! Við Birna förum gjarnan í gönguskíðaferðir á veturna. Þú skalt slást í för með okkur!

JOYCE: Það væri alveg ljómandi tækifæri til að æfa mig betur og sækja í mig veðrið ...

BIRNA: Og til að skemmta okkur saman!

Vocabulary notes

íþróttaiðkun	from **iðkun (-ar, -ir)**, practice and **íþrótt/ir**, *f.pl.* sports	**þar með er upptalin/n**, *adj.* **vera spennt/ur fyrir**, *dat.*	that is the sum of be keen on, get excited about
hvíla (hvíli) sig	rest (oneself)	**fá útrás**	vent, release
vera mikið fyrir, *acc.*	like a lot	**líkam/i (-a, -ar)** **líkamleg/ur**, *adj.*	body bodily, physical
handavinn/a	handiwork (knitting, sewing, needlework, etc.)	**fyrst**, *conj.* **kyrrsetustarf (-s, -)** **hreyfa (hreyfi) sig**	since, as sedentary work move, exercise

skokka (skokka)	jog	**ómissandi,**	indispensable
komast (kemst)	get (oneself)	*adj.indecl.*	
í gott form	into shape	**snúa (sný) sér**	turn to
léttast/leggja	lose weight	**að**, *dat.*	
(legg) af		**streit/a (-u)**	stress
lyfta (lyfti), *dat.*	lift (here 'lift	**heilbrigð/ur,**	healthy
	weights')	**hraust/ur**, *adj.*	
	lyftingar, *f.pl.*	**ég má ekki vera**	I don't have
	weight lifting	**að því**	the time for it
vaxtarrækt	body-building	**gönguskíði (-s, -)**	cross-country ski
(-ar), *f.*		**að fara á**	to cross-country
lið (-s, -)	team	**gönguskíði**	ski
leggja (leggur)	be very serious/	**áhugamál (-s, -)**	interest, hobby
mikinn	ambitious	**slást (slæst) í för**	join
metnað í	about	**sækja (sæki) í**	gather strength
-mennsk/a (-u)	-manship	**sig veðrið**	

Language points

Reflexive pronouns

Icelandic has many verbs that take a reflexive pronoun for their
object. The case of the pronoun depends on each individual verb.
For the first and second person singular and plural, the reflexive
pronoun is the same as the personal pronoun:

ég hreyfi mig	I move (myself)
við hvílum okkur	we rest (ourselves)
þú skemmtir þér	you enjoy yourself
þið æfið ykkur	you train (yourselves)

The reflexive pronoun for the third person singular and plural is
sig (*acc.*)/**sér** (*dat.*)/**sín** (*gen.*) It is the same for all genders:

hann rakar sig	he shaves (himself)
hún flýtir sér	she hurrries (herself)
barnið greiðir sér	the child combs (itself, i.e. its hair)

In the imperative, the reflexive pronoun remains: **hreyfðu þig!**
'move!', **æfið ykkur!** 'practise!'. As you can see, not all verbs that
are reflexive in English are reflexive in ný Icelandic, and the other
way around.

In Lesson 10, you learned that with the third person singular and plural you had to use the genitive form of the personal pronoun to express possession: **hjólið hennar**, **bíllinn þeirra**. However, this is not always the case. There is a special possessive pronoun for the third person: **sinn** (*f.* **sín**, *n.* **sitt**), declined just like **minn** and **þinn**, but it is only used when reflexive, that is to say, when the implied owner is also the subject of the sentence. Compare the following examples:

Jón notar hjólið sitt	Jón uses his (= Jón's) bike
but	
Jón notar hjólið hans	Jón uses his (= another boy's) bike
Mamma þvær barnið sitt	Mum washes her (own) child
but	
Mamma þvær barnið hennar	Mum washes her (= another woman's) child

Whether you use the reflexive possessive pronoun **sinn** or the genitive form of the personal pronoun completely changes the meaning of the sentence.

Exercise 1

The following sentences describe what Hrafn does every morning, but the printer has got them mixed up. Can you put them in a more logical order?

1 fer í vinnu	5 fer á fætur
2 klæðir sig	6 baðar sig
3 vaknar	7 rakar sig
4 greiðir sér	8 burstar í sér tennurnar

Can you describe your own morning routine in Icelandic?

Exercise 2

Your friend's six-year-old has stayed the night with you. Now you need to wake her up and get her ready for school. Tell her what to do, using the imperative form of the following verbs:

vakna – fara á fætur – þvo sér – klæða sig – greiða sér – borða morgunmatinn – bursta tennurnar – fara í skóla – gæta sín á bílunum 'watch out for cars'

The middle voice

The middle voice is a verb form in Icelandic that is easily distinguished by its **-st** endings. In principle, the middle voice is formed by adding **-st** to the infinitive or conjugated verb forms, as appropriate, with the following changes:

- Second and third person endings **-(u)r**, **-ð**, and **-rð** are deleted.
- Dentals (**ð**, **d**, **t**) are deleted before middle voice **-st** where deleted also in pronunciation.

Examples:

fá	**fást**	**koma**	**komast**	**breyta**	**breytast**
fæ	fæst	kem	kemst	breyti	breytist
færð	fæst	kemur	kemst	breytir	breytist
fær	fæst	kemur	kemst	breytir	breytist
fáum	fáumst	komum	komumst	breytum	breytumst
fáið	fáist	komið	komist	breytið	breytist
fá	fást	koma	komast	breyta	breytast

The middle voice is used to express the following:

1 Reflexivity

The middle voice can replace a reflexive pronoun, as in, for instance, the following:

Barnið meiðir sig = Barnið meiðist
the child hurts itself

Hann ætlar að gifta sig = Hann ætlar að giftast
He plans to get married

Note, however, that not all reflexive constructions can be replaced by a middle voice.

2 Reciprocity

The middle voice can add the meaning of 'each other' to a main verb:

Jón kveður Pal og Páll kveður Jón = Jón og Páll kveðjast
Jón and Páll take leave of each other

Þór hittir Hörpu og Harpa hittir Þór = Þór og Harpa hittast
Þór and Harpa meet each other

Kjartan talar við Sif og Sif talar við Kjartan = Kjartan og Sif talast við
Kjartan and Sif talk to each other

Við sjáumst!
(*lit.* 'We'll see each other')

3 Separate meaning or only existing form of the verb
The middle voice can give a verb a different meaning altogether:

koma come	**komast** get there
taka take	**takast** work, succeed
gera do	**gerast** happen

The middle voice often occurs in prepositional phrases and/or sayings, as we saw for instance in Dialogue 1: **fást við** 'take on', 'tackle', **slást í hópinn** 'join'. Another example: **búast við** (*dat.*) 'to expect'. The middle voice is also common in impersonal constructions, such as **mér finnst** and **mér leiðist**. In some cases, the middle voice is the only existing form of a verb, as is the case with, for instance, **ferðast** 'travel' and **nálgast** 'approach'.

4 Passive
This use of the middle voice will be dealt with in the next lesson.

Exercise 3

Fill in the blanks with the correct middle voice form of the verbs in brackets.

1 Hvað er að __________ (gera) hér?
2 Barninu __________ (leiða) heimaverkefnin.
3 Kemur hann bráðum? Ég __________ (búa) við því.
4 Áhugamál hans __________ (breyta) stöðugt.
5 Flugvélin __________ (nálgast) flugvöllinn.
6 Honum __________ (finna) erfitt að __________ (venja) tölvum.
7 Mér __________ (sýna) veðrið verða gott í dag.
8 Íslendingar sem __________ (þekkja) __________ (kyssa) þegar þeir __________ (hitta).

Dialogue 2

Áhugamál

At Áslaug's party, Þór and Harpa are talking about their interests with Kjartan and Sif from Vopnafjörður in Eastern Iceland. What instrument would Kjartan like to play? What kind of music does

Harpa like? Does Sif get the chance to go to the theatre in Vopnafjörður?

KJARTAN: Hvað segirðu Þór, ertu að læra á selló?

ÞÓR: Já, ég sæki sellótíma í tónlistarskólanum. Leikurðu á hljóðfæri?

KJARTAN: Nei, en mig langar að læra það.

ÞÓR: Hvaða hljóðfæri heillar þig mest?

KJARTAN: Ég heillast helst af píanói . . .

SIF: Og dundar sér oft við píanóið hans afa og reynir að kenna sjálfum sér að spila!

KJARTAN: En þú Harpa, heldur þú mikið upp á tónlist?

HARPA: Já, ég geri það svo sannarlega. Ég nýt lífsins helst þegar ég hlusta á klassíska, djass eða blús tónlist. Tónlist er í miklu uppáhaldi á okkar heimili!

HARPA: Hver eru þín áhugamál Sif?

SIF: Ég hef mikinn áhuga á mynd og leiklist.

ÞÓR: Þú færð þá sennilega ekki oft tækifæri til að sinna áhugamálum þínum þarna á Vopnafirði?

SIF: Oftara en fólk heldur. Áhuginn er að aukast meðal fólks á staðnum til að taka sig saman og skipuleggja ýmislegt. Það er afar öflugt félagslíf, og síðastliðið vor var til dæmis mikið um að vera.

ÞÓR: Eins og?

SIF: Eins og þorrablót, árshátíðir, starfsemi kórsins og leik-félagsins, myndlistarsýning Errós, dansleikir, prjóna-klúbburinn . . .

HARPA: Það kemur á óvart!

SIF: Það er mikil þörf fyrir tilbreytingu því á veturna er mun dýrara fyrir okkur að fara á leiksýningar í Reykjavík heldur en fólk sem býr á Akureyri eða Egilsstöðum!

Vocabulary notes

hljóðfæri (-s, -)	musical instrument	**svo sannarlega**, *adv.*	absolutely, definitely
heilla (heillar), *acc.*	enchant, attract	**myndlist (-ar)**, *f.*	visual arts
		leiklist (-ar), *f.*	drama, theatre
dunda (dunda) sér við, *acc.*	play about, busy oneself with	**sennilega**, *adv.*	probably
		sinna (sinni), *dat.*	attend to
halda mikið upp á, *acc.*	like very much	**aukast (eykst)**	increase
		öflug/ur, *adj.*	strong, powerful

kór (-s, -ar)	choir	**prjónaklúbb/ur (-s, -ar)**	knitting club
Erró	one of the most important and innovative twentieth-century Icelandic visual artists	**koma (einhverjum) á óvart**	surprise (someone)
		mun dýrara	quite a lot dearer
dansleik/ur (-ar, -ir)	dance		

Language points

Adverbs and intensifiers

Adverbs are among the easier aspects of Icelandic for the learner as they are not declined and are fairly easy to construct. The following are the main points to keep in mind about adverbs in Icelandic:

1 Adverbs can be derived from verbs, nouns or adjectives. Most end in **-lega**:

venja	custom	→ **venjulega**	customarily
hugsa	think	→ **hugsanlega**	conceivably
nýr	new	→ **nýlega**	lately

2 The position of the adverb in a regular sentence (i.e., a direct, affirmative sentence where the word order is subject – verb(s) – (prep.) – object) is:

- after the conjugated (modal) verb: **amma saknar** *oft* **stráksins** ...
- if the verb takes two objects, the adverb goes in between: **afi gefur krökkunum** *oft* **sælgæti**
- if the object is a pronoun not governed by a prepositional phrase, the pronoun takes precedence: **hún saknar hans** *oft* 'she often misses him'
- when the adverb qualifies an adjective or other adverb, it will precede that part of speech: **ég fer að hitta** *ákaflega* **þreyttan mann** 'I am going to meet a very tired man'; **við erum** *ekki* **oft heima** 'we aren't often home'
- finally, like adverbial phrases, adverbs also occur at the end of a sentence: **hún syngur lagið ágætlega** 'she sings the song quite well'.

3 Some common adverbs that do not end in **-lega** are:

góður → **vel**	**snemma**	early	**bráðum**	soon
vondur → **illa**	**varla**	hardly	**sjaldan**	seldom
seinn → **seint**	**svo(na)**	so, thus	**afar/mjög**	very
hraður → **hratt**	**gjarna(n)**	gladly	**stundum**	sometimes
hægur → **hægt**	**núna**	now	**alveg**	quite
	ansi, býsna	pretty	**frekar**	rather
	harla	extremely	**fjandi**	darned

Intensifiers

Adverbs are often used as intensifiers, particularly in daily speech, and can be very useful tools for the learner with an as yet limited vocabulary to make a point, express an emotional reaction, or simply to 'spice up' one's speech a little. Aside from the more neutral intensifying **mjög**, **afar** and **alveg**, many popular stronger intensifiers are based on adjectives and nouns which express an intensified emotion or state of being. You already encountered some in Lesson 8. Here are some more:

voði	danger	→ **voða(lega): þetta er voða(lega) skemmtilegt**
hræða	frighten	→ **hræðilega: hann syngur lagið hræðilega illa**
ósköp	something awful	→ **óskaplega (ósköp): það var óskaplega/ósköp indælt**
ákafur	enthusiastic	→ **ákaflega: hann er ákaflega þreyttur**
ferlegur	monstrous	→ **þau eru ferlega fátæk**
ótrúlegur	unbelievable	→ **barnið er ótrúlega klárt**

Note that with certain adjectives that already have a very strong meaning (such as **yndislegur** 'delightful', **stórbrotinn** 'magnificent', **gómsætur** 'delicious'), intensifiers are not really used, with the notable exception of **alveg**.

Exercise 4

The following is a description of an Icelandic holiday impression. Imagine it is yours and you want to spice it up a bit to make sure that your Icelandic friends know just how much you have enjoyed their country. Can you add the necessary intensifiers at the *, making sure to create effect without overdoing it or becoming too repetitive?

Landslagið er * fallegt, loftið er * hreint og fólkið * indælt. Það er * mikið að gera: * fallegar gönguleiðir alls staðar, og * skemmtilegt er að fara í hestaferðir á sumrin eða skíðaferðir á veturna. Það er líka * gaman að fara í sund: sundlaugarnar eru * góðar og heitu pottarnir * yndislegir(!) Maturinn er líka * góður, og það eru margir * fínir veitingastaðir í Reykjavík. Svo eru mörg og * áhugaverð söfn og gallerí í höfuðborginni, sem er * gott sérstaklega af því að veðrið getur stundum verið * leiðinlegt. Það versta er bara hvað allt er * dýrt!

Vocabulary notes

heitur pottur   hot pot (Icelandic swimming pools all have at least one 'hot pot' filled with water up to 42° C to sit in and relax. They are very popular with Icelanders and foreigners alike and often also function as a social gathering point.)

Reading 1

Besta fótboltastelpan

Hún skoraði glæsilegt mark í fyrri landsleik Íslendinga og Englendinga haustið 1994 og var þar með búin að sanna að hún er ein helsta knattspyrnukona Íslands. Margrét Ólafsdóttir var kjörin efnilegasti leikmaður ársins 1993 og besti leikmaðurinn 1994. Hún er bæði í landsliðinu U 20 og í aðalliðinu, en hún kippir sér augsýnilega ekki upp við velgengnina og telur mikilvægt að ofmetnast ekki. Margrét stundar nám við Verslunarskóla Íslands en ver mestu af frítíma sínum í fótboltaæfingar. Þegar Margrét er spurð hvað sé svona heillandi við fótboltann nefnir hún félagsskapinn. 'Mér finnst svo gaman að spila fótbolta', bætir hún við og brosir. 'Það fer auðvitað mikill tími í æfingar en ég held góðu sambandi við vini mína. ...' Margrét sér framtíðina fyrir sér áfram í fótboltanum. Hana langar að fara til útlanda og læra meira í fótbolta. Þýskaland eða Norðurlöndin eru ofarlega í huga hennar, en hún hefur ekki kynnt sér hvar hægt er að komast í atvinnumennsku í knattspyrnu. Hvað þarf til að verða svona góð knattspyrnukona? 'Það þarf til að leggja á sig mikla ástundun, æfa af fullum krafti og lifa heilbrigðu lífi. Einnig er nauðsynlegt að skipuleggja tímann vel til að komast yfir bæði æfingar og nám', segir Margrét og bætir við að foreldrar hennar séu einnig mikið íþróttafólk.

*Abridged from Elísabet Þorgeirsdóttir, 'Besta fótboltastelpan', *Nýtt líf,* 8.17 (1994): 94

Vocabulary notes

skoraði, past tense of **skora**	score
landsleik/ur (-s, -ir)	international match
kjörin/n, *adj.*	elected
leik-mað/ur (-manns, -menn)	player
kippa (kippi) sér ekki upp við, *acc.*	be unaffected by
ofmetnast (ofmetnast)	become arrogant
Verslunarskóli Íslands	secondary school in Reykjavík
verja (ver), *dat.*	use, spend
spurð/ur, *adj.*	asked
ofarlega, *adv.*	high up, in the forefront
ástundun (-ar), *f.*	diligence
kraft/ur (-s, -ar)	force
komast (komast) yfir, *acc.*	get a grip on, gain possession of

Exercise 5

Can you tell if the following statements about the text above are right or wrong?

	Rétt	Rangt
1 Margrét Ólafsdóttir hefur ofmetnast.	☐	☐
2 Hún er ekki lengur í skóla.	☐	☐
3 Hún heillast af knattspyrnu.	☐	☐
4 Allur tími hennar fer í fótboltaæfingar.	☐	☐
5 Hún hefur áhuga á að læra meira í fótbolta.	☐	☐
6 Hún er ákveðin að fara til Þýskalands eða Norðurlanda.	☐	☐
7 Það er mikilvægt að lifa heilbrigðu lífi.	☐	☐
8 Það er ekki hægt að stunda bæði nám og fótboltaæfingar.	☐	☐

Language points

Comparative and superlative

The comparative and superlative forms of adjectives are formed by adding an appropriate ending to the stem of the adjective.

Comparative: 'more'

The basic comparative ending is **-(a)r/i: rík/ur → ríkar/i, bjart/ur → bjartar/i**
Note, however, the following changes that may occur:

1 Adjectives with a two-syllable stem lose the second stem vowel: **fyndin/n → fyndnar/i**. Exceptions include adjectives ending in **-leg/ur** which become **-legr/i: falleg/ur → fallegr/i**.
2 With adjectives ending in **-l/l** or **n/n** (but not **-in/n** as under 1), the comparative **-r** is assimilated into **-l** or **-n: fín/n → fínn/i, sæl/l → sæll/i**.
3 Adjectives of which the stem ends in a vowel take double **-r: grá/r → grárr/i**.
4 I-shift may occur where stem vowels are susceptible: **fár → færr/i, stór → stærr/i, lang/ur → lengr/i, ung/ur → yngr/i**.

The comparative ending **-i** remains the same for all genders and cases in the singular and the plural except the neuter singular, where it changes to **-a**:

gjöfin er dýrar*i* – **húsið er dýrar*a***

The conjunction **því ... því** is used with the comparative in Icelandic where English uses 'the ... the': **því meira því betra** 'the more the better'.

Superlative

The basic superlative ending is **-ast/ur: rík/ur – ríkar/i – ríkast/ur, bjart/ur – bjartar/i – bjartast/ur, fyndin/n – fyndnar/i – fyndnast/ur, falleg/ur – fallegr/i – fallegast/ur, fínn – fínn/i – fínast/ur, sæl/l – sæll/i- sælast/ur, grá/r – grárr/i – gráast/ur**.
Note, however, the following:

1 **-j-** insertion occurs between **-æ-** or **-ý-** and **-astur**: **ný/r – nýrr/i
– nýjast/ur**.
2 Many adjectives subject to the I-shift only take **-stur**: **fæst/ur,
stærst/ur, lengst/ur, yngst/ur**.

Unlike the comparative, superlative adjectives are declined according to the regular strong or weak declension patterns. The **-a-** in **-ast/
ur** is subject to a U-shift: **bíllinn hans er dýrastur, gjöfin hennar er
dýrust**. Note, too, that superlatives tend to get the strong declension
in nominal predicates, and the weak one in other positions:

hann er sterkastur   –   hann er sterkasti maður heims

The following adjectives have irregular comparatives and superlatives:

góður	**betri**	**bestur**
slæmur/vondur	**verri**	**verstur**
mikill	**meiri**	**mestur**
lítill	**minni**	**minnstur**
margir	**fleiri**	**flestir**
gamall	**eldri**	**elstur**

Adjectives which only exist in the comparative and superlative:

nærri	**næstur**	near/est
fyrri	**fyrstur**	first, earlier
síðari	**síðastur**	later, last
efri	**efstur**	upper/most
neðri	**neðstur**	lower/most
skárri	**skástur**	a little better/best of a bad thing

Finally, indeclinable adjectives, mostly those ending in a vowel
(notably **-andi**) do not have comparative and superlative forms.
Instead, the adverbs **meira** and **mest** are used.

A few more things about adverbs

1 The adverbs used to qualify the comparative and superlative are
miklu and **lang-** or **al-** respectively: **hann er miklu ríkari en ég, en hún
er langríkust**. Instead of **miklu**, **mun** is also found (see Dialogue 2).

2 Some adverbs can in themselves occur in comparative and
superlative forms. These forms correspond to those of adjectives:
-(a)ra and **-(a)st**:

Hann hleypur lengra en ég, en hún hleypur lengst af öllum.

The following are irregular comparative and superlative adverbs:

vel	betur	best
illa	verr	verst
mjög	meir(a)	mest
snemma	fyrr	fyrst
varla	síður	síst
gjarna(n)	heldur	helst

Similarity and dissimilarity

When comparing dissimilarities, Icelandic uses the conjunction **en** 'than': **hann er stærri *en* ég**. When comparing similarities, you can use **jafn** plus **og** or the dative case, or **eins** followed by **og** 'as … as': **hún er jafnstór mér** or **hún er eins stór og ég = við erum jafnstórar** 'we are the same height'. **Sem** is also found: **sterkur sem naut** 'strong as an ox'.

For things that are alike, there is **lík/ur** (strong adjective) plus dative case: **hann er líkur pabba sínum** 'he's like his dad'. For things that are the same, you can use **sama (og)** 'the same (as)' (weak adjective declension) or **eins** 'the same':

Enginn er eins	No one person is the same
Það er sama sagan hér	It's the same story here
Mér er sama	It's all the same to me, I don't care

Exercise 6

Arrange the following in order of size as suggested by the prompt and express this in the form of a sentence, using the comparative and superlative. The last three have no set answer.

Dæmi: *skemmtilegur* **Charlie Chaplin, Goldie Hawn, Mr Bean: Chaplin er skemmtilegur, Goldie Hawn er skemmtilegri, en Mr Bean er alskemmtilegastur**

stór	Ísland	Frakkland	Kanada
lítill	köttur	fugl	mús
gamall	Mick Jagger	Boris Jeltsin	Jón Páll II
hár	Hallgrímskirkja (R'vík)	Eiffelturninn (Paris)	Frelsisstyttan (New York)
þungur	tíu kíló	fimmtíu kíló	hundrað kíló

erfiður	málfræði	stærðfræði	leikfimi
ungur	móðir mín	bróðir/systir	ég
góður/vondur	appelsína	súkkulaði	ís

Language points

Negative pronouns

Earlier you encountered the negative pronoun **enginn**, the opposite of **einhver** and **allur** (Lesson 8), as well as **nokkur** in anticipation of a negative answer (Lesson 11). Aside from these, the constructions **ekki neinn** and **ekki nokkur** are rather common in Icelandic. They are in fact fully interchangeable with **enginn**, with **ekki nokkur** being slightly stronger in meaning than the other two. There are two exceptions:

1 **Ekki neinn** can never be used as the subject of a sentence:

enginn er heima   ***ekki neinn er heima**

2 **Enginn** should not be used after prepositional phrases:

***hún talar við engan**   **hún talar ekki við neinn**

Note the placement of the preposition.

Instead of **ekki** it is also possible to have **aldrei** (never) or **hvergi** (nowhere) in these constructions. Finally, **neinn** is declined exactly like the numeral **einn**.

The negative counterpart to the dual pronoun **báðir** is **hvorugur** 'neither', usually found in the singular and declined like a strong adjective. **Hvorugur** can be followed by a singular noun with the definite article, or by a plural noun or pronoun in the genitive (partitive):

Eru báðir strákarnir úti?
Nei, hvorugur strákurinn er úti
or **hvorugur strákanna/þeirra er úti**

The gender of **hvorugur** depends on the noun it stands with, while its case depends on its position in the sentence.

The Icelandic counterpart to 'none' is **enginn** or **ekki neinn** followed by the appropriate noun or pronoun in the genitive: **eru allir strákarnir úti? Nei, enginn strákanna/þeirra er úti.** The Icelandic for 'not ... either' is **ekki (...) heldur: Ætlar hún út? Nei, og ég ætla ekki út heldur** (or: **ég ætla heldur ekki út**).

Emphatic negation

Emphatic negation can be expressed first of all by changing the position of the negative adverb to the beginning or end of a sentence, as in the following:

ég ætla ekki að fara þangað – *ekki* **ætla** *ég* **að fara þangað!**
Ég kaupi ekki bókina – **ég kaupi bókina** *ekki!*

Ekki neinn or **ekki nokkur** can be replaced by **ekki einn einasti** for emphasis:

Hún talar ekki við einn einasta mann
She doesn't talk to a single person

Other expressions of emphatic negation are: **aldrei framar** 'never again', **aldrei á ævinni** 'never in my life', **það kemur ekki til greina/mála** 'it's out of the question', **engan veginn** 'no way', **alveg útilokað(ur)** 'out of the question'. The following expressions contain a negation but are actually emphatically affirmative: **enginn vafi (á því)** 'no doubt (about it)', **eflaus/vafalaus** 'doubtless', **engin spurning** 'no question about it'.

Reading 2
Láttu þér líða vel!

Why is lifestyle important? How can we reduce stress? How do most of us get to work? What kinds of exercise can most of us practise?

Heilsuefling og vellíðan hefjast hjá okkur. Lífsstíll hefur veruleg áhrif á það hvernig okkur líður, bæði andlega og líkamlega, en við berum ábyrgð á eigin lífsstíl. Flest okkar njóta ekki frístunda, en hvíld er jafn mikilvæg og áreynsla. Við stuðlum að vellíðan með því að láta hæfileika okkar njóta sín í starfi og leik, og fá útrás fyrir sköpunargleði í vinnu og tómstundum. Streita veldur mörgum erfiðleikum, en þegar við lærum að slaka á, til dæmis með tónlist eða íhugun, og fáum útrás fyrir spennu með líkamlegri áreynslu, finnum við minna fyrir streitu. Við keyrum flest í vinnu heldur en að ganga eða hjóla, og gefum okkur varla eða engan tíma fyrir daglega hreyfingu, líkamsrækt eða tóm til frístunda. Hreyfing og íþróttaiðkun er holl fyrir líkama og sál, og öll hreyfing, allt frá léttri göngu til þungra íþróttaæfinga hefur góð áhrif á líkamann og einnig á andlega streitu, því við það losnar um spennu. Við verðum að hreyfa okkur reglulega og þetta verður að vera hluti af daglegu lífi. Það er næstum öllum hægt að stunda göngu eða sund. Byrjaðu hægt og byggðu upp smátt og smátt.

Vocabulary notes

heilsuefling (-ar, -ar) — increasing one's health

vellíðan (-ar), *f.* — well-being

hafa áhrif á, *acc.* — have influence on

andlega, *adv.* — mentally, spiritually

bera ábyrgð á, *dat.* — be responsible for

njóta (nýt) sín — use to full capacity, come into one's own

stuðla (stuðla) að, *dat.* — work for, help achieve something

með því að, *inf.vb.* — by (. . .ing)

sköpunargleði, *f.indecl.* — creative joy

valda erfiðleikum — cause difficulties

finna (finn) fyrir, *dat.* — feel (something)

13 Ísland

Iceland

In this lesson you will learn about:

- Icelandic geography
- present and past participles
- impersonal passive construction of intransitive verbs
- enjoying the outdoors
- pro-forms
- weather and wind directions
- passive use of the middle voice

Reading 1

Ísland

Does the President live in Reykjavík? How is hot water utilized? What is the climate like? What is so special about Þingvellir?

Ísland var byggt á níundu öld, og var Ingólfur Arnarson fyrsti íslenski landnámsmaðurinn. Lýðveldið Ísland er tæplega 60 ára gamalt. Forsetinn býr á Bessastöðum á Álftanesi, fyrir sunnan Reykjavík. Helstu atvinnuvegir hafa verið sjávarútvegur og landbúnaður, en sívaxandi fjöldi fólks starfar við þjónustu og viðskipti.

Ísland er fjalllent, og á sumum hæstu fjöllunum eru jöklar. Stærsti jökullinn er Vatnajökull, sem er jafnstór Lúxemborg. Það eru einnig margar ár og mörg vötn á Íslandi, og víða í ám eru fallegir fossar, eins og Dettifoss, stærsti foss Evrópu. Í ánum er líka mikið af laxi og silungi, sem mörgum þykir gaman að veiða. Það er hins vegar lítið af trjám á Íslandi.

Inn í landið ganga margir firðir og víkur, nema á suðurströndinni, þar sem eru miklir sandar. Í hafinu umhverfis Ísland eru auðug fiskimið og víða eru góðar hafnir. Eldfjöll á Íslandi eru mörg, og sum þeirra eru virk. Frægasta eldfjallið er vafalaust Hekla, sem gaus síðast árið 2000.

Víða á Íslandi eru laugar (þegar vatnið sem kemur upp úr jörðinni er volgt) og hverir (þegar vatnið kemur upp sjóðandi). Þekktasti goshver á Íslandi er Geysir, og eru goshverir í mörgum erlendum tungumálum kenndir við hann. Heita vatnið er notað á ýmsan hátt, meðal annars í sundlaugar sem eru víða um land, og fara margir í sund á hverjum degi allt árið. Flest hús á Íslandi eru hituð upp með heitu vatni, sem og gróðurhúsin. Gufan er notuð til að framleiða rafmagn, en einnig eru sumar stórar og straum-þungar ár virkjaðar til rafmagnsframleiðslu.

Það er ekki eins kalt á Íslandi og margir halda, en veðráttan er óstöðug, og oft er margs konar veður sama daginn. Á hálendinu er kaldara en niðri á láglendi og við strendur, og þar er lítill gróður. Vegna veðurs eru samgöngur sums staðar stundum erfiðar, og oft er ófært mikinn hluta vetrar. Flogið er til flestra kaupstaða.

Þingvellir eru frægasti sögustaður á Íslandi. Árið 930 var þar stofnað Alþingi og var fundað þar árlega þangað til Ísland varð hluti norska konungsríkisins (1262–4). En þar er líka mikil og sér-stæð náttúrufegurð. Þingvellir voru friðaðir og gerðir að þjóðgarði árið 1928.

Vocabulary notes

atvinnuveg/ur (-s, -ir)	industry, area of employment
landbúnað/ur (-ar), *m.*	agriculture
sívaxandi, *adj.indecl.*	ever-increasing
fjalllent, *adj.*	mountainous (from **fjall (-s, -)** mountain)
á (-r, -r), *f.*	river
vatn (-s, -)	lake
fiskimið (-s, -)	fishing grounds
virk/ur, *adj.*	active, functioning
fræg/ur, *adj.*	famous
gjósa (gýs, gaus, gosið)	erupt
kenna (kenni, kennt) við, *acc.*	name for, name after
framleiða (framleiði, framleitt), *acc.*	produce
framleiðsl/a (-u)	production

rafmagn (-s), *n.*	electricity
straumþung/ur, *adj.*	fast-flowing, with a strong current
virkja (virkja, virkjað), *acc.*	utilize hydroelectric/geothermal power
óstöðug/ur, *adj.*	unsteady, unstable, variable
samgöngur, *f.pl.*	transport between places, communications
ófær, *adj.*	impassable, incapable
oft er ófært	often the roads are impassable
sögustað/ur (-ar, -ir)	historical site
friðað/ur, *adj.*	declared a national monument, protected area
þjóðgarð/ur (-s, -ar)	national park

Language points

Present participles

These are formed by adding the suffix **-andi** to the stem of a verb. They can be used in four different ways:

1 Adjectives: **það er mjög** *spennandi* **bók** 'it's a very exciting/thrilling book'.
2 Adverbs: **hann er** *rennandi* **blautur** 'he is soaking wet'.
3 Verbs: **barnið er** *sofandi* **en mamman er** *vakandi* 'the child is sleeping but the mother is waking'.
4 Nouns: **hún er** *nemandi* **í Íslensku fyrir** *byrjendur* 'she's a student in Icelandic for beginners'.

Note that present participles are indeclinable as adjectives. As nouns, they are declined as weak masculine nouns with an irregular **-endur** ending (see Lesson 9).

Past participles

These are slightly more complex, as their form depends on which group the verb belongs to:

    -a- group: the past participle ends in **-að**, or **-ast** in the middle voice:

        tala – talað, borða – borðað, friða – friðað, kallast – kallast

    -i- group: past participle ends in **-t**, in the middle voice the **-t** is dropped before **-st**:

> **senda – sent, hætta – hætt, reykja – reykt, kyssast – kysst, heyrast – heyrst**

all other groups: past participle ends in **-ið**, often with a vowel change in the stem:

> **skilja – skilið, fremja – framið, brjóta – brotið, fá – fengið, lesa – lesið**

Middle voice **-ist**:

> **brjótast – brotist, búast – búist**

The vowel changes that occur in past participles are not always regular. The following is a rough indication intended to help you along:

	Stem vowel	PP vowel	
-ur- group:	**-e-**	**-a-**	**semja – samið**
(and some **-ja**	**-y/ý-**	**-u/ú-**	**flýja – flúið**
verbs from **-i-**)			
strong verbs:	**-í-**	**-i-**	**bíta – bitið**
	-jó/jú/ú-	**-o-**	**fljúga – flogið**
	-e/(j)a-	**-o-**	**gjalda – goldið**
	-i-	**-u/e-**	**finna – fundið, sitja – setið**
	-e-	**-e-**	**lesa – lesið, gefa – gefið**

Not all verbs correspond to this pattern, but you will quickly pick up the most common ones.

Past participles as adjectives

When used as adjectives, past participles adapt their form to the gender of the (pro)noun they qualify. The gender forms are as follows:

	Masc.	Fem.	Neut.	
1	**-að/ur**	**-uð**	**-að**	**kallaður–kölluð–kallað**
2	**-ð/d/t/ur**	**-ð/d/t**	**-t**	**gerður–gerð–gert**

(for choice of **-ð**, **-d** or **-t**, follow the rules for imperative suffixes)

	Masc.	Fem.	Neut.	
3	**-in/n**	**-in**	**-ið**	**brotinn–brotin–brotið**

-a- and **-i-** groups are declined like regular adjectives ending in **-ur**. The others are declined like adjectives ending in **-in/n** which are subject to fraction in some cases (e.g. **opinn**, see Grammar Summary).

Impersonal passive of intransitive verbs

Impersonal constructions are common in Icelandic. You already encountered one variant in Lesson 8. Passive constructions, too, are much more common in Icelandic than, say, in English. They are used when the agent of the action expressed by the verb is of minor or no importance, i.e. who 'does' something does not really matter. What, in fact, characterizes the passive voice is that the object of the verb becomes the subject of the sentence, followed by the appropriate form of **vera** and the past participle (in its neuter form). But what if it is a verb that does not take an object, so that there is nothing to take the role of subject? In Icelandic that is not a problem: you just make do without a proper subject. This can be achieved in two different ways:

1 The word order is changed so that the subject slot left empty is filled by another part of speech, for instance an adverb or adverbial phrase:

> **Við biðum lengi** → (*... **var beðið lengi**) → *lengi* **var beðið**
> 'the wait was long'
> **Þau fljúga ekki þangað** → (*... **er ekki flogið þangað**) →
> **þangað er ekki flogið/ekki er flogið þangað** 'there are no flights (to) there'

2 The dummy subject **það** is used to fill the subject slot:

> **Við biðum lengi** → (*... **var beðið lengi**) → *það* **var beðið lengi**
> **Þau fljúga ekki þangað** → (*... **er ekki flogið þangað**) → *það* **er ekki flogið þangað**

These impersonal constructions with dummy **það** are particularly common in daily speech with prepositional phrases, and are often very difficult to translate directly into English:

Það er gert við húsið	The house is being fixed up
Það er horft alltof mikið á sjónvarpið	People watch too much television

Exercise 1

Find all participles in Reading 1. Are they present or past participles? How are they used? In what form do they occur and why?

Exercise 2

Turn each of the following active sentences into two impersonal passive ones, once using **það**, and once by changing the word order. *Dæmi:* **Við reykjum ekki á þessu heimili** → *Það er ekki reykt á þessu heimili – Á þessu heimili er ekki reykt*

1 Þeir tala mikið í símann.
2 Þau vaka alla nóttina.
3 Þær gista oft á hóteli.
4 Við hlæjum að þessu (-æj- → -eg-).
5 Við hlustum aldrei á fréttirnar.
6 Við dönsum mikið í veislunni.

Dialogue 1 ▓

Útivist

Richard phones up the Íslenskir Fjallaleiðsögumenn, who specialize in outdoors trips, to ask about guided tours into the Icelandic interior. How long does Richard want to go for? What level is he looking for? Does he need to rent a special car?

RICHARD: Góðan daginn, mig langar að fá upplýsingar um bakpokaferðir inn í óbyggðir sem standa til í lok júlí. Ég verð á Íslandi í tvær vikur og hef áhuga á að fara í nokkra daga gönguferð með ykkur ef hægt er.

LEIÐSÖGN: Já, það er hægt. Þá bjóðum við t.d. upp á fjögurra daga ferð frá Núpsstaðarskógum inn í Djúpárdal á Suðausturlandi.

RICHARD: Hvað er ferðin erfið?

LEIÐSÖGN: Hún er miðlungserfið. Þú þarft helst að vera í sæmilega góðu formi og hafa eitthvað stundað gönguferðir.

RICHARD: Það hentar ágætlega. Getur þú sagt mér aðeins meira frá ferðinni, hvenær hún verður, hvar hún byrjar og um hvaða svæði er gengið?

LEIÐSÖGN: Sjálfsagt. Ferðin byrjar í Skaftafelli. Þaðan er ekið að Núpsá og farið yfir ána á ferjubát, og síðan ekið í Núpsstaðarskóga. Svo er gengið meðfram Núpsárgljúfrum og tjaldað við Smalavað. Næsta dag er gengið að Grænalóni og þaðan vestur Beinadal. Á þriðja degi er gengið að Djúpá. Fjórða daginn göngum við til suðurs meðfram giljum og fossum niður í Djúpárdal og skoðum Djúparfoss og Fossabrekku áður en komið er í byggð. Ferðin endar með grillveislu í Skaftafelli.

RICHARD: Mér líst mjög vel á þetta. Nú verð ég í Reykjavík eftir ég kem til landsins. Hvað er langt að keyra í Skaftafell?

LEIÐSÖGN: Það eru um það bil 400 kílómetrar eftir þjóðveginum.

RICHARD: Er vegurinn fær venjulegum bílum eða ætti ég helst að leigja fjórhjóladrifinn bíl?

LEIÐSÖGN: Nei nei, það er allt í lagi að koma á venjulegum bíl.

RICHARD: Hvaða útbúnað á ég að taka með í ferðina?

LEIÐSÖGN: Ég skal taka niður heimilisfangið þitt og setja útbúnaðarlista í póst til þín.

Vocabulary notes

óbyggð (-ar, -ir)	wilderness, uninhabited area, vs. **byggð**, inhabited/cultivated area
standa (stend – staðið) til	happen, be in the works/planned
miðlungs-	average
stunda (stunda, stundað), *acc.*	pursue, practise
gil (-s, -)	ravine
grillveisla	from **grill (-s, -)**, barbecue, and **veisl/a (-u, -ur)**, party
þjóðveg/ur (-ar, -ir)	main road
fjórhjóladrifin/n, *adj.*	four-wheel drive

Exercise 3

Richard has received his equipment list and is packing for his wilderness trip, but is getting rather flustered. He has collected everything listed on the left. From the list on the right what should he remember to take as well?

Pakkað niður í bakpokann	*Hvað fleira?*
léttur og fyrirferðarlítill svefnpoki	bækur?
prímus og pottur	póstkort?
hitabrúsi	vatnsbrúsi?
drykkjarílát	hjól?
plástur	gönguskór?
hreinlætisvörur	skíði?
áttaviti	ullarpeysa?

legghlífar til að vaða yfir á	útvarp?
strigaskór til að vaða í	vasahnífur?
ullarnærföt og tvennir ullarsokkar	klósettpappír?
bómullarskyrta	vettlingar og húfa?
göngubuxur	rúm?
vasaljós	diskur?
regngallar	blóm?
nesti: þurrkaður matur	sundföt?
smávegis varamatur	sími?

Vocabulary notes

fyrirferðarlítil/l, *adj.*	compact	**hreinlætisvörur**, *f.pl.*	toiletries
brús/i (-a, -ar)	flask		
ílát (-s, -)	container	**áttavit/i (-a, -ar)**	compass
plástur (-s, -), *m.*	plaster, band-aid	**legghlíf (-ar, -ar)**	legging

Dialogue 2

Exercise 4

You too would like to experience a hiking trip through the Icelandic interior and decide to ring the Tourist Information Centre for more information. Can you fill in the gaps in the following dialogue?

UFR: Upplýsingamiðstöð ferðamála í Reykjavík, góðan dag.
YOU: (1 *Hello, I am planning to travel to Iceland in August and I would like to get information about trips into the wilderness.*)

UFR: Ertu að hugsa um gönguferð, hestaferð, skíðaferð ...
YOU: (2 *A hiking trip*)

UFR: Og hvað ætlarðu að vera lengi?
YOU: (3 *Several days*)

UFR: Ertu tilbúinn til að tjalda eða ætlarðu að gista í skála?
YOU: (4 *I'm quite ready to camp.*)

UFR: Ertu reyndur göngumaður?
YOU: (5 *I'm an average hiker.*)

UFR: Ég skal gefa þér símanúmerið hjá Útivist. Þeir bjóða upp á spennandi gönguferðir sem eru mjög vinsælar. Leiðsögumennirnir eru allir reyndir fjallamenn.

YOU: (6 *Lovely, thank you very much*)

Exercise 5

This is a description the wilderness tour guide gives you over the phone concerning a trip you are interested in. Change it into the impersonal passive, as it would appear in a tourist brochure.

Dæmi: **Við keyrum út á flugvöll → Það er keyrt út á flugvöll.**

Við *fljúgum* frá Reykjavík til Ísafjarðar, og *siglum* þaðan í Hestfjörð. Svo *göngum* við frá Hesteyri yfir í Aðalvík, og *endum* í Hornvík og *gistum* þar í sæluskála. Næsta daginn *tökum* við Fagranesið til baka til Ísafjarðar.

Exercise 6

Below are listed some of the rules of conduct for campers in Iceland. Read them and see if you can do the following:

1 Drive up, put up your gear and go to sleep.   yes/no
2 Go for a drive in the midnight sun around the area.   yes/no
3 Have a cup of tea before you go to sleep.   yes/no
4 Go for a walk at 6 in the morning.   yes/no
5 Gather up your rubbish and leave it in a bag near
   your tent.   yes/no

Umgengnisreglur á tjaldsvæðum

a   Gestir skulu tilkynna komu sína hjá umsóknarmanni og greiða dvalargjöld
b   Umferð bíla á tjaldsvæðum er ekki leyfð frá kl. 23 til kl. 07
c   Víndrykkja er bönnuð á tjaldsvæðum
d   Sorp skal láta í þar til gerð ílát
e   Ekki skal kveikja eld nema með leyfi umsjónarmanns

Language points

Pro-forms

Pro-forms are short words that take the place of nominals or parts of sentences to avoid repetition. The most familiar examples are pronouns, which replace nouns. **Það** is the most common pro-form in Icelandic. Apart from its role as a neuter singular pronoun and its function as dummy subject in passive constructions explained above, **það** is used as follows:

1 It replaces part of a sentence:

'Hann segir *að hann ætli í gönguferð á morgun.*' 'Segir hann það virkilega?'
'He says *that he is going on a hiking trip tomorrow.*' 'Does he really say *that?*'

2 Initially, it often stands in for a subject that follows later on in the sentence (English 'there's'):

Það er *mús* **í baðkerinu**	There's a mouse in the bath tub
Það gerist *eitthvað skemmtilegt* **í kvöld**	There's something fun happening tonight

3 It serves as a dummy subject in sentences without agency (most commonly weather descriptions):

Það rignir mikið í dag	It's raining a lot today
Það verður hlýtt um helgina	It's going to be warm at the weekend

Note that in all cases where **það** serves as a surrogate subject (passive, and 2 and 3 above), it is dropped whenever the word order is changed so that another part of speech fills the subject slot:

Oft er hlustað á útvarpið – Í baðkerinu er mús – Rignir mikið í dag?

Reading 2

Landshlutar

What is Snæfellsnes most famous for? Why do few people live in the West Fjords? What is special about Egilsstaðir? Why does most agriculture take place in the south? Why are there hardly any fishing towns there?

Landshlutarnir eru Vesturland, Vestfirðir, Norðurland vestra, Norðurland eystra, Austurland, Austfirðir, Suðausturland, og Suðurland. Höfuðborgarsvæðið og Reykjanes kallast Suðvesturhornið. Á Vesturlandi eru tveir stórir flóar, Faxaflói og Breiðafjörður, og gengur langt nes út milli þeirra sem heitir Snæfellsnes. Þar er einn af frægustu og fegurstu jöklum heims: Snæfellsjökull. Jules Verne skrifaði um Snæfellsjökul í bókinni sinni frægu, *Leyndardómi Snæfellsjökuls.* Vestfirðir eru strjálbýlir, vegna þess að samgöngur eru oft erfiðar og jarðvegur rýr, en þar eru margir góðir varpstaðir. Svæðið er fjalllent og landslagið stórbrotið. Aðalkaupstaðurinn er Ísafjörður. Á Norðurlandi er stærsti bær utan höfuðborgarsvæðisins, Akureyri, og einn þekktasti staðurinn á landinu, Mývatn. Landslagið þar var mótað af eldgosum, og er jarðhiti virkjaður við fjallið Kröflu. Á Austfjörðum eru há fjöll og þröngir firðir, svipað og á Vestfjörðum. Á Austurlandi er stærsti skógur á Íslandi, Hallormsstaðaskógur, sem er 2000 hektarar að stærð. Egilsstaðir eru einn fárra kaupstaða sem liggja ekki að sjó. Suðurlandið er mesta landbúnaðarsvæði á Íslandi, enda er þar mikið undirlendi og jarðhiti víða. Þar eru líka margir ferðamannastaðir, s.s. (svo sem) Skaftafell, Þórsmörk, Jökulsárlón og Hvannadalshnúkur, sem er hæsta fjall landsins (2119 m). Ströndin er að mestu hafnlaus, enda mjög hættuleg skipum, og hafa mörg farist þar.

* Adapted from Jón Gíslason and Sigríður Þorvaldsdóttir,
Landsteinar (Reykjavík 1995)

Vocabulary notes

fagur, *adj. superl.* **fegurst/ur**	beautiful
Leyndardómur Snæfellsjökuls	*Journey to the Centre of the Earth*
strjálbýl/l, *adj.*	sparsely populated
jarðveg/ur (-s), *m.*	soil
rýr, *adj.*	sparse, scanty
varpstað/ur (-ar, -ir)	breeding ground, nesting place for birds
móta (móta, mótað), *acc.*	form, mould
þröng/ur, *adj.*	narrow
skóg/ur (-ar, -ar)	forest
undirlendi (-s), *n.*	lowland
hafnlaus, *adj.*	harbourless

Language points

Vindáttir *(wind directions)*

The four wind directions in Icelandic are: **norður – austur – suður – vestur**. Their form and usage depends very much on their position and function in the sentence.

1 Adverbs

- motion towards: **norður – austur – suður – vestur**
- motion from: **(að) norðan – (að) austan – (að) sunnan – (að) vestan**
- rest: **fyrir norðan – fyrir austan – fyrir sunnan – fyrir vestan**

Comparative: **norðar/nyrst – austar/austast – syðra/syðst – vestar/vestast**

2 Nouns *norður – austur – suður – vestur*

Only used in connection with the directions themselves, however:

Roðinn í austri   the red in the East

but

Hann býr á Norðurlandi/fyrir norðan   He lives in the North

3 Prepositonal phrases followed by an object

fyrir norðan/norðan fyrir/norðan við (*acc.*) – (to the) north of . . .

- motion: **norður eftir** (*acc.*) – northwards (along, of)

4 Prepositional phrases without an object

- rest: **norður frá** (*dat.*) – (up) north

Veðrið

Climate generates its own vocabulary. In Icelandic this is clear from the preponderance of vocabulary referring to the many different kinds of winds and precipitation. A complete list could easily take up several chapters, but the following should allow you to understand enough of the weather forecast to know whether to go camping or not, or take that trip into the interior.

Vindur 'wind'
vindstig, *n.* wind force
norðanátt/norðlæg átt,
   northerly wind
logn, *n.* windstill
gol/a, breeze
hvass, *adj.* **hvassviðri**, *n.*
   windy (weather)
strekking/ur, strong wind
stinningsgol/a, wind force 4
kald/i, wind force 5
stinningskald/i, force 6
storm/ur, storm 9
rok, *n.* storm, gale 10

Himinninn 'the sky'
það þykknar upp, it's
   clouding over
sólskin, *n.* sunshine
heiðskír, *adj.* bright
það er skýjað, it's cloudy
alskýjað, clouded over
léttskýjað, slightly cloudy
skýjað með köflum,
   occasional clouds
það léttir til, it's clearing up

Úrkoma 'precipitation'
rigning, **rigna (það rignir)**,
   rain
súld, *f.* drizzle
skúr, *f.* shower
slydd/a, sleet
él, *n.* sudden fall of snow or
   hail

éljagang/ur, intermittent
   snow/hail storms
snjó/r, **snjóa (það snjóar)**,
   snow
þok/a, mist

Hitastig 'temperature'
**það er gott veður þegar það
   er:**
hlýtt, warm
heitt, hot
(veður)blíð/a, mild
**það er tuttugu og þriggja stiga
   hiti** it's twenty-three
   degrees

Kuld/i 'cold'
**það er kalt veður þegar það
   er:**
frost, frost
ískalt, icy cold
(stór)hríð, *f.* snow storm
það er þriggja stiga frost it's
   minus three

Veðurhorfur, veðurspá
   'forecast'
útlit, *n.* outlook
veðurstof/a, weather office

Miscellaneous
óveður/illviðri, very bad
   weather
veðurteppt/ur, *adj.*, be delayed
   due to the weather

Exercise 7

Listen to the forecast and fill in the temperatures expected for each region on the map below:

Now listen again and see if you can answer the following questions:

1 Where would you definitely not want to go on a hiking trip today or tomorrow?
2 Where will it be coldest tonight?
3 Where would be the best place to go for outdoor activities on Wednesday and Thursday?
4 What is the main expected wind direction?
5 What kind of clothing would you wear?
6 Where in the country is it expected to be the coolest, and where the warmest?

Exercise 8

Listen closely to the speaker and indicate on the map above where-abouts the following places are:

1 Húsavík
2 Siglufjörður
3 Sauðárkrókur
4 Bolungarvík

5 Stykkishólmur   7 Vík (í Mýrdal)
6 Þorlákshöfn   8 Djúpivogur

Language points

Impersonal passive 2: middle voice

In Lesson 12 you were introduced to the middle voice as a way to express reciprocity and reflexivity. The middle voice can also be used in a passive sense, in a way that often translates into English as 'can/could be ...':

Húsið sést ekki	The house cannot be seen
Stóllinn kemst ekki	The chair cannot get through
Pennar týnast sífellt hér og finnast ekki aftur	Pens keep getting lost here and aren't found again

The middle voice is mostly used to express the passive where there is no real agency at all. This can be illustrated with the following examples:

Dótið okkar er geymt í skáp
Our stuff is kept in a cupboard (someone keeps it there but who is unimportant)

but **Mjólkin geymist í kæliskáp**
Milk keeps in the fridge (no agency: no one 'keeps' it)

Exercise 9

Put the verbs in brackets in the appropriate middle voice form into the following passive sentences:

1 Hún __________ við gönguna (hressa).
2 Tölvan mín __________ oft; hún er að __________ (bila, elda).
3 Buxurnar __________ í þvotti (stytta).
4 Ferskt grænmeti __________ ekki vel í þessum hita; þú verður að geyma það í kæli, annars __________ það (geyma, skemma).

14 Saga og þjóð

Story, history and people

> **In this lesson you will learn:**
>
> - some Icelandic history and culture: sagas and folk tales
> - the simple and continuous past
> - writing letters, reporting events: recent past
> - expressing possibility and ability: **geta**, **kunna**, **þekkja**, **vita**, **vera hægt**

Reading 1

Sálin hans Jóns míns (þjóðsaga)

Why won't Jón's soul get into heaven? How does the woman answer St Peter and the Virgin Mary? How does she manage to get the soul into heaven after all?

Einu sinni bjuggu saman karl og kerling. Var karlinn heldur erfiður og óvinsæll og þar að auki latur og ónýtur á heimili sínu. Líkaði kerlingu hans það mjög illa og ámælti hún honum oft. En þótt þeim kæmi ekki vel saman í sumu elskaði þó kerling karl sinn mikið.

Eitt sinn varð karlinn veikur og var þungt haldinn. Kerling vakti yfir honum, en þegar honum batnaði ekki fór hún að hugsa að hann væri ekki svo vel búinn undir dauða sinn, og vafamál hvort hann næði inngöngu í himnaríki. Hún tók þá poka og hélt honum fyrir munni á karlinum, og er hann gaf upp öndina fór hún í pokann, en kerling batt fyrir. Síðan fór hún til himna með pokann, kom að dyrum himnaríkis og drap á dyr. Þá kom Sankti Pétur út og spurði erindi hennar. Sæll nú, segir kerling, ég kom hingað með sálina hans Jóns míns, og ætla ég nú að biðja þig að koma honum hérna inn.

Jájá, segir Pétur, en því miður get ég það ekki; ég hef aldrei heyrt neitt gott um hann Jón þinn. Þá mælti kerling: Það hélt ég ekki Sankti Pétur að þú værir svona harðbrjósta. Ertu nú búinn að gleyma hvernig fór fyrir þér forðum þegar þú afneitaðir meistara þínum? Pétur fór svo aftur inn og læsti, en kerling varð úti fyrir.

Eftir litla stund drepur hún aftur á dyr og þá kemur María mey út. Sæl vertu heillin góð, segir kerling, ég vona að þú hleypir honum Jóni mínum inn. Því miður góða mín, segir María, ég þori það ekki af því hann var svo vondur hann Jón þinn. En veistu það ekki, segir kerling, að aðrir geta verið veikir eins og þú, eða manstu það nú ekki að þú áttir barn utan hjónabands? María vildi ekki heyra meira heldur læsti skjótast.

Í þriðja sinn barði kerling á dyrnar. Þá kom út Kristur sjálfur. Kerling mælti auðmjúk: Ég ætlaði að biðja þig að lofa vesalings sálinni hérna inn. Kristur svaraði: Það er hann Jón – nei kona, hann trúði ekki á mig. En í sama bili og hann lokaði hurðinni aftur kastaði hún pokanum með sálinni í inn hjá honum. Létti þá steini af hjarta kerlingar að Jón var kominn í himnaríki og fór hún glöð heim aftur.

Adapted from Jón Árnason's Íslenzkar þjóðsögur og ævintýri

Vocabulary notes

mæla (mæli – mælt)	say, speak **ámæla (ámæli – ámælt)**, *dat.* reproach, scold
koma saman, *imp.*	get along
þungt haldin/n	in a very bad way, seriously ill
gefa upp öndina	give up the ghost, die
batt, *past sg. of* **binda, fyrir**	bind shut
drepa (drep – drap – drápu – drepið) á dyr	knock on the door
forðum, *adv.*	before, long ago
afneita (afneita, afneitaði, afneitað), *dat.*	deny
læsa (læsi, læsti, læst), *acc.*	lock (the door)
verða úti fyrir	be left outside
heillin góð/góðin mín	my dear (to a woman)
hlaupa (hleyp, hljóp, hlupu, hlaupið) inn, *dat.*	let someone in
berja (ber – barði – barið)	hit, knock
létta (létti – létt) steini	be greatly relieved, heavy weight is lifted

Language points

Relating what happened: the past tense

The story in Reading 1 is told largely in the past tense. Go back
to the text for a moment and see if you can pick out the verbs.
Do you detect any patterns at all?

The main distinction in how the past tense is formed is between
weak and strong verbs. Weak verbs form the past tense with a **-d**,
-t, or **-ð** (depending on the preceding sound, as with the imperative suffix) followed by a singular (**-i**, **-ir**, **-i**) or plural ending (**-um**,
-uð, **-u**). The **-a-** group keeps its final **-a** so it is always followed by
-ð, whereas verbs from the **-ur-** group are subject to the following
stem vowel changes: **e** > **a**, **y** > **u** (**ý** > **ú**). Here are some examples:

	ætl-a	*læs-a*	*flyt-ja*	*ber-ja*
ég	ætl-a-ði	læs-ti	flut-ti	bar-ði
þú	ætl-a-ðir	læs-tir	flut-tir	bar-ðir
hún	ætl-a-ði	læs-ti	flut-ti	bar-ði
við	ætl-*u*-ðum	læs-tum	flut-tum	bör-ðum
þið	ætl-*u*-ðuð	læs-tuð	flut-tuð	bör-ðuð
þær	ætl-*u*-ðu	læs-tu	flut-tu	bör-ðu

Have you noticed the U-shift at work?

The past tense of strong verbs is a little trickier. The endings are
the easy part: only the second person singular has an ending, **-st**
(any preceding **-t-** in the stem will be dropped), and the plural
endings are the same as for weak verbs. Strong verbs form their
past tense mainly through a stem vowel change, one in the singular
and a different one in the plural. It is possible to chart the patterns
of these vowel changes, although there are significant exceptions
to these patterns. Strong verbs in the glossary list are followed by
the first person singular and third person plural in the past tense,
and you will be surprised how quickly you will pick up the past
tense forms of common verbs. The following chart of infinitive stem
vowels and their first person singular and plural past forms should
help as well. The past participle stem vowel is given in the final
column:

Stem vowel	1ˢᵗ p.sg.	1ˢᵗ p.pl.	PP vowel	
-í-	-ei-	-i-	-i-	bíða – beið – biðum – biðið
-jó/jú/ú-	-au-	-u-	-o-	fljúga – flaug – flugum – flogið
-e- 1	-a-	-u-	-u-	drekka – drakk – drukkum – drukkið
-e- 2	-a-	-á-	-e-	gefa – gaf – gáfum – gefið
-i- 1	-a-	-u-	-u-	finna – fann – fundum – fundið
-i- 2	-a-	-á-	-e-	sitja – sat – sátum – setið
-a-	-ó-	-ó-	-a-	fara – fór – fórum – farið
1 -a-	-é-	-é-	-a-	falla – féll – féllum – fallið
2 -á-	-é-	-é-	-á-	láta – lét – létum – látið
3 -ei-	-é-	-é-	-ei	heita – hét – hétum – heitið
-au-	-jó-	-u-	-au-	hlaupa – hljóp – hlupum – hlaupið

Athugið

1 Individual anomalies may occur in each of these patterns, such as **finna**, which has a **-d-** in the plural and past participle, and **binda** which has **batt** as its singular form. The following concern very common verbs:

    búa – bjó – bjuggum – búið
    standa – stóð – stóðum – staðið
    ganga – gekk – gengum – gengið
    fá – fékk – fengum – fengið
    deyja – dó – dóum – dáið

2 Verbs with initial **v-** lose that **v-** before the **-u-** in the plural and past participle:

    vinna – vann – *u*nnum – *u*nnið

3 Two common verbs with **-o-** as stem vowel:

    koma – kom – komum – komið
    sofa – svaf – sváfum – sofið

Some examples:

	grípa	*bjóða*	*lesa*	*láta*
ég	greip	bauð	las	lét
þú	greipst	bauðst	last	lést
hann	greip	bauð	las	lét
við	gripum	buðum	lásum	létum
þið	gripuð	buðuð	lásuð	létuð
þeir	gripu	buðu	lásu	létu

Exercise 1

List all verbs in Reading 1 that are in the past tense (only once).
Are they weak or strong? What would be their past plural (or
singular) forms?

Exercise 2

Can you give the singular and plural past tense forms of the
following verbs? You may have to check if they are weak or strong.
You can also use the glossary list to help you, but try first to derive
the forms on your own: **borða**, **gleyma**, **gera**, **velja**, **njóta**, **verða**,
taka, **leika**, **spyrja**, **gráta**, **nota**, **sjóða**.

Exercise 3

Now we go back to some Icelandic history. In Lesson 3, Exercise
7 you matched a number of Icelandic historical facts with their
correct dates. The events were phrased in the present tense (with
the exception of the verb **vera** which was left out altogether: **Biblían
(er) prentuð á íslensku**). Can you change the sentences to the past
tense, putting in the appropriate forms of **vera** where left out?

Exercise 4: Halldór Laxness

Below is a brief text about the life of Halldór Laxness, Iceland's
most famous modern author. Can you put the verbs in brackets in
their appropriate past tense form?

Halldór Kiljan Laxness _________ (fæðast) þegar 20. öldin
_________ (vera) tveggja ára gömul, og _________ (deyja)
þegar hún _________ (eiga) aðeins tvö ár eftir. Hann
_________ (vera) skírður Halldór Guðjóndsson og
_________ (búa) á bóndabæ í Mosfellssveit sem _________

(heita) Laxnes. Hann __________ (skrifa) fyrstu skáldsögu
sína, *Barn náttúrunnar*, og __________ (fara) til
Kaupmannahafnar þegar hann __________ (vera) sautján ára.
Hann __________ (ferðast) um Evrópu, __________ (dvelja)
m.a. í Þýskalandi, og __________ (taka) kaþólska trú og írska
nafnið Kiljan og __________ (ganga) í klaustur í Lúxemborg
árið 1922. Hann __________ (koma) heim til Íslands árið 1924,
og þremur árum seinna __________ (koma) út önnur skáld-
saga eftir hann, *Vefarinn mikli frá Kasmír*, sem hann
__________ (semja) árið 1925. Þetta verk __________ (vera)
ein af fyrstu módernísku skáldsögum á íslensku og __________
(vekja) mikla athygli. Halldór __________ (gefa) upp kaþólska
trú og prestanám og __________ (verða) sósíalisti þegar hann
__________ (vera) í Norður Ameríku árin 1927–9. Eftir það
__________ (byrja) hann að skrifa í alvöru og __________
(skrifa) hverja skáldsöguna eftir aðra, þ.á.m. *Sjálfstætt fólk*,
Sölku Völku, *Íslandsklukkuna*, *Atómstöðina*, *Gerplu* og
Kristnihald undir jökli, og __________ (vera) margar þeirra
þýddar og gerðar að kvikmyndum. Hann __________ (semja)
líka greinar, leikrit, smásögur og ljóð. Halldór Laxness
__________ (fá) Nóbelsverðlaunin árið 1955.

Exercise 5

In the text on Laxness you saw how you can use the past tense to
talk about somebody's (past) life. Write sentences describing your
life until now, using some of these words:

fæðast – búa – alast upp (= 'grow up', *strong verb*) – **fara í
skóla/stunda nám – vinna – keyra bíl – flytja – giftast – fara
til útlanda – fara til Íslands – læra íslensku ...**

There is a sample answer at the back of the book. How does
Jónína's life differ from yours?

The use of the past tense: simple and continuous past, recent past

The tense you have just learned to form is known as the simple
past. Not surprisingly, it is used to indicate an action or event that
is completely finished and in the past. In cases where something
happened in the past while something else was happening at that

very moment in time (past continuous), you use the past tense of the verb **vera** followed by **að** and the infinitive of the main verb:

Ég *var að horfa* **á sjónvarpið þegar hann** *kom* **inn**
I *was watching* television when he *came* in

Við *vorum að tala* **saman þegar hann** *hringdi*
We *were talking* when he *rang*

In sentences where an action or event is still linked to the present moment because it is so close in time and/or because its effects are still with us, Icelandic uses the construction **vera búin/n að** followed by the infinitive of the main verb. Note that **búin/n** has to reflect the gender and number of the subject:

Barnið *er búið að borða*
The child *has finished eating/has eaten*

Hún *er búin að sjá* **myndina**
She *has seen* the film

Krakkarnir *eru búnir að gera við* **hjólið**
The children *have mended* the bike

This construction can only be used in conjunction with situational verbs (**liggja**, **sitja**, etc.), or verbs denoting a quick and sudden action (**detta**, **vakna**), if there is an indication in the sentence of how long or how often it has happened:

*****Amma er búin að sofa** but **Amma er búin að sofa í allan dag**
Granny has been sleeping all day
*****Hann er búinn að detta** but **Hann er margoft búinn að detta af stólnum**
He has often fallen off his chair

The construction **vera búið að** is very common in the impersonal passive, especially in journalistic writing. Here are some examples:

Það er búið að tala við kennarann/Búið er að tala við kennarann
There have been talks with the teacher

Það er búið að segja frá slysinu í blöðunum/Búið er að segja frá slysinu í blöðunum
There has been an account of the accident in the newspapers

Exercise 6: Bílslys

There has been a serious car accident in a busy Reykjavík street. The police are interviewing eyewitnesses to find out exactly what happened. They want to know where everyone was and what they were doing when the accident happened. Can you write out the following police notes in complete sentences, using the continuous past where appropriate?

1 Örlygur Jónsson: – horfði í búðarglugga – heyrði brak
                        – leit (!) um öxl – slysið búið að gerast
2 María Jóhannsdóttir   – gekk niður götuna – sá bílinn keyra
                        inn í búðarglugga
3 Pétur Briem   – beið eftir umferðarljósi – bíllinn
                        keyrði framhjá
                        – horfði á eftir honum – bíllinn sveigði
                        til vinstri og skall á búðina
4 Fanney Freysdóttir   – talaði við kunningja hjá búðinni – sá
                        bílinn koma að sér
                        – horfði á bílstjórann – höfuðið datt
                        niður á stýrið

Reading 2

Bréf

Several weeks after Joyce has returned home from her Icelandic holiday, she writes her friend Áslaug the following letter. What happened during Joyce's absence? What did she have to do? What did she miss in Iceland?

Manchester, 4. Apríl 2000

Elsku Áslaug:

Fyrirgefðu hvað það hefur dregist hjá mér að skrifa þér, en ég er búin að vera svo önnum kafin. Þegar ég kom heim frá Íslandi kom í ljós að það var búið að brjótast inn í húsið! Innbrotsþjófarnir tóku tölvuna mína, geislaspilarann, sjónvarpið og myndbandstæki. Sem betur fer skildi ég enga peninga eftir í húsinu. En það var mikið vesen í kringum þetta allt saman. Snemma næsta dag varð ég að fara á lögreglustöð til að gefa skýrslu, hafa samband við tryggingarfélagið o.s.frv.

En annars er allt gott að frétta héðan. Það er brjálað að gera
hjá mér eins og alltaf en ég er ánægð í vinnunni. Foreldrum mínum
gengur líka vel, og þau biðja kærlega að heilsa þér.

Hvernig gengur svo hjá þér? Ertu búin að venjast nýju íbúðinni?
Hvernig var í veislunni hans Kjartans, var ekki bara gaman? Mér
þótti leitt að þurfa að missa af henni.

Ég þakka aftur innilega fyrir mig. Mikið var gott að sjá þig aftur!
Hafðu það sem best, og skilaðu mínum bestu kveðjum heim til þín!
Kær kveðja,
Joyce.

Vocabulary notes

hvað það hefur dregist hjá mér	how long it has taken me
dragast	be delayed
vera önnum kafin/n	be very busy
koma í ljós	appear
brjótast inn	break in, burgle
innbrotsþjófar	burglars
sem betur fer	fortunately
skilja (skil, skildi, skilað) eftir, *acc.*	leave behind
tryggingarfélag (-s, -)	insurance company
missa (missi – missti – misst) af, *dat.*	miss
innilega, *adv.*	affectionately
hafðu það sem best	all the best, be well

Exercise 7

Imagine you have just returned from a holiday in Iceland. Below
are notes from your diary covering the last week of your stay there.
Write a letter to your friend in Iceland in which you tell him or
her what you did during those final days.

5 July: took a coach to Þingvellir (!). Did some sightseeing and walked around. Very beautiful place! Went to a concert in Hallgrímskirkja in the evening.
6–7 July: Went on a two-day guided tour around the area of Njal's saga (*sögulóðir Njáls sögu*) in Fljótshlíð. Saw the exhibition about Njal's saga in (*á!*) Hvolsvöllur. Fantastic!
8 July: Went on a boat trip to Viðey and had a look at the church and the oldest house in the country.

Beautiful warm weather. Walked around the island and saw many kinds of birds.
9 July: went for a swim and went shopping in the town centre. Bought many gifts and souvenirs (*minjagrip/ur, -s, -ir*). Had dinner with Sif and Kjartan at Café Sólon Íslandus.
10 July: packed. Had a sandwich at the Nordic House and saw an Icelandic film there. Took the bus to Keflavík and said goodbye to Iceland.

Language points

Expressing ability, knowledge and possibility

The verb **geta** in Icelandic means 'can', 'be able to'. It is a strong verb, and it is also unusual in that it must always be followed by the past participle of the main verb:

Ég *get* ekki *gengið* á þessum skóm I can't walk in these shoes

Við *gátum* ekkert að því *gert* We couldn't do anything about it

Það *getur* ekki *verið*! That can't be! That's not possible!

Do you remember another way of saying 'it's not possible'? Of course: **Það er ekki hægt**.

Not all kinds of ability are covered by **geta**. The verb **kunna** is used to express any ability that is learned, i.e. you can because you have learned how to. When followed by a nominal, **kunna** governs the accusative. When followed by a verb, the verb is preceded by **að**:

Soffía kann ítölsku Soffia can (= knows how to) speak Italian

Þeir kunna ekki *að* synda   They can't (= haven't learned to) swim

The verbs **þekkja**, **vita** and **kannast við** all mean 'know', but they refer to different kinds of knowledge. **Þekkja** (**þekki** – **þekkti** – **þekkt**) means to know something or someone because of experience or previous exposure: **Hann þekkir Ítalíu vel. Hann fer þangað á hverju sumri** 'He knows Italy well. He goes there every summer'.

Kannast við is similar to **þekkja** but weaker. It refers more to recognition than to actual knowledge:

Kannastu við þetta orð? Já ég hef séð það en ég veit ekki hvað það þýðir

Do you recognize this word? Yes I have seen it but I don't know what it means

Kannast is the middle voice form of **kanna** 'investigate', 'explore' and is a regular weak **-a** verb.

The verb **vita** refers to factual knowledge. It governs the accusative case when followed by a nominal. It can also be followed by a subordinate clause, in which case it is followed by **að** or by an interrogative such as **hvort**, **hvar**, **hvað**, **hvernig**:

Ég veit ekki *hver* hann er, *hvar* hann býr og *hvaðan* hann kemur

I do not know *who* he is, *where* he lives or *where* he comes *from*

Þau vita ekki *að* hún ætlar til útlanda

They do not know *that* she intends to go abroad

Note that **vita** must be followed by something – it cannot be left on its own as happens in English 'I know'. **Ég veit það**.

Kunna and **vita** are rather irregular verbs. These are their present and past tense conjungations:

	kunna		**vita**	
	present	*past*	*present*	*past*
ég	kann	kunni	veit	vissi
þú	kannt	kunnir	veist	vissir
hann	kann	kunni	veit	vissi
við	kunnum	kunnum	vitum	vissum
þið	kunnið	kunnuð	vitið	vissuð
þeir	kunna	kunnu	vita	vissu

Exercise 8

Here's a little test of your knowledge of Iceland. Can you answer the following questions? (In complete Icelandic sentences, of course!)

1 Þekkir þú Ísland vel?
2 Þekkir þú Ólaf Ragnar Grímsson?
3 Kanntu (að tala) íslensku?
4 Kannastu við *Njáls sögu*?
5 Er hægt að fara kringum Ísland með lest?
6 Veistu hvenær Háskóli Íslands var stofnaður?
7 Veistu hvað Ísland er stórt (í ferkílómetrum)?
8 Veistu hvar Fljótshlíð er?
9 Veistu hver samdi *Njáls sögu*?

Reading 3

Úr Brennu Njáls sögu

The Icelandic sagas are classics of medieval European literature. Among the most renowned are the Íslendingasögur, vivid and dramatic stories about Icelanders set during the age of settlement. The sagas are characterized by a terse, laconic, realistic narrative style that is unique among its European contemporaries. The following is a fragment from The Saga of Burnt Njall, written around the thirteenth century. Gunnar, farmer and main hero of the saga, has been exiled at the Althing but has chosen not to leave his country, thereby forfeiting his life. A group of men arrives at his farm, led by Gissur hvíti, to seek justice by killing him. How did Þorgrímur find out Gunnar was at home? How many men has Gunnar killed? What does he need Hallgerður's hair for? Does he get it?

Gunnar svaf í lofti einu í skálanum og Hallgerður og móðir hans. En er þeir komu að bænum vissu þeir eigi hvort Gunnar mundi heima vera. Gissur mælti að nokkur skyldi fara heim á húsin og vita hvað af kannaði en þeir settust niður á völlinn meðan. Þorgrímur austmaður gekk upp á skálann. Gunnar sér að rauðan kyrtil ber við glugginum og leggur út með atgeirinum á hann miðjan. Þorgrími skruppu fæturnir og varð laus skjöldurinn og hrataði hann ofan af þekjunni. Gengur hann síðan að þeim Gissuri þar er þeir sátu á vellinum. Gissur leit við honum og mælti: 'Hvort er Gunnar heima?'

'Vitið þér það en hitt vissi eg að atgeir hans var heima.' segir Austmaðurinn.

Féll hann þá niður dauður. Þeir sóttu þá heim að húsunum.

Gunnar is married to the proud and temperamental Hallgerður, who has never forgiven her husband for slapping her face in public.

Í þessu bili hleypur upp á þekjuna Þorbrandur Þorleiksson og höggur í sundur bogastrenginn Gunnars. Gunnar þrífur atgeirinn báðum höndum og snýst að honum skjótt og rekur í gegnum hann atgeirinn og kastar honum dauðum á völlinn. Þá hljóp upp Ásbrandur bróðir hans. Gunnar leggur til hans atgeirinum og kom hann skildi fyrir sig. Atgeirinn renndi í gegnum skjöldinn og svo meðal handleggjanna. Snaraði Gunnar þá svo fast atgeirinn að skjöldurinn klofnaði en brotnuðu báðir handleggirnir og féll hann út af vegginum. Áður hafði Gunnar særða átta menn en vegið þá tvo. Þá fékk Gunnar sár tvö og sögðu það allir menn að hann brygði sér hvorki við sár né við bana.

Hann mælti til Hallgerðar:

'Fá mér leppa tvo úr hári þínu og snúið þið móðir mín saman til bogastrengs mér.'

'Liggur þér nokkuð við?' segir hún.

'Líf mitt liggur við,' segir hann, 'því að þeir munu mig aldrei fá sóttan meðan eg kem boganum við.'

'Þá skal eg nú,' segir hún, 'muna þér kinnhestinn og hirði eg aldrei hvort þú verð þig lengur eða skemur.'

'Hefir hver til síns ágætis nokkuð,' segir Gunnar, 'og skal þig þessa eigi lengi biðja.'

Rannveig mælti: 'Illa fer þér og mun þín skömm lengi uppi.'

Vocabulary notes

eigi = ekki		**höggva (högg/**	cut, hew, chop
vita hvað af	find out,	**hegg, hjó,**	
kannaði	investigate	**hjuggu, hoggið),**	
kyrtil/l (-s, -ar)	tunic, gown	*acc.*	
atgeir (-s, -ar),	halberd	**bogastreng/ur**	bow string
m.		**(-s, -ir)**	
hrata (hrata,	stumble, topple	**þrífa (þríf, þreif,**	grab, clean
hrataði, hratað)		**þrufum, þrifið),**	
þekj/a (-u, -ur)	roof	*acc.*	
vitið þér	find out (for	**snara (snara –**	snare
= kannið þið	yourselves)	**snarað), *acc.***	

vega (veg, vó, vógu, vegið), *acc.*	slay
brygði, *past subj. of* **bregða** (**bregð, brá, brugðu, brugðið**) **sér við**, *acc.*	react to, flinch at
ban/i (-a)	death
lepp/ur (-s, -ar)	piece, lock
liggur þér nokkuð við?	does anything depend upon it for you?
þeir munu mig aldrei fá sóttan	they will never get me
kinnhest/ur (-s, -ar)	slap in the face
hirða (hirði, hirti, hirt) um, *acc.*	care about
verja (ver, varði, varið) sig	defend oneself, hold out
lengur eða skemur	for a longer or a shorter time
hafa til síns ágætis	have to one's distinction
fara e-m illa	it is unbecoming, it doesn't become one
mun skömm þín lengi uppi	your shame will be long-lived

15 Höfuð, herðar, hné og tær

Head and shoulders, knees and toes

In this lesson you will learn about:

- the human body
- health
- more impersonal constructions: how are you feeling?
- visiting a doctor: aches, pains and afflictions
- present perfect: what has happened before, what happened a long time ago
- demonstrative pronouns: **þessi**, **sá**, **hinn**

Dialogue 1

Hvernig hefurðu það?

What is the matter with Áki? Has he been to the doctor's? What does Hrafn tell him to do?

HRAFN: Góðan og blessaðan daginn Áki minn, hvernig hefurðu það?

ÁKI: Ekki svo gott.

HRAFN: Nú, hvað er að? Ertu lasinn?

ÁKI: Ég er kominn með kvef, held ég. Ég er með hálsbólgu, ég er stíflaður í nefinu, og mér er ferlega illt í höfðinu. Mér líður alveg ömurlega.

HRAFN: Ertu með hita?

ÁKI: Ég veit það ekki, það getur vel verið. Ég er eitthvað svo slappur og of þreyttur til að gera nokkuð.

HRAFN: Þú ættir að kúra undir sæng frekar en að labba um hérna í kuldanum! Kannski er það alls ekki bara kvef heldur flensa. Það er einhver hræðileg pest að ganga. Ertu búinn að fara til læknis?

ÁKI: Nei, en ég fékk mér hóstasaft og töflur til að draga úr sárindum í hálsi.

HRAFN: Komdu þér heim maður, skríddu í rúmið og láttu þér batna!

ÁKI: Já, kannski er best ég geri það.

Vocabulary notes

kvef (-s), *n.*	cold	**flens/a (-u)**	flu
hálsbólg/a (-u)	sore throat	**það er pest að**	there's a bug
stíflað/ur	congested, *pp. of*	**ganga**	going around
	stífl/a plug (up)	**hóstasaft**	from **hóst/i**
mér er illt í	my head hurts, I		'cough', *and*
höfðinu	have a		**saft (-s)**
	headache		'juice'
ömurlega, *adv.*	miserably	**tafl/a (-u, -ur)**	tablet, pill
hit/i (-a)	temperature, fever	**draga úr**, *dat.*	take away,
slapp/ur, *adj.*	weak, without		withdraw
	energy	**sárindi**, *n.pl.*	pain, hurt

Vocabulary

Líkaminn: the body

In the course of the previous lessons you have already encountered a number of words to do with the human body. You may remember **auga**, **eyra**, **hár** ... Here are some other useful ones. Of how many can you guess the meaning, using the context of the words to help you?

1 *Höfuðið:*   tvö *eyru*, tvö *augu*
tvær *varir*, ein *tunga* og margar *tennur* í
einum *munni*
eitt *nef*, ein *haka*

Karlmenn eru með *skegg* þegar þeir eru með
hár á hökunni og/eða efri vör

Hálsinn tengir höfuðið við *herðar* og *bol*

2 **Bolurinn:**	tveir *handleggir:* tvær *hendur* og tíu *fingur*
	tveir *fætur:* tvö *hné*, tveir *ökklar*, tíu *tær*
Að framan:	eitt eða tvö *brjóst*
	einn *magi*
Að aftan:	eitt *bak*
	einn *rass*

Líkaminn er þakinn *húð* og sums staðar *hári*. Það rennur *blóð* í gegnum hann allan.

Could you derive the gender and nominative singular form of each of these new nouns, looking at their form and that of their qualifiers in the sentence?

Language points

Body parts: how to use them in Icelandic

Some Icelandic body parts are notoriously irregular in their declension patterns. **Auga**, **eyra**, **hjarta** and **lunga** ('lung') are weak neuter nouns which all have **-a** as a singular ending in each of the four cases, and **-u**, **-u**, **-um**, **-na** in the plural. The irregular ones you should know are:

		Masculine		*Feminine*		
		fótur	*fingur*	*hönd*	*tönn*	*tá*
sg.	*nom.*	fót-ur	fingur-	hönd-	tönn-	tá-
	acc.	fót-	fingur-	hönd-	tönn-	tá-
	dat.	fæt-i	fingr-i	hend-i	tönn-	tá-
	gen	fót-ar	fingur-s	hand-ar	tann-ar	tá-ar
pl.	*nom.*	fæt-ur	fingur-	hend-ur	tenn-ur	tæ-r
	acc.	fæt-ur	fingur-	hend-ur	tenn-ur	tæ-r
	dat.	fót-um	fingr -um	hönd-um	tönn-um	tá-m
	gen.	fót-a	fingr -a	hand-a	tann-a	tá-a

It is worth noting that in Icelandic, one does not 'own' the parts of one's body, that is to say, they are never used in combination with the possessive verb **eiga**, and only rarely with a possessive pronoun. Instead, you use the prepositional phrase **vera með** + *acc.* (**ég er með ljóst krullað hár** 'I have blond curly hair'), or the definite article (**mér er kalt á fótunum** 'My feet are cold', *lit.* 'I am cold on the feet'). If there is a specific need to indicate whose body the part belongs to, it is common to have it followed by the preposition **í** or **á** (depending on where the part is located) and the owner in the dative case:

Hárið á honum er skítugt
His hair is dirty

Kerlingin hélt poka fyrir *munni á karlinum*
The old woman held a bag before the old man's mouth

Exercise 1: Mannlýsingar 

One of the shops in the shopping centre Kringlan has had some of its merchandise stolen. An eyewitness who thinks she saw the shoplifter close up as he ran out gives the police the following description:

Þetta var hávaxinn maður, með sítt rautt hár. Það var slétt og bundið í tagl. Augun í honum voru græn, og hann var með stóran munn og mikið skegg. Hann var með eyrnalokk í vinstra eyranu og marga gullhringa á fingrunum. Hann var með ansi stóran maga, já, feitur myndi ég segja. Fæturnir á honum voru frekar stórir. Hann var í bol og stuttbuxum, og það var stórt ör* á hægra hnénu.

***ör (-s, -),** *n.*   scar

The policeman taking down the description is new to the job and a little flustered. He writes down the following statements. Are they correct?

1 Hárið á manninum var stutt   já/nei
2 Hann var með græn augu   já/nei
3 Maðurinn var með skartgripi   já/nei
4 Hann var skeggjaður   já/nei
5 Hann var grannur ('slim')   já/nei
6 Það var vetur   já/nei

Exercise 2

How would you describe the following people in Icelandic?

1 Elvis Presley   5 Arnold Schwarzenegger
2 Mick Jagger   6 Marilyn Monroe
3 Diana Ross   7 Fidel Castro
4 Queen Elizabeth II   8 Yourself

Dialogue 2 ▣

Hjá lækni

Áki spends a few days at home but isn't getting any better, so he decides to take Hrafn's advice and see his doctor. Does Áki often see a doctor? What does the doctor say is the matter with him? What must Áki do to get better?

LÆKNIR: Góðan daginn Áki, gjörðu svo vel. Það er langt síðan ég hef séð þig! Hvað gengur að þér, þú ert ekki vel frískur?

ÁKI: Nei, mér líður alls ekki vel.

LÆKNIR: Geturðu lýst einkennunum fyrir mig?

ÁKI: Ég hef verið með hálsbólgu í nokkra daga, nefgöngin eru alveg stífluð og ég er síhóstandi og alveg máttlaus. Svo hefur þessi voðalegi höfuðverkur lagst á mig.

LÆKNIR: Færðu oft höfuðverk?

ÁKI: Nei, það gerist sjaldan, sem betur fer.

LÆKNIR: Það lítur út fyrir að vera slæmt kvef. Ertu búinn að mæla þig?

ÁKI: Já, ég var með 40 stiga hita í morgun.

LÆKNIR: Nú, hvað! Er sárt þegar þú hóstar?

ÁKI: Já, það er það.

LÆKNIR: Viltu gjöra svo vel að fara úr skyrtunni og leyfa mér að hlusta og líta í hálsinn á þér. Jæja Áki, þú beiðst einum of lengi að koma til mín, og nú ertu kominn með lungnabólgu. Þú skalt fara heim strax og halda þig í rúminu þangað til ég kem og skoða þig aftur eftir nokkra daga. En ef þér versnar, láttu senda eftir mér strax! Gefðu konunni þinni þennan lyfseðil til að ná í lyf handa þér. Af stað með þig, Áki, og farðu nú vel með þig og taktu þér hvíld!

ÁKI: Þakka þér fyrir, ég skal gera það.

Vocabulary notes

hvað gengur að þér?	what's the matter?	**leggjast (leggst – lagðist – lagst) á**, *acc.*	strike, attack
einkenni (-s, -)	characteristics, symptoms	**mæla (mæli – mælt)**, *acc.*	measure, take temperature
máttlaus, *adj.*	feeble, weak, without energy	**lungnabólg/a (-u)**	pneumonia

versna (versna – get worse	**lyf (-s, -)**	medicine
versnað), *imp.*	**af stað með þig!**	off you go!
lyfseðil/l (-s, -ar) prescription	**fara vel með sig**	look after oneself

Vocabulary

Veikindi, meðferðir og lækningar: *illnesses, treatments and cures*

You have now learned some of the more common afflictions. Here are some other ones that are useful to know:

matareitrun (-ar), *f.*	food poisoning
sykursýki, *f.indecl.*	diabetes
taugaáfall (-s), *n.*	shock, nervous breakdown
útbrot (-s, -), *n.*	rash, outbreak

The following suffixes are commonly used for aches and pains:

pín/a (-u), *f.*, as in **tannpína** 'toothache'
verk/ur (-jar, -ir), *m.*, as in **höfuðverkur** 'headache' and
   túrverkir 'menstrual pains'
kramp/i (-a, -ar), *m.*, as in **vöðvakrampi** 'muscle cramp'

What do I tell the doctor? Some useful verbal expressions:

ég finn til í, *dat.* **ég finn til**	my stomach hurts
í maganum	
ég er með verk í, *dat.* **ég**	my back hurts
er með verk í bakinu	
það er sárt	it hurts
ég er með, *acc.* **ég er með**	I have diarrhoea
niðurgang	
kasta (kasta – kastað) upp	be sick, vomit
meiða (meiddi, meitt), *acc.*	injure, hurt
meiða sig	hurt oneself

Finally, some common adjectives:

slapp/ur – hress
lasin/n – frísk/ur
veik/ur – heilbrigð/ur
marin/n, bruised
bólgin/n, inflamed, swollen

vera -brotin/n, have a broken ..., as in
Ég er fót/ökkla/handleggsbrotinn I have a broken leg/ankle/arm

Now, what can be done about it?

fara í (læknis)skoðun	go for a check-up
fara í meðferð (við ...)	get treatment (for ...)
fara í uppskurð/vera skorinn up	have an operation
láta sprauta sig	get an injection

Language points

More impersonal constructions

Impersonal constuctions are often used when describing a physical state. The following in particular are quite common:

mér er óglatt	I feel nauseous, sick
mér líður vel/illa	I am feeling well/unwell
mér er illt í ..., *dat.*	I'm ill to my ...
mér batnar	I am getting better
mér versnar	I am getting worse
mig verkjar í ..., *acc.*	I have a pain in my ...

Did you notice how in Dialogue 1 Hrafn told Áki: **láttu þér batna!** 'get better soon!'? Because impersonal constructions have no real subject and therefore no agent, the imperative is formed with the help of the verb **láta**: **láttu þér líða vel!**

Exercise 3

The following tourists are in the **biðstofa** or waiting room of the **heilsugæslustöð**, the local health centre where one goes to see a doctor. None of these people speak Icelandic, so you offer to translate. Can you tell the doctor in Icelandic what is wrong with each of them?

1 Nilgün: feels nauseous, is sick directly after having eaten and has diarrhoea. It could be food poisoning.
2 Umberto: fell during a hiking trip and his ankle hurts. It is bruised and swollen and he is afraid it is broken.
3 Merja: backache and stomach cramps. Can hardly walk or eat.
4 Janós: has a dreadful headache which happens rarely. Feels weak. He has taken his temperature, but has no fever.

Dialogue 3

Í apótekinu

Joyce goes to the local pharmacist. What has happened to Joyce?
What does she want for it? Why does she buy the thermometer?
What else does she get while she's there?

APÓTEKARI: Góðan dag, hvað get ég gert fyrir þig?

JOYCE: Góðan daginn, mig vantar sárabindi og plástur, og
einhver sótthreinsandi efni.

APÓTEKARI: Nú, meiddirðu þig?

JOYCE: Já, ég datt í sundlauginni og hruflaði mig á hnénu,
og það er ferlega sárt.

APÓTEKARI: Þessi joðáburður hérna er mjög góður.

JOYCE: Fínt, þá ætla ég að fá hann, og líka verkjatöflur, og
lyf við nefstíflu.

APÓTEKARI: Gjörðu svo vel. Fleira nokkuð?

JOYCE: Já, hitamæli, takk. Sá gamli týndist. Og meðan ég er
hér ætla ég líka að fá mér andlitskrem. Ég er búin
að fara svo oft í sund að húðin er orðin alveg þurr.

APÓTEKARI: Prófaðu þetta, það er mjög gott, mýkjandi krem sem
hefur reynst vel hjá mörgum.

Vocabulary notes

sárabindi (-s, -)	gauze	**verkjatafl/a**	painkiller
sótthreinsandi,	disinfectant	**(-u, -ur)**	
adj.		**hitamæl/ir**	thermometer
hrufla (hrufla,	scrape one's	**(-is, -ar)**, *m.*	
hruflaði,	skin	**andlitskrem**	from **andlit (-s, -)**,
hruflað) sig			'face' and **krem**
joðáburður	from **joð (-s)**		**(-s, -)** 'cream'
	'iodine' and	**mýkja (mýki,**	'soften'
	áburð/ur (-ar)	**mýkti, mýkt)**,	
	'ointment',	*acc.*	
	'cream'		

Dialogue 4

Exercise 4

While in Iceland you have caught a bad cold, so you visit a pharmacy to get some medicine. Fill in the gaps in the following dialogue.

APÓTEKARI: Get ég aðstoðað þig?
YOU: (1 *Yes, thank you. I have a cold and I need something against nasal congestion.*)

_______________________________.

APÓTEKARI: Nefúða já. Nokkuð fleira?
YOU: (2 *Yes, I would like painkillers. I have such a bad headache.*) _______________________________.
APÓTEKARI: Gjörðu svo vel. Er þá allt komið?
YOU: (3 *No, I would also like a cough syrup, and do you have anything to relieve a sore throat?*)

_______________________________.

APÓTEKARI: Sjálfsagt. Þessar fjallagrasahálstöflur eru til dæmis ágætar. Í þeim eru náttúruleg efni sem mýkja hálsinn.
YOU: (4 *Are they very expensive?*)
_______________________________?

APÓTEKARI: Þær eru á sama verði og flestar aðrar hálstöflur.
YOU: (5 *Good, then I'll take them. That will be everything, thank you.*)

_______________________________.

Language points

Present perfect: what has happened, what happened a long time ago

As in English, the present perfect is formed with the auxiliary verb **hafa** followed by the past participle of the main verb. It is used to indicate past tense but with reference to the present, for example because it concerns an action or event that has repeated itself and may be repeated in the future, or something that is still the case:

Hann hefur aldrei komið til Íslands
He has never been to Iceland

Ég hef séð þessa mynd áður
I have seen this film before

Hefurðu nokkurn tíma heyrt annað eins?
Have you ever heard anything like it?

Ég tek verkjatöflu þegar ég hef borðað
I'll take an aspirin when I've eaten

Note that in the present perfect the past participle does not change.

The use of the present perfect here is very much like that of **vera búinn að**, which has a similar link to the present. Indeed, in the examples above, the two constructions are interchangeable. Where they differ is in the use of the present perfect to indicate something that happened a long time ago, something that cannot be done with **vera búinn að**:

Hann hefur komið til Íslands fyrir mörgum árum
He visited Iceland many years ago

Ég hef séð myndina fyrir löngu
I saw this film a long time ago

Það er langt síðan við höfum farið til Noregs
It has been a long time since we went to Norway

Note that in the last example, Icelandic has the present perfect in a different place from English.

Usually, the context makes clear whether the present perfect refers to the present (in the form of such adverbs as **oft**, **aldrei**, **áður**, etc.) or to a long gone past (**í fyrra**, **fyrir löngu**). Generally, if there is no such indication in the sentence, the present perfect refers to something that happened a long time ago. The following sentences, for instance, both mean the same:

Amma er *margoft* búin að fara til læknis
Amma hefur *margoft* farið til læknis
Granny has *often* been to the doctor

while these sentences mean two different things:

Amma er búin að fara til læknis
Granny has been to the doctor

Amma hefur farið til læknis
Granny went to the doctor (a long time ago)

In the past tense, the perfect is used to indicate one point in the past in relation to another past event that is closer to the present:

Hann *hafði farið* til læknis áður en hann *fékk* slag
He *had been* to the doctor before he *had* a stroke

Ég *hafði séð* myndina þegar ég loksins *las* bókina
I *had seen* the film when I finally *read* the book

Here, **vera búinn að** is again fully interchangeable with the present perfect:

Hann var búinn að fara til læknis áður en hann fékk slag
Ég var búin að sjá myndina þegar ég loksins las bókina

Finally, note also the following use of the present perfect in Icelandic:

Eftir að hafa lesið bókina var myndin ekki eins skemmtileg
After having read the book, the film was not as enjoyable

Honum batnaði eftir að hafa fengið lyf
He became better after he got some medicine

Exercise 5

Translate the following sentences into Icelandic. Sometimes there is more than one possibility.

1 I have never been (!) to Italy.
2 I had been to the doctor's before I went to the pharmacy.
3 He has smoked for (!) many years.
4 Granddad had a stroke a long time ago but he hasn't been ill since.
5 After having taken the medicine I felt much better.
6 I had not visited Iceland until I learned Icelandic.
7 It has been a long time since we saw you.
8 How long have you been in Iceland?

Language points

Demonstrative pronouns: 'this', 'that'

Icelandic distinguishes between two different demonstrative pronouns: **þessi**, used for something within visual range, and **sá**, when referring to something that occurs earlier or later on in a sentence or passage:

> **Þessi hundur hérna er ofsalega stór**
> (You can point to it and show just how big it is.)

> **Mig vantar** *hitamæli.* *Sá* **gamli týndist**
> (You refer back to something you mentioned earlier.)

Then there's **hinn**, which can mean various things. It is often used in combination with **þessi**, where **þessi** means 'this' and **hinn** 'that', 'the other'. In this instance, it can be followed by a noun plus definite article, or it can stand on its own:

> **Þessi hundur er stór og** *hinn* **er lítill**
> *This* dog is big and *the other* is small

> **Ég þekki** *þessa* **stelpu en ekki** *hinar stelpurnar*
> I know *this* girl but not *the other girls*

> **Hitt og** *þetta*
> *This* and *that*

Hinn also functions as a separate definite article for special emphasis, in formal speech and in certain set expressions. As it is related to the suffixed article in Icelandic, it follows the exact same declension pattern except that as a separate word it has **h-** for its initial letter. Some examples:

hið opinbera	*lit.* 'the public', i.e. the government
Þetta er hið minnsta mál	This is no problem whatsoever

Note, however, that when **hinn** is used to mean 'that' (above), its neuter singular form is not **hið** but **hitt**, as in **hitt og þetta**.

Demonstrative pronouns function grammatically like definite articles, that is to say, if you use a demonstrative pronoun, any accompanying adjectives will be in the weak declension, and the following noun(s) will not have a suffixed definite article. The one exception is **hinn** when it is used to mean 'that', 'the other'. These are the declension patterns:

	þessi			**sá**		
	masc.	*fem.*	*neut.*	*masc.*	*fem.*	*neut.*
sg.	þessi	þessi	þetta	sá	sú	það
	þennan	þessa	þetta	þann	þá	það
	þessum	þessari	þessu	þeim	þeirri	því
	þessa	þessarar	þessa	þess	þeirrar	þess

pl.	þessir	þessar	þessi	þeir	þær	þau
	þessa	þessar	þessi	þá	þær	þau
	þessum	þessum	þessum	þeim	þeim	þeim
	þessara	þessara	þessara	þeirra	þeirra	þeirra

Exercise 6

Fill in the gaps with the appropriate demonstrative pronoun in its correct form:

1 Ég hef ekki lesið ______ bók eftir Laxness en ég hef lesið ______ bækurnar hans.
2 Gefðu konunni ______ lyfseðil.
3 Hann fór til Frakklands í ______ von að hitta vinkonu sína.
4 Ég get ekki gengið í ______ skóm, ég ætla að nota ______ skóna í staðinn.
5 ______ safn hérna tengist *Njáls sögu*. ______ saga er heimsfræg.
6 Hann fór þangað á ______ fallega gamla bíl sem afi hans gaf honum.
7 Sagnfræðikennarinn okkar segir svo skemmtilega frá ______ og ______ sem gerðist hér á landi í gamla daga.
8 Ekki ætla ég að synda í Rín. Hún er ______ skítugasta fljót Evrópu!

Reading 1

Fréttagrein

The following article on p. 256 is from Morgunblaðið, *the largest Icelandic daily newspaper, and discusses the price of medicine in Iceland. As you will notice, the word order is not always the same as that used in daily speech, and impersonal constructions tend to occur frequently. How much more expensive is medicine in Iceland? What is the reason, according to the pharmaceutical companies? What is the name of the Minister of Health? What does she think should be done?*

Óhjákvæmilegt að lyf séu eitthvað dýrari hér á landi

FORSVARSMENN lyfjafyrirtækjanna vilja ekki kannast við það að lyf séu 26% dýrari hér á landi en í nágrannalöndunum. Segja þeir að skráð hámarksverð, sem lagt er til viðmiðunar þessum útreikningum, eigi ekkert skylt við raunverulegt verð á lyfjum hér á landi, þó að það sé vissulega rétt að lyf séu vegna smæðar markaðarins dýrari á Íslandi en í viðmiðunarlöndunum.

Fram kom m.a. í ræðu Ingibjargar Pálmadóttur heilbrigðisráðherra við utandagskrárumræðu um lyfjakostnað hins opinbera á Alþingi í síðustu viku að lyfjaverð væri 26% hærra hér á landi og að vinna þyrfti að því að lækka það hlutfall.

Sagði Þórir Haraldsson, aðstoðarmaður ráðherra, í samtali við Morgunblaðið að hér væri stuðst við upplýsingar frá Tryggingastofnun og Lyfjaverðsnefnd.

From *Morgunblaðið*, 1. Apríl 2000, bls. 16

Vocabulary notes

forsvarsmað/ur	spokesperson
skráð/ur, *pp.*	from **skrá** 'registered', 'recorded'
hámarksverð (-s, -)	maximum price
viðmiðun (-ar, -ir), *f.*	reference, norm, criterion
útreikning/ur (-s, -ar)	calculation
eiga skylt við, *acc.*	have to do with, bear relation to
smæð (-ar)	smallness
markað/ur (-ar, -ir)	market
utandagskrárumræða	from **utan-** 'outside of', **dagskrá (-r, -r)** 'agenda', **umræð/a (-u, -ur)** 'discussion'
þyrfti *past subj. of* **þurfa**	need
hlutfall (-s, -)	proportion, rate, ratio
styðja (styð – studdi – stutt) við	base on, rely on

Exercise 7

Find the words in the article that mean the following, bringing them back to their nominative form where necessary:

1 pharmaceutical companies
2 neighbouring countries
3 minister of health
4 assistant
5 (Social) Insurance Department
6 Committee for the Prices of Medicine

16 Gangi þér vel!

Good luck!

In this lesson you will learn about:

- hopes and dreams: what if . . . ?
- subjunctive: past and present
- living in Iceland
- 'I said I would . . .': indirect speech
- hosts and guests: expressing politeness

Dialogue 1

Happdrætti

There are various lotteries in Iceland, from the small **skafmiða-happdrætti** *or 'scratch-and-win' lotteries to the ones with very large prizes. Buying lottery tickets and imagining what you would do if you won is a very popular pastime. Áslaug, Sif and Kjartan are discussing their chances over a coffee. Does Sif play the lottery? What would Áslaug do if she won? Why would Kjartan not want to win the 20 million?*

ÁSLAUG: Jæja, eruð þið búin að kaupa lottómiða?

SIF: Ekki ég, ég spila eiginlega aldrei í lottó nema stundum þegar ég kaupi mér fimmtíu króna skafmiða.

ÁSLAUG: Lottóspilið mitt er nú ekki meira en svo að ég held við einni röð og kaupi röðina 10 vikur í senn. En vinningurinn er nú orðinn fimmfaldur! Hugsið ykkur, að vinna 20 milljónir!

KJARTAN: Hvað mundirðu gera ef þú ynnir?

Áslaug: Sko, ef ég ynni 20 milljóna króna vinning flytti ég í glæsilegt húsnæði, og yrði alveg kaupsjúk! Ég fengi mér alls konar fallegar flíkur, færi út í heimsreisu, lifði góðu lífi og léki mér þangað til allir peningarnir yrðu búnir.

Sif: Og þú, Kjartan?

Kjartan: Ég vildi sannarlega ekki lenda í því óláni að fá svo háan vinning. Ég held að ég myndi örugglega óska nafnleyndar! En ef um verulega upphæð væri að ræða væri gaman að geta spilað skynsamlega úr góðum vinningi. Ég eyddi ekki þessu öllu strax í vitleysu. Ég sæi bara eftir því seinna að hafa ekki farið betur með peningana!

Áslaug: Í alvöru Kjartan, en leiðinlegt! Hvað um þig, Sif?

Sif: Ætli ég fengi mér ekki mjög flottan bíl og byði öllum vinum mínum út að borða á mjög fínum veitingastað! Og svo legði ég fyrir til að mæta óvæntum útgjöldum og þyrfti aldrei meir að hafa áhyggjur af næsta Vísareikningi!

Vocabulary notes

happdrætti (-s, -)/lottó (-s, -)	lottery
halda (held, hélt, héldum, haldið), *acc./subj.*	think, believe (**halda við** 'keep', 'stick to')
röð (-ar, -ir)	row, order, series, here of course referring to the numbers
í senn, *adv.*	at a time
vinning/ur (-s, -ar)	prize, winnings
fimmfald/ur, *adj.* fivefold	here 'five times the original winning'
sjúk/ur, *adv.*	sick, ill (nowadays often used in colloquial daily speech to mean 'crazy', as in **kaupsjúkur**, *lit.* 'buy crazy', or **vera sjúkur í**, *acc.* 'be crazy about')
lenda (lendi, lenti, lent) í, *dat.*	end up, land in
ólán (-s)	misfortune
nafnleynd (-ar), *f.*	secrecy of name
eyða (eyði, eyddi, eytt), *dat.*	spend
leggja (legg, lagði, lagt) fyrir, *acc.*	put aside
útgjöld, *n.pl.*	costs, expenses

Language points

Subjunctive: saying what could or might be

The subjunctive is a special verb form used to indicate something unreal in the broadest sense of the word. It has different forms for the present and the past.

The present subjunctive is used:

1 to express a wish or exhortation, as in the title of this chapter: *gangi þér vel!*
2 in present tense **að**-clauses after certain verbs, notably those expressing reported speech (**segja**), or a non-factuality in the form of a wish (**óska**), hope (**vona**), belief (**halda**), expectation (**búast við**), fear (**óttast, vera hræddur um**), or suspicion (**gruna**): **hún segir að hann** *komi*; **ég vona að þeir** *fari*; **býstu við að ég** *lesi* **þetta?; mig grunar að hann** *ljúgi*;
3 in present tense interrogative clauses after **spyrja: Jón spyr hvort þú** *ætlir* **í bíó**;
4 in present tense clauses after certain conjunctions: **nema** 'unless', **þó að/þótt** 'although', **svo að** 'so that', **til þess að** '(in order) to': **ég kem þótt ég** *sé* **veik.**

The present subjunctive is derived from the infinitive form of the verb. What makes the present subjunctive easy to recognize in many cases is the **i**-ending (except the first person plural) and the fact that no I-shift occurs. Here are some paradigms of weak and strong verbs as well as **vera**, which has an irregular present subjunctive:

	spila	*flytja*	*fara*	*sjá*	*koma*	*vera (irr.)*
ég	spil-i	flyt-j-i	far-i	sjá-i	kom-i	sé
þú	spil-ir	flyt-j-ir	far-ir	sjá-ir	kom-ir	sért
hann	spil-i	flyt-j-i	far-i	sjá-i	kom-i	sé
við	spil-um	flyt-j-um	för-um	sjá-um	kom-um	séum
þið	spil-ið	flyt-j-ið	far-ið	sjá-ið	kom-ið	séuð
þeir	spil-i	flyt-j-i	far-i	sjá-i	kom-i	séu

The past subjunctive is used:

1 in past tense **að**-clauses, interrogative clauses and after certain conjunctions (see 2, 3 and 4 above);
2 in imaginary conditional clauses (which is why you often encountered it in Dialogue 1). Sometimes the conjunction **ef** precedes

these clauses, but often it is omitted, although in those cases the word order remains reversed: **Ef ég *ynni* í lottó *færi* ég í ferðalag – *Ynni* ég í lottó,** *færi* **ég í ferðalag.** Note that the occurrence of **ef** does not automatically signal a following subjunctive, but only if it concerns an imaginary condition. Compare, for instance: **ég geri það ef ég get** ('I'll do it if I can' = not imaginary);

3 in polite requests, often in combination with such verbs as **mega**, **vilja**, and **geta** (see below).

Whereas no I-shift occurs in the present subjunctive, the I-shift is the most prominent feature of the past subjunctive. The past subjunctive is derived from the plural past indicative form of the verb. It is essential to remember this, because the vowel of this form determines whether and what I-shift will occur. This means that for strong verbs, you will need to know the vowel of the past tense plural. Here are the paradigms for the past subjunctive:

	spiluðum	**fluttum**	**fórum**	**sáum**	**koma**	**vera**
		u > y	**ó > æ**	**á > æ**	(*irr.*)	(*irr.*)
ég	spilað-i	flytt-i	fær-i	sæ-i	kæm-i	vær-i
þú	spilað-ir	flytt-ir	fær-ir	sæ-ir	kæm-ir	vær-ir
hún	spilað-i	flytt-i	fær-i	sæ-i	kæm-i	vær-i
við	spiluð-um	flytt-um	fær-j-um	sæ-um	kæm-um	vær-um
þið	spiluð-uð	flytt-uð	fær-j-uð	sæ-uð	kæm-uð	vær-uð
þær	spiluð-u	flytt-u	fær-j-u	sæ-u	kæm-u	vær-u

Exercise 1

Go back to Dialogue 1 and find all the subjunctive forms. Can you tell whether they are in the present or past subjunctive? What are the infinitive forms?

Exercise 2

Put the verbs in brackets in the appropriate subjunctive form. In each case, think why the subjunctive is used, and whether you need a present or past subjunctive.

1 Strákurinn spurði hvar mamma sín ______ (vera).
2 Ég vona að ég ______ (sjá) ekki eftir þessu.
3 Hann hélt að hún ______ (gráta) af sorg frekar en af hlátri.
4 Óttast er, að ferðamennirnir ______ (hafa) týnst í stórviðrinu.
5 Hún sagði að börnin ______ (detta) niður stigann.

6 _____ (koma) að verkfalli, _____ (verða) afleiðingar alvarlegar.
7 _____ (fara) hann til fjandans!
8 Hann kemur ekki nema hún _____ (koma) líka.

Exercise 3

This is what Þór would do if he won the lottery. Write it in Icelandic.

Dæmi: **He would go on a trip** – *Hann færi í ferðalag*

1 He would get himself an expensive car.
2 He would continue to work.
3 He would pay all his bills.
4 He would dress in fancy clothes.
5 He would count all his money.
6 He would drink champagne every day.
7 He would not tell anyone about it.
8 He would give his wife a big present.

What would you do if you won the lottery?

Reading 1

Exercise 4: Reykjavík

The following words have been taken out of the Reykjavík text below. Can you put them back in their appropriate spot? Use the form of each word to help you determine where it might fit:

íbúar – útivistar – sjávarútvegi – ferðamenn – hús – byggingar – sumarsins – gömul – höfn – höfuðborg – sögu – sveitum

Reykjavík er _____(1)____ Íslands, og eina borg landsins. Íbúar hennar eru rúmlega 100.000. Hún er stærsta _____(2)____, og þar eru líka helstu menningar- og viðskiptastofnanir landsins. Þótt Reykjavík sé ekki stór borg miðað við milljónaborgir heimsins ber hún vissulega alþjóðlegt yfirbragð.

Reykjavíkurborg er ekki _____(3)____, þótt hún sé byggð á túni fyrsta landnema Íslands, Ingólfs Arnarsonar, sem reisti þar bú kringum 874. Eftir það kemur Reykjavík lítið við sögu öldum saman, en mun þar þó hafa verið verslunarstaður snemma á 16. öld. Árið 1786 voru Reykjavík veitt verslunarréttindi. Voru ____ (4)____ þá um 167. Elsta _____(5) ____ borgarinnar, Aðalstræti 10, er frá þessu tímabili.

Árið 1845 var Alþingi endurreist í Reykjavík, og á síðustu árum 19. aldar byrjaði ör og mikil þróun í ____(6)____ með komu vélbáta og togara, sem stuðlaði að því að auka vöxt og gengi borgarinnar. Árið 1904 var framkvæmdavaldið flutt frá Kaupmannahöfn til Reykjavíkur. Mikill fólksflutningur átti sér stað frá ____(7)____ til borgarinnar á fjórða og fimmta áratugnum, sem átti mikinn þátt í því að gamla íslenska bændasamfélagið breyttist í nútímasamfélag á örstuttum tíma. Árið 1950 hafði íbúatalan aukist frá 5800 um aldamótin í 56.000.

Reykjavík hefur aðdráttarafl fyrir bæði innlenda og erlenda ____ (8)____ þótt af ólíkum toga sé. Í borginni blómstrar mannlíf og menningarlíf, sérstaklega á sumrin, hvort heldur er í miðbænum, á kaffihúsum eða í menningarhúsum. Menningarnótt í miðborginni er nú hápunktur ____(9)____. Alþingishúsið, Dómkirkjan, og Ráðhúsið eru dæmi um merkar ____(10)____, gamlar og nýjar, og í Þjóðminjasafni og Árbæjarsafni er hægt að kynna sér ____(11) ____ landsins og borgarinnar. En þó þarf ekki heldur að fara langt til að njóta ____(12)____, því það eru margar náttúruperlur í borgarlandinu þar sem hægt er að draga sig í hlé frá ysi og þys borgarlífsins.

Vocabulary notes

miðað við	compared to
endurreisa	resurrect (from **reisa (reisi – reist)**, *acc.* 'raise', 'build')
ör, *adj.*	rapid, fast (also prefix 'very')
togari (-a, -ar)	trawler
stuðla (stuðla, stuðlað) að, *dat.*	help towards, assist
framkvæmdavald (-s, -)	executive power
fólksflutning/ur (-s, -ar)	migration
eiga sér stað	take place, occur
á fjórða og fimmta áratugnum	in the 1930s and 1940s
eiga mikinn þátt í, *dat.*	play an important part in
hafa aðdráttarafl fyrir, *acc.*	be attractive to
af ólíkum toga (spunninn)	of a different kind/origin
draga sig í hlé	retreat, withdraw
ys og þys	tumult, hustle and bustle

Exercise 5

Look at the listings below of what is on in Reykjavík. Write six sentences in Icelandic saying what you would do or where you would go if you were there right now (note that this is an imaginary situation). There are of course no set answers to this exercise; it depends on your interests.

■ Laugardagurinn

-Sumartónleikar í Skálholts-kirkju. Árni Heimir Ingólfsson flytur erindið Guð vor faðir, vér þökkum þér. Margrét Bóasdóttir sópran, Jorg Söndermann sembal og orgel og Nora Kornbluch selló flytja trúarleg einsöngs og orgelverk eftir m.a. Hildegaard von Bingen, Johannes Koch, Samuel Schneidt o.fl. Andrew Manze leikur verk fyrir einleiksfiðlu eftir J.S Bach og samtímamenn hans.

-Norræn þjóðdansasýning. Í tilefni af norrænu þjóðdansamóti í Reykjavík kemur Þjóðdansafélagið ásamt norrænum félögum í heimsókn og verður dansað á safnsvæðinu kl. 15:00

-Sumarsýning í Hallgrímskirkju. Verk eftir Tryggva Ólafsson. Opnunin verður klukkan 12:15.

FERÐAFÉLAG ÍSLANDS

MÖRKINNI 6 – SÍMI 568-2533

Dagsferð Ferðafélagsins: Laugardagur 16. ágúst kl. 09.00 Langavatnsdalur Öku- og gönguferð á Árbók arslóðir. Verð kr. 2.800. Forvitni leg ferð á fáfarnar slóðir. Brottfö frá Umferðarmiðstöðinni, aust anmegin, og Mörkinni 6.

■ Þriðjudagurinn 18. ágúst

-Tónleikar í Iðnó sem hefjast klukkan 20:30.

-Afmæli Reykjavíkur. Reykjavík fékk kaupstaðarréttindi þann 18. ágúst 1786. Í tilefni afmælisins er ókeypis aðgangur þennan dag í Árbæjarsafni.

-Sumartónleikar í Listasafni Sigurjóns Ólafssonar. Flytjendur Elisabeth Zeuthen, fiðla og Halldór Haraldsson píanó. Verk eftir J.P.E Hartmann, Emil Hartmann og Carl Nielsen. Tónleikarnir hefjast klukkan 20:30.

■ Fimmtudagurinn 20. ágúst

-Tónleikar í Kaffileikhúsinu, Hlaðvarpanum. Flytjandi Signý Sæmundsdóttir. Tónleikarnir hefjast klukkan 21:00.

■ Laugardagurinn 22. ágúst

-Menningarnótt í Reykjavík. Söfn, gallerí, kirkjur, kaffihús, veitingarstaðir, búðir og önnur fyrirtæki verða opin fram á nótt. Boðið verður upp á sýningar, tónleika, leiksýningar og aðrar menningar uppákomur. **Á miðnætti verður flugeldasýning við Tjörnina.**

-Skemmtun fyrir börn í Árbæjarsafni.

-4X4 jeppa sýning í Reykjavík.

■ Sunnudagurinn 23.ágúst

-Tónleikar í Hallgrímskirkju. Organisti Hörður Áskelsson. Tónleikarnir hefjast klukkan 20:30.

-Tónleikar í Árbæjarsafni. Þjóðlegir tónleikar í húsinu Lækjargötu 4 kl 15:00. Auk þess verður harmonikan þanin á safnsvæðinu og Dillonshús býður upp á ljúffengar veitingar. Handverksfólks við störf í ýmsum húsum.

-Rally Kross við Kapelluhraun

■ Þriðjudagurinn 25. ágúst

-Sumartónleikar í Listasafn Sigurjóns Ólafssonar. Kristjana Helgadóttir leikur á flautu og Daric Macaluso á gítar. Verk eftir Maurc Giuliani, Astor Piazzolla, Þorke Sigurbjörnsson, Alberto Ginastera Heitor Villa-Lobos og Riccardc Malipiero.

-Tónleikar í Iðnó klukkan 20:30

■ Fimmtudagurinn 27. ágúst

-Ganga um Elliðarárdal til að kanna slóðir drauga, álfa og afbrota manna. Leiðsögn frá Árbæjarsafn klukkan 22:00.

-Tónleikar í Kaffileikhúsinu Hlaðvarpanum. Flytjandi Hulda B Garðarsdóttir.

■ Laugardagurinn 29. ágúst

-Sýning á gömlum leikföngum Árbæjarsafni. Skemmtanir og marg: konar uppákomur.

-Light Nights. Sýning í Tjarnarbíói Leiksýning byggð á Íslendinga sögunum. Sýningin hefst klukkar 21:00.

-Kvartmílan í Reykjavík

Dialogue 2

Húsnæði

Þórey has had to move from her home town Egilsstaðir to Reykjavík, where she will be going to university. She has found herself a small flat and has just moved in. She is phoning her mother to tell her the news.

Þórey: Sæl mamma. Nú er ég flutt inn í nýju íbúðina mína!

Mamma: Til hamingju með það elskan. Hvernig er íbúðin, og hvernig líkar þér?

Þórey: Þetta er ágætis íbúð þó ekkert stórglæsileg. Hún er í fjölbýlishúsi, á þriðju hæð, og þetta er tveggja herbergja íbúð. Hún er lítil en björt, og á mjög góðum stað í borginni nálægt háskólanum. Og svo er lítið en þægilegt eldhús með ísskáp og eldavél, og ég hef aðgang að þvottahúsi niðri í kjallaranum.

Mamma: Hvernig er leigan, er hún mjög há?

Þórey: Ekki svo mjög: 30.000 á mánuði.

Mamma: Og ertu búin að fá húsgögn?

Þórey: Það er enn býsna tómt hérna inni. En ég keypti mér gamlan sófa og stól, og ég er með lítið eldhúsborð sem þjónar sem skrifborð. Ég er ekki með rúm ennþá, en vinkona mín lánaði mér dýnu.

Mamma: Ertu með skápa?

Þórey: Það er pínulítill fataskápur í svefnherberginu, og nokkrir skápar í eldhúsinu.

Mamma: Heyrðu Þórey, við pabbi ætlum að keyra suður um næstu helgi með alls konar dót úr hjólhýsinu gamla sem við notum ekki lengur: potta, pönnur, diska, bolla, skálar, hnífapör, rúmföt, handklæði, viskustykki ...

Þórey: Elsku mamma mín, það liggur ekkert á, þetta reddast, hafðu engar áhyggjur!

Mamma: Ég veit það, en við sögðumst koma með dót handa þér þegar þú værir búin að finna þér íbúð, og við erum ákveðin í því að gera það sem allra fyrst!

Þórey: Allt í lagi þá! Ég hlakka til að sjá ykkur!

Vocabulary notes

ágætis-	fine	**aðgang/ur (-s)**	access, entrance
hæð (-ar, -ir)	floor	**húsgögn**, *n.pl.*	furniture

dýn/a (-u, -ur)	mattress	**þetta reddast**	it'll be okay
dót (-s)	stuff	**sem allra fyrst**	as soon as possible
hjólhýsi (-s, -)	caravan		

Vocabulary connected with housing

1 *Hýbýli*
einbýlishús single home
fjölbýlishús duplex/
 triplex . . .
íbúð flat, apartment
blokk block of flats, apartment building

2 *Herbergi*
stofa living room
borðstofa dining room
gangur hallway
stigi stairs, staircase
svefnherbergi bedroom
baðherbergi bathroom
salerni/klósett WC
loft attic
gluggi window
kjallari cellar, basement
veggur wall
gólf floor
þak roof

3 *Tæki*
(upp)þvottavél (dish)washing
 machine
örbylgjuofn microwave
kæliskápur, ísskápur fridge
eldavél stove
samstæða music centre
hárþurrka hair dryer
rakvél razor
tengill, klór plug, plug-in

4 *Húsgögn*
sófi sofa
(bóka)skápur (book) case,
 cupboard
arinn, *m.* fireplace
teppi carpet
hilla shelf
kommóða chest of drawers
skúffa drawer
gluggakista window sill
gardína/gluggatjald curtain
rúmföt bed linen
koddi pillow
spegill mirror
sturta shower
sápa soap
ofn heater, radiator, oven
(tann)bursti, greiða
 (tooth)brush, comb
handklæði towel
vaskur, krani sink, tap
(vekjara)klukka (alarm) clock

5 *Búsáhöld*
diskur plate
bolli cup
hnífapör (hnífur – gaffall –
 skeið) cutlery ('knife',
 'fork', 'spoon')
pottur pot
panna pan
skál bowl
viskustykki dish cloth, tea
 towel

Exercise 6

Write a description of your own home in Icelandic (you may want to brush up on prepositions and their cases before doing this exercise). There is a sample answer at the back. Compare Áslaug's flat to your own – how are they different?

Language points

Reported speech

Reporting what someone said can be done in two ways in Icelandic: Whenever people report what they themselves said, Icelandic uses the middle voice, usually of the verb **segja**, followed by the infinitive of the main verb. This way, repetition of the subject (as in English 'I said I ...') is avoided. You have already encountered an example in Dialogue 2: **við** *sögðumst ætla* **að koma** '*we* said *we* would come'. In these instances, there is no need to use the subjunctive because you use an infinitive. Here are some more examples:

> *Ég* **sagði:** '*Ég* **fer ekki í bæinn í dag'** > *Ég* *sagðist* ekki *fara í* **bæinn í dag**
> *I* said *I* would not go into town today

> *Þeir* **segja:** '*Við* **nennum því ekki'** > *Þeir* *segjast* ekki *nenna* því
> *They* say *they* don't care to/don't feel like it

Reporting what someone else said usually involves a so-called **að**-clause (**Hann** *sagði að* **...** 'He said that...'), or, if it concerns a question, an **interrogative** clause (**Hún** *spurði* **hvort/hvar/hvenær ...** 'She asked whether/where/when...'). Earlier in this lesson you learned that these clauses take a subjunctive. The question is when to use which tense. If the 'reporting verb' (i.e., **segja**, **spyrja**, etc.) is in the present tense, then the subordinate clause will have the present subjunctive, and if it is in the past tense, the subordinate clause will have the past subjunctive:

> **Þórey** *segir:* **'Íbúðin** *er* **ágæt'** > **Þórey** *segir* **að íbúðin** *sé* **ágæt**
> **Þórey** *says* her flat *is* fine

> **Þau** *spurðu:* **'Er hún dýr?'** > **Þau** *spurðu* **hvort hún** *væri* **dýr**
> They *asked* whether it *was* expensive

If what is reported is in the past tense, however, the subordinate clause will be in the present perfect with auxiliary **hafa** in the subjunctive. The tense of the subjunctive will be the same as that of the reporting verb:

Þórey *segir:* **'Íbúðin** *var* **ágæt'** > **Þórey** *segir* **að íbúðin** *hafi* *verið* **ágæt**
Þórey *says* that her flat *has been* fine

Þau *spurðu:* **'Var hún dýr?'** > **Þau** *spurðu* **hvort hún** *hefði* *verið* **dýr**
They *asked* whether it had *been* expensive

If what is reported has an impersonal construction or a possessive pronoun in it that refers to the 'reporter', you cannot use the middle voice construction. Instead, you use a subordinate clause according to the rules outlined above, but in which the pronoun in question is made reflexive:

Áki segir: **'***Mér* **liður ekki vel'** > **Áki segir að** *sér* **liði ekki vel**
Þórey sagði: **'Íbúðin** *mín* **er björt'** > **Þórey sagði að íbúðin** *sín* **væri björt**

Exercise 7

Rephrase the following sentences, using indirect (reported) speech. Remember to pay attention to tense, subjunctive or middle voice, and pronouns referring to the subject:

Dæmi: **Jón segir: 'Mig langar í ís'** > *Jón segir að sig langi í ís*

1 Ég segi: 'Ég hef aldrei komið til Íslands áður.'
2 Barnið sagði: 'Mér finnst grænmeti vont.'
3 Mamma spyr: 'Hvar varstu í gærkvöldi?'
4 Pabbi spurði: 'Af hverju horfðirðu svo einkennilega á mig (!)?'
5 Þórey spurði: 'Komið þið á morgun?'

Exercise 8

Go back to Exercise 6. Imagine Áslaug described her flat to you and you want to tell a mutual friend what she said. Report her description using indirect speech (present tense).

Dialogue 3

Gestir í kaffi

Þórey has invited her landlord and landlady Jóhann and Guðbjörg, an elderly couple living on the ground floor of the house, for afternoon coffee, so they can see the flat and get to know her a little better. Why does Guðbjörg want to sit in the chair? What would she like with her coffee? What would Þórey like to see fixed in her flat?

ÞÓREY: Komið þið sæl og blessuð, og gangið í bæinn.

JÓHANN: Sæl vertu, Þórey, og þakka þér fyrir.

ÞÓREY: Gjörið þið svo vel og fáið ykkur sæti.

GUÐBJÖRG: Gæti ég fengið mér sæti hér í þessum stól? Ég er svo slæm í bakinu og kæmist örugglega ekki aftur upp úr sófanum.

ÞÓREY: Að sjálfsögðu, Guðbjörg, gjörðu svo vel. Jæja, hérna er kaffið. Þætti ykkur gott að fá rjóma út í það?

JÓHANN: Já, takk, það væri mjög gott.

GUÐBJÖRG: Mætti ég biðja um molasykur? Mér þykir molasykur svo góður með kaffinu.

ÞÓREY: Sjálfsagt, ég skal ná í hann, en gjörið svo vel og fáið ykkur kökusneið.

JÓHANN: Takk fyrir. Þetta er alveg fyrirtakskaka, Þórey mín! Það var mjög fallegt af þér að bjóða okkur í kaffi.

GUÐBJÖRG: Já, rétt er það. Vildirðu rétta mér kökudiskinn, Þórey, takk.

JÓHANN: Hvernig líkar þér svo Þórey? Er ekki allt í lagi með íbúðina?

ÞÓREY: Jú jú, hún er fín, ég er mjög ánægð. Það þyrfti kannski aðeins að laga frárennslið, það virðist vera svolítið stíflað.

JÓHANN: Það gæti vel verið, já. Ég skal athuga það í fyrramálið. Jæja, Þórey, við Guðbjörg ættum að koma okkur. Það er orðið framorðið. Þakka þér kærlega fyrir kaffið.

GUÐBJÖRG: Já, takk fyrir mig elskan, þetta var indælt.

ÞÓREY: Verði ykkur að góðu, og takk fyrir komuna.

Vocabulary notes

fá út í (kaffið), *acc.*   have in one's coffee

molasykur (-s), *m.*   lump sugar traditionally held between the teeth while drinking coffee

fyrirtaks-	excellent
það var fallegt af þér	it was very nice of you
frárennsli (-s, -)	drain

Language points

Hosts and guests: ways of expressing politeness

It is probably clear to you by now that Icelandic has slightly different ways of expressing politeness than English. When talking to strangers, in shops, or with friends, elaborate politeness is considered rather unnecessary. This does not mean, however, that politeness is not an issue. For instance, one could argue that while Icelanders don't go out of their way to say 'please', they generally do tend to express their thanks more elaborately and on more occasions than happens in English.

Politeness is expressed through greater formality when dealing with people you don't know very well, particularly when the people concerned are older than you are, as in the dialogue above, or the situation is rather formal. Certain formulaic phrases of formality are used in such situations, most of which you already learned at the beginning of this course, and requests and invitations are couched in the non-assertive or tentative past subjunctive. The auxiliary verbs used in these situations are: **geta**, **vilja**, **mega**, **þykja**, **þurfa**, **eiga að** 'should'. It is thus worthwhile to know these verbs in their past subjunctive forms. You already encountered them in Dialogue 3. Another way of sounding more polite is to add the phrase **gjöra/gera svo vel að** . . . 'please be so good as to . . .', either in combination with **vilja** or in the imperative:

Viltu gjöra svo vel að rétta mér kökudisk
Would you please (be so good as to) hand me a cake dish

or

Gjörðu svo vel og réttu mér kökudisk
Hand me a cake dish, would you, please

Exercise 10

The following requests would be appropriate in an informal situation. Can you rephrase them for a more formal occasion?

1 Réttu mér mjólkina.
2 Gefðu mér eld.
3 Mér þykir gott konfekt með kaffinu
4 Má ég fá meira kaffi?
5 Get ég fengið vatnsglas?
6 Á ég að koma með þér?
7 Viltu dansa?

Reading 2

Fyrsta þakíbúð á Íslandi opnuð almenningi

Einar Jónsson (1874–1954) is one of Iceland's most famous sculptors. Several of his sculptures, depicting prominent figures from Icelandic history, adorn central Reykjavík. The museum dedicated to his work is also located in Reykjavík. When will the flat be open to the public? What's so special about the flat? What's currently happening to it? What is remarkable about the flat's furniture?

Frá og með deginum í dag verður íbúð Einars Jónssonar myndhöggvara opin gestum safnsins. Íbúðin er í Listasafni Einars Jónssonar, en þar bjuggu hjónin Einar og Anna kona hans frá 1923 til 1954 þegar Einar lést.

'Það má segja að þetta sé fyrsta þakíbúð á Íslandi,' segir Hrafnhildur Schram forstöðumaður listasafnsins. 'Íbúðin verður nú hluti af safninu og opin gestum. Það er mjög skemmtilegt að opna hana, það færir gesti safnsins nær persónu Einars.' Einar innréttaði íbúðina og teiknaði mikið af húsgögnum sem eru í henni. 'Hann teiknaði m.a. bókaskápa sem eru stuðlabergsformaðir, og það er mjög ríkur þáttur í verkum hans. En raunar má segja að húsið sjálft sé stærsti skúlptúr Einars.'

Listasafn Einars Jónssonar verður 75 ára á næsta ári og af því tilefni var ráðist í viðgerðir á húsinu að utan. 'Húsið var mjög illa farið. Nú er verið að skipta um glugga og gera við vegginn. Það þurfti að gera við allar sprungur, skipta um járnverk og síðan verður settur kvarsmulningur yfir alla bygginguna.' Framkvæmdirnar munu koma til með að kosta 27 milljónir og hafa þær gengið eftir áætlun.

From Morgunblaðið, 14. ágúst 1997, bls. 2

Vocabulary notes

myndhöggvar/i (-a, -ar)	sculptor
forstöðumað/ur	leader, director
innrétta (innrétta, innréttaði, innréttað), *acc.*	furnish, install
stuðlaberg (-s, -)	columnar basalt
ráðast (ræðst, réðst, réðust, ráðist) í, *acc.*	decide to have
viðgerð (-ar, -ir)	renovations, repairs
illa farið	in bad condition
sprung/a (-u, -ur)	crack
járnverk (-s, -)	metal work
kvarsmulning/ur (-s)	quartz dust
koma til með að kosta	will cost
eftir áætlun	according to plan, on schedule

Grammar summary

Nouns and definite articles

Masculine declensions

sg.					
nom.	hattur	dagur	trefill	fugl	
acc.	hatt	dag	trefil	fugl	
dat.	hatti	degi	trefli	fugli	
gen.	hatts	dags	trefils	fugls	

pl.					
nom.	hattar	dagar	treflar	fuglar	
acc.	hatta	daga	trefla	fugla	
dat.	höttum	dögum	treflum	fuglum	
gen.	hatta	daga	trefla	fugla	

sg.					
	mælir	staður	köttur	skóli	þátttakandi
	mæli	stað	kött	skóla	þátttakanda
	mæli	stað	ketti	skóla	þátttakanda
	mælis	staðar	kattar	skóla	þátttakanda

pl.					
	mælar	staðir	kettir	skólar	þátttakendur
	mæla	staði	ketti	skóla	þátttakendur
	mælum	stöðum	köttum	skólum	þátttakendum
	mæla	staða	katta	skóla	þátttakenda

With definite article

sg.			
	hattur-inn	mælir-inn	skóli-nn
	hatt-inn	mæli-nn	skóla-nn
	hatti-num	mæli-num	skóla-num
	hatts-ins	mælis-ins	skóla-ns

pl.			
	hattar-nir	mælar-nir	skólar-nir
	hatta-na	mæla-na	skóla-na
	höttu-num	mælu-num	skólu-num
	hatta-nna	mæla-nna	skóla-nna

Feminine declensions

sg.			
borg	skeið	spurning	stöð
borg	skeið	spurningu	stöð
borg	skeið	spurningu	stöð
borgar	skeiðar	spurningar	stöðvar

pl.			
borgir	skeiðar	spurningar	stöðvar
borgir	skeiðar	spurningar	stöðvar
borgum	skeiðum	spurningum	stöðvum
borga	skeiða	spurninga	stöðva

sg.			
helgi	strönd	rót	saga
helgi	strönd	rót	sögu
helgi	strönd	rót	sögu
helgar	strandar	rótar	sögu

pl.			
helgar	strendur	rætur	sögur
helgar	strendur	rætur	sögur
helgum	ströndum	rótum	sögum
helga	stranda	róta	sagna

With definite article

sg.		
borg-in	spurning-in	saga-n
borg-ina	spurningu-na	sögu-na
borg-inni	spurningu-nni	sögu-nni
borgar-innar	spurningar-innar	sögu-nnar

pl.		
borgir-nar	spurningar-nar	sögur-nar
borgir-nar	spurningar-nar	sögur-nar
borgu-num	spurningu-num	sögu-num
borga-nna	spurninga-nna	sagna-nna

Neuter declensions

sg.			
glas	herbergi	auga	tré
glas	herbergi	auga	tré
glasi	herbergi	auga	tré
glass	herbergis	auga	trés

pl.			
glös	herbergi	augu	tré
glös	herbergi	augu	tré
glösum	herbergjum	augum	trjám
glasa	herbergja	augna	trjáa

With the definite article

sg.	herbergi-ð	auga-ð	tré-ð
	herbergi-ð	auga-ð	tré-ð
	herbergi-nu	auga-nu	tré-nu
	herbergis-ins	auga-ns	trés-ins

pl.	herbergi-n	augu-n	tré-n
	herbergi-n	augu-n	tré-n
	herberju-num	augu-num	trjá-num
	herbergja-nna	augna-nna	trjá-nna

Adjectives: strong declension

Singular nominative endings

Masculine	Feminine	Neuter
_______ur	$a > ö/u$ ____0	_______t
_______ll		____(ð > t) t
_______nn		____(V)tt
_______r		____(C + d > t)
		____(C + t)0

sg.	Masculine			Feminine			Neuter		
	hvítur	heill	hár	hvít	heil	há	hvítt	heilt	hátt
	hvítan	heilan	háan	hvíta	heila	háa	hvítt	heilt	hátt
	hvítum	heilum	háum	hvítri	heilli	hárri	hvítu	heilu	háu
	hvíts	heils	hás	hvítrar	heillar	hárrar	hvíts	heils	hás

pl.	Masculine			Feminine			Neuter		
	hvítir	heilir	háir	hvítar	heilar	háar	hvít	heil	há
	hvíta	heila	háa	hvítar	heilar	háar	hvít	heil	há
	hvítum	heilum	háum	hvítum	heilum	háum	hvítum	heilum	háum
	hvítra	heilla	hárra	hvítra	heilla	hárra	hvítra	heilla	hárra

irregular

sg.	Masculine		Feminine		Neuter	
	mikill	stór	mikil	stór	mikið	stórt
	mikinn	stóran	mikla	stóra	mikið	stórt
	miklum	stórum	mikilli	stórri	miklu	stóru
	mikils	stórs	mikillar	stórrar	mikils	stórs

pl.						
	miklir	stórir	miklar	stórar	mikil	stór
	mikla	stóra	miklar	stórar	mikil	stór
	miklum	stórum	miklum	stórum	miklum	stórum
	mikilla	stórra	mikilla	stórra	mikilla	stórra

Like **mikill** goes **lítill**; like **stór** go all adjectives without an ending, including **laus**, **jafn**, etc.

sg.	fagur	fögur	fagurt	opinn	opin	opið
	fagran	fagra	fagurt	opinn	opna	opið
	fögrum	fagurri	fögru	opnum	opinni	opnu
	fagurs	fagurrar	fagurs	opins	opinnar	opins
pl.	fagrir	fagrar	fögur	opnir	opnar	opin
	fagra	fagrar	fögur	opna	opnar	opin
	fögrum	fögrum	fögrum	opnum	opnum	opnum
	fagurra	fagurra	fagurra	opinna	opinna	opinna

Like **fagur** go adjectives with two-stem syllables and without an ending. Like **opinn** go all adjectives with two syllables ending in **-inn**, including past participles.

Adjectives: weak declension

		masculine	*feminine*	*neuter*
sg.	nom.	_____i	_____a	_____a
	acc.	_____a	U-shift _____u	_____a
	dat.	_____a	U-shift _____u	_____a
	gen.	_____a	U-shift _____u	_____a
pl.			U-shift _____u	

(for all genders and cases)

Personal pronouns

sg.	ég	þú	hann	hún	það
	mig	þig	hann	hana	það
	mér	þér	honum	henni	því
	mín	þín	hans	hennar	þess
pl.	við	þið	þeir	þær	þau
	okkur	ykkur	þá	þær	þau
	okkur	ykkur	þeim	þeim	þeim
	okkar	ykkar	þeirra	þeirra	þeirra

Possessive pronouns

	masc.	fem.	neut.	masc.	fem.	neut.
sg.	minn	mín	mitt	þinn	þín	þitt
	minn	mína	mitt	þinn	þína	þitt
	mínum	minni	mínu	þínum	þinni	þínu
	míns	minnar	míns	þíns	þinnar	þíns
pl.	mínir	mínar	mín	þínir	þínar	þín
	mína	mínar	mín	þína	þínar	þín
	mínum	mínum	mínum	þínum	þínum	þínum
	minna	minna	minna	þinna	þinna	þinna

	masc.	fem.	neut.
sg.	sinn	sín	sitt
	sinn	sína	sitt
	sínum	sinni	sínu
	síns	sinnar	síns
pl.	sínir	sínar	sín
	sína	sínar	sín
	sínum	sínum	sínum
	sinna	sinna	sinna

Demonstrative pronouns

þessi: **sá:**

	masc.	fem.	neut.	masc.	fem.	neut.
sg.	þessi	þessi	þetta	sá	sú	það
	þennan	þessa	þetta	þann	þá	það
	þessum	þessari	þessu	þeim	þeirri	því
	þessa	þessarar	þessa	þess	þeirrar	þess
pl.	þessir	þessar	þessi	þeir	þær	þau
	þessa	þessar	þessi	þá	þær	þau
	þessum	þessum	þessum	þeim	þeim	þeim
	þessara	þessara	þessara	þeirra	þeirra	þeirra

hinn   *Interrogative pronoun:* **hver**

sg.	hinn	hin	hitt/hið	hver	hver	hvert/hvað
	hinn	hina	hitt/hið	hvern	hverja	hvert/hvað
	hinum	hinni	hinu	hverjum	hverri	hverju
	hins	hinnar	hins	hvers	hverrar	hvers

pl.	hinir	hinar	hin	hverjir	hverjar	hver
	hina	hinar	hin	hverja	hverjar	hver
	hinum	hinum	hinum	hverjum	hverjum	hverjum
	hinna	hinna	hinna	hverra	hverra	hverra

Dual and plural indefinite pronouns

		allir		***nokkrir***		
sg.	*masc.*	*fem.*	*neut.*	*masc.*	*fem.*	*neut.*
	allur	öll	allt	nokkur	nokkur	nokkuð/nokkurt
	allan	alla	allt	nokkurn	nokkra	nokkuð/nokkurt
	öllum	allri	öllu	nokkrum	nokkurri	nokkru
	alls	allrar	alls	nokkurs	nokkurrar	nokkurs
pl.	allir	allar	öll	nokkrir	nokkrar	nokkur
	alla	allar	öll	nokkra	nokkrar	nokkur
	öllum	öllum	öllum	nokkrum	nokkrum	nokkrum
	allra	allra	allra	nokkurra	nokkurra	nokkurra

		báðir		***ýmsir***		
pl.	*masc.*	*fem.*	*neut.*	*masc.*	*fem.*	*neut.*
	báðir	báðar	bæði	ýmsir	ýmsar	ýmis
	báða	báðar	bæði	ýmsa	ýmsar	ýmis
	báðum	báðum	báðum	ýmsum	ýmsum	ýmsum
	beggja	beggja	beggja	ýmissa	ýmissa	ýmissa

Negative pronouns: *enginn*

sg.	*masc.*	*fem.*	*neut.*	*pl.*	*masc.*	*fem.*	*neut.*
	enginn	engin	ekkert		engir	engar	engin
	engan	enga	ekkert		enga	engar	engin
	engum	engri	engu		engum	engum	engum
	einskis	engrar	einskis		engra	engra	engra

Numerals

sg.	*masc.*	*fem.*	*neut.*	*pl.*	*masc.*	*fem.*	*neut.*
	einn	ein	eitt		einir	einar	ein
	einn	eina	eitt		eina	einar	ein
	einum	einni	einu		einum	einum	einum
	eins	einnar	eins		einna	einna	einna

All plural numerals (**tvennir, þrennir, fernir**) decline like **einir**.

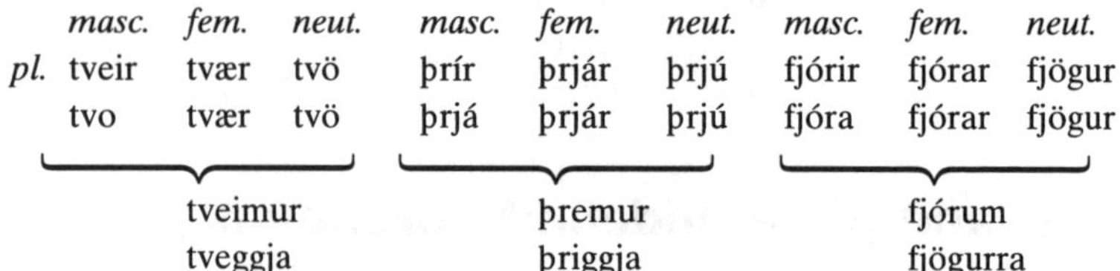

	masc.	fem.	neut.	masc.	fem.	neut.	masc.	fem.	neut.
pl.	tveir	tvær	tvö	þrír	þrjár	þrjú	fjórir	fjórar	fjögur
	tvo	tvær	tvö	þrjá	þrjár	þrjú	fjóra	fjórar	fjögur
	tveimur			þremur			fjórum		
	tveggja			þriggja			fjögurra		

I-shift

a	changes to	e	as in	**taka – tek, fara – fer**
o	changes to	e	as in	**koma – kem**
ö	changes to	e	as in	**dökkur – dekkri, köttur – kettir**
á	changes to	æ	as in	**fá – fæ**
ó	changes to	æ	as in	**stór – stærri**
ú				**búa – bý**
jú	changes to	ý	as in	**fljúga – flýg**
jó				**brjóta – brýt**
u	changes to	y	as in	**ungur – yngri, sonur – synir**
au	changes to	ey	as in	**auka – eyk**

Verbs: weak

Pres.	*ætla*	*heyra*	*þegja*	*velja*
ég	ætla	heyri	þegi	vel
þú	ætlar	heyrir	þegir	velur
hún	ætlar	heyrir	þegir	velur
við	ætlum	heyrum	þegjum	veljum
þið	ætlið	heyrið	þegið	veljið
þær	ætla	heyra	þegja	velja
Past	ætlaði	heyrði	þagði	valdi
	ætlaðir	heyrðir	þagðir	valdir
	ætlaði	heyrði	þagði	valdi
	ætluðum	heyrðum	þögðum	völdum
	ætluðuð	heyrðuð	þögðuð	völduð
	ætluðu	heyrðu	þögðu	völdu

Pres.	hafa	þvo	snúa	ná
	hef	þvæ	sný	næ
	hefur	þværð	snýrð	nærð
	hefur	þvær	snýr	nær
	höfum	þvoum	snúum	náum
	hafið	þvoið	snúið	náið
	hafa	þvo	snúa	ná
Past	hafði	þvoði	snéri	náði
	hafðir	þvoðir	snérir	náðir
	hafði	þvoði	snéri	náði
	höfðum	þvoðum	snérum	náðum
	höfðuð	þvoðuð	snéruð	náðuð
	höfðu	þvoðu	snéru	náðu

Verbs: strong

Pres.	bíta	ljúga	stökkva	sofa	sitja
ég	bít	lýg	stekk	sef	sit
þú	bítur	lýgur	stekkur	sefur	situr
hann	bítur	lýgur	stekkur	sefur	situr
við	bítum	ljúgum	stökkvum	sofum	sitjum
þið	bítið	ljúgið	stökkvið	sofið	sitjið
þeir	bíta	ljúga	stökkva	sofa	sitja
Past	beit	laug	stökk	svaf	sat
	beist	laugst	stökkst	svafst	sast
	beit	laug	stökk	svaf	sat
	bitum	lugum	stukkum	sváfum	sátum
	bituð	luguð	stukkuð	sváfuð	sátuð
	bitu	lugu	stukku	sváfu	sátu
Pres.	falla	hlaupa	fá	fara	búa
	fell	hleyp	fer	fæ	bý
	fellur	hleypur	ferð	færð	býrð
	fellur	hleypur	fer	fær	býr
	föllum	hlaupum	förum	fáum	búum
	fallið	hlaupið	farið	fáið	búið
	falla	hlaupa	fara	fá	búa

Past	féll	hljóp	fór	fékk	bjó
	féllst	hljópst	fórst	fékkst	bjóst
	féll	hljóp	fór	fékk	bjó
	féllum	hlupum	fórum	fengum	bjuggum
	félluð	hlupuð	fóruð	fenguð	bjugguð
	féllu	hlupu	fóru	fengu	bjuggu

Verbs: subjunctive

Pres.	spila	flytja	fara	sjá	koma	vera (irr.)
ég	spili	flytji	fari	sjái	komi	sé
þú	spilir	flytjir	farir	sjáir	komir	sért
hann	spili	flytji	fari	sjái	komi	sé
við	spilum	flytjum	förum	sjáum	komum	séum
þið	spilið	flytjið	farið	sjáið	komið	séuð
þeir	spili	flytji	fari	sjái	komi	séu

Past	spiluðum	fluttum	fórum	sáum	koma	vera
		u>y	ó>œ	á>œ	(irr.)	(irr.)
ég	spilaði	flytti	færi	sæi	kæmi	væri
þú	spilaðir	flyttir	færir	sæir	kæmir	værir
hún	spilaði	flytti	færi	sæi	kæmi	væri
við	spiluðum	flyttum	færum	sæjum	kæmum	værum
þið	spiluðuð	flyttuð	færuð	sæjuð	kæmuð	væruð
þær	spiluðu	flyttu	færu	sæju	kæmu	væru

Verbs: past participles

-a- group: **-að**, or **-ast** (middle voice): **ætla – ætlað, kallast – kallast**
-i- group: **-t** (middle voice: **-t** dropped before **-st**): **senda – sent, kyssast – kysst**
All other groups: past participle ends in **-ið** (middle voice **-ist**) with the
following vowel changes:

	Stem vowel	PP vowel		
weak verbs	-e-	-a-	semja – samið	
	-y/ý-	-u/ú-	flýja – flúið	
strong verbs	-í-	-i-	bíta – bitið	
	-jó/jú/ú-	-o-	fljúga – flogið	
	-e/(j)a-	-o-	gjalda – goldið	
	-i-	-u/e-	finna – fundið, sitja – setið	
	-e-	-e-	lesa – lesið, gefa – gefið	

Glossary of grammatical terms

accusative case (form) indicating an object position of a noun or other nominal with a verb or preposition governing this case (usually direct object)

adjective describes a noun, e.g. 'a *clean* table', where 'clean' describes the noun 'table'

adverb describes any part of speech other than a noun

agent subject performing the action described by the (main) verb

antonym word which has an opposite meaning to another word

article: definite *Engl.* 'the'; indefinite, *Engl.* 'a(n)'

cardinal number regular number denoting quantity (*Engl.* 'one, two, three, . . .')

cases different forms nominals take on to reflect their position in a sentence. There are four in Icelandic, one for the subject position (nominative) and three for objects (accusative, dative, genitive), where the verb or preposition in the sentence determines which of three object cases the nominal takes on

comparative form of adjective or adverb indicating a higher degree (*Engl.* 'more', '-er')

compound word made up of two or more individual words (*Engl.* 'toothpaste')

conjugation process whereby a verb is given different endings to reflect the person (first, second or third) and number (singular or plural) of the subject

conjunction word used to connect sentences, clauses and words (*Engl.* 'and', 'but' . . .)

dative case (form) indicating one of three object positions of a noun or other nominal (the indirect object where applicable)

declension process whereby a nominal takes on different forms, reflecting case, gender and number. The *strong* (adjectives) declension pattern is used when the adjective describes an indefinite noun (i.e., without the definite article, demonstrative or possessive pronoun); the *weak* (adjectives) declension pattern is used when the adjective describes a definite noun (*with* definite article, demonstrative or possessive pronoun, or a personal name) or is a superlative or an ordinal number. In the weak declension, all endings consist of vowels

direct object see **object**

demonstrative see **pronoun, demonstrative**

ending final part of a word which changes as a result of declension or conjugation

fraction dropping of the second stem vowel of nouns and adjectives when an ending beginning with a vowel is added to the stem

genitive case (form) of a noun or other nominal indicating ownership or an object position where the verb or preposition governs the genitive

imperative verb form telling people what to do and what not to do, as in English 'Go!'

impersonal construction sentence or clause where the supposed subject is in an object case

indeclinable nominal which is not subject to declension, i.e. does not change its form

indirect object see **object**

indirect speech sentence where someone's words are related by someone else (*Engl.* 'She says that …')

infinitive basic verb form which does not reflect any person, number, tense etc. ('dictionary form' of the verb)

intensifier word (often an adverb, adjective or prefix) used to give special force or emphasis

interjection exclamation (as part of speech)

interrogative word used to formulate a question, particularly asking for specific information (*Engl.* 'wh-' words, *Icel.* 'hv-' words)

intransitive verb verb that does not take an object

middle voice Icelandic verb form ending in '-st', used in many instances to indicate reciprocity, reflexivity or a passive

nominal noun or behaving like a noun, i.e. its form reflects gender, number and case

nominative case (form) indicating the subject position of a noun or other nominal; also the form which appears in dictionaries and glossaries

noun word that indicates ('names') someone or something (*Engl.* 'chair', 'dog', 'child', 'John'). In Icelandic, all nouns have gender and take on different number and case forms, which in turn determine the form of many other nominals in the sentence

number singular (one) or plural (more than one)

object part of speech filled by a nominal, indicating the object of the action expressed by the verb. A distinction is made between the 'direct' object that undergoes or suffers the action directly, and an 'indirect' object, representing the recipient of the action

ordinal form indicating a number in a series (*Engl.* 'first, second, third, …')

participle word formed from a verb: present, formed with a specific suffix (*Engl.* '-ing', *Icel.* '-andi') to use as an adjective, noun or adverb, indicating something going on in the present (*Engl.* 'the *singing* cook'); past, formed with suffix and, in the case of strong verbs, with vowel change, to use as an adjective or noun, indicating something that was or has resulted from a past action, e.g. 'I have *finished*'

passive verbal construction (made with a form of the verb 'to be' and the past participle) where the object becomes the subject to indicate a lack or irrelevance of agency, e.g. 'The novel is read (by X)' is the passive of 'X reads the novel'

past: *simple* verb form indicating something that happened in the past, as in 'she *left*'; *continuous*, verbal construction made with a form of the verb 'to be' indicating an action (usually temporary or instantaneous) that was happening in the past, as in 'she *was leaving*'

perfect compound tense (i.e. formed with more than one word) denoting a fully completed action in the past, constructed with a form of the verb 'to have' and the past participle of the main verb (*Engl.* 'I have/had eaten')

plural noun noun which only ever occurs in the plural form (*Engl.* 'trousers', 'spectacles')

possessive indicates ownership; see also **pronoun, possessive**

prefix element added to the beginning of a word to qualify or adjust its meaning

preposition word denoting the direction of the action expressed by the verb (*Engl.* 'on', 'in')

present: *simple* verb form indicating something that happens in the present, as in 'she *leaves*'; *continuous* verbal construction made with a form of the verb 'to be' indicating an action (usually temporary or instantaneous) that is happening at this moment, as in 'she *is leaving*'

pro-form short word replacing a part of speech, clause or sentence, e.g. 'She is gone. Is *that* so?', where 'that' replaces the previous sentence

pronoun a short word replacing a noun and behaving exactly like it
personal Engl. 'I', 'you', 'he', 'she', 'it', 'we', 'they'
plural pronoun only, or predominantly, occurring in the plural form (*Engl.* 'all')
dual same as a plural pronoun but exclusively denoting a plurality of two (*Engl.* 'both')
indefinite pronoun denoting a generality (*Engl.* 'some')
reflexive object pronoun referring back to the subject (*Engl.* 'myself', 'yourself')

possessive pronoun indicating ownership (*Engl.* 'my/mine', 'your(s)'
demonstrative pronoun used to indicate something within visual range
or to indicate something mentioned earlier or to be mentioned shortly
(*Engl.* 'this', 'that')

reciprocity expressing a mutuality or mutual action (*Engl.* 'each other')

reflexive verb or sentence where the action expressed by the verb is performed on the subject of the verb (*Engl.* 'she hurt *herself*')

stem the root or main part of a word which remains unchanged (except for vowel changes and fraction)

subject part of speech indicating the performer (agent) of the action expressed by the verb

subjunctive verb form indicating a non-factuality, i.e. wish, exhortation, incertitude, report, imaginary situation, etc.

subordinate clause a secondary or 'sub'sentence which does not constitute a sentence in itself but modifies the main sentence

suffix element added to the end of a word

superlative form of adjective or adverb indicating the highest degree (*Engl.* 'most', '-est')

verb word denoting an action

   impersonal a verb denoting an action that is not conceived to have any agency and thus has no subject

   strong category of verbs which form their past tense with the help of a vowel change (*Engl.* 'leave – left')

   weak category of verbs which form their past tense with the help of a suffix (*Engl.* 'walk – walk*ed*')

Key to exercises

Lesson 1

Á flugstöð Leifs Eiríkssonar   In Reykjavík; right outside the terminal

Exercise 1   flugvöllur = *m.* taska = *f.* bíll = *m.* dagur = *m.* kona = *f.* íslenska = *f.* Englendingur = *m.* stafur = *m.* hjálp = *f.* hótel = *n.* flugstöð = *f.*

Exercise 2   flugvöllurinn, taskan, bíllinn, dogurinn, konan, íslenskan, Englendingurinn, stafurinn, hjálpin, hótelið, flugstöðin.

Dialogue 2   From Canada; to the Blue Lagoon

Exercise 3   1 Góðan daginn 2 Fyrirgefðu, getur þú sagt mér hvar Dómkirkjan er? 3 Þakka þér kærlega fyrir 4 Já, ég er Englendingur. 5 Þakka þér fyrir. Vertu blessaður.

Exercise 4   Hvað er þetta? Þetta er 1 rúta 2 steinn 3 borð 4 stóll 5 kirkja 6 (karl)maður 7 rós 8 kona 9 verslun 10 bíll

Exercise 5   rútan, steinninn, borðið, stóllinn, kirkjan, maðurinn, rósin, konan, verslunin, bíllinn

Exercise 6   1 hún er að vinna 2 hann er að lesa 3 barnið er að drekka 4 barnið (það) er að borða

Exercise 7   There are no set answers for this exercise, it depends on you. Here are some sample answers: 10 a.m. ég er að vinna, 1 p.m. ég er að borða, 5 p.m. ég er að fara, 9 p.m. ég er að lesa

Símtal   Eimskip; Aberdeen, Scotland

Exercise 8   Women: Helga Björg, Ingigerður, Jakobína, Kristín; Men: Helgi Hlynur, Hjalti, Ingimar, Kristinn. Ingimar and Kristín have family names (Schram and Blöndal).

Exercise 9   1 Gunnþóra/Hún heitir fullu nafni Gunnþóra Gunnarsdóttir 2 Hrafn er Ólafsson 3 Þóra er Einarsdóttir 4 Ég heiti ... 5 Ég er ... -dóttir/-son

Lesson 2

Spjall   Elva lives in Gimli in Canada; Guðrún lives in Húsavík; Elva is Western Icelandic

Exercise 1   Tæland, Suður Afríka, Færeyskur/Færeyingar, Rússarnir, Sviss, Rúmeníu/rúmenska, Holland, Ástralíu, Noregur, Malasíu, Skotland, Ítalíu, Frakklandi/franskan, Bandaríkin, Þýskaland, England, Mexíkó, Kanada, Danmörk, Belgía, Ísrael, Svíþjóð, Austurríki, Finnland

Exercise 2   1 sænskur 2 spænskur 3 indverskur 4 skoskur 5 ítalskur 6 franskur 7 ástralskur 8 þýskur 9 grískur 10 kínverskur 11 kanadískur 12 rússneskur 13 japanskur 14 bandarískur

Spjall 2   Elva is writing an article about Reykjavík; Guðrún is on a computer course

Exercise 3   1 Róm er ítölsk borg 2 sænsk 3 þýsk 4 rússnesk 5 indversk 6 hollensk 7 írsk 8 ensk

Exercise 4   Dialogue 1: íslensk = *f.* > ég = Guðrún; laust = *n.* > sæti; íslenskt = *n.* > nafn; vestur-íslensk = *f.* > ég = Elva; íslenskur = *m.* > pabbi Dialogue 2: skemmtileg = *f.* > borg; lífleg = *f.* > borg

Exercise 5   1 appelsínan er appelsínugul 2 bananinn er gulur 3 grasið er grænt 4 himinninn er blár 5 rósin er rauð 6 hundurinn er brúnn 7 kaffið er svart 8 vínberið er fjólublátt 9 svanurinn er hvítur 10 fíllinn er grár 11 svínið er bleikt

Hvernig líkar þér hérna?   She is a marketing director; yes she does; at the Italian Embassy; it is expensive to live in Iceland.

Exercise 6   kalt = *n.* > veðrið; leiðinlegt = *n.* > veðrið; fallegt = *n.* > landið; indælt = *n.* > fólkið; óvenjulegur = *m.* > maturinn; dýrt = *n.* > það; gott = *n.* > starf; margt = *n.* > fólk; skemmtilegt = *n.* > starfsfólkið. Dýr has no ending in the masculine.

Exercise 7   flugstjóri = captain (on an aeroplane), skipstjóri = captain (on a ship), fiskifræðingur = ichthyologist; bókari = bookkeeper/accountant; bílasali = car salesman, læknaritari = medical secretary; píanóleikari = piano player; rútubílstjóri = coach driver

Exercise 8   1 Björk er söngkona. 2 Ólafur Ragnar Grímsson er ekki hjúkrunarkona, hann er forseti. 3 Halldór Laxness er ekki forseti, hann er rithöfundur. 4 Sigmund Freud er sálfræðingur. 5 Leifur Eiríksson er ekki alþingismaður, hann er landkönnuður. 6 Florence Nightingale er ekki málari, hún er hjúkrunarkona. 7 Nelson Mandela er ekki rithöfundur, hann er alþingismaður. 8 Edvard Munch er ekki tölvufræðingur, hann er málari. 9 Gérard Dépardieu er leikari. 10 Bill Gates er ekki landkönnuður, hann er tölvufræðingur.

Exercise 9   1 Björk er íslensk. 2 Ólafur Ragnar Grímsson er íslenskur. 3 Halldór Laxness er íslenskur. 4 Sigmund Freud er austurrískur. 5 Leifur Eiríksson er íslenskur. 6 Florence Nightingale er ensk. 7 Nelson Mandela er suður-afrískur. 8 Edvard Munch er norskur. 9 Gérard Dépardieu er franskur. 10 Bill Gates er bandarískur.

Exercise 10   hún vinnur, hann les, barnið drekkur, barnið borðar, 10 am ég vinn, 1 pm ég borða, 5 pm ég fer, 9 pm ég les

Exercise 11   Ég heiti Mark. Ég er kanadískur/Kanadamaður. Ég er rithöfundur og er frá Calgary. Ég vinn heima. Ég tala ensku og er að læra íslensku. Calgary er skemmtileg borg. Það er alltaf mikið um að vera og fólkið er indælt.

Exercise 12   1 skáldið skrifar 2 kokkurinn eldar 3 kennarinn kennir 4 nemandinn lærir 5 ritarinn vélritar 6 sölumaðurinn selur 7 sjómaðurinn fiskar 8 píanóleikarinn spilar á píanó

Exercise 13   1 heiti 2 er 3 er 4 er 5 kenni 6 kenni 7 heitir 8 vinnur 9 er 10 spila 11 les 12 eldar 13 er

Exercise 14   1 Þetta er Tom. Hann er frá Ástralíu/ástralskur/Ástrali. Hann er hávaxinn og ljóshærður. Hann er giftur. Hann er bakari og vinnur í Brisbane. 2 Þetta er Helen. Hún er frá Glasgow. Hún er Skoti/skosk. Hún er háskólanemi og er að læra lögfræði. Hún er gift. Maðurinn hennar er írskur.

Lesson 3

Á Akureyri   No they don't; in Sigurhæðir; it's morning.

Exercise 1   1 Jú við tölum íslensku. 2 Jú við förum þangað. 3 Já þau eiga húsið. 4 Jú við kennum tölvufræði. 5 Jú þær vinna. 6 Já þeir ganga niður í bæ. 7 Jú við lærum íslensku. 8 Já við erum í fríi á Íslandi.

Exercise 2   fjórir-sex-fjórir fjórtán núll-níu; fimm-sex-átta fimmtán fjörutíu-og-þrír; fjórir-átta-sjö ellefu sjötíu-og-tveir; fjórir-fimm-einn þrjátíu-og-tveir sextíu-og-átta; fimm-sex-sex sjötíu-og-einn tuttugu-og-þrír; átta-fimm-fjórir þrjátíu-og-sjö áttatíu-og-níu
Listening comprehension: 561 84 77; 453 67 52; 437 12 93; 561 5871; 857 2393

Exercise 3   3+2=5, 6+4=10, 1+7=8, 100+100=200, 18–5=13, 12–3=9, 30–20=10, 5000–2000=3000

Exercise 4   bílar – blöð – kirkjur – pennar – ömmur – rósir – brauð – tölvur – kennarar – nöfn – fyrirtæki – þakkir – konur – spjöll – búðir – störf bíllinn – bílarnir; blaðið – blöðin; kirkjan – kirkjurnar; penninn – pennarnir; amman – ömmurnar; rósin – rósirnar; brauðið – brauðin; tölvan – tölvurnar; kennarinn – kennararnir; nafnið – nöfnin; fyrirtækið – fyrirtækin; þökkin – þakkirnar; konan – konurnar; spjallið – spjöllin; búðin – búðirnar; starfið – störfin

Enn á Akureyri   most Icelandic plants; Laxdalshús; to a café

Exercise 5   ein-tvær-þrjár-fjórar borgir; einn-tveir-þrír-fjórir Íslendingar; einn-tveir-þrír-fjórir fílar; ein-tvær-þrjár-fjórar appelsínur; eitt-tvö-þrjú-fjögur sæti; einn-tveir-þrír-fjórir bananar; einn-tveir-þrír-fjórir sjómenn; eitt-tvö-þrjú-fjögur skáld

Exercise 6   tvö hundruð og sextíu kr.; fjögur þúsund þrjú hundruð sjötíu og þrjár kr.; sex hundruð og fjörutíu kr.; sautján þúsund sjö hundruð og fimmtíu kr.; þrjú hundruð sjötíu og tvö þúsund fjögur hundruð sextíu og fimm kr.; fjórar miljónir kr.
Listening comprehension: 83 kr.; 2.000.000 kr.; 12.674 kr.; 8.381 kr.

Exercise 7

874	Ingólfur Arnarson byggir bæ sem heitir Reykjavík
1000	Kristnitaka á Íslandi – Leifur Eiríksson finnur Norður Ameríku
1402–(til)1404	Svartidauði á Íslandi – ⅓ Íslendinga deyr
1550	Jón Arason biskup hálshöggvinn, Ísland tekur lútherska trú
1584	Biblían prentuð á íslensku
1700	Íslendingar taka upp gregoríanskt tímatal
1750	Tveir íslenskir stúdentar ganga fyrstir upp á Heklutind
1787	Verslun á Íslandi gefin frjáls
1874	1000 ára byggð á Íslandi – Ísland fær stjórnarskrá
1886	Um 2000 Íslendingar flytja til Kanada
1940	Englendingar hernema Ísland
1944	Ísland verður sjálfstætt lýðveldi
1949	Ísland gengur í NATO
1955	Halldór Laxness fær Nóbelsverðlaun
1980	Vigdís Finnbogadóttir verður forseti Íslands
1986	Reagan og Gorbatsjof funda í Reykjavík
2000	Heklugos

Exercise 8   1 tvö kíló(grömm) 2 fjórir lítrar 3 fimmtán hundruð fjörutíu og þrjú grömm 4 þrjú þúsund eitt hundrað og fimmtán kílómetrar 5 fimmtán hundruð þrjátíu og einn kílómetri 6 fjórtán hundruð sextíu og fjórir kílómetrar

Hvað eigum við að gera?   No, only on Sundays; yes she does; no, they can't.

Exercise 9   There are of course no set answers to this exercise. Here are some sample answers:
1 Klukkan er þrjú. 2 Ég fer að vinna klukkan átta. 3 Ég kem heim klukkan sex. 4 Ég fer að sofa klukkan ellefu. 5 Búðirnar opna klukkan níu. 6 Rútan fer af stað klukkan tvö.

Exercise 10   1 Já, ég vinn um helgar/Nei, ég vinn ekki um helgar. 2 Já, ég er í fríi á sumrin/Nei, ég er ekki í fríi á sumrin. 3 Já, ég er heima á virkum dögum/Nei, ég er ekki heima á virkum dögum. 4 Ég á afmæli í (janúar, febrúar, mars ...).

Exercise 11   1 Já, hann er opinn um helgar. 2 Nei, bara laugardaga/á laugardögum. 3 Það er ekki opið þriðjudaga/á þriðjudögum. 4 Já, það er opið um helgar. 5 Já, það er opið á sumrin.

Exercise 12   1 grár fiskur – gráir fiskar; 2 skemmtilegt blað – skemmtileg blöð; 3 falleg mynd – fallegar myndir 4 hátt borð – há borð 5 gamall maður – gamlir menn 6 löng vika – langar vikur 7 indæl fjölskylda – indælar fjölskyldur 8 rauð rós – rauðar rósir 9 þungur steinn – þungir steinar 10 sterk kona – sterkar konur.

Exercise 13   1 Eigum við að fara og skoða Alþingishúsið? (Nei,) Förum frekar upp Laugarveg og skoðum búðirnar. 2 Það er laugardagur í dag og búðirnar opna ekki fyrr en klukkan tíu, förum þangað eftir hádegi. 3 Við skulum fara (Förum) í þjóðminjasafnið. Það er langt héðan, eigum við ekki frekar að skoða Ráðhúsið og fá okkur kaffi þar? 4 Hvar er Ráðhúsið? (Það er) Þarna niður frá 5 Góð hugmynd, göngum niður eftir og gerum það!

Lesson 4

Í bókabúð   She plans to drive along the ringroad around Iceland; it's not detailed enough; she needs to buy stamps at the post office.

Exercise 1   hluti-hluta-hluta-hluta, hlutar-hluta-hlutum-hluta; skeið-skeið-skeið-skeiðar, skeiðar-skeiðar-skeiðum-skeiða; kort-kort-korti-korts, kort-kort-kortum-korta.

Exercise 2   fá, *acc.*: póstkort-0; út á, *acc.*: land-0; vantar, *acc.*: leiðsöguhandbók-0; með, *dat.*: vegakort-i; heimsækja, *acc.*: landshlut-a; um, *acc.*: landshlut-a; leigja, *acc.*: bíl-0; keyra, *acc.*: hringveg-0-inn; sýnir, *dat.*: mann-i, *acc.*: aðalveg-i-na, merkisstað-i; frá, *dat.*: einkenn-um; í, *dat.*: landslag-i-nu; yfir, *acc.*: hálendi-ð, Sprengisandsleið-ina; þarftu, *acc.*: leiðsögn-0; skoða, *acc.*: bók-ina; á, *dat.*: pósthús-i-nu.

Exercise 3   1 hóteli, Íslandi, Ítalíu, ítölskuna, aðalgötunni 2 myndirnar, merkisstaðina, Hallgrímskirkju 3 glugganum 4 fisk 5 konunni

Exercise 4   1 ég ætla að ganga niður í bæ 2 ég ætla á Austurvöllinn 3 ég ætla að skoða Alþingishúsið og Dómkirkjuna 4 ég ætla í bókabúð 5 ég ætla að kaupa póstkort 6 ég ætla á kaffihús 7 ég ætla að skrifa póstkortin 8 ég ætla að ganga upp Laugaveginn 9 ég ætla að skoða

búðirnar 10 ég ætla að heimsækja forsetann á Bessastöðum (least likely)
11 ég ætla að . . .

Exercise 5   Á morgun ætla ég að . . .

Exercise 6   1 Góðan daginn. 2 Er til kaffi hér?/Fæst kaffi hér? 3 Er
hægt að fá hamborgara? 4 Þá ætlum við að fá þrjár kók og . . . áttu til
ávaxtasafa?/Ertu með ávaxtasafa? 5 . . . og eitt Trópíkana, og svo þrjár
pylsur og einn ís. 6 Já. Hvað verður þetta mikið? 7 Hérna eru 2000 8
Takk.

Á pósthúsinu   until after the weekend; no, with friends

Exercise 7   1 Listasafn Íslands er á Fríkirkjuvegi. 2 Ráðhúsið er á
Tjarnargötu. 3 Hallgrímskirkja er á Skólavörðustíg. 4 Hljómskálinn er
á Sóleyjargötu (á Skothúsvegi). 5 Maður tekur rútu á Vatnsmýrarvegi.
6 Margir strætisvagnar stoppa á Lækjartorgi. 7 Kristín býr á Hringbraut.
8 Einar á heima í Espimel. 9 Ég bý/á heima í/á . . .

Lesson 5

Göngufatnaður   the Vatnajökull; tomorrow; woollen underwear and a
woollen sweater

Exercise 1   1 Konan er í úlpu, peysu, buxum og kuldaskóm. Hún er
með húfu, poka og trefil. 2 Konan er í jakka og pilsi (í dragt), blússu,
sokkabuxum og skóm. Hún er með úr, hálsfesti, tösku og síma.
3 Maðurinn er í jakkafötum, skyrtu, vesti (með hnöppum/tölum), og
spariskóm. Hann er með hring og bindi.

Exercise 2   1 Konan fer í úlpuna, peysuna, buxurnar og kuldaskóna.
Hún setur á sig húfuna og trefilinn. 2 Konan fer í jakkann og pilsið (í
dragtina), blússuna, sokkabuxurnar og skóna. Hún setur á sig úrið og
hálsfestina. 3 Maðurinn fer í jakkafötin, skyrtuna, vestið, og spariskóna.
Hann setur á sig hringinn og bindið.

Exercise 3   There are no set answers to this exercise, as it depends on
you.

Exercise 4   1 svartur jakki – svartan jakka – svörtum jakka – svarts
jakka/svartir jakkar – svarta jakka – svörtum jökkum – svartra jakka

2 skrautlegt pils – skrautlegt pils – skrautlegu pilsi – skrautlegs pilss/skrautleg pils – skrautleg pils – skrautlegum pilsum – skrautlegra pilsa 3 fínn kjóll – fínan kjól – fínum kjól – fíns kjóls/fínir kjólar – fína kjóla – fínum kjólum – fínna kjóla 4 þykk peysa – þykka peysu – þykkri peysu – þykkrar peysu/þykkar peysur – þykkar peysur – þykkum peysum – þykkra peysa 5 ljótt bindi – ljótt bindi – ljótu bindi – ljóts bindis/ljót bindi – ljót bindi – ljótum bindum – ljótra binda 6 ný dragt – nýja dragt – nýrri dragt – nýrrar dragtar/nýjar dragtir – nýjar dragtir – nýjum drögtum – nýrra dragta

Exercise 5   1 bláan 2 nýja, gráa 3 hvítri, svörtum, nýjum 4 gulri, brúnu, gulum, grænum 5 rauða, hlýja, langan, stóra

Exercise 6   Some sample answers: 1 ég ætla að vera í hlýjum fötum: í þykkri peysu, buxum, kuldaskóm, ullarsokkum og úlpu. Ég ætla að vera með trefil, vettlinga og húfu. 2 ég ætla að vera í skyrtu, léttum buxum og léttum jakka, bómullarsokkum og skóm. 3 ég ætla að vera létt-klædd/ur: í bol og stuttbuxum eða pilsi, og í klossum eða strigaskóm. Ég ætla að vera með sólgleraugu og hatt. 4 ég ætla að vera í léttri peysu og buxum, sokkum, stígvélum og regnkápu (regngöllum) með hettu.

Exercise 7   1 jöklar 2 trefla 3 gamlar 4 fallegan 5 opin 6 lykilinn, lyklana 7 litlir, sætir 8 stóra vindla.

Draumur um brúðkaup í hvítum kjól   from a small beach town; to find her love and get married in white

Exercise 8   1 eitt, tvö, þrjú, fjögur hjól 2 einni, tveimur, þremur, fjórum peysum 3 einn, tvo, þrjá, fjóra jakka 4 eina, tvær, þrjár, fjórar myndir 5 ein, tvær, þrjár, fjórar krónur 6 eins, tveggja, þriggja, fjögurra landa.

Exercise 9   1–0; 2–1; 1–0; 12–0.

Exercise 10   1 Hvar er pósthúsið? 2 Hvað kostar þetta? 3 Hvað segirðu? 4 Hvenær ferðu? 5 Hver er þetta? 6 Hvert ertu að fara? 7 Hverju klæðist hún? 8 Hvers saknar hann?

Exercise 11   góður/ágætur-vondur/slæmur, hlýr – svalur, svartur – hvítur, síður/langur – stuttur, heitur – kaldur, nýr – gamall, lítill – stór/mikill, fölur – skær, ljós – dökkur, léttur – þungur, skemmtilegur – leiðinlegur, fallegur – ljótur, druslulegur – snyrtilegur, erfiður – auðveldur

Exercise 12   Some possibilities are: hár: sítt, dökkt, grátt, stutt; munnur: stór, þunnur, rauður, fallegur; veður: svalt, hlýtt, leiðinlegt, vont; bíomynd: falleg, slæm, löng, gömul

Exercise 13   1 ullarsokkar 2 bómullarsokkar, bómullarjakki, bómullar-bolur 3 leðurskór, leðurbuxur, leðurstígvél 4 gallabuxur, gallajakki 5 gúmmískór, gúmmístígvél 6 lopasokkar 7 plastpoki 8 tréskór 9 gullhringur
1 sólgleraugu 2 sparikjóll 3 brúðarkjóll 4 vasaúr 5 hárspenna, hárband 6 hettupeysa 7 teygjuefni 8 vetrarfrakki

Exercise 14   on sale are trainers and fleece jumpers; expected before the weekend are white, black and blue jumpers; no: sleeping bags

Skuggi skammdegisins   January; only at Christmas; autumn

Lesson 6

Að panta flug   tomorrow morning; Wednesday; one day; 6:30 a.m.

Exercise 1   tuttugu og fimm mínútur yfir sex; hálf sjö (átján þrjátíu); tíu mínútur yfir þrjú (fimmtán tíu); korter í fimm; fimm mínútur í eitt (tólf fimmtíu og fimm); tuttugu og fimm mínútur í tólf (tuttugu og þrjú þrjátíu og fimm); tuttugu mínútur yfir fimm; tuttugu mínútur í níu (tuttugu fjörutíu); tíu mínútur í ellefu; níu (tuttugu og eitt); korter yfir ellefu

Exercise 2   11:05; 11:45; 3:30; 9:03; 7:35; 12:30; 3:15; 5:50; 18:50; 14:40

Exercise 3   1 Það er flogið kl. hálf níu, kl. tólf og kl. hálf sjö (átján þrjátíu). 2 Já, það er hægt að fljúga kl. korter í sjö á laugardags-morgnum. 3 Það er flogið þrisvar á viku til Færeyja. 4 Kvöldrútan/hún fer tuttugu of fimm mínútur yfir níu. 5 Þú kemur til Borgarness kl. korter í tíu.

Exercise 4   1 Ég er næst/ur, góðan daginn. 2 Ég ætla að ferðast til Hafnar í Hornafirði með rútu, ef hægt er. 3 Klukkan hvað? 4 Klukkan hvað kemur rútan til Hafnar? 5 Hvað kostar miðinn? 6 Kemur rútan við í Jökulsárlóni? 7 Nú er það/Nújá. Er hægt að kaupa miða til Hafnar núna? 8 Nei, aðra leið, ég ætla að fljúga til baka. 9 Í fyrramálið. 10 Gjörðu svo vel, þakka þér kærlega fyrir.

Exercise 5 1 Í morgun ætla ég að ganga um bæinn. 2 Eftir það ætla ég að fá kaffi. 3 Fyrir hádegi ætla ég að fá upplýsingar um skoðunarferðir á Vatnajökul og að Jökulsárlóni. 4 Í hádeginu ætla ég að borða hádegismat. 5 Eftir hádegi ætla ég að skoða safnið. 6 Í fyrramálið ætla ég í skoðunarferð. 7 Annað kvöld ætla ég að taka rútu til Egilsstaða. 8 . . .

Exercise 6 1 at 18:21 2 at 18:29 3 at 10:34 4 3400 kr. 5 20 kr. 6 200 kr.

Exercise 7 1 Vagn númer sex/hann fer að Breiðholtskjöri og að (Eiðisgranda við) Öldugranda. 2 Já, hann stoppar á Laugavegi. 3 Farið kostar 120 kr. 4 Þá bið ég vagnstjórann um skiptimiða. 5 '(Ég ætla að fá) skiptimiða, takk'. 6, 7 and 8 These depend of course on you.

Exercise 8 1 henni 2 þau eru sein 3 þær skoða þá 4 það fer til hennar 5 þeir taka hana

Exercise 9 Þær, hún, hún, þau, hann, hann, þær, þau, hún, hann, þeir, þau, hún

Útvarp og sjónvarp á Íslandi the news; foreign programmes; not any longer

Exercise 10 1 comedy film 2 cartoon (animated film) 3 documentary 4 western 5 thriller, action film 6 detective, 'whodunnit' 7 epic 8 horror film

Exercise 11 1 aðalhlutverk 2 þýðandi og þulur 3 söngleikur 4 tilnefnd til Óskarsverðlauna 5 bein útsending 6 barna- og unglingaþáttur

Exercise 12 1 Dagskráin byrjar kl. 11:30. 2 Já, bresk sakamálamynd er sýnd í Sjónvarpinu, og myndin 'Geimveran' er synd á Stöð 2. 3 Fyrstu fréttir kvöldsins byrja kl. sjö. 4 Dagskráin á Stöð 2 er búin kl. korter í eitt. 5 Heimildarmyndin kemur frá Frakklandi. 6 Fimm erlendir þættir eru sýndir í sjónvarpinu. 7 . . .

Lesson 7

Dagur í lífi íslenskrar fjölskyldu one; five; Jón at home, Sigríður at a bank; Jón and Sigríður; Jón

Exercise 1   1 verður, stendur 2 sker 3 ferð, flýg 4 býr 5 fæ 6 sofa, sefur 7 býður 8 gangið, göngum, geng, ek

Exercise 2   2 hann fer á fætur kl. korter yfir sjö 3 hann borðar morgunmat og drekkur kaffi, og hann klæðir sig 4 hann tekur strætó í vinnu 5 hann vinnur á skrifstofu 6 hann fer út í búð og fær sér samloku kl. tólf 7 hann fer á fund eftir hádegi, og sér um matarinnkaup 8 hann kemur heim kl. sjö 9 hann eldar matinn og horfir á fréttir 10 hann tekur til og les yfir skjöl 11 hann háttar kl. hálf tólf 12 hann sefur eins og steinn alla nóttina . . .

Exercise 3   2 hún er 3 hún rekur 4 hún sér 5 hún býr 6 hún á 7 hún nýtur 8 hún fær 9 hún vaknar 10 hún vinnur 11 fer hún 12 kemur hún

Samtal við nýbúa   in Ísafjörður; nature, the air, doing different things in one place, partying; cold and darkness of winter, expense; well

Exercise 4   1 húsið 2 útlanda 3 skólanum 4 mig 5 húsanna 6 gólfinu 7 borðinu 8 veginum 9 afa og ömmu 10 hjálpina 11 honum 12 veðurs

Exercise 5   1 eftir/í 2 hjá/fyrir/nálægt 3 við, á 4 í 5 með, til 6 úr, í 7 í 8 úr, í, af, úr, á, í, í, úr, í, í, með

Exercise 6   1 false 2 true 3 true 4 false 5 false 6 true 7 false 8 true 9 true 10 false

Lesson 8

Í matarbúð   Þór finds it too much of a bother; a pasta dish; tomato sauce, skyr, bread and milk

Exercise 1   There are no set answers to this exercise.

Exercise 2   1 þig 2 okkur 3 barninu 4 Jónínu 5 honum 6 hana 7 ykkur 8 manninum 9 konunni 10 þá

Exercise 3   1 mér finnst/þykir mjólk ofsalega góð 2 mér finnast/þykja epli mjög góð 3 mér finnast/þykja franskar kartöflur óætar 4 mér finnst/þykir appelsínusafi ofsalega vondur 5 mér finnst/þykir reyktur lax æðislega góður 6 mér finnast/þykja pylsur hryllilega vondar 7 mér finnst/þykir ofnbakaður kjúklingur ljúffengur 8 mér finnst/þykir svart kaffi mjög vont

*Exercise 4*A: 1 – ii; 2 – iv; 3 – i; 4 – v; 5 – iii; *B*: 1 – iii; 2 – v; 3 – i; 4 – ii, iv. Adjusted menu: pasta without the nuts, pancakes without the cream.

Á veitingarstað   the food is exceptional at the Hótel; a bottle of red wine; a little overcooked; coffee and cognac

Exercise 5   sweet; tender; juicy; soft; tasteless/bland; soggy; spoiled/off; undercooked/raw; bad-tasting; lean

Exercise 6   1 stór eða lítill, rauður, safaríkur, mjúkur, svolítið sætur, . . . 2 stór, gul, súr, safarík, hörð . . . 3 stór, hvít, sæt, mjúk, feit, bragðgóð . . . 4 lítil, brún, sæt, þurr, seig . . . 5 brúnt eða svart, beiskt (sætt með sykri út í) . . . 6 hvítur, sætur, mjúkur, bragðgóður 7 brúnt eða svart, beiskt, hart, seigt, soðið . . . 8 lítil, bleik, meyr, safarík, soðin . . .

Exercise 7   1 tómatur 2 hvalkjöt 3 gulrót 4 lax

Exercise 8   eina samloku, tvo (skammta) af frönskum, þrjá ostborgara, eina pítu, fjórar kók, tvo kaffi og þrjú mjólk(-urglös!)

Exercise 9   1 Má ég fá matseðil? 2 Síðdegisseðil, takk 3 Einn kaffi og gulrótakökustykki 4 Kakó og vöfflur 5 Eina grænmetissamloku og eina kók 6 Tvöfaldan espresso og stórt súkkulaðikökustykki!

Exercise 10   1 einhver, enginn 2 eitthvað 3 einskis 4 engan 5 einhverja 6 einhverjum 7 eitthvert, engin 8 engan

Lesson 9

Fjölskyldan mín   she is the second oldest; two; Jón and Lilja; her mother; Hjálmar and Jón

Exercise 1   1 það heitir Ragnar Hjálmarsson og Eyrún Jónsdóttir 2 hann heitir Hjálmar Sveinsson 3 þau heita Ragnar Hjálmarsson og Eyrún Jónsdóttir 4 hún heitir Hulda Jónsdóttir 5 föðursystir (frænka)

Exercise 2   1 bróðir 2 systir 3 föðurbróðir (frændi) 4 dóttir 5 mágkona 6 mágur 7 mæðgin 8 feðgar

Exercise 3   There is of course no set answer to this exercise.

Exercise 4 1 bræður, systur 2 systur 3 mæðurnar 4 feðranna 5 syni 6 dætur

Question dætur is a noun which indicates exclusively a family relation.

Exercise 5 1 á 2 eiga 3 hefur 4 er með, á 5 er með 6 hefur

Exercise 6 1 þetta er útvarpið hennar 2 þetta er skápurinn okkar 3 þetta eru börnin þeirra 4 þetta eru fötin ykkar 5 þetta eru peningarnir mínir

Exercise 7 1 já, þetta er peysa stráksins 2 já, þetta er penni kennarans 3 já, þetta er bolti barnanna 4 já, þetta er hús fólksins 5 já, þetta eru myndir ömmu

Brúðkaup Dagný's brother; yes; Dagný's father's relatives; to a meeting

Exercise 8 1 já, þetta er taskan mín 2 nei, þetta er bíll mömmu minnar, þetta er bíllinn hennar mömmu 3 nei, þetta er bók bróður míns, þetta er bókin hans bróður míns 4 nei, þetta er úlpa frænku minnar, þetta er úlpan hennar frænku minnar 5 já, þetta eru gleraugun mín 6 nei, þetta eru dætur systur minnar, þetta eru dætur (!) hennar systur minnar

Exercise 9 1 Sæll (og blessaður)! 2 Allt gott, takk, en hjá þér? 3 þetta er mamma mín. 4 Hún er að heimsækja mig hér. 5 Hún er búin að vera hér í einn dag. 6 En við verðum víst að halda áfram. 7 Við ætlum að hitta vinkonu mína, hana Brynju, niðri í bæ, 8 og á eftir ætlum við (að fara) í skoðunarferð inn í Ásbirgi (við ætlum í skoðunarferð inn í Ásbirgi á eftir). 9 Þakka þér fyrir, Magnús. 10 Vertu blessaður (bless bless).

Lesson 10

Er Hrafn Jökulsson við? on Wednesday afternoon; meet for dinner at Hótel Óðinsvé

Exercise 1 sautjándi júní; fyrsti maí; tuttugasti og fimmti desember; tuttugasti og níundi febrúar; annar ágúst

Exercise 2 1 síðustu 2 nýja 3 næsta 4 stóra 5 stóra 6 bandaríska

Exercise 3   1 Ég kem (á) mánudaginn þriðja september 2 Ég fer heim í næstu viku 3 á föstudaginn 4 Ég ætla að heimsækja foreldra mína á sunnudaginn 5 Hann á afmæli annan apríl 6 Ég ætla að hitta vini mína á morgun(daginn) um áttaleytið.

Að panta tíma   the dentist called Sigurjón; he's working

Bréf   from the Icelandic Embassy; a catalogue and information about orders and payment

Exercise 4   1 (1 11 00) 2 (1 11 00) 3 (0112) 4 (2 12 30) 5 (04) 6 (03)

Komdu með mér í bíó   There's a brilliant Spanish film showing; he has to finish an assignment; to make sure they get tickets

Exercise 5   1 bræddu, bræðið 2 láttu, látið 3 saxaðu, saxið 4 settu, setjið 5 hitaðu, hitið 6 búðu, búið 7 skerðu, skerið 8 sjóddu, sjóðið 9 hrærðu, hrærið 10 kryddaðu, kryddið 11 blandaðu, blandið 12 berðu, berið

Exercise 6   1 skulið 2 skal 3 munt 4 skalt 5 mun

Lesson 11

Að panta herbergi   double rooms with a bath; only one; an extra bed in the room

Exercise 1   1 þriggja hæða 2 tveggja metra 3 fjögurra herbergja (!) 4 tuttugu mínútna 5 (eins) dags 6 það er sextíu og sjö ára gamalt 7 hún er um það bil sjö hundruð ára gömul 8 . . .?

Á ferðaskrifstofu   a weekend; Friday; no, not at the special fare

Exercise 2   a Snartartunga, Brekkulækur b Bær, Melstaður, Barkarstaðir c Staðarskáli, Brekkulækur d Melstaður e Breiðavík, Alviðra, Snartartunga, Melstaður, Barkarstaðir
1 Áttu/Eigið þið herbergi laust í júní? 2 Er hægt að panta fjögurra daga dvöl (gistingu) fyrir einn/er hægt að panta einbýli í fjórar nætur? 3 Mig langar að fá uppbúið rúm, ef hægt er. 4 Er til eldunaraðstaða? 5 Hvað kostar gistingin? 6 Ég ætla að panta herbergið núna.

Exercise 3 1 ein, tvenn, þrenn, fern gleraugu 2 einir, tvennir, þrennir, fernir vettlingar 3 ein, tvenn, þrenn, fern skæri 4 eitt, tvö, þrjú, fjögur armbandsúr 5 einar, tvennar, þrennar, fernar buxur 6 einar, tvennar, þrennar, fernar dyr

Exercise 4 1 já ég kaupi marga ávexti 2 já ég borða marga rétti 3 já, ég sé marga ísbirni 4 já, ég þekki marga nemendur 5 já ég kem við á mörgum flugvöllum 6 já ég skoða margar sýningar 7 já ég heyri í margar flugvélar 8 já ég les margar bækur 9 já ég er með margar skemmdar tennur 10 já ég fer í margar sundlaugar

Exercise 5 1 frá Akureyri til Víkur er fimm hundruð sextíu og einn kílómetri 2 frá Borgarnesi til Ísafjarðar eru þrjú hundruð áttatíu og fjórir kílómetrar 3 frá Grindavík til Reykjavíkur eru fimmtíu og tveir kílómetrar 4 frá Selfossi til Þingvalla eru fjörutíu og fjórir kílómetrar 5 frá Kirkjubæjarklaustri til Egilsstaða eru fjögur hundruð og fjörutíu kílómetrar 6 frá Ólafsfirði til Akureyrar er sextíu og einn kílómetri 7 frá Þingvöllum til Borgarness eru níutíu og fimm kílómetrar

Hringferð um Grænland árið 2000 two weeks; the millennium of Inuit settlement in Greenland; one million krónur; *For Him Magazine*

Lesson 12

Íþróttaiðkun She has little time and takes her work home with her; he wants to get into shape and lose weight; exercising (working out)

Exercise 1 3–5–6–7–2–8–4–1. Ég vakna kl. … Ég fer á fætur kl. … Ég baða mig og klæði mig og svo …

Exercise 2 vaknaðu – farðu á fætur – þvoðu þér – klæddu þig – greiddu þér – borðaðu morgunmatinn – burstaðu tennurnar – farðu í skóla – gættu þín á bílunum

Exercise 3 1 gerast 2 leiðist 3 býst 4 breytast 5 nálgast 6 finnst, venjast 7 sýnist 8 þekkjast, kyssast, hittast

Áhugamál the piano; classical, jazz and blues; yes, there's a local theatre company

Exercise 4   you have a choice out of a range of adverbs; the following is a sample answer: ótrúlega, mjög, alveg, ofsalega, voðalega, æðislega, óskaplega, afar, alveg (the only option here), ákaflega, ofsalega, afar, mjög, hryllilega, hræðilega.

Exercise 5   1 wrong 2 wrong 3 right 4 wrong 5 right 6 wrong 7 right 8 wrong

Exercise 6   Ísland er stórt, Frakkland er stærra en Kanada er alstærst; köttur er lítill, fugl er minni en mús er langminnst; Mick Jagger er gamall, Boris Jeltsin er eldri en Jóhannes Páll II er langelstur; Hallgrímskirkja er há, Eiffelturninn er hærri en Frelsisstyttan er alhæst; tíu kíló eru þung, fimmtíu kílo eru þyngri en hundrað kíló eru langþyngst.

Láttu þér líða vel   It affects how we feel mentally and physically; by moving/exercising; driving; walking and swimming

Lesson 13

Ísland   no, in Bessastaðir; to heat up houses and greenhouses; not all that cold but unsettled; the first Icelandic parliament was founded and held there

Exercise 1   byggt (past, n.sg.nom., land), verið (past), vaxandi (present, adj., fjöldi), sjóðandi (present, adv., kemur upp), kenndir (past, m.pl.nom., hverir), notað (past, n.sg.nom., vatnið), hituð (past, n.pl.nom., hús), notuð (past, f.sg.nom., gufan), virkjaðar (past, f.pl.nom., ár), flogið (past), stofnað (past, n.sg.nom., Alþingi), fundað (past), friðaðir and gerðir (past, m.pl.nom., vellir)

Exercise 2   1 Það er talað mikið í símann/mikið er talað í símann 2 Það er vakað alla nóttina/alla nóttina er vakað 3 Það er oft gist á hóteli/oft er gist á hóteli 4 Það er hlegið að þessu/að þessu er hlegið 5 Það er aldrei hlustað á fréttirnar/aldrei er hlustað á fréttirnar 6 Það er mikið dansað í veislunni/mikið er dansað í veislunni

Útivist   several days; medium/average; no

Exercise 3   vatnsbrúsi, gönguskór, ullarpeysa, vasahnífur, klósettpappír, vettlingar og húfa, diskur, sundföt

Exercise 4 1 Góðan daginn. Ég ætla að fara/ferðast til Íslands í ágúst og mig langar að fá upplýsingar um ferðir inn í óbyggðir 2 Gönguferð 3 Nokkra daga 4 Ég er alveg tilbúin(n)/til í að tjalda 5 Ég er miðlungsgöngumaður 6 Fínt, þakka þér (kærlega) fyrir.

Exercise 5 *Það er flogið* frá Reykjavík til Ísafjarðar, og *siglt* þaðan (*þaðan er siglt*) í Hestfjörð. Svo *er gengið* frá Hesteyri yfir í Aðalvík, og *endað* í Hornvík og *er gist* þar í skála. Næsta daginn *er* Fagranesið *tekið* til baka til Ísafjarðar.

Exercise 6 1 no 2 no 3 yes 4 yes 5 no

Landshlutar its glacier; connections are difficult and soil is sparse; it's one of few towns not on the coast; it has most of the lowland; it's very dangerous to ships

Exercise 7 SW and W: 9–15 (day), 6 to 8 (night); West Fjords and NE: 3–6 (night), 5–9 (day), E and East Fjords: 3–9; SE: 7–13; interior: 0–6. 1 North-east and interior 2 interior 3 Western Iceland 4 North-easterly 5 sweater and raincoat 6 coldest: north-eastern peninsulas; warmest: SW and W.

Exercise 8 1 NE Iceland, north of Mývatn and NE of Akureyri 2 on northern coast, W of Húsavík, between Eyjafjord and Skagafjord 3 on Skagafjord in NW 4 in West Fjords at Ísafjarðardjúp north of Ísafjörður 5 on northern side of Snæfellsnes peninsula from where one can sail to Flatey 6 on southern Reykjanes peninsula from where one can sail to the Westmen Islands 7 on the south coast not far from Mýrdals glacier and Mýrdal sands 8 in East Fjords from where one can sail to Papey.

Exercise 9 1 hressist 2 bilast, eldast 3 styttast 4 geymist, skemmist

Lesson 14

Sálin hans Jóns míns he has been a bad man; she reminds them of their past sins; she throws in a bag with the soul in it.

Exercise 1 bjuggu (irr.-bjó), var (irr.-voru), líkaði (W-líkuðu), ámæltu (W-ámælti), elskaði (W-elskuðu), varð (S-urðu), vakti (W-vöktu), batnaði (W-bötnuðu), fór (S-fóru), tók (S-tóku), hélt (S-héldu), gaf (S-gáfu), batt (S-bundu), kom (S-komu), drap (S-drápu), spurði (W-spurðu), afneitaði

(W-afneituðu), læsti (W-læstu), áttir (*irr.*, áttu), vildi (W-vildu), barði (W-börðu), ætlaði (W-ætluðu), svaraði (W-svöruðu), trúði (W-trúðu), lokaði (W-lokuðu), kastaði (W-köstuðu), létti (W-léttu)

Exercise 2 1 borðaði/ir/ir-borðuðum/uð/u 2 gleymdi/ir/i-gleymdum/uð/u 3 gerði/ir/i-gerðum/uð/u 4 valdi/ir/i-völdum/uð/u 5 naut-naust-naut-nutum-nutuð-nutu 6 varð-varðst-varð-urðum-urðuð-urðu 7 tók-tókst-tók-tókum-tókuð-tóku 8 lék-lékst-lék-lékum-lékuð-léku 9 spurði/ir/i-spurðum/uð/u 10 grét-grést-grét-grétum-grétuð-grétu 11 notaði/ir/i-notuðum/uð/u 12 sauð-sauðst-sauð-suðum-suðuð-suðu

Exercise 3 1 (var), tók 2 (var) 3 gengu 4 byggði, hét 5 fékk 6 fluttu 7 fann 8 gekk 9 dó 10 (var) 11 hernámu 12 funduðu 13 varð 14 (gaus) 15 fékk 16 varð 17 tóku

Exercise 4 fæddist, var, dó, átti, var, bjó, hét, skrifaði, fór, var, ferðaðist, dvaldi, tók, gekk, kom, kom, samdi, var, vakti, gaf, varð, var, byrjaði, skrifaði, voru, samdi, fékk

Exercise 5 Ég fæddist árið 1943 og var skírð Jónína Jónsdóttir. Ég bjó í Fáskrúðsfirði þegar ég var lítil, í litlu húsi sem hét Framnes. Ég ólst upp og fór í skóla á Egilsstöðum þangað til ég var sextán ára. Þá fór ég aftur til Fáskrúðsfjarðar til að vinna þar í fiski. Ég giftist Einari, manninum mínum, þegar ég var átján ára. Við fluttum í stærra hús sem Einar byggði handa okkur, og við eignuðumst þrjú börn. Ég lærði aldrei að keyra bíl, og ferðaðist aldrei, en þegar börnin voru orðin stór skildum við Einar og ég flutti til Reykjavíkur til að stunda nám. Ég lærði ensku og spænsku og fór til útlanda í fyrsta sinn þegar ég var þrjátíu og sex ára gömul. Ég tók kennarapróf þegar ég var þrjátíu og níu og fékk vinnu sem tungumálakennari.

Exercise 6 1 Örlygur Jónsson var að horfa í búðarglugga þegar hann heyrði brak. Þegar hann leit um öxl var slysið búið að gerast. 2 María Jóhannsdóttir var að ganga niður götuna þegar hún sá bílinn keyra inn í búðarglugga. 3 Pétur Briem var að bíða eftir umferðarljósi þegar bíllinn keyrði framhjá. Hann var að horfa á eftir honum þegar bíllinn sveigði til vinstri og skall á búðina. 4 Fanney Freysdóttir var að tala við kunningja hjá búðinni þegar hún sá bílinn koma að sér. Hún var að horfa á bílstjórann þegar höfuðið datt niður á stýrið.

Bréf the house was burgled; go to the police station and contact the insurance company; Kjartan's party

Exercise 7 Fimmta júlí tók ég (fór með) rútu til Þingvalla. Ég fór í skoðunarferð og gekk um. Mjög fallegur staður! Svo fór ég á tónleika um kvöldið. Daginn eftir fór ég í tveggja daga ferð með leiðsögn (leiðsöguferð) um söguslóðir Njáls sögu í Fljótshlíð. Ég sá sýninguna um Njáls sögu á Hvolsvelli. Það var alveg frábært! Áttunda júlí fór ég í bátsferð til Viðeyjar og skoðaði kirkjuna og elsta hús landsins. Það var fallegt og hlýtt veður. Ég gekk um eyjuna og sá marga (margs konar) fugla. Daginn eftir fór ég í sund og verslaði í miðbænum. Ég keypti margar gjafir og marga minjagripi. Á eftir borðaði ég kvöldmat með Sif og Kjartani á Sólon Íslandus (kaffihúsi). Tíundi júlí var síðasti dagur minn á Íslandi. Ég pakkaði niður og borðaði samloku í Norræna húsinu og sá íslenska kvikmynd þar. Svo tók ég rútuna til Keflavíkur og kvaddi Ísland.

Exercise 8 1 Já, ég þekki Ísland mjög/frekar vel, svolítið/nei, ég þekki Ísland ekki vel 2 Nei, ég þekki ekki Ólaf Ragnar Grímsson (en ég veit hver hann er) 3 Já, ég kann íslensku! 4 Já, ég kannast við Njáls sögu (nei, ég kannast ekki við ...) 5 Nei, það er ekki hægt af því að það eru engar lestir á Íslandi 6 Ja, hann var stofnaður árið 1911 (nei, það veit ég ekki) 7 Já, Ísland er 103.000 km² að stærð (ég veit það ekki) 8 Já, Fljótshlíð er á Suðurlandi 9 Nei, enginn veit hver samdi Njáls sögu!

Úr Brennu Njáls sögu he was fatally stabbed by him; two; to make a new bow string; no

Lesson 15

Hvernig hefurðu það? he has a headache, a sore throat and congestion; no; go home and crawl into bed

Exercise 1 1 nei 2 já 3 já 4 já 5 nei 6 nei

Exercise 2 Some indications: 1 hann var hávaxinn og þybbinn (jafnvel feitur). Hann var með mikið svart hár og var alltaf með marga skartgripi, svo sem hringa og hálsfesti. 2 Hann er hávaxinn og mjög grannur. Hann er með blá augu og svart, slétt hár, og hann er með mjög stóran munn. 3 Hún er grönn, með mikið sítt, svart, krullað hár og mjög falleg brún augu. Hún er oft með skartgripi og er oftast í fallegum síðum kjól. 4 Hún er lágvaxin og þybbin, með grátt, liðað, stutt hár og gleraugu. Hún er alltaf með handtösku og oft með sjal, og hún klæðist fínum fötum. 5 Hann er hávaxinn og mjög sterkur, og hann er með stórt brjóst, stóra handleggi og stóra fætur. Hann er með ljósbrúnt, stutt hár og blá augu. 6 Hún var grönn og var með mjög ljóst, stutt, liðað hár, blá augu og rauðar varir. 7 Hann er með stutt, grátt hár og stutt grátt skegg. Hann er lágvaxinn og grannur, og hann er oftast með hatt og í herfötum. 8 ...?

Hjá lækni   no; he's got pneumonia; stay in bed and take his medicine.

Exercise 3   1 henni er óglatt, hún kastar upp strax eftir að hafa borðað, og hún er með niðurgang. Það getur verið matareitrun. 2 hann datt í gönguferð og hann finnur til (er með verk) í ökklanum. Hann er marinn og bólginn og hann er hræddur um að hann er brotinn. 3 hún er með bakverki og magakrampa. Hún getur varla gengið eða borðað. 4 honum er ferlega illt í höfðinu, sem gerist sjaldan. Hann er slappur/máttlaus. Hann er búinn að mæla sig en hann er ekki með hita.

Í apótekinu   she fell and scraped her knee; a disinfectant, gauze and plaster; she's lost her old one; facial cream.

Exercise 4   1 Já takk. Ég er með kvef og mig vantar lyf við nefstíflu 2 Já, ég ætla að fá verkjatöflur. Mér er svo ferlega illt í höfðinu 3 Nei, ég ætla líka að fá hóstasaft, og áttu til eitthvað til að draga úr sárindum í hálsi? 4 Eru þær mjög dyrar? 5 Fínt, þá ætla ég að fá þær. Þá er það komið, þakka þér fyrir.

Exercise 5   1 Ég hef aldrei komið til Ítalíu 2 Ég hafði farið til læknis áður en ég fór í apótekið 3 Hann hefur reykt/er búinn að reykja í mörg ár 4 afi hefur fengið slag fyrir löngu en hann er ekki búinn að vera veikur síðan 5 eftir að hafa tekið lyfin leið mér miklu betur 6 ég hafði ekki komið til Íslands þangað til ég lærði íslensku 7 það er langt síðan við höfum séð þig 8 hvað ertu búinn að vera lengi á Íslandi?

Exercise 6   1 þessa, hinar 2 þennan 3 þeirri 4 þessum, hina 5 þetta, sú 6 þeim 7 hinu, þessu 8 hið

Fréttagrein   26%; the smallness of the market; Ingibjörg Pálmadóttir; work at lowering the rate

Exercise 7   1 lyfjafyrirtæki 2 nágrannalönd 3 heilbrigðisráðherra 4 aðstoðarmaður 5 Tryggingastofnun 6 Lyfjaverðsnefnd

305

Lesson 16

Happdrætti   only the occasional scratch-and-win; move into a magnificent house, buy and spend until all the money is gone; he fears the
publicity and spending such a high sum unwisely.

Exercise 1   ynnir, ynni (*past*, vinna); flytti (*past*, flytja); yrði (*past*,
verða); fengi (*past*, fá); færi (*past*, fara); lifði (*past*, lifa); léki (*past*, leika);
yrðu (*past*, verða); vildi (*past*, vilja); myndi (*past*, munu); væri (*past*,
vera); eyddi (*past*, eyða); sæi (*past*, sjá); fengi (*past*, fá); byði (*past*,
bjóða); legði (*past*, leggja); þyrfti (*past*; þurfa)

Exercise 2   1 væri 2 sjái 3 gréti 4 hafi 5 dyttu 6 komi, verði 7 fari
8 komi

Exercise 3   1 hann fengi sér dýran bíl 2 hann héldi áfram að vinna 3 hann
borgaði/greiddi alla reikningana sína 4 hann klæddi sig/færi í fín/flott föt
5 hann teldi alla peningana sína 6 hann drykki kampavín á hverjum degi
7 hann segði engum frá þessu 8 hann gæfi konunni sinni stóra gjöf

Exercise 4   1 höfuðborg 2 höfn 3 gömul 4 íbúar 5 hús 6 sjávarútvegi
7 sveitum 8 ferðamenn 9 sumarsins 10 byggingar 11 sögu 12 útivistar

Exercise 5   There are no set answers to this exercise.

Exercise 6   Ég bý í tveggja herbergja íbúð í fjölbýlishúsi í miðbænum.
Íbúðin er á fyrstu hæð, og í henni eru stofa, svefnherbergi, eldhús og
baðherbergi. Kringum húsið er stór og fallegur garður. Í stofunni eru
sófi og kaffiborð, og við vegginn eru bókaskápar. Arinn er á móti
bókaskápunum og á árinhillunni eru blómapottar og kerti. Við gluggann eru fjórir stólar og borð, og við hlíðina á borðinu er samstæða. Í
horninu hjá borðinu er kommóða og á henni eru sjónvarpstæki og
lampi. Myndir hanga á veggjunum. Eldhúsið er stærsta herbergi í
íbúðinni. Það er bjart, með mörgum eldhússkapum, eldhúsborði og
stólum, eldavél, örbylgjuofni, og þvottavél. Mér finnst mjög fallegt
útsýnið frá eldhúsinu í garðinn. Svefnherbergið er jafnstórt stofunni.
Þar eru rúm og fataskápar. Svefnherbergið þjónar líka sem skrifstofa,
og í horninu eru skrifborð, tölva og margar hillur fullar af pappírsdóti,
möppum og skjölum. Baðherbergið er hvítt og blátt á litinn, og í því
eru bað, sturta, vaskur og klósett. Auk þess eru lítill skápur, handklæði
og hreinlætisvörur. Ég er ánægð með íbúðina. Mér líður mjög vel hér,
og ég ætla ekki að flytja héðan.

Exercise 7 1 Ég segist aldrei hafa komið til Íslands áður. 2 Barnið sagði að sér fyndist grænmeti vont. 3 Mamma spyr hvar ég hafi verið í gærkvöldi. 4 Pabbi spurði af hverju ég hefði horft svo einkennilega á sig. 5 Þórey spurði hvort við kæmum á morgun.

Exercise 8 Áslaug segist búa í tveggja herbergja íbúð í fjölbylishúsi í miðbænum. Hún segir að íbúðin sé á fyrstu hæð, og að í henni séu stofa, svefnherbergi, eldhús og baðherbergi, og stór og fallegur garður sé kringum húsið. Svo segir hún að í stofunni séu sófi og kaffiborð, og að við vegginn séu bókaskápar. Hún segir að arinn sé á móti bókaskápunum og á árinhillunni séu blómapottar og kerti. Við gluggann séu fjórir stólar og borð, segir hún, við hlíðina á borðinu sé samstæða, og í horninu hjá borðinu sé kommóða og á henni séu sjónvarpstæki og lampi. Hún segir að myndir hangi á veggjunum. Svo segir hún að eldhúsið sé stærsta herbergi í íbúðinni, og að það sé bjart, með mörgum eldhússkapum, eldhúsborði og stólum, eldavél, örbylgjuofni, og þvottavél. Hún segir að sér finnist mjög fallegt útsýnið frá eldhúsinu í garðinn. Svo segir hún að svefnherbergið sé jafnstórt stofunni, og að þar séu rúm og fataskápar. Hún segir að svefnherbergið þjóni líka sem skrifstofa, og að í horninu séu skrifborð, tölva og margar hillur fullar af pappírsdóti, möppum og skjölum. Baðherbergið sé hvítt og blátt á litinn, og í því séu bað, sturta, vaskur og klósett. Auk þess segir hún að það séu lítill skápur, handklæði og hreinlætisvörur. Hún segist vera ánægð með íbúðina. Hún segir að sér líði mjög vel þar, og hún segist ekki ætla að flytja þaðan.

Gestir í kaffi she has a bad back; lump sugar; the drain

Exercise 10 1 viltu (gjöra svo vel að)/vildir þú rétta mér mjólkina 2 viltu (gjöra svo vel að)/vildir þú gefa mér eld 3 mér þætti gott konfekt með kaffinu 4 mætti ég fá meira kaffi? 5 gæti ég fengið vatnsglas? 6 ætti ég að koma með þér? 7 vildirðu dansa?

Fyrsta þakíbúð á Íslandi opnuð almenningi as of today; it's the first penthouse; it's being renovated; Einar installed and drew much of the furniture.

Glosses of reading passages

Lesson 1

Fjölskylda frá Íslandi: *a family from Iceland*

Einar Gunnarsson is an Icelander. His father is called Gunnar, and therefore Einar is Gunnarsson (Gunnar's son). Granddad's name is Jónas, and therefore Gunnar is Jónasson. In Iceland that is how it is.

Einar is a husband. That means that he is married. His wife is called Birna. She is Einar's wife, but she is nevertheless not called Gunnarsson because she isn't Gunnar's son. She is Ólafsdóttir, because her father's name is Ólafur. Granddad is called Hrafn, and therefore Ólafur is Hrafnsson.

Birna and Einar have a child. The child is called Þóra. What is the child doing? She is playing. Where is Einar? He is not at home. He is working. He is a salesman. And what is Birna doing? She is working at home. She is reading a play. She is an actress and she is preparing [for] a part.

Lesson 5

Árstíðir á Íslandi: *seasons in Iceland*

The winter is from January until March. It is long and rather cold. Often there are intermittent snowstorms, snow and frost, and often it is very windy. The days are short in midwinter.

The spring is from April until June. Then it starts to become warmer, the days become longer, and the golden plover comes to the country. Nature wakes from its winter sleep and all begins to bloom.

The summer is from July until September. Then it is bright around the clock, and when the sun shines it is often very warm and comfortable, up to 20–25 degrees. There are many outdoor festivals, and many go camping. But it can also be cool, even cold, especially in the interior; and one can always expect precipitation. In August and September people go berry-picking.

The autumn is from October until December. The autumn colours are beautiful, but in the autumn it also starts to get cold and it is often rainy and windy.

Draumur um brúðkaup í hvítum kjól: *dream about a wedding in a white dress*

The Australian comedy film, *Muriel's Wedding*, which is now being shown in the Háskólabíó, is about a girl who lives in a small beach town. The girl is called Muriel and her greatest wish is to find her love and get married in a white wedding dress. Unfortunately it turns out to be difficult for Muriel to have her wish fulfilled because she is timid and unsure of herself.

The music of the Swedish band ABBA is important in Muriel's life. There, existence is so bright and carefree and completely different from the one Muriel has to struggle with.

Hogan is a great fan of ABBA and spared himself no trouble to get permission of the band members to play the music in the film.

Muriel's Wedding has been well received both here and abroad.

Skuggi skammdegisins: *midwinter's shadow*

Hermann Ragnar, dance teacher: I find the autumn a lovely time. Then the schools and the theatres start their activities. The autumn colours are so beautiful and the larches in my garden become a beautiful yellow-brown. I always look forward to Christmas, but when the Christmas lights have been turned off at Epiphany a more difficult time approaches.

Sóley, actress: I am rather cheerful by nature but in the autumn I become lazy and depressed. Then I look forward most to snuggling down in bed all day. I also notice that my children have a harder time waking up in the morning. Christmas raises my spirits but at the beginning of February I become lazy again.

Nína Björk: I experience depression at the beginning of spring when it starts to brighten again. I feel good on the other hand in the twilight by candlelight. Therefore autumn is the nicest time of year and September my favourite month.

Lesson 6

Útvarp og sjónvarp á Íslandi: *radio and television in Iceland*

The Icelandic radio station, called the Icelandic National Broadcasting (RÚV) since 1934, was founded in the year 1928. Since 1983 RÚV runs two channels, Channel 1 and Channel 2. Channel 1 runs a varied programme which emphasizes news, education, music and Icelandic subjects. Channel 2 is on the air 24 hours a day and presents mainly popular music and chat shows. The main news broadcasts on both channels are the midday news at noon and the evening news at seven, and they enjoy the greatest popularity on the radio. Initially, the RÚV had a monopoly, but since the radio and television channels were deregulated in 1985 several private stations have been founded. Many of them only broadcast in the greater Reykjavík area.

The first television broadcasts in Iceland came from the American army base in Keflavík. The year 1966 saw the first broadcast in Icelandic when the National Television Station, or Sjónvarpið, began its activities. Its daily programme was short for a very long time, four to five hours per evening, and there was no broadcast on Thursdays. Nowadays there is, apart from Sjónvarpið, Channel 2, a private station which one has to pay for. Due to lack of money the majority of the programmes is foreign material, mostly from Britain and the United States, which is shown with Icelandic sub-titles; children's programmes are dubbed into Icelandic. The most important new stations which have broadcast since 1995 are Sýn, Bíórásin and Skjár 1. The principal stations' main programme is the news at seven ('Fréttir' on Sjónvarpið and '19>20' on Channel 2).

Lesson 7

Dagur í lífi íslenskrar fjölskyldu: *a day in the life of an Icelandic family*

Jón Grétarsson and Sigríður Ólafsdóttir live in Kópavogur, which is right near Reykjavík. They live in a large flat in a block and together have a daughter, Halla. Sigríður is divorced and also has Ásgeir from a previous marriage, and Jón has Einar from a previous relationship. The boys live with them. Sigríður is a branch manager with Íslandsbanki, and Jón is a carpenter but is presently working as a full-time dad (a 'housedad').

The day begins with Jón and Sigríður waking up and getting up at 7 o'clock, and while Sigríður has a shower and dresses, Jón wakes up the children and gives them their breakfast in the kitchen, and lets them take their fish liver oil. He also makes coffee for the two of them. Before Sigríður goes to work she helps Jón to dress the children. After Sigríður is gone Jón and the children go for a walk. At noon the family eats sandwiches at the kitchen table and listens to the midday news. Then the time comes to take the children to kindergarten. Jón returns home, cleans up, hoovers/vacuums and buys groceries.

Sigríður is very busy at work. The day is booked solid and she is continually at meetings, but she still likes it at work. Her colleagues are energetic and fun, and they meet for a coffee or eat lunch together when the opportunity presents itself.

When Sigríður comes home at 7 o'clock after a long day's work Jón has cooked dinner and she goes straight to the dinner table. The family chats together – the children talk about what they did in school today. Then they thank [their parents] for the meal and go out to play or do their homework for tomorrow. Sigríður clears the table, does the dishes and folds the laundry while Jón watches the news on television. Then they all wish each other good night and go to bed.

Hátíðir og merkisdagar á Íslandi: *holidays and feast days in Iceland*

Bun day used to be the Monday before Lent. On Bun day people have coffee and eat cream buns.

Shrove Tuesday (*lit.* 'exploding day') was the last day before Lent. It is an old custom to eat as much meat as possible and other things that were prohibited during Lent. Many eat salt meat and peas on Shrove Tuesday.

Ash Wednesday was the first day of Lent and is now a public holiday in Iceland.

Easter. There are not many Icelandic traditions that are connected to Easter outside the church holiday. Nowadays people eat chocolate eggs (Easter eggs) but that is not a very old custom.

Many ancient traditions seem on the other hand to be connected to the *first day of summer*, which has long been an important holiday in Iceland. It was an old custom that people gave summer gifts. The first day of summer is the first Thursday after 18 April and is still a holiday today. On the first day of summer people wish each other a happy summer.

Fishermen's day is the first Sunday in June, first celebrated officially in 1938. There are many outdoor festivals, and fishermen, shipowners and the Minister of Fisheries deliver speeches.

Seventeenth of June is Iceland's national day. Iceland became a republic on 17 June 1944, and 17 June is a great feast day all across the country. There is a large gathering at Parliament House on Austurvöllur in Reykjavík where the President of Iceland and the Prime Minister deliver speeches and the Mountain Lady delivers an address. In the afternoon there are all kinds of festivities.

Bank holiday weekend is the first weekend in August. The Monday is a public holiday, and many go on pleasure trips, camping and to outdoor festivals.

Christmas. 23 December is Thorlák's Mass. In many places across the country people eat skate on this day. People also cut 'leaf bread', particularly in northern Iceland. On Christmas Eve, 24 December, at 6 o'clock the bells ring in Christmas. People eat festively, the traditional Christmas porridge, ptarmigans or some other festive food, and then open their gifts. On Christmas Eve the last Christmas lad also arrives. There are thirteen Christmas lads and they come to town to give the children gifts, the first one thirteen days before Christmas. Then they leave again, the first one on Christmas Day. On Christmas Day many eat smoked lamb and drink Christmas ale, and all are dressed up. If you do not get new clothes for Christmas, the Christmas cat will come and eat all your Christmas food, and you too if he gets the chance!

New Year. New Year's Eve and New Year's Day. At night the elves, 'hidden people', move house. Nowadays there are New Year's Bonfires on New Year's Eve, and at midnight there are also many fireworks.

Epiphany (Twelfth Night). The last day of the Christmas season. Then there are elf-fires and people dance around the bonfires disguised as elves and trolls.

Lesson 9

Fjölskyldan mín: *my family*

My name is Kristín Ragnarsdóttir. I am seventeen years old. My father is called Ragnar Hjálmarsson. He is a printer, just like Sveinn, my great-grandfather. My mother's name is Eyrún Jónsdóttir. She is a school secretary. I have three siblings, two brothers and one sister. My brother Jón is the eldest. He is twenty years old and is at sea (i.e. he is a fisherman). He is married to Lilja. I am next, and then comes my sister Soffía. She has just turned sixteen, and has started grammar school. Little Palli (Páll) is the youngest. He is still in elementary school. My niece, Hulda, is the first grandchild of mum and dad. Jón and Lilja have just had her. My sister-in-law Lilja is the same age as I am, and we are good friends.

My family and I live in Selfoss, which is a town in southern Iceland. We live in an old house in the town centre. Dad's workshop is at the side of the house. Mum is very much into horses. She has several horses, and often when we come out of school we, mother and daughter, go riding.

Granddad Hjálmar and Granny Soffía have a farm out in the country. My great-grandmother Sigurbjörg lives with them. We often go to visit them when we are on holiday. They have many sheep and cows, and it's always fun to go there. I was named after granny Kristín, who lives in Reykjavík with Gústaf, my mum's stepfather. My grandfather died when mum was still small. We always visit them when we go to Reykjavík.

Mum is an only child, but I have many aunts, uncles and cousins on dad's side. We are going to a family reunion next summer, and I am looking forward to meeting all my relatives there.

Lesson 10

Bréf: *a letter*

Dear Þórhallur, Sigrún Jónsdóttir from the Icelandic Embassy in Washington advised me to contact you. I am learning Icelandic on my own, because there are no Icelandic courses offered here in the area (neighbourhood). The problem is that I need books to practise the language. Would you please send me a catalogue and information about (mail) orders and payment.

Thank you very much in advance, Yours sincerely, John Anderson.

Lesson 11

Hringferð um Grænland árið 2000: *a trip around Greenland in the year 2000*

The Akureyri travel agency plans in the millennial year 2000 to offer a two-week plane trip around Greenland with stops at over twenty places.

There the participants will be given the opportunity to see polar bear settlements, historically famous fjords and enjoy a view over glacial run-off areas. The trip around Greenland costs one million krónur and is organized on the occasion of the millennium of Inuit settlement in Greenland.

The round trip has caught the attention of people abroad if we may take seriously a study of exciting adventure trips by *For Him* magazine. In a list of one hundred exciting travel possibilities for those who want to try something new, it is in second place.

Among other exciting trips on the list may be mentioned rapid sailing down the river Ganges, a trip down to the *Titanic*, an eight-month coach trip around Bali and a bike trip around Cuba.

Lesson 12

Besta fótboltastelpan: *the best female footballer*

She scored a magnificent goal in the former international match between Iceland and England in the autumn of 1994 and had thereby proved that she was one of the most important Icelandic female footballers. Margrét Ólafsdóttir was elected the most promising player of the year 1993 and the best player in 1994. She is both in the international league U 20 and in the main league, but she is obviously unaffected by her success and considers it important not to become arrogant. Margrét studies at the Business School of Iceland but spends most of her free time football training. When Margrét is asked what is so attractive about football she mentions the company. 'I so much enjoy playing football' she adds and smiles. 'Training takes up a lot of time of course but I keep in close (*lit.* 'good') contact with my friends ...' Margrét sees herself continuing in football in the future. She would like to go abroad and learn more about football. Germany and the Nordic countries are uppermost in her mind, but she has not informed herself yet where it is possible to get into football professionally. What does it take to become such a good football player? 'One needs to apply oneself diligently, train vigorously and live a healthy life. It is also necessary to organize one's time well in order to tackle both training and studying', says Margrét, and adds that her parents are also great sports people.

Láttu þér líða vel! *Allow yourself to feel well!*

Improving one's health and well-being begins with ourselves. Lifestyle has a real influence on how we feel, both mentally and physically, and we are responsible for our own lifestyle. Most of us do not enjoy free time, but rest is as important as exercise. We increase our own well-being by letting our talents come into their own in work and play, and find a release for our creativity at work and in our spare time. Stress causes many difficulties, but when we learn to relax, for instance with music or meditation, and release tension through physical exertion we feel less stress. Most of us drive to work rather than walking or cycling, and give ourselves hardly any time for daily exercise or room for leisure. Exercise and participating in sports are healthy for body and soul, and all movement, from a light walk to heavy sports training, has a good influence on the body and also on mental stress, because then tension is released. We must exercise regularly and this must be a part of daily life. It is possible for almost everyone to practise walking or swimming. Begin slowly and build it up little by little.

Lesson 13

Ísland: *Iceland*

Iceland was settled in the ninth century, and the first settler was Ingólfur Arnarson. The Republic of Iceland is almost sixty years old. The president lives at Bessastaðir in Álftanes, south of Reykjavík. The main areas of employment have been the fishing industry and agriculture, but an ever-growing number of people work in service industries and business.

Iceland is mountainous, and on some of the highest mountains there are glaciers. The largest glacier is Vatnajökull, which is as large as Luxemburg. There are also many rivers and many lakes in Iceland, and in the rivers are many beautiful waterfalls, such as Dettifoss, the largest waterfall in Europe. There is also much salmon and trout in the rivers, which many enjoy catching. There are on the other hand few trees in Iceland.

Many fjords and bays run into the country, except on the southern coast, where there are large sandy deserts. In the sea around Iceland there are rich fishing grounds and good harbours are widespread. There are many volcanoes in Iceland, and some of them are active. The most famous volcano without a doubt is Hekla, which last erupted in 2000.

In Iceland hot springs (where the water coming out of the earth is warm) and geysers (when the water comes up boiling) are widespread. The best-known geyser in Iceland is Geysir, and in many foreign languages geysers have been named after it. The hot water is used in various ways, among other things in swimming pools which are all around the country, and many people go for a swim every day all year round. Most houses in Iceland are heated with hot water, as are the greenhouses. The steam is used to produce electricity, and large and fast-flowing rivers are also utilized for the production of electricity.

It is not as cold in Iceland as many think, but the climate is unsettled, and often people see (*lit.* 'there are') many different kinds of weather in one day. In the interior it is colder than down in the lowlands and on the coast, and there is little growth. Because of the weather, communications (including traffic) are difficult in some areas, and often roads are impassable during the greater part of the winter. There are flights to most towns.

Þingvellir is the most famous historic site in Iceland. In 930 the Icelandic Parliament (Alþingi) was founded there and held meetings there every year until Iceland became a part of the Norwegian crown (1262–4). But it also has much unique natural beauty. Þingvellir was declared a protected area and became a national park in 1928.

Landshlutar: *parts of the country*

The parts of the country are the West, the West Fjords, the North-West, the North-East, the East, the East Fjords, the South-East, and the South. The capital area and the Reykjanes peninsula are called the South-Western corner. In the West there are two large bays, Faxaflói and Breiðafjörður, and a long peninsula runs out (into the sea) in between them which is called Snæfellsnes. There is one of the most famous and most beautiful glaciers in the world: Snæfellsjökull. Jules Verne wrote about Snæfellsjökull in his famous book *Journey to the Centre of the Earth*. The West Fjords are sparsely populated, as transport links are often difficult and the soil is scanty, but there are many good nesting places for birds. The area is mountainous and the landscape magnificent. The main town is Ísafjörður. In the North is situated the largest town outside the capital area, Akureyri, and one of the best-known places in the country, Mývatn. The landscape there has been moulded by volcanic eruptions, and the heat of the earth is utilized at Mt Krafla. In the East Fjords are high mountains and narrow fjords, similar to the West Fjords. In the East there is the largest forest in Iceland, Hallormsstaðaskógur, which is 2,000 hectares in size. Egilsstaðir is one of the few towns that is not situated on the coast. The South is the greatest agricultural area in Iceland, where is after all most of the lowland as well as heated earth. There are also many tourist destinations, such as Skaftafell, Þórsmörk, Jökulsárlón and Hvannadalshnúkur, which is the highest mountain in the country (2119 m). The coast is largely without harbours since it is very dangerous to ships, and many have perished there.

Lesson 14

Sálin hans Jóns míns (þjóðsaga): *the soul of my Jón (a folk tale)*

Once upon a time an old man and an old woman lived together. The old man was rather difficult and unpopular and on top of that he was lazy and useless around the house. His old lady did not like this at all and often scolded him. But although they did not get along well in some respects, the old woman still loved her old man very much.

Then one time the old man became very ill and was in a very bad way. The old woman kept vigil but when he did not get better she started thinking that he was not so well prepared for his death, and it was a matter of doubt whether he would get entrance into the kingdom of heaven. She then took a bag and held it in front of the man's mouth, and when he gave up the ghost, it went into the bag, and the woman tied it shut. Then she went to the heavens with the bag, came to the door and knocked on it. St Peter then came out and asked her what her business was. 'Hello', says the old woman, 'I've come here with the soul of my Jon and intend to ask you to let him in here.' 'Yes, yes', says Peter, 'but unfortunately I cannot do that, I have never heard anything good about your Jon.' Then the old woman said: 'I didn't think, St Peter, that you would be so hard-hearted. Have you forgotten what happened to you in the old days when you denied your master?' Peter went inside again and locked the door, and the old woman was left outside.

After a little while she knocked on the door once more and then the Virgin Mary came out. 'Hello there, my dear', says the old woman, 'I hope that you will let my Jon inside.' 'Unfortunately, love', says Mary, 'I don't dare to because he was so bad, your Jon.' 'But don't you know', says the old woman, 'that others can be weak like you, or don't you remember that you had a child outside of wedlock?' Mary didn't want to hear any more and quickly locked the door.

For the third time the old woman knocked on the door. Then Christ himself came out. The old woman spoke humbly: 'I wanted to ask you to promise this poor soul entrance here.' Christ answered: 'That is your Jon – no, woman, he didn't believe in me.' But at the same moment that he closed the door again, the old woman threw the bag with the soul inside past him. Then a heavy weight was lifted from the old woman's heart knowing that her Jon had gone to heaven and she returned home happy.

Bréf: *a letter*

Dear Áslaug:
I apologize for how long I have been delayed in writing to you, but I have been so very busy. When I came home from Iceland it appeared that my house had been broken into! The burglars took my computer, CD player, television and video recorder. Fortunately I left no money behind. But there was a lot of bother surrounding it all. Early the next day I had to go to the police station to give a statement, get in touch with the insurance company, etc.

Otherwise everything is fine here. It is insanely busy as always but I am happy in my work. My parents are also doing well and they pass on their regards.

How are things going for you? Have you become used to your new flat? How was Kjartan's party, wasn't it fun? I was sorry to miss it.

I warmly thank you once again for everything. It was wonderful to see you again! Be well, and pass on my best regards to your family.

Sincerely,
Joyce.

Úr Brennu Njáls sögu: *from the story of burnt Njáll*

Gunnar was sleeping in one loft in the lodge as well as Hallgerður and his mother. And when they came to the farm they did not know whether Gunnar would be at home. Gissur said that someone should go to the (farm)houses and find out, and in the meantime they sat down in the field. Þorgrímur from the East went up onto the lodge. Gunnar sees a red tunic appear at the window and ventures out with his halberd through his middle. Þórgrímur's feet slipped and the shield came loose and he toppled off the roof. Then he walks to Gissur and the men where they were sitting in the field. Gissur looked at him and said: 'Is Gunnar home?' 'You find out for yourselves, but what I do know is that his halberd was at home.' says the Eastman. Then he fell down dead. They went to them at their houses.

At this moment Þorbrandur Þorleiksson jumps up on the roof and cuts in two Gunnar's bowstring. Gunnar grabs his halberd with both hands and turns quickly towards him and strikes the halberd through him and throws him dead on to the field. Then his brother Ásbrandur leapt up. Gunnar puts his halberd to him and he put up a shield in front of him. The halberd ran through the shield and then between the arms. Gunnar then snared his halberd so tight that the shield split and both arms broke and he fell off the wall. Before this Gunnar had wounded eight men and slain these two. Then Gunnar received two wounds and all men said that he flinched neither at the wounds nor at death.

He said to Hallgerður: 'Get me two locks from your hair and turn them into a bowstring for me, you and my mother.' 'Does anything depend upon it?' she says. 'My life depends upon it,' he says, 'because they will never get me while I have the chance to use my bow.' 'Then I will now,' she says, 'remind you of the slap in my face and I'll never care whether you defend yourself for a longer or a shorter time.' 'Everyone has something to their distinction,' says Gunnar, 'and I will not ask you for this any longer.' Rannveig said: 'This ill becomes you, and your shame will be long-lived.'

Lesson 15

Óhjákvæmilegt að lyf séu eitthvað dýrari hér á landi: *inevitable that medicine is somewhat more expensive here in Iceland*

Spokespersons for the pharmaceutical companies do not want to recognize that medicine is 26 per cent more expensive in Iceland than in neighbouring countries. They say that a registered maximum price, which is proposed as a reference for these calculations, has nothing in common with a realistic price for medicine in this country, although it is certainly true that medicine is, due to the smallness of the market, more expensive in Iceland than in the countries referred to.

It appeared amongst other things in a speech of Ingibjörg Pálmadóttir, Minister of Health, during a discussion held outside the agenda about the cost of medicine by the government in parliament last week that the price of medicine was 26 per cent higher here and that work was needed to lower this rate.

Þórir Haraldsson, assistant to the Minister, said in an interview with *Morgunblaðið* that this was based on information from the (Social) Insurance Department and the Committee for the Prices of Medicine.

Lesson 16

Reykjavík

Reykjavík is the capital of Iceland and the country's only city. Its population is about 100,000. It has the largest harbour, and the main cultural and business institutions in the country are also to be found there. Although Reykjavík is not a big city compared to the cities of millions around the world it definitely has an international flavour.

The city of Reykjavík is not old, although it was built on the home field of the first settler in Iceland, Ingólfur Arnarson, who set up a farm there around 874. After this Reykjavík appears little on the scene for centuries on end, although there is supposed to have been a trading centre there early in the sixteenth century. In 1786 Reykjavík was granted a trading licence. There were then about 167 inhabitants. The city's oldest house, Aðalstræti 10, dates from this time.

In 1845 the Alþingi was resurrected in Reykjavík, and during the last years of the nineteenth century there began a rapid and great development in the fishing industry with the arrival of motorized boats and trawlers, which helped to increase the growth and success of the city. In 1904 executive power was moved from Copenhagen to Reykjavík. A great migration from the countryside to the city took place during the 1930s and 1940s, which played an important part in changing the old Icelandic farmers' society into a modern society within a very short time. In 1950 the number of inhabitants had increased from 5,800 around the turn of the century to 56,000.

Reykjavík is attractive to both domestic and foreign tourists, although in different ways. In the city social and cultural life flourish, particularly in the summer, whether it is in the city centre, the cafes or the cultural institutions. Cultural Night in the city centre is now a high point of the summer. The parliament building, the cathedral, and the town hall are examples of remarkable buildings, old and new, and in the Ethnographic Museum and the Árbær open air museum it is possible to become acquainted with the history of the country and the city. And yet one need never go far either to enjoy the outdoors, because there are many pearls of nature in the city landscape where it is possible to retreat from the hustle and bustle of city life.

Fyrsta þakhúsið á Íslandi opnuð almenningi: *the first penthouse in Iceland opened to the public*

As from today the flat of Einar Jónsson, the sculptor, will be open to museum guests.The flat is in the Einar Jónsson museum, where the couple Einar and Anna, his wife, lived from 1923 until 1954 when Einar died.

'It can be said that this is the first penthouse in Iceland,' says Hrafnhildur Schram, director of the museum. 'The flat will now be a part of the museum and open to guests. It is a lot of fun to open it; it brings museum visitors closer to the person Einar was.' Einar furnished the flat and designed much of the furniture which is in it. 'He designed amongst other things book cases which are formed like columnal basalt, which plays a rich part in his works. Indeed it may be said that the house itself is Einar's largest sculpture.'

The Einar Jónsson Museum is 75 years old next year and for that occasion it was decided to renovate the outside of the house. 'The house was in a very bad state. Now we are changing the windows and mending the wall. We had to repair all the cracks and change the metal work, and now quartz dust will be put to all of the building.' The work will cost 27 million krónur and has gone according to plan.

Icelandic–English glossary

að vísu — to be sure
að, *prep. + dat.* — (up) to, towards
aðal- — main
aðallega, *adv.* — mainly
aðdáand/i (-a, -ar), *m.* — fan
aðeins, *adv.* — only, just
aðgang/ur (-s), *m.* — access, entrance
aðstoða (aðstoða, aðstoðaði, aðstoðað), *acc.* — assist
af hverju — why
af því að — because
af, *prep. + dat.* — off
af/i (-a, -ar), *m.* — grandfather
afar, *adv.* — very, most
afgreiðslu-mað/ur (-manns, -menn), *m.* — shop assistant
afleiðing (-ar, -ar), *f.* — consequence
afmæli (-s, -), *n.* — birthday
afskipti, *n.pl.* — dealings
afslátt/ur (-ar), *m.* — discount
aftur, *adv.* — again
   aftur á móti — on the other hand
aka (ek, ók, óku, ekið), *dat.* — drive
akstur (-s), *m.* — driving

alast (elst, ólst, ólust, alist) upp — grow up
aldeilis, *adv.* — totally, absolutely
aldrei, *adv.* — never
all/ur, *adj.* — all
   allt, *adv.* — completely, totally
   með öllu — the works
   allt í lagi — all right, okay
   alls staðar — everywhere
alltaf, *adv* — always
almenning/ur (-s), *m.* — general public
alþingi (-s), *n.* — parliament
alþingis-mað/ur (-manns, -menn), *m.* — Member of Parliament
alþjóðleg/ur, *adj.* — international
alvarleg/ur, *adj.* — serious
   í alvöru — seriously
alveg, *adv.* — quite, about to
amm/a (-u, -ur), *f.* — grandmother
andartak (-s, -), *n.* — moment
andlega, *adv.* — mentally, spiritually
andlit (-s, -), *n.* — face
annars — by the way
ansi, *adv.* — pretty
apótek (-s, -), *n.* — pharmacy

appelsín/a (-u, -ur), *f.* orange

appelsínugul/ur, *adj.* orange

athuga (athuga, athugaði, athugað), *acc.* check, look into

athygli, *f.indecl.* attention

atvinn/a (-u), *f.* work, employment

auðmjúk/ur, *adj.* humble

auðug/ur, *adj.* rich, wealthy

auðveld/ur, *adj.* easy

aug/a (-a, -u), *n.* eye

augnablik (-s, -), *n.* moment

auk, *prep. + gen.* apart from

auk þess in addition

auka, *acc./***aukast (eykst, jókst, jukust, aukist),** *intrans.* increase

auka-, *pref.* extra, additional

austur, *adv.* east

fyrir austan, *acc.* to the east of

á (-r, -r), *f.* river

á, *prep. + dat./acc.* on, per

áætlun (-ar, -ir), *f.* plan, schedule

áberandi, *adj.indecl.* striking

áburð/ur (-ar), *m.* ointment, cream

ábyrgð (-ar), *f.* responsibility

áður, *adv.* before

ágæt/ur, *adj.* fine, okay

ágætlega, *adv.* fine

áhersl/a (-u, -ur), *f.* emphasis

leggja áherslu á emphasize

áhrif, *n.pl.* influence

áhug/i (-a, -ar), *m.* interest

áhugamál (-s, -), *n.* interest, hobby

áhyggja (-u, -ur), *f.* care, worry

ákveða (ákveð, ákvað, ákváðum, ákveðið) (sér), *acc.* decide

álegg (-s, -), *n.* luncheon meat

án, *prep. + gen.* without

ánægð/ur, *adj.* content, happy

ánægj/a (-u), *f.* pleasure;

mín var ánægjan the pleasure was all mine

ár (-s, -), *n.* year

áramót, *n.pl.* New Year

áratug/ur (-s, -ar), *m.* decade

áreynsl/a (-u), *f.* effort, exertion

árshátíð (-ar, -ir), *f.* annual celebration, staff party

árstíð (-ar, -ir), *f.* season

ást (-ar, -ir), *f.* love

ávaxtasaf/i (-a, -ar), *m.* fruit juice

bað (-s, -), *n.* bath, bathroom

baða (baða, baðaði, baðað) sig bathe

baðherbergi (-s, -), *n.* bathroom

bak (-s, -), *n.* back

baka (baka, bakaði, bakað), *acc.* bake

bakarí (-s, -), *n.* bakery

bakpok/i (-a, -ar), *m.* backpack

banan/i (-a, -ar), *m.*   banana

Bandaríkin, *n.pl.*   the United States

Bandaríkja-mað/ur (-manns, -menn), *m.*   person from the US

bandarísk/ur, *adj.*   American, from the US

bank/i (-a, -ar), *m.*   bank

banna (banna, bannaði, bannað) *dat. + acc.*   prohibit

barn (-s, -), *n.*   child

barnabarn (-s, -), *n.*   grandchild

batna (batnar, batnaði, batnað), *imp.*   get better

baun (-ar, -ir), *f.*   pea, bean

bát/ur (-s, -ar), *m.*   boat

bein/n, *adj.*   straight, direct

bera (ber, bar, báru, borið), *acc.*   carry

   bera fram   serve

   bera fram af borðinu   clear the table

berja (ber, barði, barið), *acc.*   hit, knock

berjamó/r (-s): fara í berjamó   go berry-picking

biblía (-u, -ur), *f.*   bible

biðja (bið, bað, buðu, beðið) um, *acc.*   ask for

   biðja að heilsa   give one's regards

biðstof/a (-u, -ur), *f.*   waiting room

bil (-s, -), *n.*   moment

   um það bil   around

   í bili   at the moment

binda (bind, batt, bundu, bundið), *acc.*   bind, tie

   binda fyrir   bind shut

bindi (-s, -), *n.*   tie

birta (birti, birti, birt)   brighten

biskup (-s, -ar), *m.*   bishop

bíða (bíð, beið, biðu, biðið)   wait

   bíða eftir, *dat.*   wait for

bíl/l (-s, -ar), *m.*   car

bílstjór/i (-a, -ar), *m.*   driver

bíó (-s, -), *n.*   cinema

bjart/ur, *adj.*   bright

bjóða (býð, bauð, buðu, boðið), *dat. + acc.*   offer, wish

bjór (-s, -ar), *m.*   beer

blað (-s, -), *n.*   paper

blaða-mað/ur (-manns, -menn), *m.*   journalist

blaðsíð/a (-u, -ur), *f.*   page

blanda (blanda, blandaði, blandað), *dat.*   blend

   blanda sér inn í, *acc.*   interfere, involve oneself

blaut/ur, *adj.*   wet

blá/r (blátt, n.) *adj.*   blue

bleik/ur, *adj.*   pink

blessað/ur, *adj.* (**blessuð**), *f.* komdu blessaður — hello, how do you do;

vertu blessaður — goodbye

blokk (-ar, -ir), *f.* — block of flats

blotna (blotna, blotnaði, blotnað), *intrans.* — get wet

blóð (-s, -), *n.* — blood

blóm (-s, -), *n.* — flower, plant

blómleg/ur, *adj.* — flourishing

blómstra (blómstra, blómstraði, blómstrað) — bloom, flourish

bol/ur (-s, -ir), *m.* — torso, shirt

boll/i (-a, -ar), *m.* — cup

borð (-s, -), *n.* — table

borða (borða, borðaði, borðað), *acc.* — eat

borg (-ar, -ir), *f.* — city

borga (borga, borgaði, borgað), *dat. + acc.* — pay

bók (-ar, bækur), *f.* — book

bókabúð (-ar, -ir), *f.* — bookshop

bókhald (-s), *n.* — book-keeping

bómull (-ar), *f.* — cotton

bónd/i (-a, bændur), *m.* — farmer

bóndabæ/r (-jar, -ir), *m.* — farm

bragð (-s, -), *n.* — taste

bragðast (bragðast, bragðaðist, bragðast), *intrans.* — taste

brak (-s), *n.* — crash

brauð (-s, -), *n.* — bread

bráðum, *adv.* — soon

bregða (bregð, brá, brugðu, brugðið) sér við, *acc.* — react to, flinch at

brennivín (-s, -), *n.* — Icelandic aquavit

Bretland (-s), *n.* — Britain

breyta (breyti, breytti, breytt), *dat.* — change

breytast (breytist, breyttist, breyst), *intrans.* — change

breytileg/ur, *adj.* — changeable

bréf (-s, -) *n.* — letter

brjálað/ur, *adj.* — crazy

brjóst (-s, -), *n.* — chest, breast

brjóta (brýt, braut, brutu, brotið), *acc.* — break

brjóta saman, *acc.* — fold

brjótast inn — break in

brottför (-ar), *f.* — departure

bróð/ir (-ur, bræður), *m.* — brother

brú (-ar, brýr), *f.* — bridge

brúðkaup (-s, -), *n.* — wedding

brún/n, *adj.* — brown

bræða (bræði, bræddi, brætt), *acc.* — melt

bursta (bursta, burstaði, burstað), *acc.* — brush

bursta (í sér) tennurnar — brush one's teeth

búa (bý, bjó, bjuggu, búið) — live

búin/n (búið), *n.* — finished, done

vera búinn að — be finished doing

búa til, *acc.* — prepare

búast við, *dat.* — expect

búð (-ar, -ir), *f.* — shop

byggð (-ar, -ir), *f.* — settlement, habitat, inhabited area

bygging (-ar, -ar), *f.* — building

byggja (byggi, byggði, byggt), *acc.* — build, settle

byrja (byrja, byrjaði, byrjað) — begin

byrja á, *dat.* — start with, begin by

byrjun (-ar, -ir), *f.* — beginning

bæði, *n. of* **báðir** — both

bæ/r (-jar, -ir), *m.* — town

bæta (bæti, bætti, bætt) við, *dat.* — add

dag/ur (-s, -ar), *m.* — day

í dag — today

nú á dögum — nowadays

dagbók (-ar, -bækur), *f.* — diary

dagsetning (-ar, -ar), *f.* — date

dagskrá (-r, -r), *f.* — programme

dansa (dansa, dansaði, dansað) — dance

dansleik/ur (-ar, -ir), *m.* — dance

dauði (-a), *m.* — death

detta (dett, datt, duttu, dottið) — fall

deyja (dey, dó, dóu, dáið) — die

disk/ur (-s, -ar), *m.* — plate, disk

doll/a (-u, -ur), *f.* — pot

dós (-ar, -ir), *f.* — tin

dót (-s), *n.* — stuff

dótt/ir (-ur, dætur), *f.* — daughter

draga (dreg, dró, drógu, dregið), *acc.* — draw, delay

draga úr, *dat.* — take away, withdraw

draum/ur (-s, -ar), *m.* — dream

drekka (drekk, drakk, drukku, drukkið) *acc.* — drink

drepa (drep, drap, drápu, drepið), *acc.* — kill

drepa á dyr — knock on the door

drífa (dríf, dreif, drifu, drifið) sig — hurry (up), get going

drusluleg/ur, *adj.* — sloppy

dugleg/ur, *adj.* — diligent, industrious

dunda (dunda, dundaði, dundað) sér við, *acc.* — play about, busy oneself with

dvelja (dvel, dvaldi, dvalið) — stay

dvöl (-ar, -ir), *f.* — stay

dyr, *f.pl.* — door

dýr, *adj.* — expensive

dæmi (-s, -), *n.* — example

dökkhærð/ur, *adj.* — dark-haired

eða, *conj.* — or

eðli (-s), *n.* — nature

  eðlisfar (-s, -), *n.* — nature, disposition

eðlileg/ur, *adj.* — natural

efling (-ar, -ar), *f.* — increase

efni (-s, -), *n.* — material

efnileg/ur, *adj.* — promising

efri, *adv.comp.* — upper

eftir, *prep. + dat./acc.* — after

eiga (á, átti, átt), *acc.* — have, own

  eiga til, *acc.* — have available/ in one's possession

  eiga að — have to, should

  eiga heima — live

  eiga von á, *dat.* — expect

  eiga eftir — have left

eigin, *adj.indecl.* — (one's) own

eiginkon/a (-u, -ur), *f.* — wife

eigin-að/ur (-manns, -menn), *m.* — husband

einbýli (-s, -), *n.* — single room

ein/n (eitt, n.), *num./adj.* — one, alone

  einu sinni — once upon a time

einhver (eitthvað, n.), pron. — someone

einka-, *pref.* — private

einkabarn (-s, -), *n.* — only child

einkenni (-s, -), *n.* — characteristics

einmitt, *adv.* — exactly

einnig — also

eins, *conj.* — as

  eins og — like, such as, as . . . as

einstak/ur, *adj.* — unique

eitthvað (n. of einhver) — something

ekkert (n. of enginn) — nothing

ekki — not

eld/ur (-s, -ar), *m.* — fire

elda (elda, eldaði, eldað), *acc.* — cook

eldast (eldist, eltist, elst) — become older

eldavél (-ar, -ar), *f.* — cooker, stove

eldfjall (-s, -), *n.* — volcano

eldhús (-s, -), *n.* — kitchen

elska (elska, elskaði, elskað), *acc.* — love

elst/ur, *adj.superl.* — oldest

en, *conj. comp. excl.* — but, and; than

  en . . . ! — how/what . . . !

enda (enda, endaði, endað) — end

enda, *conj.* — and what's more, in fact

endilega — by all means
endur-, *pref.* — again, re-
enginn (ekkert, n.) pron. — no (one)
Englending/ur (-s, -ar), m. — English person
ennþá, *adv.* — still, yet
ensk/a (-u), f. — English
erfið/ur, *adj.* — difficult
erfiðleik/i (-a, -ar), m. — difficulty
erindi (-s, -), n. — business, errand
erlend/ur, *adj.* — foreign
erlendis, *adv.* — abroad
ey (-jar, -jar)/ eyja (-u, -ar), f. — island
eyða (eyði, eyddi, eytt), *dat.* — spend
eyr/a (-a, -u), n. — ear
ég, *pron.* — I
fagur, *adj.* — beautiful
falla (fell, féll, féllu, fallið) — fall
falleg/ur, *adj.* — beautiful
far (-s, -), n. — ride, passage
fara (fer, fór, fóru, farið) — go
fara eftir, *dat.* — depend on
fara í, *acc.* — go (in)to, put on
fara úr, *dat.* — take off
farþeg/i (-a, -ar), m. — passenger
fá (fæ, fékk, fengu, fengið), *dat. + acc.* — get, obtain
fá sér — get/have oneself
fást, *acc.* — be available
fást við — take on

fegurð (-ar, -ir), f. — beauty
feimin/n, *adj.* — shy
feit/ur, *adj.* — fat
ferð (-ar, -ir), f. — trip, journey
ferða-maður (-manns, -menn), m — traveller, tourist
ferðaskrifstof/a (-u, -ur), f. — travel agency
ferðast (ferðast, ferðaðist, ferðast) — travel
fern/a (-u, -ur), f. — carton
félagslíf (-s), n. — social life, social activity
fimmtudag/ur (-s, -ar), m. — Thursday
fingur (-s, -), m. — finger
finna (finn, fann, fundu, . fundið), acc. — find
finnast, *imp.* — find, think
finna fyrir, *dat.* — feel (something)
finna til í, *dat.* — hurt
fisk/ur (-s, -ar), m. — fish
fiska (fiska, fiskaði, fiskað), vb. — fish
fiski (-jar), f. — fishing
fiskimið (-s, -), n. — fishing grounds
fiskveið/i (-ar, -ar), f. — fishing
fíl/l (-s, -ar), m. — elephant
fín/n, *adj.* — fine, elegant, posh
fjall (-s, -), n. — mountain
fjalla (fjalla, fjallaði, fjallað) um, *acc.* — deal with, be about

fjandi, *adv.* — darned
fjand/i (**-a, ar**), *n.* — devil
fjólublá/r (**fjólublátt**, *n.*), *adj.* — purple
fjórhjóladrifin/n, *adj.* — four-wheel drive
fjórir (**fjórar**, *f.* **fjögur**, *n.*) — four
fjölbreytt/ur, *adj.* — varied, diverse
fjöld/i (**-a, -ar**), *m.* — large number, crowd
fjöllótt/ur, *adj.* — mountainous
fjölskyld/a (**-u, -ur**), *f.* — family
fjör (**-s**), *n.* — vitality, fun
fjörð/ur (**fjarðar, firðir**), *m.* — fjord
flask/a (**-u, -ur**), *f.* — bottle
fleiri, *comp.* (**eitthvað/ nokkuð**) **fleira?** — more / anything else?
flens/a (**-u**), *f.* — flu
flest/ir, *pl.superl.* — most
flink/ur, *adj.* — good, adept (at something)
flík (**-ar, -ur**), *f.* — piece of clothing
fljót (**-s, -**), *n.* — river
fljót/ur, *adj.* — fast, quick
fljótt, *adv.* — quickly
fljúga (**flýg, flaug, flugu, flogið**) — fly
fló/i (**-a, -ar**), *m.* — large bay
flott/ur, *adj.* — great, 'cool'
flugeld/ar (**-a**), *m.pl.* — fireworks
flugpóst/ur (**-s**), *m.* — air mail
flugstöð (**-var, -var**), *f.* — airport terminal
flugvél (**-ar, -ar**), *f.* — aeroplane
flug-völl/ur (**-vallar, -vellir**), *m.* — airport
flytja (**flyt, flutti, flutt**), *acc.* — deliver, recite, move house
flýta (**flýti, flýtti, flýtt**) **sér** — hurry (up)
forðum, *adv.* — before, long ago
foreldr/ar, *m.pl.* — parents
form (**-s, -**), *n.* — form, shape
formleg/ur, *adj.* — formal
forsætisráðherra (**-, -r**), *m.* — Prime Minister
forset/i (**-a, -ar**), *m.* — president
forstöðu-mað/ur (**-manns, -menn**), *m.* — leader, director
foss (**-, -ar**), *m.* — waterfall
fólk (**-s**), *n.* — people
fót/ur (**-ar, fætur**), *m.* — foot, leg
fara á fætur — get up (out of bed)
fótbolt/i (**-a**), *m.* — football
frakk/i (**-a, -ar**), *m.* — men's overcoat
Frakkland (**-s**), *n.* — France
fram, *adv.* — forwards, on(wards)
framhjá, *adv.* — past
framkvæma (**framkvæmi, framkvæmdi, framkvæmt**), *acc.* — carry out, execute

framleiða   produce
  (framleiði,
  framleiddi,
  framleitt), *acc.*
framleiðsl/a   production
  (-u), *f.*
framorðið   late
fransk/ur, *adj.*   French
  franskar   chips, french
  (kartöflur), *f.pl.*   fries
frá, *prep. + dat.*   from
frábær, *adj.*   wonderful,
    great
fráskilin/n, *adj.*   divorced
frekar, *adv.*   rather
fremur, *adv.*   rather
fréttir, *f.pl.*   news
friðað/ur, *adj.*   declared a
    national
    monument,
    protected area
frí (-s, -), *n.*   holidays,
    vacation, time
    off
frímerki (-s, -), *n.*   stamp
frísk/ur, *adj.*   healthy, feeling
    well
frjáls, *adj.*   free
frost (-s), *n.*   frost
fræði, *n.pl.*   studies *(f.indecl.*
    as last
    element
    of a
    compound,
    '-ology')
fræg/ur, *adj.*   famous
frænd/i (-a,   male relative
  -ur), *m.*
frændfólk (-s), *n.*   relatives
frænka (-u,   female relative
  -ur), *f.*
fugl (-s, -ar), *m.*   bird

full-, *pref.*   very
full/ur, *adj.*   full, drunk
  á fullu   very busy
fund/ur (-ar,   meeting
  -ir), *m.*
funda (funda,   hold a meeting
  fundaði,
  fundað)
fylla (fylli,   fill
  fyllti, fyllt),
  acc.
fyndin/n, *adj.*   funny, witty
fyrir utan, *acc.*   apart from,
    outside of
fyrir, *prep.*   for, ago
  + dat./acc.
fyrirfram   in advance
fyrir-gefa (-gef,   forgive
  -gaf, -gáfu,
  -gefið), *acc.*
  fyrirgefðu   excuse me
fyrirtæki   company, firm
  (-s, -), *n.*
fyrirtaks-, *pref.*   excellent
fyrr (en), *adv.*   before, until
  í fyrramálið   tomorrow
    morning
  fyrri, *comp.adj.*   previous,
    former
fyrst, *adv.*   first
  fyrst/ur, *adj.*
fyrst, *conj.*   since, as
fæðast (fæðist,   be born
  fæddist, fæst)
færa (færi,   move, bring
  færði, fært),
  acc. + dat.
föðurnafn   patronymic
  (-s, -), *n.*
föl/ur, *adj.*   pale
föstudag/ur (-s,   Friday
  -ar), *m.*

föt, *n.pl.* — clothes, clothing

gallabux/ur, *f.pl.* — jeans

gamal/l (gömul, f.) *adj.* — old

gamaldags, *indecl.adj.* — old-fashioned

gaman (-s), *n.* — fun

gamanmynd (-ar, -ir), *m.* — comedy film

gang/ur (-s, -ar), *m.* — hallway

ganga (geng, gekk, gengu, gengið) — walk, go

garð/ur (-s, -ar), *m.* — garden, park

gat/a (-u, -ur), *f.* — street

gefa (gef, gaf, gáfu, gefið), *dat. + acc.* — give

gegnum, *prep. + acc.* — through

geislaspilar/i (-a, -ar), *m.* — CD player

gengi (-s), *n.* — going, success

gera (geri, gerði, gert), *acc.* — do, make

gera við, *acc.* — fix

gera að, *dat.* — turn into

gerast — happen

gest/ur (-s, -ir), *m.* — guest

gestgjaf/i (-a, -ar), *m.* — host

geta (get, gat, gátu, getið), *acc.* — can

geyma (geymi, geymdi, geymt), *acc.* — keep

gift/ur, *adj.* — married

gifta sig/giftast (giftist, giftist, gifst), *dat.* — get married, marry

gifting (-ar, -ar), *f.* — wedding (ceremony)

gil (-s, -), *n.* — ravine

girnileg/ur, *adj.* — appetizing

gista (gisti, gisti, gist) — stay overnight

gistihús (-s, -), *n.* — guesthouse

gisting (-ar, -ar), *f.* — accommodation

gjald (-s, -), *n.* — fee, charge

gjarnan, *adv.* — gladly

gjósa (gýs, gaus, gusu, gosið) — erupt

gjöf (-ar, -ir), *f.* — gift, present

gjöra — see **gera**

gjörðu svo vel — here you are, be my guest, go ahead

glað/ur, *adj.* — happy, cheerful

gleði, *f.indecl.* — joy

gleraugu, *n.pl.* — glasses, spectacles

gleyma (gleymi, gleymdi, gleymt), *dat.* — forget

glugg/i (-a, -ar), *m.* — window

glæsileg/ur, *adj.* — elegant, magnificent

gos (-s, -), *n.* — eruption, soft drink

gosdrykk/ur (-jar, -ir), *m.* — soft drink

góð/ur, *adj.* — good

góðan dag(inn) — good morning, good afternoon

góði minn/góða mín — my dear

góðgæti (-s, -), *n.* delicacy

gólf (-s, -), *n.* floor

gramm (-s, -), *n.* gram

grann/ur, *adj.* slim

gras (-s, -) *n.* grass

graut/ur (-s, -ar), *m.* porridge

grá/r (grátt, *n.*) *adj.* grey

gráta (græt, grét, grétu, grátið) cry

greiða (greiði, greiddi, greitt), *dat. + acc.* pay

  greiða sér comb one's hair

greiðsla (-u, -ur), *f.* payment

greiðslukort (-s, -), *n.* credit card

grein (-ar, -ar), *f.* article

greinileg/ur, *adj.* obvious

grill (-s, -), *n.* barbecue, grill

grípa (gríp, greip, gripu, gripið), *acc.* seize, grab

gróður (-s), *m.* growth

gróðurhús (-s, -), *n.* greenhouse

gruna (grunar, grunaði, grunað), *imp.acc.* suspect

grunnskól/i (-a, -ar), *m.* elementary school

græn/n, *adj.* green

grænmetisæt/a (-u, -ur), *f.* vegetarian

guf/a (-u, -ur), *f.* steam

gul/ur, *adj.* yellow

gull (-s, -), *n.* gold

gælunafn (-s, -), *n.* pet name

gæta (gæti, gætti, gætt) sín á, *dat.* watch out for

gönguferð (-ar, -ir), *f.* hiking trip, walk

gönguskíði (-s, -), *n.* cross-country ski

hafa (hef, hafði, haft), *acc.* have

hagstæð/ur, *adj.* economical

hak/a (-u, -ur), *f.* chin

halda (held, héld, héldu, haldið), *dat.* hold, *acc.* think

  halda áfram, *dat.* continue, go on

  halda við keep, stick to

  halda upp á, *acc.* celebrate, like

hamborgar/i (-a, -ar), *m.* hamburger

hamingj/a (-u), *f.* happiness

  til hamingju (með, *acc.*) congratulations (on ...)

handa, *prep. + dat.* for (someone)

handavinn/a (-u), *f.* handiwork

handklæði (-s, -), *n.* towel

handlegg/ur (-s, -ir), *m.* arm

hanga (hangi, hékk, héngu, hangið) hang

hangikjöt (-s), *n.* smoked lamb

hann, *pron.* he

happdrætti (-s, -), *n.* lottery

harðbrjósta, *adj.indecl.* — hard-hearted

harla, *adv.* — extremely

hatt/ur (-s, -ar), *m.* — hat

haus (-s, ar), *m.* — (animal) head

haust (-s, -), *n.* — autumn

há/r, *adj.* — high, tall

hádegi (-s), *n.* — noon
  eftir hádegi — (in the) afternoon

hádegismat/ur (-ar), *m.* — lunch

hálftím/i (-a, -ar), *m.* — half an hour

háls (-, -ar), *m.* — neck, throat

hálsbólg/a (-u), *f.* — sore throat

hár (-s, -), *n.* — hair

háskól/i (-a, -ar), *m.* — university

hátíð (-ar, -ir), *f.* — feast, festival, holiday

hátíðahöld, *n.pl.* — festivities

hátta (hátta, háttaði, háttað) — go to bed

hávaxin/n, *adj.* — tall (of build)

hefðbundin/n, *adj.* — traditional

hefja (hef, hóf, hófu, hafið), *acc.* — begin, commence

heil/l, *adj.* — whole

heilbrigð/ur, *adj.* — healthy

heilla (heilla, heillaði, heillað), *acc.* — enchant, attract

heils/a (-u), *f.* — health

heilsa (heilsa, heilsaði, heilsað), *dat.* — greet

heilsugæslustöð (-var, -var), *f.* — health centre

heima, *adv.* — at home

heimili (-s, -), *n.* — home

heimilisfang (-s, -), *n.* — address

heimsækja (heimsæki, heimsótti, heimsótt), *acc.* — visit

heimsókn (-ar, -ir), *f.* — visit

heit/ur, *adj.* — hot

heita (heiti, hét, hétu, heitið) — be called

heitin/n eftir — called after

heldur, *adv.* — rather
  ekki heldur — neither

helgi (-ar, -ar), *f.* — weekend

hella (helli, hellti, hellt), *dat.* — pour

helming/ur (-s, -ar), *m.* — half

helst, *adv.* — preferably
  adv.superl. — most prominent

hengja (hengi, hengdi, hengt), *acc.* — hang up

hennar, *pron.* — her

henta (hentar, hentaði, hentað), *dat.* — suit

heppni, *f.indecl.* — luck

her (-s, -ir), *m.* — army

herbergi (-s, -), *n.* — room

herðar, *f.pl.* — shoulders

hest/ur (-s, -ar), *m.* — horse
  fara á hestbak — (go) riding

heyra (heyri, heyrði, heyrt), *acc.* — hear
  heyrðu! — listen!

héðan, *adv.* from here

hér(na), *dem.* here

hill/a (-u, -ur), *f.* shelf

him-in/n (-ins, -nar), *m.* sky

himnaríki (-s, -), *n.* heaven

hingað, *adv.* to here (hither)

hinn (hitt, n.), *pron.* the, the other one

hins vegar on the other hand

hissa, *adj.indecl.* surprised

hit/i (-a), *m.* heat, (above zero) tempera-ture, fever

hitabrús/i (-a, -ar), *m.* thermos

hitamæl/ir (-is, -ar), *m.* thermometer

hitta (hitti, hitti, hitt), *acc.* meet

hjart/a (-a, -u), *n.* heart

hjá, *prep. + dat.* next to, with

hjálp (-ar), *f.* help

hjálpa (hjálpa, hjálpaði, hjálpað), *dat.* help

hjól (-s, -), *n.* bicycle

hjón, *n.pl.* couple

hjónaband (-s, -), *n.* marriage

hjúkrunar-fræðing/ur (-s, -ar), *m.* (registered) nurse

hlakka (hlakka, hlakkaði, hlak-kað) til, *gen.* look forward to

hlaupa (hleyp, hljóp, hlupu, hlaupið) run

hlaupa inn, *dat.* let someone in

hlátur (-s), *m.* laughter

hlé (-s, -), *n.* pause, interval

hlið (-ar, -ar), *f.* side

við hliðina á, *dat.* to the side of

hljoðfæri (-s, -), *n.* musical instrument

hljómsveit (-ar, -ir), *f.* orchestra, band

hljóta (hlýt, hlaut, hlutu, hlotið), *acc.* receive, must

hlusta (hlusta, hlustaði, hlustað) á, *acc.* listen to

hlut/i (-a, -ar), *m.* part

hlut/ur (-ar, -ir), *m.* thing

hlutfall (-s, -), *n.* proportion, rate, ratio

hlutverk (-s, -), *n.* part, role

hlý/r, *adj.* warm

hlýna (hlýna, hlýnaði, hlýnað), *intrans.* get warm

hlæja (hlæ, hló, hlógu, hlegið) laugh

hné (-s, -), *n.* knee

hníf/ur (-s, -ar), *m.* knife

holl/ur, *adj.* healthy

horfa (horfi, horfði, horft) á, *acc.* watch

hópur (-s, -ar), *m.* group

hópferð (-ar, -ir), *f.* group trip

hósta (hósta, hóstaði, hóstað)	cough
hótel (-s, -), *n.*	hotel
hratt, *adv.*	fast
hrein/n, *adj.*	clean
hreinlætisvörur, *f.pl.*	toiletries
hress, *adj.*	energetic, fit
hressast (hressist, hresstist, hresst)	become fit, refresh, recover
hreyfa (hreyfi, hreyfði, hreyft) sig	move, exercise
hrifin/n af, *adj. + dat.*	very taken/ infatuated with
hring/ur (-s, -ar), *m.*	ring
hringja (hringi, hringdi, hringt), *acc.*	ring
hryllilega, *adv.*	dreadfully
hrædd/ur, *adj.*	afraid
hugmynd (-ar, -ir), *f.*	idea
hugsa (hugsa, hugsaði, hugsað), *acc.*	think
huldufólk (-s), *n.*	elf, elfin people
hund/ur (-s, -ar), *m.*	dog
hundrað (-s, -), *n.*	hundred
húð (-ar, -ir), *f.*	skin
húf/a (-u, -ur), *f.*	woollen hat
hún, *pron.*	she
húsgögn, *n.pl.*	furniture
húsnæði (-s), *n.*	accommodation, lodging
hvað (*n. of* **hver**) *inter*	what
hvað ... [adj.]?	how ...?
hvaða, *inter.*	what kind of
hvaðan, *inter.*	where ... from
hval/ur (-s, -ir), *m.*	whale
hvar, *inter.*	where
hvass, *adj.*	windy, blowing hard
hver (hvað, *n.*), *inter.*	who
hvers konar	what kind of
hver (-s, -ir), *m.*	hot spring, geyser
hvergi, *adv.*	nowhere
hvernig, *inter.*	how
hvert, *inter.*	where to
hvíla (hvíli, hvíldi, hvílt) sig	rest (oneself)
hvít/ur, *adj.*	white
hvorki ... né	neither ... nor
hvort, *inter.*	whether, which (of two)
hyggjast (hyggst, hugðist, hugast)	intend, plan
hæð (-ar, -ir), *f.*	floor, storey
hæfileik/i (-a, -ar), *m.*	talent, ability
hæg/ur, *adj.*	slow, possible
hægri	right
höfðing/i (-ja, -jar), *m.*	leader
höfn (-ar, -ir), *f.*	harbour
höfuð (-s, -), *n.*	head
höfuðstað/ur (-ar, -ir), *m.*	capital
höfuðverk/ur (-jar, -ir), *m.*	headache
höggva (högg/ hegg, hjó, hjuggu, hoggið), *acc.*	cut, hew, chop

hönd (handar, hendur), *f.* — hand, arm

  fara í hönd — approach

illa, *adv.* — badly

indæl/l, *adj.* — friendly, lovely, delightful

inn (*dat.* **inni**), *adv.* — in, into, inside

innan, *prep. + gen.* — within

inngang/ur (-s, -ar), *m.* — entrance

innifalin/n, *adj.* — included

innilega, *adv.* — affectionately

í, *prep. + dat./acc.* — in(to)

  í kring(um), *prep. + acc.* — around

  í senn, *adv.* — at a time

  í sundur, *adv.* — apart, in two pieces

íbúð (-ar, -ir), *f.* — flat

íbú/i (-a, -ar), *m.* — inhabitant

íhugun (-ar), *f.* — reflection, meditation

ís (-s, -ar), *m.* — ice-cream

ísbjörn (ísbjarnar, ísbirnir), *m.* — polar bear

Ísland (-s), *n.* — Iceland

íslensk/a (-u), *f.* — Icelandic

ísskap/ur (-s, -ar), *m.* — fridge

ítarleg/ur, *adj.* — detailed

íþrótt/ir, *f.pl.* — sports

já — yes

jafn, *adv.* — equally

jakk/i (-a, -ar), *m.* — jacket

jarðveg/ur (-s), *m.* — soil

jól, *n.pl.* — Christmas

jólasvein/n (-s, -ar), *m.* — one of the thirteen Icelandic Christmas lads/elves

jæja — well

jörð (-ar, -ir), *f.* — earth

kaffi (-s), *n.* — coffee

  kaffisop/i (-a, -ar), *m.* — sip of coffee, a coffee

kak/a (-u, -ur), *f.* — cake

kald/ur (kalt, n.), *adj.* — cold

kalla (kalla, kallaði, kallað), *acc.* — call

kannast (kannast, kannaðist, kannast) við, *acc.* — recognize

kannski, *adv.* — perhaps

karl (-s, -ar), *m.* — (old) man

kartafl/a (-u, -ur), *f.* — potato

kasta (kasta, kastaði, kastað), *dat.* — cast, throw

  kasta upp — vomit

kaupa (kaupi, keypti, keypt), *acc.* — buy

  kaupa í mat — buy groceries

kaupstað/ur (-ar, -ir), *m.* — town

káp/a (-u, -ur), *f.* — coat

kenna (kenni, kenndi, kennt), *dat. + acc.* — teach

  kenna við — name after

kennar/i (-a, -ar), *m.* — teacher

keppa (keppi, keppti, keppt) — compete

kerling (-ar, -ar), *f.* old woman

kerti (-s, -), *n.* candle

keyra (keyri, keyrði, keyrt), *acc.* drive

kíló(gramm) (-s, -), *n.* kilo(gram)

kind (-ar, -ur), *f.* sheep

kjallar/i (-a, -ar), *m.* cellar, basement

kjól/l (-s, -ar), *m.* dress

kjósa (kýs, kaus, kusu, kosið), *acc.* vote

kjörin/n, *adj.* elected

kjöt (-s), *n.* meat

kjötkraft/ur (-s), *m.* meat bouillon, stock

klaustur (-s, -ar), *m.* monastery, cloister

klára (klára, kláraði, klárað), *acc.* finish

klæðast (klæðist, klæddist), *dat.* wear, be dressed in

klæða sig dress, get dressed

klukk/a (-u, -ur), *f.* clock

klukkutim/i (-a, -ar), *m.* one hour

knattspyrn/a (-u), *f.* football

kokk/ur (-s, -ar), *m.* cook

koma (kem, kom, komu, komið) come

koma sér af stað get going

(þá er það) komið that's it

komin/n með, *acc.* have got, have caught

koma á óvart, *dat.* surprise

koma saman, *imp.* get along

koma í ljós appear

koma við, *acc.* touch, call on

koma fram behave, appear

komast get there

kon/a (-u, -ur), *f.* woman

kort (-s, -), *n.* map

korter (-s, -), *n.* quarter (of an hour)

kosta (kosta, kostaði, kostað), *acc.* cost

kost/ur (-ar, -ir), *m.* choice, chance, advantage

gefast kostur á, *dat.* be offered the possibility of

að minnsta kosti at least

kók (-s), *n.* cola

kólna (kólna, kólnaði, kólnað), *intrans.* cool down, get cold

konungsríki (-s, -), *n.* kingdom

kór (-s, -ar), *m.* choir

kraft/ur (-s, -ar), *m.* force

krem (-s, -), *n.* cream

kristnitaka (-u), *f.* christianization

krón/a (-u, -ur), *f.* crown (Icelandic currency unit)

krullað/ur, *adj.* curly

krydd (-s, -), *n.* spice

kuld/i (-a), *m.* cold

kunna (kann, kunni, kunnað) know how to

kunna vel/illa við, *acc.* like/dislike

kunning/i (-ja, -jar), *m.* acquaintance

kveðja (kveð, kvaddi, kvatt), *acc.* say goodbye

kvef (-s), *n.* cold

kveikja (kveiki, kveikti, kveikt), *acc.* light

kveikja á, *dat.* turn on

kvöld (-s, -), *n.* evening

í kvöld tonight

kvöldmat/ur (-ar), *m.* supper

kynna (kynni, kynnti, kynnt), *acc.* introduce

kynnast (kynnist, kynntist, kynnst), *dat.* meet, get to know

kynning (-ar, -ar), *f.* introduction

kýr (-, -), *f.* cow

kær, *adj.* dear

kærast/a (-u, -ur), *f.* girlfriend

kærast/i (-a, -ar), *m.* boyfriend

kærlega, *adv.* kindly

kött/ur (kattar, kettir), *m.* cat

labba (labba, labbaði, labbað) walk

lag (-s, -), *n.* song

laga (laga, lagaði, lagað), *acc.* brew, fix

lagast get better

lamb (-s, -), *n.* lamb

lamp/i (-a, -ar), *m.* lamp

land (-s, -), *n.* country, land

landbúnað/ur (-ar), *m.* agriculture

landnám (-s, -), *n.* settlement

landshlut/i (-a, -ar), *m.* part of the country, area

landslag (-s, -), *n.* landscape

lang/ur, *adj.* long (horizontally)

langt síðan a long time since

lasin/n, *adj.* under the weather, ill

lat/ur, *adj.* lazy

laug (-ar, -ar), *f.* hot spring

laugardag/ur (-s, -ar), *m.* Saturday

laus, *adj.* free, not taken

lauslega, *adv.* loosely, roughly

lax (-, -ar), *m.* salmon

lágvaxin/n, *adj.* short (built)

lána (lána, lánaði, lánað), *acc. + dat.* lend

láta (læt, lét, létu, látið), *acc.* let, behave

látast pass away

leður (-s, -), *n.* leather

leggja (legg, lagði, lagt), *acc.* lay, put

leggja á sig take pains

leggja af lose weight

leggja til, *gen.* put to

leggja fyrir, *acc.* put aside

leggjast lay down

leggjast á, *acc.* strike, attack

leið (-ar, -ir), *f.* route
  aðra leið single (ticket)
  báðar leiðir return
  á leiðinni on the way
leiðinleg/ur, *adj.* dull, umpleasant, boring
leiðsögn (-ar, -ir), *f.* guidance
  leiðsögu-mað/ur (-manns, -menn), *m.* guide
leig/a (-u), *f.* rent
leigja (leigi, leigði, leigt), *dat. + acc.* rent
leik/ur (-s, -ir), *m.* game, match
leika (leik, lék, léku, leikið), *acc.* play
  leika sér play
leikar/i (-a, -ar), *m.* actor, player
leikfimi, *f.indecl.* gymnastics
leikhús (-s, -), *n.* theatre
leikkon/a (-u, -ur), *f.* actress
leiklist (-ar), *f.* drama, theatre
leik-mað/ur (-manns, -menn), *m.* player
leikrit (-s, -), *n.* play
leikskól/i (-a, -ar), *m.* kindergarten
leita (leita, leitaði, leitað) að, *dat.* look for
lenda (lendi, lenti, lent) í, *dat.* end up, land in
lengi, *adv.* long (of time)

lengjast (lengist, lengdist, lengst), *intrans.* become longer
lesa (les, las, lásu, lesið), *acc.* read
  lesa undir, *acc.* prepare, study for
lest (-ar, -ir), *f.* train
leyfa (leyfi, leyfði, leyfð), *dat. + acc.* allow, permit
leyfi (-s, -), *n.* permission, licence, leave
leynd (-ar), *f.* secrecy
leyndardóm/ur (-s, -ar), *m.* mystery
létt/ur, *adj.* light (weight)
létta (létti, létti, létt), *dat. + acc.* lighten
léttast (léttist, lést), *intrans.* become lighter
lið (-s, -), *n.* league, team
liggja (lá, lágu, legið) lie
  það liggur ekkert á there's no hurry
listamað/ur (-manns, -menn), *m.* artist
listasafn (-s, -), *n.* art museum
lit/ur (-ar, -ir), *m.* colour
líf (-s), *n.* life
lífleg/ur, *adj.* lively
lífsvenjur, *f.pl.* customs
líka (líkar, líkaði, líkað), *imp.dat.* like
  líka vel/illa like/dislike
líkam/i (-a, ar), *m.* body
líklega, *adv.* probably, likely

lín/a (-u, -ur), *f.* line

líta (lít, leit, litu, litið) út look (like)

líta um öxl look back

lítil/l (lítið), *n.*, *adj.* little

lítr/i (-a, -ar), *m.* litre

ljóð (-s, -), *n.* poem

ljómandi, *adj.indecl.* wonderful

ljós (-s, -), *n.* light

ljóshærð/ur, *adj.* fair-haired, blond

ljót/ur, *adj.* ugly

ljúffeng/ur, *adj.* delicious

ljúga (lýg, laug, lugu, logið), *dat.* (tell a) lie

lofa (lofa, lofaði, lofað), *dat. + acc.* promise

loft (-s, -), *n.* air, loft

logn (-s), *n.* windstill weather

loka (loka, lokaði, lokað), *dat.* close

lopapeys/a (-u, -ur), *f.* Icelandic jumper

losna (losna, losnaði, losnað) við, *acc.* lose, get rid of

lúthersk/ur, *adj.* Lutheran

lyf (-s, -), *n.* medicine

lyfsal/i (-a, -ar), *m.* pharmacist

lyfseðil/l (-s, -ar), *m.* prescription

lyfta (lyfti), *dat.* **(-u, -ur)**, *f.* lift

lykt (-ar), *f.* smell

lýðveldi (-s, -), *n.* republic

lýsa (lýsi, lýsti, lýst), *dat.* describe

lýsi (-s), *n.* fish liver oil

lækka (lækka, lækkaði, lækkað), *acc.* decrease, lower

lækn/ir (-is, -ar), *m.* doctor, GP

læra (læri, lærði, lært), *acc.* learn, study

læsa (læsi, læsti, læst), *acc.* lock (the door)

lögfræðing/ur (-s, -ar), *m.* lawyer

lögregl/a (-u), *f.* police

lögg/a (-u), *f.* the cops

lögreglustöð (-var, -var), *f.* police station

mað/ur (manns, menn), *m.* person, man

mag/i (-a, -ar), *m.* stomach, belly

magnað/ur, *adj.* brilliant, super

mamm/a (-u, -ur), *f.* mum(my)

marg/ir, *adj.pl.* many

margs konar many kinds of

mark (-s, -), *n.* goal

markað/ur (-ar, -ir), *m.* market

mat (-s), *n.* estimation, assessment

að þínu mati in your estimation/ opinion

matarskeið (-ar, -ar), *f.* table spoon

matseðil/l (-s, -ar), *m.* menu

mat/ur (-ar), *m.* food, meal

mál (-s, -), *n.* matter, problem, case

mála (málaði, málað), *acc.* paint

mánuð/ur (-ar, -ir), *m.* — month

mánudag/ur (-s, -ar), *m.* — Monday

máta (máta, mátaði, mátað), *acc.* — try on

með, *prep.* + *dat./acc.* — with, along

meðal, *prep.* + *gen.* — among

meðan, *conj.* — while

meðferð (-ar, -ir), *f.* — treatment

mega (má, mátti, máttu, mátt) — may

megrun (-ar), *f.* — diet

meiða (meiði, meiddi, meitt) sig — hurt oneself

meira að segja — what's more

meirihlut/i (-a, -ar), *m.* — majority

menning (-ar), *f.* — culture

menntaskól/i (-a, -ar), *m.* — grammar school

menntun (-ar, -ir), *f.* — culture, education

merk/ur, *adj.* — distinctive, remarkable

merkisstað/ur (-ar, -ir), *m.* — sight

metnað/ur, *adj.* — ambition

metr/i (-a, -ar), *m.* — metre

mey (-jar, -jar), *f.* — maid, virgin

meyr, *adj.* — tender

mið/ur, *adj.* — centre, middle

miðað við — compared to

miðbæ/r (-jar, -ir), *m.* — city centre, town centre

miðlungs-, *pref.* — average

miðnætti (-s), *n.* — midnight

miðvikudag/ur (-s, -ar), *m.* — Wednesday

mikil/l (mikið, n.), *adj.* — much, large, important

mikilvæg/ur, *adj.* — important

miljón (-ar, -ir), *f.* — million

milli, *prep.* + *gen.* — between

minjagrip/ur (-s, -ir), *m.* — souvenir

minn, *poss.* — my, mine

minni, *comp.* — less, smaller

missa (missi, missti, misst) af, *dat.* — miss

mínút/a (-u, -ur), *f.* — minute

mjólk (-ur), *f.* — milk

mjög, *adv.* — very

morgunmat/ur (-ar), *m.* — breakfast

móta (móta, mótaði, mótað), *acc.* — form, mould

móttak/a (-u, -ur), *f.* — reception

muna (man, mundi, munað), *acc.* — remember; *dat.* remind

munn/ur (-s, -ar), *m.* — mouth

munu (mun, mundi, *subj.* myndi) — will

mús (-ar, mýs), *f.* — mouse

mýkja (mýki, mýkti, mýkt), *acc.* — soften

myndarleg/ur, *adj.* — handsome

myndbandstæki (-s, -), n. video recorder

myndhöggvar/i (-a, -ar), m. sculptor

myndlist (-ar), f. visual arts

mæla (mæli, mælti, mælt), acc. say, speak, measure, take temperature

mæla með, dat. recommend

mæta (mæti, mætti, mætt) dat. appear, turn up; meet

möguleik/i (-a, -ar), m. possibility

nafn (-s, -), n. name

nauðsynleg/ur, adj. necessary

ná (næ, náði, náð), dat. pass, catch

ná í acc. reach, get

nágrann/i (-a, -ar), m. neighbour

nágrenni (-s), n. neighbourhood

nákvæm/ur, adj. precise

nálægt, prep. + dat. close to, nearby

nálgast (nálgast, nálgaðist, nálgast), acc. approach

nám (-s, -), n. studies

námskeið (-s, -), n. course

náttúr/a (-u), f. nature

náttúr(u)lega, adv. naturally, of course

nef (-s, -), n. nose

nefnilega, adv. namely, you see

nei no

neikvæð/ur, adj. negative

nema (nem, nam, námu, numið), acc. study, settle

nema, adv. except

ekki nema not unless, only

nem-and/i (-anda, -endur), m. also **nem/i (-a, -ar), m.** student

nenna (nenni, nennti, nennt), dat. feel like

nes (-s, -), n. promontory

nesti (-s, -), n. provisions, meal box

neyðar-, pref. emergency

niður (dat. niðri), adv. down

niðurdregin/n, adj. down, depressed

njóta (nýt, naut, nutu, notið), gen. enjoy

njóta sín use to full capacity, come into one's own

nokkr/ir, m.pl. several

norðurland (-s), m. northern Iceland

nota (nota, notaði, notað), acc. use

nóg/ur, adj. enough

nú, interj. well, really

númer (-s, -), n. number, size

núna now, presently

ný-, pref. newly, just

ný/r (nýtt, n.), adj. new

nýbú/i (-a, -ar), m. immigrant to Iceland

nýlega, adv. lately

nær, adj. closer

nærföt, *n.pl.* — underwear

ofarlega, *adv.* — high up, in the forefront

ofn (-s, -ar), *m.* — heater, radiator, oven

ofnæmi (-s), *n.* — allergy

ofsa(lega), *adv.* — tremendously, awfully

oft, oftast, *adv.* — often

og, *conj.* — and

  og svo framvegis — etcetera

olí/a (-u, -ur), *f.* — oil

opin/n (**opið**, *n.*), *adj.* — open

opinber, *adj.* — public

opna (**opna, opnaði, opnað**), *acc.* — open

orð (-s, -), *n.* — word

ost/ur (-s, -ar), *m.* — cheese

óbyggð (-ar, -ir), *f.* — wilderness, uninhabited area

ófær, *adj.* — impassable, incapable

ófrísk, *adj.* — pregnant

ógeðsleg/ur, *adj.* — disgusting

óhjákvæmileg/ur, *adj.* — inevitable

ókunnug/ur, *adj.* — strange, unknown

ólán (-s), *n.* — misfortune

ólík/ur, *adj.dat.* — unlike, different from

ómissandi, *adj.indecl.* — indispensable

ónýt/ur, *adj.* — useless, incompetent

ósjálfráð/ur, *adj.* — involutary, unintentional

ósk (-ar, -ir), *f.* — wish

óska (**óska, óskaði, óskað**), *dat. + gen.* — wish

óskaplega, *adv.* — tremendously

óttast (**óttast, óttaðist, óttast**), *acc.* — fear

óvenjuleg/ur, *adj.* — unusual

óvænt/ur, *adj.* — unexpected

pabb/i (-a, -ar), *m.* — dad(dy)

pakka (**pakka, pakkaði, pakkað**) **niður**, *dat.* — pack

pakkaferð (-ar, -ir), *f.* — package trip

pakk/i (-a, -ar), *m.* — package

pann/a (-u, -ur), *f.* — pan

panta (**panta, pantaði, pantað**), *acc.* — book, reserve

pappír (-s, -ar), *m.* — paper

passa (**passa, passaði, passað**), *acc.* — suit, fit

  passa sig — watch out

páskar, *m.pl.* — Easter

pening/ur (-s, -ar), *m.* — money

penn/i (-a, -ar), *m.* — pen

pest (-ar, -ir), *f.* — epidemic, 'bug'

pipar (-s), *m.* — pepper

plast (-s, -), *n.* — plastic

plástur (-s, -ar), *m.* — band-aid, plaster

prenta (**prenta, prentaði, prentað**), *acc.* — print

prest/ur (-s, -ar), *m.* minister, pastor

prjóna (prjóna, prjónaði, prjónað), *acc.* knit

próf (-s, -), *n.* exam, diploma

prófa (prófa, prófaði, prófað), *acc.* try (out), test

punkt/ur (-s, -ar), *m.* point, dot

pyls/a (-u, -ur), *f.* hot dog, wiener

pöntun (-ar, ir), *f.* reservation, order

pönnukak/a (-u, -ur), *f.* pancake

rafmagn (-s), *n.* electricity

raka (raka, rakaði, rakað) sig shave

rass (-, -ar), *m.* bottom, behind

rauðróf/a (-u, -ur), *f.* beet

rauð/ur (rautt, n.), *adj.* red

raunar, *adv.* as a matter of fact, indeed

raunveruleg/ur, *adj.* realistic

ráðherra (-, -r), *m.* minister

ráðhús (-s, -), *n.* town hall

ráðleggja (ráðlegg, ráðlagði, ráðlagt), *dat. + acc.* advise

rás (-ar, -ar), *f.* channel

redda (redda, reddaði, reddað), *dat.* work out, fix

reið/ur, *adj.* angry

reikning/ur (-s, ar), *m.* bill

reisa (reisi, reisti, reist), *acc.* raise, build

reka (rek, rak, ráku, rekið), *acc.* run, strike

renna (renn, rann, runni, runnið) turn, (let) flow, glide

reykja (reyki, reykti, reykt), *acc.* smoke

reyna (reyni, reyndi, reynt), *acc.* try

reynast turn out to be, prove to be

reyndar, *adv.* in fact, as a matter of fact

rétt áðan, *adv.* just now

rétt/ur, *adj.* right, correct
rétt, *adv.* just, right

rétta (rétti, rétti, rétt), *dat. + acc.* hand

réttindi *n.pl.* rights, licence

réttur (-ar, -ir), *m.* dish

rigna (rignir, rigndi, rignt) rain

rigning (-ar), *f.* rain

ristað brauð, *n.* toast

ritar/i (-a, -ar), *m.* secretary

ritföng, *n.pl.* writing materials, stationery

rithöfund/ur (-ar, -ar), *m.* novelist, author

ríða (ríð, reið, riðu, riðið) ride a horse

rjóm/i (-a, -ar), *m.* cream

rós (-ar, -ir), *f.* rose

rúm (-s, -), *n.* bed

rút/a (-u, -ur), *f.* coach

ryksug/a (-u, -ur), *f.* **(ryksuga, ryksugaði, ryksugað)** hoover, vacuum

rýr, *adj.* sparse, scanty

ræð/a (-u, -ur), *f.* speech

ræða (ræði, ræddi, rætt), *acc.* discuss

rækta (rækta, ræktaði, ræktað), *acc.* grow, cultivate

rækt (-ar), *f.* cultivation

röð (-ar, -ir), *f.* row, order, series

rökkur (-s), *n.* twilight

sadd/ur, *adj.* full, eaten one's fill

saf/i (-a, -ar), *m.* juice

safn (-s, -), *n.* museum, collection

sag/a (-u, -ur), *f.* history, story

sakna (sakna, saknaði, saknað), *gen.* miss

saman, *adv.* together

samband (-s, -), *n.* contact, connection, relationship

sameiginleg/ur, *adj.* common, shared

samfélag (-s, -), *n.* society

samgöngur, *f.pl.* transport between places, communications

samkom/a (-u, -ur), *f.* gathering

samlok/a (-u, -ur), *f.* sandwich

sammála, *adj.indecl.* + *dat.* agreed, agree with

samt *adv.* nevertheless, still, yet

samtal (-s, -), *n.* dialogue, conversation

sand/ur (-s, -ar), *m.* sand, sandy desert

sann/ur (satt, *n.*), *adj.* true

sannarlega, *adv.* truly, definitely

saxa (saxa, saxaði, saxað), *acc.* chop

sál (-ar, -ir), *f.* soul

sálfræðing/ur (-s, -ar), *m.* psychologist

sáp/a (-u, -ur), *f.* soap

sár (-s, -), *n.* wound

sárabindi (-s, -), *n.* gauze

segja (segi, sagði, sagt), *dat.* + *acc.* say, tell

hvað segirðu 1 how are you 2 really, is that so

segja frá, *dat.* relate, tell of

sein/n, *adj.* late

seinni partinn in the afternoon

seinkað/ur, *adj.* delayed

selja (sel, seldi, selt), *acc.* sell

sem, *conj.* — which, that, as
  sem betur fer — fortunately
semja (sem, samdi, samið), *acc.* — compose, write
senda (sendi, sendi, sent), *dat. + acc.* — send
sendiráð (-s, -), *n.* — embassy
sennilega, *adv.* — probably
setja (set, setti, sett), *acc.* — put
  setja á sig — put on
  setjast — sit down
sé/séu, *pres.subj.* **vera** — be
sér-, *pref.* — special, particularly
sérstak/ur, *adj.* — special
sérstæð/ur, *adj.* — unusual
sið/ur (-ar, -ir), *m.* — custom
sigling (-ar, -ar), *f.* — sailing (trip)
silung/ur (-s, -ar), *m.* — trout
sinna (sinni, sinnti, sinnt), *dat.* — attend to
sinnep (-s), *n.* — mustard
sitja (sit, sat, sátu, setið) — sit
sí-, *pref.* — ever-
síðan, *adv.* — since, then
síðast/ur, *adj.* — last
síðdegis — in the afternoon
sífelld, *adv.* — constantly
sím/i (-a, -ar), *m.* — telephone
símsvar/i (-a, -ar), *m.* — answering machine
símtal (-s, -), *n.* — telephone conversation
síróp (-s), *n.* — syrup

sjaldan, *adv.* — seldom
sjá (sé, sá, sáu, séð), *acc.* — see
  sjá um, *acc.* — look after, take care of
  sjá eftir, *dat.* — regret
sjálf/ur — (one)self
sjálfsagt (að sjálfsögðu) — of course, naturally
sjálfstæð/ur, *adj.* — independent
sjávarútveg/ur (-s), *m.* — fishing industry
sjó/r (sjávar, -ir), *m.* — sea
  vera á sjó — be at sea (as a fisherman)
sjóða (sýð, sauð, suðu, soðið), *acc.* — boil
sjó-mað/ur (-manns, -menn), *m.* — fisherman
sjónvarp (-s, -), *n.* — television
sjúk/ur, *adj.* — ill
  vera sjúkur í (coll.), *acc.* — be crazy about
sjúkrahús (-s, -), *n.* — hospital
skammdegi (-s), *n.* — short days of winter, midwinter
skammt/ur (-s, -ar), *m.* — portion
skartgrip/ur (-s, -ir), *m.* — piece of jewellery
skál (-ar, -ar), *f.* — bowl, toast
skál! — cheers!
skál/i (-a, -ar), *m.* — lodge, cabin
skáld (-s, -), *n.* — poet
skáldsag/a (-u, -ur), *f.* — novel

skáp/ur (-s, -ar), *m.* cupboard

skegg (-s, -), *n.* beard

skeið (-ar, -ar), *f.* spoon

skella (skell, skellti, skellt) á, *acc.* slam, crash

skemmta (skemmti, skemmti, skemmt) sér have fun, have a good time

skemmtileg/ur, *adj.* enjoyable, fun

skera (sker, skar, skáru, skorið), *acc.* cut

skila (skila, skilaði, skilað), *dat.* pass on, give back, hand in

skilja (skil, skildi, skilið), *acc.* separate, understand

skilja eftir, *acc.* leave behind

skip (-s, -), *n.* ship

skipta (skipti, skipti, skipt), *dat.* change, exchange

skiptimið/i (-a, -ar), *m.* transfer ticket

skipulagð/ur, *adj.* organized

skíði (-s, -), *n.* ski

fara á skíðum, *v.* ski

skína (skín, skein, skinu, skinið) shine

skírð/ur, *adj.* christened

skítug/ur, *adj.* dirty

skjal (-s, -), *n.* file, document

skjótast (skjótt), *adv.* quickly

sko, *interj.* look, you see

skoða (skoða, skoðaði, skoðað), *acc.* (have/take a) look at

skoðun (-ar, -ir), *f.* examination, check-up

skokka (skokka, skokkaði, skokkað) jog

skó/r (-s, -r), *m.* shoe

skóg/ur (-ar, -ar), *m.* forest

skól/i (-a, -ar), *m.* school

skrá (skrái, skráði, skráð), *acc.* register, record

skreppa (skrepp, skrapp, skruppu, skroppið) pop out

skrifa (skrifa, skrifaði, skrifað), *dat. + acc.* write

skrifstof/a (-u, -ur), *f.* office

skríða (skríð, skreið, skriðu, skriðið) crawl

skulu (skal, *subj.* **skyldi)** shall

við skulum … let's …

skynsamlega, *adv.* wisely, sensibly

skyr (-s), *n.* milk curds

skýjað, *adj.* cloudy

skýra (skýri, skýrði, skýrt) explain

skýra frá, *dat.* give an account of

skýrsl/a (-u, -ur), *f.* report, statement

skæri, *n.pl.* scissors

sköpun (-ar), *f.* creation, creativity

slaka (slaka, slakaði, slakað) á relax, unwind

slapp/ur, *adj.* weak, without energy

slappa (slappa, slappaði, slappað) af relax

sleppa (sleppi, sleppti, sleppt), *dat.* leave undone, let pass, let go

slétt/ur, *adj.* smooth, flat; straight (hair)

slóð (-ar, -ir), *f.* trail, area

slys (-s, -), *n.* accident

slæm/ur, *adj.* bad

slökkva (slekk, slökkti, slökkt) á turn off, extinguish

smakka (smakka, smakkaði, smakkað) *acc.* taste

smá/r, *adj.* small

smátt og smátt little by little

smámynt (-ar, -ir), *f.* change

smástund (-ar, -ir), *f.* a while

smekkleg/ur, *adj.* tasteful

smjör (-s), *n.* butter

smjörlíki (-s), *n.* margarine

snarl (-s), *n.* snack

snemma, *adv.* early

snjó/r (-s, -ar), *m.* snow

snjóa (snjóar, snjóaði, snjóað) snow

snúa (sný, snéri, snúið), *dat.* turn

snúa sér að, *dat.* turn to

snyrtileg/ur, *adj.* neat, smart

snyrting (-ar, -ar), *f.* toilet, washroom

sofa (sef, svaf, sváfu, sofið) sleep

sofna (sofna, sofnaði, sofnað), *intrans.* fall asleep

son/ur (-ar, synir), *m.* son

sorg (-ar, -ir), *f.* sorrow, grief

sorp (-s, -), *n.* rubbish, garbage

sóf/i (-a, -ar), *m.* sofa, couch

sól (-ar), *f.* sun

sólarhring/ur (-s), *m.* 24 hours, around the clock

sólbað (-s, -), *n.* sunbath

sós/a (-u, -ur), *f.* sauce, gravy

sótthreinsandi, *adj.indecl.* disinfectant

spari-, *pref.* dress

spariföt, *n.pl.* dressing-up clothes

sparsam/ur, *adj.* economical, thrifty

spá (-ar, -r), *f.* forecast

spegil/l (-s, -ar), *m.* mirror

spenna (-u, -ur), *f.* tension, clasp

spennandi, *adj.indecl.* exciting

spennt/ur, *adj.* keen, excited

spila (spila, spilaði, spilað), *acc.* play

spjald (-s, -), *n.* card, sign, book of tickets

spjall (-s, -), *n.* chat

spjalla (spjalla, spjallaði, spjallað) — chat

spurning (-ar, -ar), *f.* — question

spyrja (spyr, spurði, spurt), *acc.* — ask

stað/ur (-ar, -ir), *m.* — place

fara/leggja af stað — depart

í staðinn — instead

eiga sér stað — take place

staðgreiða (-greiði), *acc.* — pay cash

staf/ur (-s, -ir), *m.* — letter

standa (stend, stóð, stóðu, staðið) — stand

það stendur — it says

sem stendur — as it is, right now

standa til — happen, be in the works/planned

starf (-s, -), *n.* — job, employment

starfsfólk (-s), *n.* — employees

starfsemi, *f.indecl.* — activity, work

stefnumót (-s, -), *n.* — appointment

steikja (steiki, steikti, steikt), *acc.* — fry

stein/n (-s, -ar), *m.* — stone

sterk/ur, *adj.* — strong

stig (-s, -), *n.* — level, degree

stinga (sting, stakk, stungu, stungið) upp á, *dat.* — suggest

stífla (stífla, stíflaði, stíflað), *acc.* — plug (in)

stig/i (-a, -ar), *m.* — stairs, staircase

stíl/l (-s, -ar), *m.* — style

stjúp/i (-a, -ar), *m. from* **stjúpfaðir** — stepfather

stof/a (-u, -ur), *f.* — living room

stofnað/ur, *adj.* — founded

stofnun (-ar, -ir), *f.* — foundation, institution

stoppa (stoppa, stoppaði, stoppað) — stop

stól/l (-s, -ar), *m.* — chair

stór (stór, *adj. f.*) — big, large

stórborg, (-ar, -ir), *f.* — metropolis

stórbrotin/n, *adj.* — magnificent

straum/ur (-s, -ar), *m.* — current, stream

strax, *adv.* — immediately

streit/a (-u), *f.* — stress

strjálbýl/l, *adj.* — sparsely populated

strætisvagn (-s, -ar, strætó), *m.* — city bus

strönd (strandar, strendur), *f.* — coast, beach

stuðla (stuðla, stuðlaði, stuðlað) að, *dat.* — help towards, assist

stunda (stunda, stundaði, stundað), *acc.* — pursue, practise

sturt/a (-u, -ur), *f.* — shower

stúlk/a (-u, -ur), *f.* — girl, young woman

styðja (styð, support
studdi, stutt),
acc.
  styðja við base on, rely on
stytta (stytti, shorten
stytti, stytt), *acc.*
stýri (-s, -), *n.* steering wheel
stöðug/ur, *adj.* steady,
   continuous
stöðugt, *adv.* continually
stökkva (stekk, jump
stökk, stukku,
stokkið)
sult/a (-u, -ur), *f.* jam
sumar (-s, -), *n.* summer
sumir, *m.pl.* some
sund (-s), *n.* swimming
  fara í sund (go) swimming
sundlaug (-ar, swimming pool
-ar), *f.*
sunnudag/ur Sunday
(-s, -ar), m.
súkkulaði (-s), *n.* chocolate
súp/a (-u, -ur), *f.* soup
svakalega, *adv.* terribly,
   tremendously
svang/ur, *adj.* hungry
svara (svara, answer
svaraði,
svarað), *dat.*
svartur (svört, *f.* black
svart, *n.*), *adj.*
svefnherbergi bedroom
(-s, -), *n.*
svefnpok/i (-a, sleeping bag
-ar), *m.*
sveigja (sveigi, bend, turn
sveigði, sveigt),
acc.
sveit (-ar, -ir), *f.* countryside
svipstund (-ar, instant
-ir), *f.*

svín (-s, -), *n.* pig
Svíþjóð (-ar), *f.* Sweden
svo(na), *adv.* thus, so, such,
   like that
svolítið a little
svæði (-s, -), *n.* area
sykur (-s), *m.* sugar
synda (syndi, swim
synti, synt)
syngja (syng, sing
söng, sungu,
sungið), *acc.*
syst/ir sister
(-ur, -ur), *f.*
systkini, *n.pl.* siblings
sýna (sýni, sýndi, show
sýnt), *dat. + acc.*
sýning (-ar, show
-ar), *f.*
sækja (sæki, pick up, collect
sótti, sótt), *acc.*
sæmilega, *adv.* fairly well,
   reasonably
sæng (-ar, -ur), *f.* duvet
sænsk/ur, *adj.* Swedish
særa (særi- hurt, wound
særði-sært),
acc.
sæt/ur, *adj.* sweet, cute
sæti (-s, -), *n.* seat
sölu-mað/ur sales person
(-manns,
-menn), *m.*
söluturn (-s, kiosk that also
-ar), *m.* sells snacks,
   ice cream, etc.
sömuleiðis likewise
söngvar/i (-a, singer
-ar), *m.*
söngkon/a
(-u, -ur), *f.*
tafl/a (-u, -ur), *f.* tablet, pill, board

tagl (-s, -), *n.*	ponytail, horsetail
taka (tek, tók, tóku, tekið), *acc.*	take
taka til	clean up
takast, *imp.*	succeed
takast á við	struggle
takk (fyrir)	thanks
tala (tala, talaði, talað), *acc.*	talk, speak
tannlækn/ir (-is, -ar), *m.*	dentist
task/a (-u, -ur), *f.*	bag, case
tá (-ar, tær), *f.*	toe
te (-s, -), *n.*	tea
teikna (teikna, teiknaði, teiknað), *acc.*	draw
telja (tel, taldi, talið), *acc.*	count, consider
tengja (tengi, tengdi, tengt), *acc.*	connect
tengjast, *dat.*	be connected/related to
teppi (-s, -), *n.*	carpet, blanket
teskeið (-ar, -ar), *f.*	teaspoon
text/i (-a, -ar), *m.*	text
til(búin/n), *adj.*	ready, set, prepared
til, *prep. + gen.*	to
til dæmis (t.d.)	for example
tilboð (-s, -), *n.*	offer
tilbreyting (-ar, -ar), *f.*	change
tilefni (-s, -), *n.*	occasion
tilkynna (tilkynni, tilkynnti, tilkynnt), *acc.*	announce
tilver/a (-u), *f.*	existence
tím/i (-a, -ar), *m.*	time, class
tímabil (-s, -), *n.*	period
tjald (-s, -)	tent
tjalda (tjalda, tjaldaði, tjaldað)	camp (in tent)
togari (-a, -ar), *m.*	trawler
tóm/ur, *adj.*	empty
tónleikar (-a), *m.pl.*	concert
tónlist (-ar), *f.*	music
traust/ur, *adj.*	reliable, solid
trefil/l (-s, -ar), *m.*	woollen scarf
tré (-s, -), *n.*	tree, wood
trésmið/ur (-s, ir), *m.*	carpenter
trú (-ar, -ir), *f.*	faith, belief
trúa (trúi, trúði, trúað), *dat.* á, *acc.*	believe (in)
tryggingarfélag (-s, -), *n.*	insurance company
tung/a (-u, -ur), *f.*	tongue
tungumál (-s, -), *n.*	language
turn (-s, -ar), *m.*	tower
tún (-s, -), *n.*	(hay)field
tveir (tvær, *f.* tvö, *n.*)	two
týna (týni, týndi, týnt), *dat.*	lose
tæki (-s, -), *n.*	appliance
tækifæri (-s, -), *n.*	opportunity
tæplega, *adv.*	barely, not quite
tölv/a (-u, -ur), *f.*	computer
tönn (tannar, tennur), *f.*	tooth

ull (-ar), *f.* — wool

um, *prep. + acc.* — about, around
  um það bil (u.þ.b.) — around

umferð (-ar, -ir), *f.* — traffic

umhverfis, *prep. + acc.* — surrounding

umræð/a (-u, -ur), *f.* — discussion

umsóknar- mað/ur (-manns, -menn), *m.* — admissions person

undan, *prep. + dat.* — from under

undir, *prep. + dat./acc.* — under

undirlendi (-s), *n.* — lowland

ung/ur, *adj.* — young

upp (*dat.* **uppi**), *adv.* — up

uppáhalds-, *pref.* — favourite

upphaflega, *adv.* — initially

upphæð (-ar, -ir), *f.* — sum

upplýsing (-ar, -ar), *f.* — information

upplýsingamið- stöð (-svar), *f.* — tourist information centre

uppskurð/ur (-ar, -ir), *m.* — operation

upptekin/n, *adj.* — busy

utan, *prep. + gen.* — outside of

úlp/a (-u, -ur), *f.* — parka, winter coat

úr (-s, -), *n.* — watch

úr, *prep. + dat.* — out (of)

úrkom/a (-u), *f.* — precipitation

útflutning/ur (-s, -ar), *m.* — export

útgerðar-mað/ur (-manns, -menn), *m.* — (fishing) shipowner

útgjöld, *n.pl.* — costs, expenses

úti, *adv.* — outside, outdoors

útileg/a (-u), *f.* — camping

útivist (-ar), *f.* — outdoors (i.e. hiking, camping, etc.) activities

útlending/ur (-s, -ar), *m.* — foreigner

útlit (-s, -), *n.* — outlook

útlönd, *n.pl.* — abroad

útrás (-ar, -ir), *f.* — vent, release

útsending (-ar, -ar), *f.* — broadcast

útsýni (-s, -), *n.* — view

útvarp (-s, -), *n.* — radio (broadcast)

vaða (veð, óð, óðu, vaðið) — wade, ford

væntanleg/ur, *adj.* — expected, due

vafamál (-s, -), *n.* — matter of doubt

vaka (vaki, vakti, vakað) — be/stay awake, keep watch

vakna (vakna, vaknaði, vaknað), *intrans.* — wake up

valda (veld, olli, ollu, valdið), *dat.* — cause

vand/i (-a, -ar), *m.* — problem

vanta (vanta, vantaði, vantað), *impers. acc.* — lack, need, want

vara-, *pref.* — spare, extra

varla, *adv.* — hardly
varlega, *adv.* — carefully
vas/i (-a, -ar), *m.* — pocket
vasaljós (-s, -), *n.* — flash light, torch
vaska (vaska, vaskaði, vaskað) upp — do the dishes
vatn (-s, -), *n.* — water, lake
veðrátt/a (-u), *f.* — climate
veður (-s, *def.* veðrið), *n.* — weather
veg/ur (-ar/-s, -ir), *m.* — road
vegakort (-s, -), *n.* — road map
vegg/ur (-jar, -ir), *m.* — wall
vegna, *prep.* + *gen.* — due to, because of
veiða (veiði, veiddi, veitt), *acc.* — hunt, fish
veik/ur, *adj.* — sick, weak
veikleik/i (-a, -ar), *m.* — weakness
veisl/a (-u, -ur), *f.* — party, feast
veita (veiti, veitti, veitt), *acc./dat.* — give, grant, offer
veitingastað/ur (-ar, -ir), *m.* — restaurant
veitingasal/ur (-ar, -ir), *m.* — restaurant
vekja (vek, vakti, vakt), *acc.* — wake (someone) up
vel, *adv.* — well
vél (-ar, -ar), *f.* — machine, engine
velgengni, *f.indecl.* — success, prosperity

velja (vel, valdi, valið), *acc.* — choose
velkomin/n, *adj.* — welcome
vellíðan (-ar), *f.* — well-being
venj/a (-u, -ur), *f.* — habit
venjast (venst, vandist, vanist), *dat.* — get used to
vera (er, var, voru, verið) — be
  mikið um að vera — a lot going on
  vera eftir — be left
  vera með, *acc.* — carry, have (on you)
  vera til — exist
  vera að — be the matter, wrong
  vera mikið fyrir, *acc.* — like a lot
  vera áfram — continue to be
  vera í, *dat.* — wear
verð (-s, -), *n.* — price
verða (verð, varð, urðu, orðið) — become, will be
  verða að — must, have to
verðlaun, *n.pl.* — prize
verja (ver, varði, varið), *dat.* — use, spend protect, *acc.* defend
verk (-s, -), *n.* — work
verk/ur (-jar, -ir), *m.* — pain
verkefni (-s, -), *n.* — task, project, assignment
verkfall (-s, -), *n.* — strike
verkjatafl/a (-u, -ur), *f.* — painkiller
verkstæði (-s, -), *n.* — workshop
vesalings, *adv.* — poor

verslun (-ar, -ir), *f.* — shop, trade

versna (versna, versnaði, versnað), *imp.* — get worse

verst/ur, *adj.superl.* — worst, awful

vesen (-s), *n.* — bother, fuss, trouble

veski (-s, -), *n.* — wallet, purse

vetrarsvefn (-s), *n.* — winter sleep

vettling/ur (-s, -ar), *m.* — mitten

vet-ur (-rar, -ur), *m.* — winter

við, *prep. + acc. pron.* — at, up against we

viðskiptafélag/i (-a, -ar), *m.* — business associate

viðskipti, *n.pl.* — business;
  eiga viðskipti við, *acc.* — do business/ have dealings with

viðurkenna (viðurkenni, viðurkenndi, viðurkennt), *acc.* — admit

vik/a (-u, -ur), *f.* — week

vikudag/ur (-s, -ar), *m.* — weekday

vin/ur (-ar, -ir), *m.* **vinkon/a (-u, -ur)**, *f.* — friend

vind/ur (-s, -ar), *m.* — wind

vinna (vinn, vann, unnu, unnið), *acc.* — work, win

vinning/ur (-s, -ar), *m.* — prize, winnings

vinnsl/a (-u), *f.* — (fish) processing

vinnufélag/i (-a, -ar), *m.* — colleague

vinnustof/a (-u, -ur), *f.* — work room, studio, workshop

vinsæl/l, *adj.* — popular
  vinsældir, *f.pl.* — popularity

vinstri — left

virðast (virðist, virtist, virst) — seem

virðingarfyllst, *adj.superl.* — respectfully

virk/ur, *adj.* — active, functioning
  virkur dagur — work day

virkileg/ur, *adj.* — real, true

virkja (virkja, virkjaði, virkjað), *acc.* — utilize (hydro-electric/ geothermal power)

viss, *adj.* — sure, certain

víst — surely

vita (veit, vissi, vissu, vitið), *acc.* — know

vitleys/a (-u), *f.* — foolishness, nonsense

víða, *adv.* — widely

vík (-ur, -ur), *f.* — small bay, inlet

vín (-s, -), *n.* — spirits, liquor

volg/ur, *adj.* — lukewarm

vona (vona, vonaði, vonað), *acc.* — hope

vond/ur (vont, n.), *adj.* — bad

vor (-s, -), *n.* — spring

vöfflur, *f.pl.* — waffles

vör (-ar, -ir), *f.* — lip

vöxt/ur (-ar, -ir), *m.* — growth

yfir, *prep. + dat./acc.* — over

yfirbragð (-s, -), *n.* flavour
yfirleitt, *adv.* generally
yndisleg/ur, *adj.* delightful, lovely
yngst/ur, *adj.superl.* youngest
ýmsir, *m.pl.* various
ýs/a (-u, -ur), *f.* haddock
það, *pron.* it
  það er/eru there is/are
þaðan, *adv.* from there
þak (-s, -), *n.* roof
þakka (þakka, þakkaði, þakkað), *dat. + acc.* thank
þangað, *adv.* to there (thither)
  þangað til until
þannig að so that
þar, *dem.* there
  þar sem, *conj.* where, as
  þar á meðal among them
  þar að auki, *conj.* besides, moreover
þarna, *dem.* there
þau, *pron.* they (*n.*)
þátt-takand/i (-a, -tekendur), *m.* participant
þáttur (-ar, þættir), *m.* part, show
  taka þátt í take part in
þegar, *adv.* when
þegja (þegi, þagði, þagað) be quiet
þeir, *pron.* they (*m.*)
þekja (þek, þakti, þakið), *dat.* cover
þekkja (þekki, þekkti, þekkt), *acc.* know

þess vegna therefore
þessi (*n.* þetta), *dem.* this
þið, *pron.* you (*pl.*)
þjóð (-ar, -ir), *f.* people, nation
þjóð(ar)-, *pref.* national
þjóðsaga (-u, -ur), *f.* folk tale
þjóðveg/ur (-ar, -ir), *m.* main road
Þjóðverj/i (-a, -ar), *m.* German
þjónust/a (-u), *f.* service
  þjóna (þjóna, þjónaði, þjónað), *dat.* serve
þola (þoli, þoldi, þolað), *acc.* bear, endure, stand
þora (þori, þorði, þorað), *acc.* dare, risk
þorna (þorna, þornaði, þornað), *intrans.* (get) dry
þorsk/ur (-s, -ar), *m.* cod
þó (að) (also þótt), *conj.* (al)though
þriðjudag/ur (-s, -ar), *m.* Tuesday
þrífa (þríf, þreif, þrifum, þrifið), *acc.* grab, clean
þrír (þrjár, *f.* þrjú, *n.*) three
þróun (-ar, -ir), *f.* development
þröng/ur, *adj.* narrow
þung/ur, *adj.* heavy
þurfa (þarf, þurfti, þurft) að need to

þurr, *adj.* — dry
þú, *pron.* — you
þúsund (-s, -), *n.* — thousand
því miður — unfortunately
þvo (þvæ, þvoði, þvegið), *acc.* — wash
þvo sér — wash oneself
þvott/ur (-s, -ar), *m.* — laundry
þybbin/n, *adj.* — chubby, stout
þykja (þykir, þótti, þótt), *imp.* — think, find
þykk/ur, *adj.* — thick
þýða (þýði, þýddi, þýtt), *acc.* — mean, translate
þægileg/ur, *adj.* — comfortable
þær, *pron.* — they (*f.*)
þökk (-ar, -ir), *f.* — thanks
þörf (-ar, -ir), *f.* — need
æfa (æfi, æfði, æft) sig í, *dat.* — practise (oneself) in
æfing (-ar, -ar), *f.* — exercise, training
ætla (ætla, ætlaði, ætlað), *acc.* — intend/plan to

ætt (-ar, -ir), *f.* — family lineage, kin
ættarnafn (-s, -), *n.* — family name
ættingi (-ja, -jar), *m.* — relative
öðruvísi, *adj.indecl.* — different
öflug/ur, *adj.* — strong, powerful
ökkl/i (-a, -ar), *m.* — ankle
öld (-ar, -ir), *f.* — century
öldum saman — for centuries on end
ömurlega, *adv.* — miserably, wretchedly
önn (-ar, -ir), *f.* — work, term
vera önnum kafin/n — be very busy
ör (-s, -), *n.* — scar
adj. — rapid, fast
pref. — very
örbylgjuofn (-s, -ar), *m.* — microwave
örugg/ur (með sig), *adj.* — sure (of oneself)
örugglega, *adv.* — surely, certainly

English–Icelandic glossary

about	**um**	as ... as	**eins ... og**
abroad	**erlendis**	ask	**spyrja**
accident	**slys**	asleep	**sofnaður**
accommodation	**gisting, húsnæði**	fall asleep	**sofna**
acquaintance	**kunningi**	aspirin	**verkjatafla**
address	**heimilisfang**	assist	**aðstoða**
aeroplane	**flugvél**	at	**við**
after	**(á) eftir**	Australian, *adj.*	**ástralskur**
afternoon	**(eftir) hádegi,**	author	**(rit)höfundur**
	seinni partinn	autumn	**haust**
airport	**flugvöllur,**	awake	**vakandi**
	flugstöð	be/stay awake	**vaka**
	(terminal)	back	**aftur, til baka,**
all right	**allt í lagi**		*adv.* **bak,** *n.*
all	**allur**	backpack	**bakpoki**
allow	**láta, leyfa**	bad	**vondur, slæmur**
alone	**einn**	bag	**poki, taska**
also	**líka, einnig**	bake	**baka**
always	**alltaf**	banana	**banani**
among	**meðal**	bank	**banki**
and	**og**	bath	**bað**
answer	**svara**, *n.* **svar,** *v.*	bathroom	**baðherbergi**
appear	**koma í ljós**	beard	**skegg**
apple	**epli**	beautiful	**fallegur**
appointment	**stefnumót**	because	**(af) því að,**
area	**svæði**		**vegna þess að**
arm	**handleggur**	become	**verða**
around	**um, (í)**	bed	**rúm**
	kring(um), um	bedroom	**svefnherbergi**
	það bil	beer	**bjór**
arrive	**koma (til)**	before	**fyrr en, áður**
art	**list**		**(en), áðan**
as	**sem**	begin	**byrja, fara að**

believe	**trúa**		**viðskipti**
beside	**hjá**		(dealings)
between	**(á) milli**	busy	**upptekinn**
big	**stór, mikill**	butter	**smjör**
bike	**hjól**	cafe	**kaffihús**
bill	**reikningur**	cake	**kaka**
birthday	**afmæli**	call	**kalla**
my birthday	**ég á afmæli ...**	be called	**heita**
is ...		can	**geta** (+ *pp.*),
biscuit	**smákaka, kex**		**kunna, vera**
black	**svartur**		**hægt, mega**
blond	**ljóshærður**		can you tell
blood	**blóð**		me ...,
blue	**blár**		**geturðu sagt**
body	**líkami**		**mér ...**
boil	**sjóða**	candle	**kerti**
book	**bók**	capital	**höfuðborg**
bookshop	**bókabúð**	car	**bíll**
book	**bóka, panta,**	cash	**staðgreitt**
booking	**pöntun**	cat	**köttur**
boring	**leiðinlegur**	centre	**mið-, miður**
born	**fæddur**		*adj.,*
(be) born	**fæðast**		**miðja** *n.*
bottle	**flaska**	century	**öld**
boy	**strákur, piltur,**	in the ...	**á ... öld**
	drengur	century	
boyfriend	**kærasti**	chair	**stóll**
bread	**brauð**	champagne	**kampavín**
break	**brjóta**	chance	**kostur**
break down	**bila**	change	**breyta(st), skipta**
breakfast	**morgunmatur**		*v.;* **tilbreyting,**
bright	**bjartur,**		*n.*
(colour)	**skær**	chat	**spjall**, *n.* **spjalla,**
bring	**koma með,**		*v.*
	færa	cheap	**ódýr**
brother	**bróðir**	check	**athuga**
brown	**brúnn**	cheers!	**skál!**
build	**byggja**	cheese	**ostur**
building	**bygging**	cheque	**ávísun, tékki**
bus	**strætisvagn**	child	**barn**
	(strætó)	chips	**franskar**
business	**fyrirtæki** (firm),		**(kartöflur)**

chocolate	**súkkulaði**
choose	**velja**
Christmas	**jól**
church	**kirkja**
cinema	**bíó**
city	**borg**
city centre	**miðbær**
climate	**veðrátta**
close	**loka**, *v.* **nálægur**, *adj.*
close by	**nálægt**
clothing	**föt**
cloud	**ský**
cloudy	**skýjað**
coach	**rúta**
coast	**strönd**
coat	**frakki**, *m.*, **kápa**, *f.*, **úlpa** (winter coat)
coffee	**kaffi**
cold	**kaldur**
colleague	**vinnufélagi**
colour	**litur**
come	**koma**
comfortable	**þægilegur**
company	**fyrirtæki**
computer	**tölva**
concert	**tónleikar**
congratulations	**til hamingju**
connection	**samband**
contact	**samband**, *n.*, **hafa samband við**, *v.*
continue	**halda áfram**
conversation	**samtal**
cook	**elda**, *v.* **kokkur**, *n.*
cool	**svalur** (*temp.*)
cost	**kosta**
count	**telja**
country	**land**
countryside	**sveit**
course	**námskeið**
cream	**rjómi, krem**
credit card	**greiðslukort, visa, krítarkort**
crowd	**fjöldi**
culture	**menning**
cup	**bolli**
cupboard	**skápur**
curly	**krullað**
custom	**(lífs)venja, siður**
cut	**skera**
cycle	**hjóla**
daily	**daglega**
dance	**dansa**, *v.*, **dans, dansleikur**, *n.*
dark	**dökkur** (colour), **dimmur** (light), **dökkhærður** (hair)
date	**dagsetning, mánaðardagur**
daughter	**dóttir**
day	**dagur**
dear	**kær**
degree	**(hita)stig**
delicious	**ljúffengur**
dentist	**tannlæknir**
depart	**leggja af stað**
departure	**brottför**
different	**öðruvísi**
differing	**mismunandi**
difficult	**erfiður**
diligent	**duglegur**
dirty	**skítugur**
discuss	**ræða**
dish	**réttur**
diverse	**fjölbreyttur**
do	**gera**
doctor	**læknir**
dog	**hundur**
door	**hurð, dyr**

down	**niður** (motion), **niðri** (static)	exercise	**æfing**, *n.*; **hreyfa sig**, *v.*
draw	**teikna**	exhibition	**sýning**
dream	**draumur**, *n.* **dreyma** (*imp, v.*)	expect	**búast við**
		expensive	**dýr**
		explain	**(út)skýra**
dress	**kjóll**, *n.*; **klæða**, *v.*; get dressed, **klæða sig**; be dressed in, **vera í**	extra	**auka-**
		face	**andlit**
		fall	**detta**
		family	**fjölskylda**
		famous	**frægur**
drink	**drykkur**, *n.*; **drekka**, *v.*	fancy	**fínn, flottur**
		far	**langt (í burtu)**
drive	**keyra, aka**	fare	**fargjald**
driver	**bílstjóri, vagnstjóri**	farm	**bóndabær**
		fast	**fljótur**, *adj.*; **fljótt**, *adv.*
dry	**þurr**		
ear	**eyra**	fat	**feitur**
early	**snemma**	father	**pabbi, faðir**
east	**austur, fyrir austan**	favourite	**uppáhalds-**
		feel	**finna (til), finnast** (*imp.*), **líða** (*imp*)
easy	**auðveldur**		
eat	**borða**		
education	**menntun**	fill out	**fylla út**
electricity	**rafmagn**	find	**finna(st**, *imp.*)
elegant	**fínn, glæsilegur**	to be found	**má finna**
emergency	**neyðar-, neyðartilfelli**	fine	**ágætur, ágætlega**
		finger	**fingur**
empty	**tómur**	finish	**klára**
enjoy oneself	**skemmta sér**	first	**fyrst, fyrstur**
enjoyable	**skemmtilegur**	fish	**veiða, fiska** (commercially), *v.* **fiskur**, *n.*
enough	**nógur**		
even	**jafnvel**, *adv.*; **jafn**, *adj.*		
every	**hver**	fix	**laga, gera við**
everyday	**á hverjum degi, daglegur**	flash light	**vasaljós**
		flat	**íbúð**
example	**dæmi**; for example, **til dæmis**	flight	**flug**
		floor	**gólf, hæð** (storey)
excuse me	**fyrirgefðu, afsakið**	flower	**blóm**
		fly	**fljúga**

English	Icelandic	English	Icelandic
food	matur	say goodbye	kveðja
football (soccer)	knattspyrna, fótbolti	grandfather	afi
		grandmother	amma
for	fyrir, handa	green	grænn
foreign	erlendur, útlenskur	greet	heilsa
		grey	grár
foreigner	útlendingur	guest	gestur; be my guest, gjörðu svo vel
forest	skógur		
forget	gleyma		
free	frjáls, laus	guest house	gistihús
fridge	ísskápur	guide	leiðsögn, leiðsögumaður
friend	vinur (*m.*), vinkona (*f.*)		
friendly	indæll	guided tour	ferð með leiðsögn
from	frá		
fruit	ávöxtur	guidebook	leiðsöguhandbók
fun	gaman, skemmtilegur	hair	hár
game	leikur	hand	hönd; on the other hand, hins vegar; rétta, *v.*
garbage	sorp, rusl		
garden	garður		
generally	yfirleitt, almennt		
get	fá	hang	hanga
get up	fara á fætur	hang up	hengja
girl	stelpa, stúlka	happen	gerast, koma fyrir
girlfriend	kærasta		
glass	glas, gler (material)	happy	ánægður
		hardly	varla
glasses	gleraugu	hat	hattur, húfa (woollen)
go	fara		
going on	um að vera	have	eiga, hafa, vera með
it goes well	það gengur vel		
		have to	eiga að, verða að
get going	koma sér af stað		
		he	hann
go ahead	gjörðu svo vel	head	höfuð
good	góður	headache	höfuðverkur
good morning/ afternoon	góðan dag(inn)	health	heilsa
		healthy	heilbrigður, hollur
goodbye	vertu blessaður (*m.*)/blessuð (*f.*)	hear	heyra
		heavy	þungur

hello	**(komdu) sæll** **(***m.***), sæl (***f.***)**	Iceland	**Ísland**
help	**hjálpa,** *v.* **hjálp,** *n.*	Icelandic	**íslenskur**
here	**hér(na), hingað** (motion to), **héðan** (motion from); here you are, **gjörðu svo vel**	Icelander	**Íslendingur**
		immediately	**strax**
		important	**mikilvægur**
		in(to)	**í**
		included	**innifalinn**
		information	**upplýsingar** (*pl.*)
		inhabitant	**íbúi**
		inside	**inn** (motion), **inni** (static)
high	**hár**		
hike	**ganga**; hiking **. . ., göngu-**	instead	**í staðinn**
		instrument	**verkfæri,** **hljóðfæri** (musical)
historic	**sögu-, sögulegur**		
hobby	**áhugamál**		
holiday	**hátíð, frídagur**	intend to	**ætla að**
holidays	**frí**	interest	**áhugi**
home	**heimili,** *n.*; **heim,** *adv.*; at home, **heima**	I am interested in	**ég hef áhuga á**
		introduce	**kynna**
		introduction	**kynning**
hope	**vona,** *v.* **von,** *n.*	Irish, *adj.*	**írskur**
horse	**hestur, hross**	island	**ey, eyja**
(horse)riding	**fara á hestbak**	it	**það**
hospital	**sjúkrahús**	jacket	**jakki**
hour	**(klukku)tími**	job	**starf, atvinna**
house	**hús**	journey	**ferð, ferðalag**
how	**hvernig**; how . . . (*adj.*)?, **hvað** . . .?; how . . . ! **en . . .!**; how are you? **hvað segirðu gott?**	juice	**safi**
		jumper	**peysa**
		just	**bara**
		kaffi	**coffee**
		keep	**geyma**
hundred	**hundrað**	kilogram	**kíló(gramm)**
hungry	**svangur**	kilometre	**kílómetri**
hunt	**veiða**	kindly	**kærlega**
hurry up	**flýta sér, drífa sig**	kitchen	**eldhús**
		knife	**hnífur**
hurt	**finna til í, vera sárt, meiða sig**	know	**vita, þekkja, kunna**
husband	**(eigin)maður**	lake	**vatn**
I	**ég**	lamb	**lamb, lambakjöt**
ice-cream	**ís**	lamp	**lampi**

landscape	**landslag**
large	**stór**
last	**síðasti, síðastur**
late	**seinn, framorðið**; later, **seinna**
laugh	**hlæja**
law	**lög, lögfræði** (study)
lay	**leggja**
lay down	**leggjast**
learn	**læra**
least	**síst, minnst**
at least	**að minnsta kosti**
leave	**fara/leggja af stað**
left	**(til) vinstri**
let	**láta**
let go	**sleppa**
letter	**bréf, stafur** (alphabet)
lie	**liggja**
life	**líf**
lift	**far** (ride), **lyfta** (elevator)
light	**bjartur, ljós** (colour), **léttur** (weight)
light	**ljós**, *n.*; **kveikja**, *v.*
like	*conj.* **sem, eins og**; *adj.* **líkur**
like	*v.* **líka vel við** (*imp.*); would like, **langa í** (*imp.*), **ætla að fá**
likewise	**sömuleiðis**
listen (to)	**hlusta (á)**
litre	**lítri**
little	**lítill**
a little (bit)	**svolítið**
live	**lifa** (be alive), **búa** (reside)
lively	**líflegur**
living room	**stofa**
lock	**læsa**
long	*adj.* **langur** (hor.), **síður** (vert.); *adv.* **lengi** (time), **langt** (distance)
long time ago	**langt síðan, fyrir löngu**
look (have/take a …) at	**skoða**
look forward to	**hlakka til**
look after	**sjá um**
lose	**týna**
love	**elska**, *v.* **ást**, *n.*
lovely	**indæll, yndislegur**
lunch	**hádegismatur**
magnificent	**glæsilegur, stórbrotinn** (land)
main	**aðal-**
make	**gera, framleiða**
many	**margir**
map	**kort**
marriage	**hjónaband**
get married	**giftast, gifta sig**
married	**giftur**
marry	**gifta**
material	**efni**
may	**mega**
mean	**þýða, meina**
meat	**kjöt**
medicine	**lyf**
meet	**hitta**
meeting	**fundur**

menu	**matseðill**
milk	**mjólk**
minute	**mínúta**
moment	**andartak, augnablik**
money	**peningar**
month	**mánuður**
morning	**morgunn**
mother	**mamma, móðir**
mountain	**fjall**
moustache	**yfirskegg**
mouth	**munnur**
move	**færa** (transp.), **hreyfa sig, flytja** (house)
much	**mikill (mikið,** *n.***)**
museum	**safn**
music	**tónlist**
must	**verða að, hljóta að**
name	**nafn,** *n.*; my name is, **ég heiti**
narrow	**þröngur**
nation	**þjóð** (people), **ríki**
national	**þjóð(ar)-**
nature	**náttúra**
nearby	**nálægt**
neccesary	**nauðsynlegur**
need	**þurfa, vanta** (*imp.*)
neither	**(ekki) heldur**
neither ... nor	**hvorki ... né**
nevertheless	**samt, eigi að síður**
New Year	**nýársdagur, áramót**
new	**nýr**; what's new with you? **hvað er að frétta (af þér)?**
news	**frétt, fréttir**
no	**nei; enginn (ekkert,** *n., ind.pron.***)**
noon	**hádegi**
north	**norður, fyrir norðan**
not	**ekki**
nothing	**ekkert**
novel	**skáldsaga**
now	**núna**
nowhere	**hvergi**
number	**númer**
nurse	**hjúkrunarfræðingur**
of course	**auðvitað, sjálfsagt**
off	**af**
offer	**bjóða**
on offer	**í boði**
office	**skrifstofa**
often	**oft(ast)**
okay	**allt í lagi**
old	**gamall**
once	**einu sinni**
one	**einn** (number); **maður,** *imp.*
only	**bara, aðeins**
open	**opna,** *v.* **opinn,** *adj.*
opportunity	**tækifæri**
opposite	**á móti**
or	**eða**
orange	**appelsína**
outdoors	**útivist**
outside	**úti, fyrir utan**
over	**yfir**
pack	**pakka niður**
package	**pakki**
pain	**verkur, pína**
paper	**pappír, blað**
park	**(skrúð)garður**

parliament	**þing**	post office	**pósthús**
(Icelandic)	**alþingi**	practise	**æfa (sig í)**
parliament		preferably	**helst**
part	**hluti**	pregnant	**ófrísk**
party	**veisla**	prepare	**búa til** (make),
past	**framhjá**		**lesa undir**
pay	**borga, greiða**;		(study),
	payment,		**undirbúa**
	greiðsla	prescription	**lyfseðill**
pen	**penni**	present	**gjöf**
pencil	**blýantur**	president	**forseti**
people	**fólk, menn**	previous	**fyrri**
perhaps	**kannski, ef til**	previously	**(áður) fyrr**
	vill (e.t.v.)	price	**verð**
permit	**leyfi**	print	**prenta**
person	**maður**	probably	**líklega, sennilega**
pharmacy	**apótek**	programme	**dagskrá, þáttur,**
picture	**mynd, kvikmynd**		**efni**
	(film),	project	**verkefni**
	ljósmynd	promise	**lofa**
	(photo)	public	**opinber,** *adj.*;
take a picture	**taka mynd**		**almenningur,**
piece	**stykki**		*n.*
pill	**tafla**	put	**setja**
plan	**ætla,** *v.* **áætlun,**	put on	**fara í, setja á**
	n.		**sig**
plaster	**plástur**	question	**spurning**
plate	**diskur**	quick	**fljótur,** *adj.*
play	**leika sér, spila,**	quit	**hætta**
	v.; **leikrit,** *n.*	radio	**útvarp**
pleasant	**skemmtilegur,**	rain	**rigning,** *n.*;
	góður		**rigna,** *v.*
pocket	**vasi**	rather	**frekar, heldur**
poem	**ljóð**	reach	**ná í**
poet	**skáld**	read	**lesa**
police	**lögregla, lögga**	ready	**(til)búinn,**
popular	**vinsæll**		**kominn**
possibility	**möguleiki**	reception	**móttaka**
possible	**hægt**	red	**rauður**
post	**póstur** *n.* **setja í**	relative	**ættingi**
	póst, *v.*	relax	**slappa af, slaka**
postcard	**póstkort**		**á**

remember	**muna**
rent	**leigja**, *v.* **leiga**, *n.*
rest	**hvíla sig**
restaurant	**veitingastaður**
return	**koma aftur,** *v.*
	báðar leiðir (ticket)
ride	**far**
right away	**strax**
right	**(til) hægri**
right	**réttur,** *n.* **réttur,** *adj.*
ring	**hringur**
river	**á, fljót**
road	**vegur**
road map	**vegakort**
room	**herbergi**
rose	**rós**
route	**leið**
row	**röð**
run	**hlaupa, reka** (a business)
sail	**sigla**
salesperson	**afgreiðslumaður**
sandwich	**samloka**
scarf	**trefill** (woollen), **sjal**
schedule	**áætlun**
school	**skóli**
Scottish	**skoskur,** *adj.* **Skoti,** *n.*
seat	**sæti**
see	**sjá**
see you	**við sjáumst**
seem	**virðast** (*imp.*), **sýnast** (*imp.*)
seldom	**sjaldan**
sell	**selja**
send	**senda**
serve	**þjóna, bera fram**
service	**þjónusta**
several	**nokkrir**

shall/should	**skulu, eiga að**
shave	**raka sig**
she	**hún**
shine	**skína**
ship	**skip**
shirt	**bolur, skyrta** (buttoned)
shoe	**skór**
shop	**búð, verslun**
short	**stuttur, lágvaxinn** (built)
show	**sýning,** *n.*; **sýna,** *v.*
shower	**sturta**
have a shower	**fara í sturtu**
siblings	**systkini**
sick	**veikur, lasinn**
sight	**merkisstaður**
sightseeing (go/do ...)	**fara í skoðunarferð**
sightseeing trip	**skoðunarferð**
since	**síðan**
sing	**syngja**
single (room)	**einbýli**
sister	**systir**
sit	**sitja**
sit down	**setjast**
size	**númer**
ski	**skíði,** *n.* **fara á skíðum,** *v.*
skin	**húð**
sky	**himinn**
sleep	**sofa,** *v.* **svefn,** *n.*
sleeping bag	**svefnpoki**
slim	**grannur**
slow	**hægur, seinn**
smart	**flottur, fínn**
snack	**snarl**
snow	**snjór,** *n.*; **snjóa,** *v.*
so	**svo(na), þannig**

so that	svo að, þannig að	suggest	stinga upp á
some	sumir	suit	passa, *v.* jakkaföt, *n.*
someone	einhver	summer	sumar
something	eitthvað	sun	sól
sometimes	stundum	sunshine	sólskin
son	sonur	supper	kvöldmatur
sorry	fyrirgefðu, afsakið	surely	víst, örugglega
		sweet	sætur
south	suður, fyrir sunnan	swim	synda, fara í sund
souvenir	minjagripur	swimming pool	sundlaug
speak	tala	table	borð; lay the table, **leggja á borðið**
spend	eyða		
sports	íþróttir		
spring	vor	take	taka
stamp	frímerki	take off	fara úr, taka af sér
start	byrja, fara að		
stay	dvöl, *n.*; **gista** (overnight), **dvelja** (longer time), **vera áfram, verða áfram** (remain)	talk (to)	tala (við)
		tall	hár, hávaxinn (built), **stór**
		taste	smakka (*trans.*), **bragðast** (*intrans.*), *v.*; **bragð**, *n.*
still	ennþá	tea	te
stomach	magi	teacher	kennari
stone	steinn	telephone	hringja í, *v.*; **sími**, *n.*
stop	stoppa, stansa, *v.* **viðkomu-staður, stoppistöð**, *n.*	television	sjónvarp
		tell	segja frá
		temperature	hitastig
story	saga	tent	tjald, *n.* tjalda, *v.*
street	gata	thank	þakka
stress	streita, stress	thank you	þakka þér fyrir, takk (fyrir)
strong	sterkur		
student	nemandi, stúdent		
		theatre	leikhús
studies	nám	there	þarna (*dem.*), þar (*ref.*), þangað (motion to),
study	læra, lesa		
stuff	dót, efni		
sugar	sykur		

	þaðan (motion from)	trousers	**buxur**
		true	**sannur**
there is/are	**það er/eru**	try	**reyna, prófa**
is ... there?	**er ... við?**	turn off	**slökkva (á)**
therefore	**þess vegna**	turn on	**kveikja (á)**
they	**þeir** (*m.*), **þær** (*f.*), **þau** (*n.*)	under	**undir**
		unfortunately	**því miður**
thick	**þykkur**	university	**háskóli**
think	**hugsa, halda, þykja**	unpleasant	**leiðinlegur**
		until	**(þangað) til**; not ..., **ekki fyrr en...**
thirsty	**þyrstur**		
this	**þessi, þetta** (*n.*)		
thousand	**þúsund**	up	**upp** (motion), **uppi** (static)
throw	**kasta**		
ticket	**(far)miði, farseðill**	use	**nota**
		various	**ýmsir**
time	**tími**	very	**mjög**
to	**til**	view	**útsýni**
toast	**skála (fyrir)**	visit	**heimsækja,** *v.*; **heimsókn,** *n.*
today	**í dag**		
together	**saman**	wait	**bíða**
toilet	**snyrting, salerni, klósett**	wake	**vekja**
		wake up	**vakna**
toiletries	**hrein- lætisvörur**	walk	**ganga**
		go for a walk	**fara í gönguferð**
tomorrow	**á morgun**		
tonight	**í kvöld**	want	**vilja**
tourist	**ferðamaður**	warm	**hlýr**
towards	**að**	wash	**þvo (sér)**
town	**bær, kaupstaður**	watch	**úr,** *n.* **horfa á,** *v.*
town centre	**miðbær**	water	**vatn**
trade	**verslun**	waterfall	**foss**
traditional	**hefðbundinn**	we	**við**
traffic	**umferð**	weather	**veður**
traffic light	**umferðarljós**	week	**vika**
train	**æfa sig** (*v.*)	weekend	**helgi**
translate	**þýða**	welcome	**velkominn**
travel agency	**ferðaskrifstofa**	you're welcome	**það var lítið, ekkert að þakka**
travel	**ferðast**		
treatment	**meðferð**		
tree	**tré**	west	**vestur, fyrir vestan**
trip	**ferð**		

wet	**blautur**
what	**hvað**
what kind of	**hvaða, hvernig**
when	**hvenær**
where	**hvar, hvert** (motion to), **hvaðan** (motion from); **þar sem** (conj.)
which	**sem**
while	**á meðan**
a little while	**smástund**
white	**hvítur**
who	**hver**
whole	**heill**
why	**af hverju, hvers vegna**
wife	**(eigin)kona**
wind	**vindur**
windy	**hvass**
window	**gluggi**
wine	**léttvín (rauðvín, hvítvín)**
winter	**vetur**
wish	**óska**, v. **ósk**, n.
with	**með, hjá**
woman	**kona**
wood	**viður, tré**
work	**vinna, starfa**
worry	**áhyggja**, n.; **hafa áhyggjur**, v.
write	**skrifa**
wrong	**rangur**
what's wrong	**hvað er að**
year	**ár**
yellow	**gulur**
yes	**já, jú** (in reponse to neg.)
yesterday	**í gær**
you	**þú** (sg.), **þið** (pl.)
young	**ungur**

Index